Samuel P. Oliner

Pearl M. Oliner

SAMUEL P. OLINER was born in Poland in the 1930s and came to the United States after World War II. He is Research Director of the Institute for Righteous Acts, Director of the Altruistic Personality Project, and Professor of Sociology at Humboldt State University.

PEARL M. OLINER is Research Director of the Altruistic Personality Project and Professor of Education, also at Humboldt State.

The
Altruistic
Personality

The Altruistic Personality

•

Rescuers of Jews in Nazi Europe

Samuel P. Oliner

Pearl M. Oliner

With Foreword by
Rabbi Harold M. Schulweis

THE FREE PRESS
A Division of Macmillan, Inc.
NEW YORK

Collier Macmillan Publishers
LONDON

The Free Press
A Division of Macmillan, Inc.
866 Third Avenue, New York, N.Y. 10022

Collier Macmillan Canada, Inc.

Printed in the United States of America

printing number
1   2   3   4   5   6   7   8   9   10

Library of Congress Cataloging-in-Publication Data

Oliner, Samuel P.
   The altruistic personality.

   Bibliography: p.
   Includes index.
   1. Righteous Gentiles in the Holocaust—Psychology.
2. World War, 1939–1945—Jews—Rescue.   3. Altruism.
4. Motivation (Psychology). I. Oliner, Pearl M.
II. Title.
D810.J40418   1988   940.54′7794′019   87–33223
ISBN 0-02-923830-7

We dedicate this book to rescuers whose acts of kindness and humanity during those dark days serve as a beacon of hope for all of us.

Contents

Foreword

Victor Frankl, the founder of logotherapy, recalls lying at night in his bunk at Auschwitz. Next to him his fellow inmate lay tossing and turning, uttering tortured screams. Frankl wondered whether he should rouse him from his dreams. But rouse him—to what? At Auschwitz reality was more frightening than nightmares. Frankl decided to let him alone.

The Holocaust is our nightmare, unprecedented in its cruelty, a world turned topsy-turvy, an admixture of fantasy and reality. But the Holocaust cannot be let alone. Wisdom requires that the world be roused from the confusion of the nightmare, its miasma entered so that the distinctions beween decency and depravity, goodness and evil can be restored. To live beyond the void of the Holocaust, cognitive and moral discriminations must be exercised. We know that even in the midst of that impenetrable darkness, there were scattered sparks of sanctity. These must be gathered, identified, and understood. To do so honestly, calmly, and with as much scientific integrity as can be mustered is of ultimate significance.

It may well be that one of the latent consequences of the Oliners' pioneering study is its challenge to many of the tacit assumptions of philosophers and social scientists about the character of human nature. According to George Santayana, the American philosopher of naturalism, "In human nature generous impulses are occasional or reversible; they are spent in childhood, in dreams, in extremities, they are often weak or soured in old age. They form amiable interludes like tearful sentiments in a ruffian, or they are pleasant self-deceptive hypocricies acted out, like civility to strangers because such is in society the path of least resistance. Strain the situation, however, dig a little beneath the surface, and you will find a ferocious, persistent, profoundly self-ish man."

This Hobbesian portrait of human nature, convinced of the duplicitous and superficial character of human benevolence, is no eccentric view. Sigmund Freud's description is no less morose. For him, "People view their neighbor in order to gratify their aggressiveness, to exploit his capacity for work without recompense, to use him sexually without his consent, to seize his possessions, to humiliate him, to cause him pain, to torture and to kill him."[1] Tear away the mask of his public persona, and his natural viciousness lies stripped bare. Scratch a saint, a villain bleeds; beneath each white man, Jim Crow dwells; behind every gentile, an anti-Semite lurks. Anna Freud doubted the authenticity of altruism because the altruist's very enjoyment of the act of self-sacrifice belies his or her selflessness. Not surprisingly, the word "altruism" emerged late in the nineteenth century, as a term coined by Auguste Comte. The secular version of original sin establishes an a priori bias against good acts and good people. It explains in part the social sciences' neglect of the subject of altruism and the uniqueness of the Altruistic Personality Project.

In the recent past, many voices expressed a wariness of such an investigation and its focus, a fear that it could mitigate the gravity and extensiveness of the devastation. The fear was that shining light on the rescue behavior of non-Jews would somehow brighten and thereby deny the darkness of the cavern. However, such understandable apprehension, made still more real by revisionist historians who minimize and even deny the existence of the Holocaust, dismisses the moral and intellectual imperatives calling for the honest documentation, analysis, and evaluation of good acts and good people. Moreover, the objections ignore the meaning of the reality of heroic people and acts for the understanding of the tragedy of destruction. The rescuers offer strong empirical refutation of the claim that nothing could be done, that individuals in totalitarian societies are helpless, and that complicity was the only alternative left to those overrun by the Nazi juggernaut. Rescuers' behavior belies the rationalizations of the bystanders, the nonrescuers delineated so effectively by the Oliners in their study. There are no heroes without villains. Through a view of the rescuers, the acts of the predators and spectators may be exposed in all their horror.

In proportion to the villainy of the perpetrators of evil and their mute conspirators, the acts of altruism are scandalously few. Given the smallness of their number, ought they then to be given so much attention? From the time of Sodom and Gomorrah throughout history, there have always been too few righteous men and women. Yet surely that does not minimize the significance of the behavior of that noble minority. Additionally, we simply do not know how many were involved in the conspiracies of goodness. No systematic search for rescuers has been instituted by any national or international body. Regretably, there are no Wiesenthals to search out the rescuers and their accomplices in protecting, hiding, feeding, and saving the hunted. A major institution, such as Yad Vashem, financially restricted in its activities, must wait upon the initiative and energy and goodwill of the rescued to come forth with evidence and testimony on behalf of the rescuers. It is forced to adopt a passive role, made more difficult by the modesty of the rescuers and the clandestine nature of their rescue during the war years. Nevertheless, the number of rescuers revealed has risen dramatically over the past 40 years. In the absence of complete information, it is specious to conclude that merely a bare handful risked their lives to help. Many of the millions of Jews who survived the slaughter could not have done so without the care and protection of non-Jews in every country the Nazis occupied.

Paradoxically, confronting goodness may be more painfully challenging than confronting evil. It is one thing to study and condemn the sadistic behavior of a Klaus Barbie but quite another to study and acknowledge the rescue behavior of a Herman Graebe. The latter presents us with a hard mirror. Would I rescue a pregnant woman, a hungry and homeless child, an aged, frightened couple—provide them with food and shelter, dispose of their refuse, and care for them in their sickness—knowing that doing so might bring disaster upon my family and myself from Nazi pursuers and their informers? The rescuers' goodness shakes the foundations of my claims to virtue. The behavior of flesh-and-blood rescuers compels me to think long and hard about my own goodness and to imaginatively rehearse my choices in analogous situations.

Now some four decades after the Holocaust there are positive indications of increased academic and popular interest in the phenomenon of gentile rescuers of Jews. The Oliners' work on the Altruistic Personality promises to consolidate a major change in

the attitudes and concerns toward this neglected group. The Altruistic Personality Project also opens up a much-neglected area
in the social sciences. It stimulates philosophers, theologians, educators, and all of us to question the nature of moral education
after the Holocaust. Are these rescuers, who transcended the circles of their own lives to defend the persecuted of other faiths and
fates the moral models we wish to present to our children as heroes to be emulated? Is altruism to be regarded as an esteemed
virtue? If so, how can the altruistic personality be fostered? Would
we encourage parents in their homes and teachers in their classrooms to point to these rescuers as exemplars to be imitated?
Given the psychological and cultural backgrounds that inform the
character education of these altruists, so carefully analyzed by the
Oliners, how would we train our children, write our texts, and live
our lives? The responses to such questions affect the very character and shape of civilization.

Robert Penn Warren wrote of "the compulsion to try to convert what now is was, back into what was is." A post-Holocaust
weariness has seduced many into accepting the bleak wisdom of
Ecclesiastes: "Only that shall happen which has happened, only
that occur which has occurred." The phenomenon of altruism, so
painstakingly analyzed in this study, lends empirical and interpre-
tive substance to the realm of human possibility. That men,
women, and children of our time were able to jump out of their
parochial skins and transcend the surrounding culture of hate or
indifference toward those different from themselves remains critical evidence that there is far more to human nature than ex-
ploitive selfishness, and more to the future than the doom of
cyclical repetition.

We began the Foreword with a dream and conclude it with
another. The disciples of the Baal Shem Tov, the founder of Has-
idism, tell of a dream he had. In the dream, the very incarnation
of the Evil Impulse appears in the form of a sinister heart. The
Baal Shem Tov seizes the heart and pounds it furiously. He would
destroy evil and redeem the world. As he pummels it, he hears an
infant's sobbing emitted from the heart. He stops beating it. In
the midst of evil is a voice of innocence; there is goodness entan-
gled in evil.

The dream may have its philosophic roots in the Zohar leg-
end: "When God came to create the world and reveal what was
hidden in the depths and disclose light out of darkness, they were

all wrapped in one another, and therefore light emerged from darkness, and from the impenetrable came forth the profound. So too from good issues evil and from mercy issues judgment, and all are intertwined, the good impulse and the evil impulse, right and left, Israel and other peoples, white and black—all depend on one another."[2] Neither evil nor good exists in a pure state. They coexist intertwined. Wisdom lies in disentangling the knots in the skein of history.

The research on altruism in our times searches to reveal valuable information lost in the debris of the Holocaust. It is a search beyond camera history. The recording of history cannot be equated with the meaning in history. History is not memory. The gathering of historical data does not interpret itself or redeem society. As historian Yoseph Yerushalmi observes in his book *Zakhor,* "the choice for Jews as for non-Jews is not whether or not to have a past but what kind of past shall one have."[3] While history is irreversible, we have the power to decide what of our past belongs in our future. To choose a past is not to dissemble, but to attend to events in a way that frees the future from the grasp of the past. To reveal the unrecorded altruistic acts of anonymous men and women and to interpret their meaning are not only projects of historical integrity but significant contributions to the morale of humankind. The history of the Holocaust requires "keeping faithfully a double memory . . . a memory of the best and of the worst" (Camus).[4] Repression of either side of the ledger both distorts history and paralyzes the future.

In calling attention to the best of those times, this book serves as a beacon for moral education and morale for post-Holocaust generations. The courage and commitment documented in the following pages should challenge the hopelessness about the future which has dispirited many among us. It is no small matter to know that there were men and women in that hell who lived Isaiah's prophesy, who were "as hiding places from the wind, and shelters from the tempest; as rivets of water in dry places as shadows of a great rock in a weary land."

Harold M. Schulweis
Founding Chairman of the Foundation
to Sustain Righteous Christians,
sponsored by the International Center
for Holocaust Studies of the ADL

Preface

On a summer dawn in 1942, a pajama-clad twelve-year-old boy lay quietly hugging the tar paper of a sloping rooftop in the Bobowa Ghetto in Poland. The squalid ghetto, in which he—like all neighboring Jews—had been forced to live for the last two months, appeared to be deserted. His father, stepmother, grandfather, stepbrother, and stepsister were gone. Under a barrage of blows they, along with all the other inhabitants of the ghetto, had been shoved onto trucks leaving for an unknown destination. As he had prepared to go with them, his stepmother, holding the small children to her breast, had whispered savagely: "Antloif mein kind, und du vest bleiben beim leben" (Run away so that you will stay alive). She had pushed him away, and he had run blindly to the rooftop on which he now lay.

He had been there for almost an entire day and night, watching the terrorized ghetto inhabitants and listening to their screams. He had seen one child stabbed with a bayonet and another thrown from a window. Gradually the shouting subsided, the occasional gunshots were heard no more, and the roaring trucks disappeared. Whereas earlier he had heard mostly German voices, toward late afternoon he detected some Polish words amid muffled laughter. He looked down to see two men dragging a mattress from the empty house behind them. One he recognized—a Pole who had done some business with his father. He waited until they left, climbed down from the roof, and carefully entered the empty houses one by one in search of some clothes to replace his pajamas. He could find no shoes.

No sooner had he managed to get dressed than he heard the sound of scuffling boot heels. He peeked cautiously around the corner of a building. Six men in German uniforms, three of whom were speaking Ukranian, were doing a house-to-house, cellar-to-cellar search. He watched one of them push open the door of a house and saw a young woman rushing out shouting that no one else was there. Then he heard a baby cry. One of the soldiers hit the woman, knocking her down, and went into the house. He heard a single pistol shot.

The boy pushed away from the wall of the house and began worming his way through the hedges along the sides of the buildings until he neared the barbed wire fence surrounding the ghetto. There he came face to face with a young Polish boy with whom he had frequently fought. "Jude!" "Jude!" (Jew! Jew!) the young Pole shouted. Intent on choking the voice giving him away, the young Jewish lad attacked him, and the Polish boy ran away. He stumbled into an old, broken-down house on the edge of the ghetto and hid in a small closet, where he spent the night. When morning came, he managed to crawl through an escape hole not far from the main gate of the ghetto, undetected by the German soldier on guard. He was now in the Polish sector of town.

He walked and walked along the muddy summertime roads in his bare feet, eventually coming upon a farmer wearing a coarse homespun jacket and wooden shoes. He asked the farmer for a bit of bread. The farmer smiled and said, "Come to my house and I'll give you some." It was from the farmer that he heard that the Germans had killed all the Jews from the Bobowa Ghetto—shooting them into a mass grave with machine guns all day long, piling dead and live bodies, which they covered with chemicals and earth. For all the boy knew, he was now the only surviving Jew from the Bobowa Ghetto, not daring to reveal to anyone who he was and having no place to go.

And then he thought of Balwina. Balwina was a Polish peasant woman who lived in the nearby village of Bystra. He did not know her well, but he knew that his father had attended school with her and that both his father and grandfather sometimes traded with her. Forced to give up all his possessions before being herded into the ghetto, his grandfather had sold their cow and horse to Balwina, and she had given him a fair price. When the boy delivered the animals to her, Balwina had invited him in and given him some milk and cookies. These fragmented warm recollections were all the lad had to go on, but he made his way to her house.

He knocked on the door and identified himself. "It's Shmulek," he said, "Aron's son." Balwina opened the door and said "For heaven's sake, what are you doing here? It's very dangerous. Where did you come from? Hurry, come on in." She bolted the door, listened to his story, dried his tears, fed him, and kept him hidden in her attic for several days. She then advised him:

> You know what I suggest? I can't keep you here because the neighbors will recognize you. You don't look Jewish. You don't have a beard yet, and you speak Polish very well, just like a Polish peasant boy. You look just like one of our Polish Christian boys, and I suggest you change your name right now and pretend to be a peasant. Find yourself a job helping out on a farm or tending cows. You mustn't cry. There is not a Jew in Poland who is not a fugitive from death itself, and tears will not help.

Balwina gave him a new name, Jusek Polewski; taught him the Polish catechism, and also taught him to read some Polish. Several days later, he left her house and hired himself out as a Polish farm helper to a childless couple living several kilometers away. Only Balwina and her family knew who and where he was. She sent her young son, Staszek, to visit him from time to time. Staszek brought news of impending threats and also served to authenticate his fabricated identity. Shmulek, alias Jusek, had many brushes with death thereafter, but he managed to survive. All his family did indeed perish, with the exception of one cousin and his wife. They had been hidden for three years by a Polish peasant family who shared with them their meager rations and bestowed on them every manner of kindness.

Today Shmulek is the senior author of this book. He is married, the father of three sons, and a professor of sociology at Humboldt State University in California. But this book is not Shmulek's story.[1] It is Balwina's and that of the Polish couple who hid his cousins. More accurately, it is a study of those people—that small percentage of people—who risked their lives to help some Jews survive the Holocaust.

World War II brought a new dimension of evil to the world; suffering, misery, and dehumanization were its hallmarks. Millions perished. Millions of defenseless Poles, Yugoslavs, Russians, Gypsies, and other noncombatants were killed. But Jews were its special victims. Defined by the Nazis as outside humanity, Jews were collectively targeted for death. Six million of them were murdered—more than 60 percent of all Jewish men, women, and children living in Nazi-occupied Europe. The grisly extermination process proceeded very rapidly and with great efficiency despite

the fact that Jews had lived in their national communities as
friends, colleagues, neighbors, and cocitizens. Its success was due
to the relentlessness with which the Nazis pursued their prey and
the collaboration of native populations, as well as to the fact that
the majority of the world's citizen's simply stood by.

Yet, in the very midst of this catastrophe, there were exemplars of great humanity. Outstanding among them are those non-
Jews who committed themselves to helping Jews despite the awesome personal risks. This group, whom we call rescuers, refused
to abdicate their responsibilities to Jews even while the majority
of their neighbors abandoned them. They undertook their task
without monetary compensation and with full cognizance that de-
tection might result in death to themselves and frequently to their
families as well. If perpetrators and collaborators constitute the
tragedy of this human experience, rescuers constitute its hope.

What enabled this group to choose its markedly divergent
path? They seem to defy what we think we know about human
nature. That people act in the service of their own self-interest is
a maxim we are quite likely to accept. We are not even startled
when they behave demonically. What we find difficult to accept
or explain are behaviors that appear self-transcendent.

Our study was designed to provide an understanding of European rescuers of Jews during World War II, but its goal transcends this particular group or European historical moment. The
world is filled with groups marked for special cruelty. The Holocaust ushered in a new death technology, as awesome in its implications as nuclear technology. Whereas nuclear warfare
threatens to turn all of us into ashes, Holocaust technology created a means whereby selected populations could be plucked out
from among their neighbors and destroyed. The Holocaust thus
points not only to the fragility of Jews but to the precariousness
of any group that might have the misfortune of being so arbitrarily designated. If we are to live in a world free from the threat of
Holocausts, we will need to create it. If we can understand some
of the attributes that distinguished rescuers from others, perhaps
we can deliberately cultivate them.

Since its inception in 1982, the project has received hundreds
of letters reflecting a wide range of interests and sentiments. Most
of them are supportive, expressing the hope that the study will
contribute to the promotion of a more caring society, enhance the
prospects of world peace, or simply serve as an antidote to an
overwhelming sense of cynicism. Still haunted by unresolved is-

sues, numerous rescuers, survivors, or their families have written to tell us of yet other rescuers who perished, and of their hopes that the study will help lay to rest many painful memories. Some letters are troubled and troubling. One letter simply states that the study is futile: The world is evil, and there is no such thing as "altruism." Others reflect ambivalence about the project's efforts to find answers and concerns about reawakening past nightmares suppressed over the years.

But the most disturbing concerns of all have been raised by some survivors. Highlighting the activity of this small minority, many say, will lull people into believing that the horrors never occurred. "Be prepared for a great deal of criticism," warned one Auschwitz survivor. "The memories of those years are too surfeited with tragedy to allow for much of goodness." Such anguish was revealed most deeply at a conference intended to honor rescuers that was sponsored by the U.S. Holocaust Memorial Council and held in Washington, D.C., in September 1984. Some fifty rescuers and many of those they rescued were among the invited and honored guests. One of the scheduled events was a dialogue between rescuers and rescued, organized along national lines—Dutch rescuers with Dutch rescued, Polish rescuers with Polish rescued, and so on. It was a pioneering effort at such communication. But no one quite foresaw the depths of the wounds. Even amid those who were acknowledged rescuers, some survivors could not restrain themselves from shouting accusations as they recalled those years during which their lives had been dominated by brutal behaviors at the hands of others.

We need to break through these walls of bitterness and recrimination, for pessimism and despair feed on themselves. Our purpose is not to bury the past but rather to help illuminate its full scope with all its dimensions. The story of rescue must be told not only for the sake of historical accuracy but also because social inquiry itself is a moral enterprise, reflecting what cultures and nations choose to remember, study, and above all leave as a message for posterity. Sholem Asch said it best of all:

> It is of the highest importance not only to record and recount, both for ourselves and for the future, the evidences of human degradation, but side by side with them to set forth evidences of human exaltation and nobility. Let the epic of heroic deeds of love, as opposed by those of hatred, of rescue as opposed to destruction, bear equal witness to unborn generations.[2]

Acknowledgments

A study of this magnitude would not have been possible without the help of many people, only a fraction of whom can be mentioned here. We are immensely grateful to all those individuals and groups who supplied us with valuable services and support.

Above all, we owe a special debt of gratitude to Dr. John Slawson, Executive Vice President Emeritus of the American Jewish Committee. Dr. Slawson, through the John Slawson Fund of the American Jewish Committee, provided the major funding for this study, without which our research would not have been possible. In a real sense he launched the project and remains its most steadfast supporter. Forty years ago he played an even more elaborate role in relation to the monumental Authoritarian Personality Study, which explored the roots of ethnocentrism and fascism, and to which he contributed conceptually, methodologically, and financially. That he should conclude what has been an unusually productive career by focusing on the study of altruism lends a particularly appropriate symmetry to his life and work. In this context we also want to thank Selma Hirsh, associate director emeritus of the American Jewish Committee and Dr. Slawson's long-time associate, for her consistent support, encouragement, and kindness.

We are also grateful for financial support given by the following foundations: the Charles H. Revson Foundation and its president, Eli Evans, the Jacob and Hilda Blaustein Foundation Inc., the May and Benjamin Swig Charity Foundation, the Sidney Stern Memorial Trust, the Volkswagen Foundation, the Johnson Foundation, and the Elliot Wolk Foundation. We owe a special debt of gratitude to Raffaello Fellah, president of the Italian Section of the World Sephardi Foundation, who helped finance the study in

Italy. Although we much appreciate the very valuable help given by the foundations mentioned here, the statements made and views expressed are solely the responsibility of the authors.

We are indebted to our international team of colleagues, who coordinated and supervised the intricate details involved in data collection in their respective countries. Sustained attention to the complexities involved in these procedures required a special type of tenacity and dedication. We are also grateful to them for providing us with a collegial community that challenged us intellectually and supported us emotionally. We thus express deep appreciation to Professor Janusz Reykowski (Poland), Professor Jürgen Falter (Germany), Professor André Kaspi (France), Dr. Richard Van Dyck (Holland), Dr. Michele Sarfatti and Professor Luisella Mortara Ottolenghi (Italy), and Susan Schwartz (Norway). We also acknowledge the help of Professor Erika Fromm, who helped us connect with Dr. Richard Van Dyck and begin the study in Holland.

The interview process required great sensitivity and skill. We were most fortunate to have acquired the services of many gifted and dedicated interviewers, including Dr. Zuzanna Smolenska, Professor Ellen Land-Weber, Professor Lawrence Baron, Anna Tarocchi, Ute Klingemann, Dr. Siegfried Schumann, Dr. Ted Linn, Marne Carmean, Mary Fullerton Farr, Viola Wdowinsky, Eva Fogelman, Marc Knobel, Claude Singer, Jean Laloum, Jean-Claude Kuperminc, Joyce Tapper, Irene Juniper, Mae Briskin, Achim von Malottki, Dalia Aminoff, Philippe Kaspi, Nathalie Weill, Trees Egberts, A. Wallace, Marguerite Mulder, Gisele Apter, Dr. Alberto Cavaglion, Marieke Van Der Eyk, M. C. Bogaards, Laura Quiercioli Mincer, Magdelena Cybulko, and Professor Aimée Langlois among others. Equally important were our translators, including Tatiana Klonowicz, Alicja Rudnicka, Dr. Maya Peretz, and Marek Szopski (Polish); Gabrielle Duebendorfer, Wilhelmine Hartnack, and Ursula Osborne (German); Marguerite Budenaers, Dr. Odette Meyers, Dr. Jeanette K. Ringold, and Le'ene Sherwood (French); Nelda Cassuto and Giulia Drew (Italian); Wiete Ter Haar, Ellen Montiere, and Catharina P. Olivares (Dutch); Gila Flam (Hebrew); and Miriam Frydman (Yiddish).

For their transcriptions, coding, typing, as well as assorted other tasks associated with managing the day-to-day operations of the project, we thank Janyce Neuman, Hadidjah Shortridge, and Gabrielle Duebendorfer. Their versatile skills and grace under pressure made it possible to do the impossible on more than one occasion.

Framing and analyzing the statistical components of our study were highly demanding tasks. We benefited greatly from the work of Professor Paul Crosbie, who helped us design the questionnaire and begin the coding procedures. We express our deep thanks to Professor Mary Gruber for unraveling our data and supervising their final preparation, participating in the ongoing demands of statistical analyses, and counseling us throughout regarding statistical procedures and data presentation. We are particularly appreciative of the notable contribution made by Professor Don Bowlus in preparing the complex summary statistical data, which strengthened and illuminated our work considerably. We are also grateful to Suzanne Bowlus for "cleaning" the data. All brought to their tasks not only high levels of competence, but also a spirit of shared excitement and grace that made the process unusually pleasurable.

To our colleagues who read the initial drafts of our manuscript and offered invaluable suggestions, we also extend our thanks. We note among them Dr. Marianne Pennekamp, Professors Susan Frances, Bill Devall, Jerry Krause, John Gai, Mary Gruber, Jack Shaffer, John Steiner, Janusz Reykowski, Rev. Douglas Huneke, Dr. Zuzanna Smolenska, Susan Allan, Mark Allan, and Joanne Sullivan.

We are grateful for the support given us at many levels by Humboldt State University. We thank the students who helped us with assorted tasks, including the qualitative coding of our data, among them most notably Wally Anderson, Roger Golec, John Mulvaney, Star Robinson, Heline Sundet, Celeste Del Grande, Linda Knopp, Michael Chandler, Edward Chevalier, Garland Garrisi, Kristin Carlson, and Tandy Oremus. We also wish to thank James Hamby and the staff of the Humboldt State University Foundation, who so ably handled the financial management of our project. We also thank Judy Hampton, Ruth Miller, Mary Roth, Nancy Wollin, and Kathy Mayer, who assisted us with assorted secretarial tasks as the need arose, and Jeannie Wielgus, who assisted us so ably at the computer.

A special word of great appreciation is due to Rabbi Harold Schulweis, founder of the Institute for Righteous Acts, who wisely urged the study of rescuers in the early 1960s; and to Seymour Fromer, director of the Judah Magnes Memorial Museum, for his sustained support and encouragement over the years and for permitting us to use the museum's facilities. We also acknowledge with special thanks the continuing support of Reverend Douglas Huneke, a trailblazer himself in the study of rescuers, who shared with us his intellectual insights as well as data and also facilitated the implementation of several critical responsibilities.

We also wish to express thanks to our board members—Mae Briskin, Harry James Cargas, Paul Crosbie, Raffaello Fellah, Howard Friedman, Seymour Fromer, Erika Fromm, Rabbi Joseph Glaser, David Gordis, Irene Juniper, William Helmreich, Rev. Douglas Huneke, Ellen Land-Weber, Aimée Langlois, George Lerski, Ted Linn, Seymour Martin Lipset, Franklin Littel, Elizabeth Midlarsky, Odette Meyers, Marianne Pennekamp, Sister Carol Rittner, David Rosenhan, John Roth, Pierre Sauvage, Rabbi Harold Schulweis, Neil Smelser, André Stein, Tina Strobos, Joyce Tapper, Nechama Tec, William Trosten, Tilla Vahanian, Selma Hirsh, and John Steiner.

Numerous other individuals have given their support and services (financial and other) including George Rynecki, Fred Knauer, Dan Enright, Dr. Elaine Dallman, Alfred Fromm, Gene Glick, Michele McKeegan, Dr. Ed Olsgaard, Elaine Deutsch, Ruth Robinson, Dr. Tina Strobos, Raffaello Fellah of the Commitato Italiano, Martha Cherkis, Jack Lumer, and the staffs of the Centre di Documentazione Ebraica Contemporanea, the Centre de Documentation Juive Contemporaine, the Jewish Historical Institute in Warsaw, and Yad Vashem in Israel as well as its director, Dr. Mordecai Paldiel.

We feel most fortunate in having had a group of colleagues who helped us directly in preparing sections of this manuscript. Lawrence Baron, author of the chapter on the historical context of rescue, was able to compress a highly complex array of facts and subtleties into a cogent and lucid analysis of the broad social conditions that constituted the background against which our respondents lived. Janusz Reykowski not only provided the theoretical framework for the analysis of the catalysts which aroused rescuers to action but, along with Zuzanna Smolenska, collaborated with us in writing that chapter. Professor Neil Smelser helped us articulate some of the methodological issues, and Professor Jack Shaffer aided us in clarifying some of the personality factors.

We are deeply grateful to Laura Wolff, senior editor at The

Free Press, whose tireless editing has greatly improved this work. Ms. Wolff brought to this endeavor her highly developed communication skills, a shared sense of the importance of the work, and knowledge of its substantive content. We feel most fortunate to have had her assistance and thank The Free Press for making her services available to us.

The above do not exhaust the names of individuals and groups who have supported this effort and enriched our lives in the process. Although we alone are responsible for the views expressed in this work and any errors contained therein, we nonetheless feel linked to all these people in a shared concern for creating a global caring community.

・

CHAPTER 1

・

Why Risk One's Life?

World War II is rightfully remembered as a time of exceeding cruelty and barbarism. Nowhere was this brutality more evident than in the treatment of Jews, six million of whom were exterminated by unprecedentedly ruthless means in a period of about five years. Yet, also during this period, somewhere between 50,000 to 500,000 non-Jews risked their lives and frequently those of their families to help Jews survive. Although they constituted but a fraction of the total population under Nazi occupation, their significance transcends their numbers.

We regard the rescue of Jews as an example of an altruistic behavior. To be sure, there were those who helped Jews out of greed and self-interest; these individuals are not the subjects of our study. The individuals we are interested in are those who helped out of humanitarian considerations alone—without material rewards of any kind. What makes their behavior of particular interest is not only the fact that it was undertaken in the context of terror but that it was undertaken on behalf of an "outsider" minority group, marginal under normal conditions and increasingly rejected and despised as the poisonous seeds of Nazism spread all over Europe.

The true number of rescuers is unlikely ever to be known. Many perished in the effort; they became another wartime casualty, their specific activities lost in a statistic of over forty million World War II deaths. Among those who survived, many refused to identify themselves even after the war was over. Some refused to do so because they did not want public recognition for doing what they thought was their simple human duty. Others were afraid of revealing their activities—"Jew lover" was an unrewarding title in many places long after the Nazi menace had abated. Some con-

1

tinue to fear the shadowy hand of threatening neo-Nazi groups.
Any counts of rescuers are thus, at best, estimates.

If the definition of rescue is limited to those who risked their
lives without monetary compensation, the lower figure of 50,000 is
more reasonable. This is the estimate given by Mordecai Paldiel,[1]
director of Yad Vashem's Department of the Righteous in Israel.
But even the highest estimate, a million,[2] represents less than one-
half of 1 percent of the total population under Nazi occupation.
Clearly, then, even many basically good and decent folk, personally sympathetic, nonetheless regarded the fate of others as separate and distinct from their own—not quite pertinent enough, not
quite important enough to compel intervention. What we need to
understand is why rescuers could not share this perception of the
fate of Europe's Jews.

Much of human behavior can be explained as the result of
broad social forces—political, economic, and social organizations
compel the assumption of social roles that shape us. Living in any
society demands submission to its organized patterns and behavioral requirements. Within such dominating structures, the individual often appears to be powerless. The existence of rescuers
informs us, however, that individuals are not entirely powerless.
We seek to understand the source of their power to resist the
forces around them and why they chose to manifest that power in
an act of altruism toward an outsider group despite the risks.

In search of answers we interviewed almost 700 persons living
in several countries in Nazi-occupied Europe—406 rescuers, 126
nonrescuers, and 150 survivors. The rescuers in our sample were
all identified as such by Yad Vashem, Israel's memorial to the victims of the Holocaust. Part of Yad Vashem's charge is to honor
those who risked their lives to rescue Jews, in fulfillment of which
a commission of eighteen members appointed by Yad Vashem in-
vestigates and determines who shall be designated a rescuer. The
commission makes its determination based on evidence submitted
by rescued survivors (or their friends and relatives), as well as an-
cillary documentation and personal interviews. Three overriding
criteria determine selection: the rescuer had to be motivated by
humanitarian considerations only, risked his or her own life, and
received no remuneration of any kind for his or her act. As of this
writing, Yad Vashem has identified some 6,000 such rescuers—at
the time of the collection of our data, the number was approximately 5,500. The important point about Yad Vashem's list is that

all those identified thereon are authenticated rescuers—their activities corroborated by external documentation—and their hu-
manistic motivations are attested to by the rescued survivors themselves. Ninety-five percent of the rescuers we interviewed are Yad
Vashem designees; the remaining 5 percent are individuals we
identified by virtue of our interviews with rescued survivors, using
criteria similar to those established by Yad Vashem.

Most of our respondents are from Poland, Germany, France,
and Holland, but also included are representatives from other
countries, including Italy, Denmark, Belgium, and Norway. Most
still live in their native countries; a few have emigrated to the
United States or Canada. We designed a questionnaire and
trained interviewers who met with each respondent for a period
of several hours. The interviews were taped and subsequently
translated into English, transcribed, coded, and analysed. Analyses
were both qualitative and quantitative in character.

Our interviews were guided by several key questions, including: Was rescue primarily a matter of opportunity—that is, a question of external circumstances? If so, what were they? Was rescue
a matter of personal attributes—particular learned values and personality characteristics? If so, what were they? Implicit in these
questions is the notion that there may exist something called an
"altruistic" personality; that is, a relatively enduring predisposition to act selflessly on behalf of others, which develops early in
life. For this reason we were interested not only in what our respondents did during the war and the circumstances of their wartime lives but also in their parents and their youthful characteristics and behaviors as well as their current behaviors.

We included a sample of nonrescuers because explanations
regarding rescue needed to address not only what rescuers may
have shared in common but also whether their particular attributes were in some way different from others. If no discernible
differences are found, then we must either conclude that rescue
behavior was a matter of chance—that is, not really explainable—
or that we have failed to look for those factors that might provide
reasonable explanations.

Our comparison group consists of people not identified as
rescuers either by Yad Vashem or our own means of corroboration
but who lived in the same countries at the same time as the rescuers did. During the course of interviewing our 126 nonrescuers,
we became aware of an important difference among the members

of this group. In response to the question of whether they had done anything out of the ordinary during the war to help other people or to resist the Nazis, 53 responded yes; it turned out that they were either members of resistance groups or had helped Jews or sometimes both. Although we had no reason to doubt their claims, we did not have corroborating external evidence. Rather than exclude them from our study, we labeled them "actives"— that is, persons who by their self-reports either participated in resistance activities or helped Jews. The remaining 72 nonrescuers said they had done nothing out of the ordinary during the war either to help other people or resist the Nazis. We labeled this group "bystanders." The statistical comparisons we report are based on two types of comparisons: (1) similarities or statistically significant differences between rescuers and all nonrescuers, including actives and bystanders, and (2) similarities or statistically significant differences between rescuers and bystanders only.

The sample of survivors served supplementary purposes only. They were helpful in illuminating some of the diversity of rescue conditions and rescuers, and we used their testimony in comparing rescuers' assertions of their reasons for rescue with survivors' perceptions of reasons.

Altruism is such a complex concept that some clarification of its historical and theoretical background is in order.

The word *altruism* is rooted in the Latin *alter,* which simply means "other." It is credited to August Comte, who coined it about 150 years ago. The word itself was widely disseminated through the works of Herbert Spencer toward the latter part of the nineteenth century.[3] Although it was favored and popularized by social reformers and explored by philosophers and theologians, with few exceptions, social scientists tended to ignore the term until recent times. Pitirim Sorokin[4] gave the concept some academic respectability in the 1940s when he turned his attention to its meaning and dimensions and began to study it as a sociopsychological phenomenon. But not until the 1960s did other social scientists begin a serious study of the phenomenon. Not coincidentally, perhaps, this period overlapped with a renewed interest in the scientific study of morality, based largely on the seminal works of Jean Piaget and Lawrence Kohlberg.

Comte conceived of altruism as devotion to the welfare of others, based in selflessness.[5] This probably comes closest to its consensual meaning as given in *Webster's Third New International Dic-*

tionary—"uncalculated consideration of, regard for, or devotion to other's interests. . . . " This suggests that the act needs to be performed entirely for its own sake apart from any considerations of self-satisfaction, pleasure, or utility. Is such behavior possible? Skeptics such as Machiavelli and Hobbes would argue that humans are incapable of acting out of any other motive than their own self-interest. Even those who might have a more benevolent view of human behavior—such as Helvetius, Plato, Marx, Freud, and mainstream psychologists[6]—suggest that people rarely act out of any motive higher than enlightened self-interest. Whereas Machiavellianism implies manipulating or even harming others for the sake of self, enlightened self-interest counsels helping others in light of reciprocal claims. Thus, what appears like altruism turns out at best to be intelligent consideration of the self.

On the other hand, Émile Durkheim believed that altruism exists in every society.[7] Altruism exists, said Durkheim, whenever individuals abnegate their interests in favor of obedience for the sake of society. No society could exist unless its members acknowledge and make sacrifices on behalf of each other. Thus, said Durkheim, altruism is not merely "a sort of agreeable ornament to social life" but its fundamental basis.

Most definitions center on selflessness and motivation as critical elements of altruism. However, the degree of selflessness necessary and the type of motivation required vary considerably. At one extreme are those who insist that the altruistic actor must have no concern for self[8] and derive no benefit from the act;[9] at the other are those who say that an act that satisfies both the self and the other can nonetheless be considered altruistic.[10] In between are those who maintain that it is sufficient that costs outweigh gratification.[11] Proposals regarding the types of motivations necessary range from mere intention to help,[12] to helping for any reasons other than external rewards,[13] to insistence on specific internal states (such as empathy,[14] or lack of concern with restitution),[15] specific values (such as love or compassion),[16] personal norms,[17] or principles of justice.[18]

Each of the above presents its own set of conceptual and pragmatic problems. For example, if we say that the actor does not benefit, does this mean that he or she must derive no *internal* pleasure from the act? And does this exclude incidental benefits, derived as unforeseen by-products of the act? How can we assess practically whether expectation or gratification is outweighed by costs or rule out the possibilities of restitution or compensation as motivating mechanisms even if people say they performed the act for other reasons? Such problems, of course, are not unique to the construct of altruism. Any attempt to characterize internal psychological states is hindered by similar difficulties in knowing or quantifying another's thoughts or feelings.

For the purpose of our study, we prefer a definition that relies on objective, measurable criteria. We characterize a behavior as altruistic when (1) it is directed towards helping another, (2) it involves a high risk or sacrifice to the actor, (3) it is accompanied by no external reward, and (4) it is voluntary. Rescue behavior in the context of the Holocaust meets these criteria. The behavior was clearly directed toward helping; it was very high risk, threatening life itself; it was accompanied by no external reward, according to the rescued survivors' Yad Vashem testimony; and it was certainly voluntary—no external coercions required it.

The above criteria could encompass a variety of altruistic behaviors, such as saving drowning people, pulling people out of burning buildings, searching for those lost on the high seas, or abandoning one's career in order to care for ailing parents. But rescue behavior in the context of the Holocaust has special dimensions that make it a particular form of altruism.

One distinguishing characteristic of Holocaust rescue activity was its duration. For a small number of rescuers, the activity was confined to a few hours or a few days—for most, though, it continued from two to five years. Second, help was extended to a group that differed from the actors in culture, ethnicity, and religion. Such differences were highlighted and exaggerated by a constant barrage of Nazi propaganda that defined Jews as outside the pale of humanity.

Finally, Holocaust rescue activity differed from altruistic behaviors rooted in approved social norms. In the context of World War II, the rescue of Jews was legally prohibited, and broad extralegal norms were at best ambivalent and at worst supportive of Nazi policies. Rescuers could anticipate little external approval. Even if they had reason to believe that intimate friends or neighbors might approve, they could not disclose their activities to them. Any rewards had to be self-administered. Thus, we are looking at a particular form of altruism—marked by life-threatening risks to self and a long duration in time, extending to a "pariah"

group marked for death, and occurring in the context of a disapproving or, at most, equivocal normative social climate.

Our study is part of an as yet small but accumulating body of
literature addressing rescue behavior, primarily the work of historians and social scientists during the last twenty years.[19] Historians
and other Holocaust scholars point to the fact that some form of
rescue activity occurred in many countries and regions under Nazi
occupation[20] and that thousands of individuals died as a consequence of helping Jews.[21] On a national level, Bulgaria,[22] Denmark,[23] and Italy[24] managed to keep Jewish victimization to a relatively low level because of the cooperation of elite officials and
local populations generally resistant to anti-Semitism. But rescue
also occurred in those countries in which local populations were
virulently anti-Semitic, themselves participated in murdering
Jews, and among which Jewish victimization was extraordinarily
high (for example, Rumania[25] and Lithuania).[26]

In some cases, rescue was undertaken by formally organized
networks. In Poland, for example, Zegota was specifically organized to help Jews, whereas in the Netherlands, the National Organization for Assistance to Divers (Landelijker Organisatie voor
Hulp aan Onderduikers, also known as the LO) sheltered Jews
along with other fugitives.[27] Religious groups representing assorted denominations also participated in rescue, including for
example, the Protestant CIMADE (Comité d'Inter-Mouvements
Auprès des Evacués) and the Huguenot congregation of Pastor
Trocmé in France, the Caritas Catholics in Germany, and Father
Marie-Bénoit's network in Italy and France.[28] Although networks
could obviously help larger numbers of victims then could individuals acting alone, single individuals sometimes masterminded the
rescue of hundreds and even thousands of Jewish lives. This was
the case, for example, with Herman Graebe,[29] Oskar Schindler[30]
and Raoul Wallenberg.[31]

Although not the focus of our study, it is important to note
that Jews themselves participated in resistance and rescue. When
allowed, they participated in general resistance groups, frequently
in disproportionate percentages,[32] and also formed their own
fighting groups, such as the Jewish Fighting Organizations of Warsaw and Bialystok in Poland, [33] the Jewish Action Groups in Holland,[34] and the Jewish Fighting Organization in France.[35] Jewish
partisan groups in Eastern Europe were not only fighting units

but also provided shelter for Jews, although they themselves were frequently the hunted targets of other, non-Jewish partisan units.[36] Jews also worked to find shelters, arrange for emigration, and relieve general suffering in such organizations as the OSE (Organisation de Secours d'Enfants) and Jewish Scouts in France[37] and DELASEM in Italy. Although increasingly attacked for their naive and misguided policies,[38] some Nazi-appointed Jewish councils nonetheless were able to help Jews emigrate and to provide other services.[39] Zionist groups such as Hashomer Hatzair and Hechalutz,[40] as well as Jewish communists and socialists and other individuals of varying political persuasions, were also engaged in such efforts.

In an effort to identify the social groups most likely to be involved in rescue, several researchers have focused on the demographic characteristics of rescuers. Thus, for example, males, older Germans, independents (particularly small businessmen), and white-collar workers were more represented than were females and blue-collar workers among *Judenfreunde* (friends of Jews) and *Rassenschänder* (those who had sexual relations with Jews) in Gestapo files at Düsseldorf.[41] Males and older Germans (born before 1910) were also more represented among seventy German helpers interviewed in 1966.[42] But although the over-forty age group and the middle class were also most likely to extend kindness to Jews in a small town in the Rhineland area of Germany, females outnumbered the males there.[43] On the other hand, socioeconomic class was found to be only weakly related to rescue in Poland.[44] Thus, at best, the demographic evidence is fragmentary—suggestive but inconclusive.

Implicitly or explicitly, investigations of human behavior are based in some theoretical explanation. Historians, sociologists, and anthropologists prefer to explain rescue activity as the result of specific events, social forces, and institutions or culture. In general, they pay scant attention to psychological processes. Because our study is more rooted in the latter, and to illuminate its context, a brief description of the five major theoretical orientations that have been applied to explain altruistic behavior follows.

According to sociobiologists, genes are the source of altruistic behaviors.[45] They maintain that no species could survive unless certain individuals within it were ready to sacrifice themselves for the welfare of the group and that such inclinations are transmitted genetically. Species that do not transmit such genetic predispositions to a sufficient proportion of their members perish. Although this hypothesis has yet to be proved conclusively, it is highly probable that biological factors do contribute to altruistic behavior. A promising avenue of research may lie in an examination of emotive and brain systems, as Panksepp has recently proposed.[46] However, it appears unlikely that biology alone accounts for altruistic behavior. Evidence suggests that not only humans but also higher animal primates learn many of their skills—aggressive as well as nurturant—from their caregivers.[47]

According to psychoanalytic theory, learning, rather than genetically transmitted predispositions, explains altruistic behaviors. It is only through identification with others and the constraints imposed by society that individuals learn to mute their innate aggressiveness and help others. Identification fosters the development of the superego, and altruistic behaviors emerge as a result of guilt for moral transgressions, imposed by the superego,[48] and through the internalization of certain values and standards,[49] largely developed in early childhood. In fact, psychoanalytic theory denies the existence of selfless motivation, for, according to Freud, all behavior is ultimately rooted in satisfying the self.[50] Psychoanalytic theory offers one of the most comprehensive explanations of human behavior, but many of its essential propositions have as yet to be validated. It has not been clearly demonstrated, for example, that the source of altruistic behaviors lies in egoistic or selfish concerns. As critics have noted, Freud was heavily influenced by the biology of his times, now disputed in many of its essentials.[51] Moreover, he made large-scale inferences based on a small number of clinical cases.

Cognitive developmental theorists such as Piaget[52] and Kohlberg[53] propose that individuals progress through stages of moral reasoning as a result of mental maturational processes interacting with experience. Kohlberg identified six stages of progressive moral reasoning, each one superior to the preceding one by virtue of more adequately resolving issues relating to justice. Evidence bearing on the relationship between articulated moral reasoning and helpful behavior indicates that the latter is only partly explained by the level of moral reasoning.[54] Long before they are capable of mature moral reasoning, some young children already exhibit helping behaviors despite cost to themselves.[55] And many adults who cannot necessarily articulate high levels of moral reasoning also display altruistic behaviors—as Iris Murdoch noted, "An unexamined life can be virtuous."[56]

Whereas psychoanalysts and cognitive developmentalists infer internal psychological processes as critical for altruistic behavior, social learning theorists prefer to concentrate on the observ-
able and demonstrable. Altruistic behaviors, they maintain, are
indeed learned, but basically through reinforcement and modeling. Learners may experience the reinforcement directly through
externally administered rewards, or vicariously, as when they observe altruistic models rewarded for their behavior.[57] Internal
states, such as values, cognition, and emotions, are not considered
to cause the behavior but are themselves the results of reinforcement.[58] Yet, in the absence of apparent external rewards, it is not
always clear where and how reinforcement occurs. We are left to
infer some internal reward system—such as pleasure in meeting
another's needs or in fulfilling some value. This suggests that external reinforcement, including the observation of models, may
be important in influencing altruistic behavior but that internal
factors need also to be considered.

Our study is rooted in a *social psychological* orientation, which
assumes that behavior is best explained as the result of an interaction between personal and external social, or situational, factors.
We view an altruistic behavior as the outcome of a decision-
making process in which the internal characteristics of actors as
well as the external environments in which they find themselves
influence each other.

Personal factors include personality characteristics and values. Situational factors are the immediate external environmental
conditions over which the actor has no control but that nonetheless affect a decision. Some decisions are more rooted in personal
dispositional factors, others are more dependent on situational
factors. A passerby, for example, might consider whether he has
the skills to save a drowning person, but he might not stop to consider his skills if the life of his child were at stake.

In studying the role of personal factors in motivating our respondents' wartime behavior, we make certain assumptions about
the stability of personality. We met our respondents forty years
after the event—forty years during which they had many experiences. Some married; others divorced and remarried; some acquired additional education and new occupations; others changed
little. Some remained in their countries of birth; others emigrated;
some became ill and disabled; others are relatively healthy. The

war itself was a traumatic event, and what they did during the war also affected them. Yet we are assuming that despite any changes, there is a basic continuity in personality that extends over a life-time—that the person we meet today is in essential ways very similar to the person of forty years ago.

Such an assumption would probably have been accepted with-out question a few years ago, when most psychologists believed that personality is formed early, that childhood plays a determi-nant role in shaping it, and—although changes occur—that it re-mains largely stable after childhood. However, the recent work of some "life-span" researchers has challenged these beliefs.[59]

These researchers find change an ongoing process through-out life, from birth to old age. They point out that individuals vary markedly in their courses of development and also vary because of their particular conditions and experiences. Rather than ac-cepting early childhood as the primary period during which indi-vidual personality is formed, they propose that any period in the life span can be a time for critical change.[60] Although some psy-chologists are not quite as ready as they once were to give stability their unqualified endorsement, nonetheless few fully reject it. The emerging view is something of a compromise—yes, some things change and some things remain the same.

Direct evidence bearing on the question of consistency in per-sonality comes from longitudinal studies that take repeated mea-sures of the same population at different times. These studies are almost unanimous in reporting a basic consistency in personality, particularly from early adulthood onward. Predispositions with re-gard to such matters as values,[61] occupational interests,[62] psycho-logical well-being,[63] neuroticism, extroversion, and openness to ex-perience,[64] as well as other self-reported personality traits, appear to change very little after the early twenties. To be sure, the evi-dence is not yet conclusive. The studies are few in number; their quality differs as do the measuring tools used and the characteris-tics investigated. But because they follow the same people over time, they offer the strongest evidence to date of a basic consist-ency in personality from young adulthood on. We therefore as-sume that despite the passage of years and change in external cir-cumstances, the people we meet today have many of the same predispositions they manifested at the outbreak of the war.

Predispositions represent an inclination toward a given behavior, not an inevitably programmed response. Thus, when we say that someone has an "altruistic personality," it means not that he or she always acts altruistically but that this person is more likely than others to make altruistic decisions. Similarly, we are not proposing that early life experiences and personality inevitably determine an altruistic response, but that they influence perceived choices.

This book examines what led rescuers to choose their particular course of action. It looks at what led them to place themselves and their families at risk on behalf of Jews—often unknown to them previously—and what experiences, values, and personality characteristics moved them to act while others stood silently by. We turn first to the political, legal, and social climate within which they acted.

CHAPTER 2

The Historical Context of Rescue

The Germans insisted that we [Jews] all be handed over to them. So we were arrested by the Italian military to save us from being handed over to the Ustases [the Croatian security police] and to the Germans. It was a measure of compassion to save us because the Italians had seen the terrible things that the Ustases did in the concentration camp in Belgrade.... One day the commanding officer came to me and said, "I think the situation is very precarious. The Germans may come any day. But I have"—and this was one of his most generous gestures—"an ambulance car here in the garage with enough gasoline to travel thirty kilometers to Italy, across the border. I have given the name of five persons to the driver because I am going on vacation and don't want you to remain unprotected. So even if the Germans should come, you will be put in an ambulance car and taken to the kingdom." I cannot imagine anyone but an Italian making such a gesture. He said, "I was always a fascist. I will not deny being a fascist, but I will never accept anti-Semitism and the persecution of the Jews."

As this rescued Croatian Jew's testimony illustrates, the response to the Holocaust differed not only from country to country but from individual to individual. To gain an understanding of how and why individuals made the difficult and dangerous decision to rescue Jews requires looking first at the general factors that enhanced or diminished the feasibility of helping Jews and the risks involved in doing so.[1] These will be set in the context of an outline of the specific historical events and conditions that affected the efforts to rescue Jews in the five principal countries in which indigenous research teams conducted interviews for the Altruistic Personality Project: Germany, Poland, the Netherlands, France, and Italy.

In assessing the relationship between wartime conditions and the victimization or protection of the Jewish community in each country, we need to distinguish between the policies and condi-

This chapter was written by Lawrence Baron.

13

tions imposed by Nazi Germany and the responses of local leaders and officials. The Third Reich sowed and cultivated the seeds of anti-Semitism by disseminating propaganda, enacting discriminatory legislation in the territories it occupied, and relentlessly pressuring its allies to participate in the crusade against European Jewry. The extent of its success in making each country *Judenrein* (purified of Jews) depended partly on the fertility of the native soil for the seeds of Nazi prejudice. In areas where political anti-Semitism was already widespread and virulent, the Germans received local cooperation in the implementation of the Final Solution or at least encountered public indifference to the plight of the Jews. In some places indigenous collaborators tried to carve out a niche for themselves and their nations in Hitler's "new order" by assisting or emulating his campaign against the Jews for ideological or pragmatic reasons. Conversely, the plan to murder European Jews sometimes failed to take root or reach fruition in countries where anti-Semitism was weak, Jewish civic equality was firmly established, German influence was limited, or the local regime and populace were or became anti-German during the war. Ultimately the nature and extent of German control over a country were the primary determinants of the toll of Jewish lives there. When the decision to exterminate the Jews was made in 1941,[2] Germany relied primarily on military force to attain this end. The greater Germany's presence and power, especially in the form of the SS—which was in charge of carrying out the Final Solution— the greater was Germany's capability to achieve its genocidal aim.[3]

Because Hitler had no coherent blueprint for organizing his empire, but rather improvised occupation regimes and alliances on the basis of changing economic, ideological, racial, and strategic considerations, Germany's system for ruling the countries it conquered and influencing its allies varied from country to country. The status accorded a nation or region in Germany's diplomatic and military realm reflected which of the above criteria Hitler deemed most crucial at a particular stage in the war.[4]

Areas subjected to direct German control and a substantial SS presence had the least chance of resisting Nazi policies successfully. Three types of governance characterized German rule in these areas. The first, entailing incorporation into the Greater German Reich, was applied to countries and territories Hitler viewed as historically and racially German, such as Alsace-Lorraine, Austria, and the Sudetenland. Here the German civil bureaucracy administered the law and the police and security apparatus of the Gestapo and SS enforced it. A second kind of rule was enforced in Poland in the newly created provinces of Danzig–West Prussia, German Silesia, and the Wartheland, which were designated for agricultural colonization by Germans. The racially "inferior" inhabitants of these provinces were slated for economic servitude or relocation by their German "superiors." All Jews were immediately to be expelled from these lands, and SS agencies headed the program of population transfers. The third form of German control was exercised through German military commanders or civilian governors who relied on SS and Wehrmacht occupation troops to exact local obedience. The territories making up this zone consisted of the remainder of Poland, the military district Südost, which included Serbia and Nazi-occupied Greece, and the occupation zones carved out of the areas wrested from the Soviet Union—Bialystok Province, the Ostland (Belorussia, Estonia, Latvia, and Lithuania), and the Ukraine. These regions became centers for the killing of Jews. German rule was harshest in the second and third types of regimes because they were located in places where battlefront conditions and remoteness prevented scrutiny by the German public or by neutral and enemy countries. Moreover, these regions were populated by nationalities the Nazis held in contempt and that contained the largest concentrations of the Nazis' main racial and ideological foes—namely, European Jewry and Russian Bolshevism.

In other defeated and occupied countries, policy was set by German authorities, utilizing the existing bureaucracies or native collaborators to assist in its implementation. Under this sort of regime, the relative strength of the SS vis-à-vis the Wehrmacht, and the degree of autonomy granted to local administrators determined the possibilities for rescuing Jews. In the Netherlands a *Reichskommissar* (high commissioner) obtained the grudging compliance of Dutch officials through reprisals and coercion frequently employed by SS police and native fascists. The situation was similar in Norway, where a *Reichskommissar* governed in conjunction with the pro-Nazi regime of Vidkun Quisling and an SS detachment. The SS was somewhat weaker in Belgium and the occupied zones of France, which were under the jurisdiction of military governors. In both countries much of the internal administration remained in the hands of the native civil service. Until 1943, Denmark enjoyed the greatest independence of all conquered and occupied countries. In return for its rapid surrender and voluntary economic exploitation, Denmark was allowed to keep its king, parliament, and armed forces, which retained a good deal of their autonomy under a relatively lenient military occupation. When Germany eventually cracked down on the Danes, its worsening fortunes in the war prevented it from sending sufficient numbers of SS troops to round up the Jews. In general, German persecution of the Jews in Western Europe evolved more subtly and gradually than in Eastern Europe.

The level of influence Germany exerted over its allies varied. In Croatia and Slovakia the Nazis created dependent and loyal satellite states by exploiting local ethnic rivalries. These proxy regimes represented authoritarian political factions that would not have come to power without Germany's support. Sustained by German aid and restrained by the proximity (Slovakia) or presence (Croatia) of Axis troops, the governments of both states exercised a precarious sovereignty that could be terminated at the first sign of insurgency, as was the case in Slovakia in 1944. Vichy France's latitude in relating to Germany was similarly circumscribed. By negotiating a truce limiting the German occupation of France, the Vichy leadership retained control over southern France and continued to play a secondary political role in the occupied sector of the country. German troops, however, remained poised to march into the "free" zone when this seemed strategically necessary— as it eventually did in November 1942. Other allies like Bulgaria, Hungary, Italy, and Rumania aided the German war effort in order to expand into territories they had long coveted. Although Germany tried to persuade them through diplomatic means to participate in the Final Solution, these countries adopted such policies only when they served their own pragmatic interests. Bulgaria and Rumania acceded to German requests for deporting Jews early in the war, when Germany's military might was at its zenith, but then became increasingly uncooperative when German power began to wane in the face of Allied offensives. Although the liquidation of native Jews had not been the goal of the discriminatory measures promulgated by Hungary, Italy, and Vichy France, these measures paved the way for the Third Reich to pursue this goal once its troops occupied all or part of these countries.

While the degree of direct control and indirect leverage Germany exerted over a country was the single most important factor

affecting the victimization rate of the Jews there, national traditions of religious tolerance and civic equality could engender sympathy for the Jews that sometimes found expression in efforts to
save them. In Northern and Western Europe the emancipation of
the Jews accompanied the overall trend of political liberalization
and economic modernization that swept this region in the eighteenth and nineteenth centuries. Consequently, by the twentieth
century, anti-Semitic and reactionary movements attracted only a
minority following there. For example, the climate of Danish democracy nurtured a national commitment to protect the rights
and lives of both refugee and native Jews alike. Similarly, the failure of Nazi racism to strike a responsive chord among the tolerant
Italians resulted in Italy's refusal to agree to deport any of the Jews
residing under its jurisdiction. In Belgium and Holland many of
the local officials serving the Germans initially protested or clan-
destinely undermined the persecution of their countries' Jewish
communities. Eighty percent of the Jews survived in Bulgaria, the
one Eastern European country where anti-Semitism had never
gained a strong foothold. To be sure, Germany often elevated anti-
Semitic groups into positions of power, but this did not necessarily
mean that their policies for dealing with the Jews were identical to
those of the Nazis. Despite the anti-Semitism of the conservative,
authoritarian leaders of Vichy France, they still respected the
French heritage of native Jews and strove to prevent their deportation while simultaneously sanctioning the deportation of foreign
Jews.[5]

The status Jews enjoyed in a country before the war had other
ramifications for the way they fared under German domination.
Jewish acculturation and socioeconomic integration often created
strong business or personal relationships with non-Jews. These relationships, in turn, provided Jews with an accessible network of
native colleagues, friends, or relatives through intermarriage who
could help them when Nazi rule or influence placed them in grave
jeopardy. Thus, the successful rescue of the Danish Jews was partly
attributable to their high level of assimilation and to close personal ties with Danish gentiles.[6] Even in countries where the population was hostile or indifferent toward Jews, certain areas or cities
with a history of hospitality to Jews became relative havens where
it was more likely for Jews to find people willing to shield them
from their Nazi tormentors. For example, though Berlin was the

capital of the Reich, it had been the cosmopolitan home of a siz-able and prominent Jewish community and served during the war as a hiding place for several thousand Jewish fugitives.[7]

Jewish chances of survival decreased in areas where indige-nous anti-Semitism had made deep political inroads before World War II. In contrast to Western Europe, Jewish emancipation in many parts of Central and Eastern Europe occurred later and was more broadly and effectively contested.[8] Here local leaders some-times equaled the Nazis in their desire to rid their countries of Jews. For example, Rumanian troops joined Germany's invasion of Russia in 1941 and shocked and surpassed their SS accomplices with their savagery in massacring 200,000 Jews. Then the Ruma-nian government crowded Jews into the Transnistria region, where approximately 150,000 died from disease and starvation. When Rumania reneged on earlier promises to hand Jews over to Germany for deportation in late 1942, as German prospects of winning the war dimmed, 50 percent of Rumanian Jewry already had been killed.[9] An even more fatal combination of circum-stances existed in Nazi extermination zones, where strong German control and native anti-Semitism complemented each other. Here the Germans recruited local personnel to assist in the persecution of the Jews, whose maltreatment engendered a mixture of enthusi-asm or indifference among the majority of the native population. For example, Lithuanian nationalism contained a significant anti-Semitic streak that intensified under German influence during the 1930s and in reaction to Jewish collaboration with Soviet occupa-tion forces in 1940. Thus, many Lithuanians responded to Germa-ny's "liberation" of their country in 1941 by slaughtering Jews on their own initiative or joining SS *Einsatzgruppen* (mobile killing squads) in executing Jews. Less than 10 percent of Lithuanian Jewry managed to survive the war.[10]

However, vocal opposition to Jewish persecution by local elites could legitimate the cause of helping the Jews for undecided citizens. Discontent over Nazi policy toward Jews often remained latent until it was vented in a public forum by respected native leaders. Such demonstrations of solidarity with the Jews some-times restrained local bureaucrats and collaborators from imple-menting unpopular measures against the Jews. The vociferous condemnation of Bulgaria's anti-Semitic laws by the Bulgarian Or-thodox clergy, various professional organizations, and prominent politicians clearly contributed to the government's lax enforcement of these laws and eventual refusal to deport native Jews.[11] Guided by instructions from their government-in-exile, the highest ranking remaining Belgian officials refused to sanction anti-Jewish policies that violated the Hague Convention. This forced the Germans to rely on municipal mayors and the Jewish Council of Belgium (Association des Juifs de Belgique) to administer Nazi programs against the Jews. When both of these groups were not entirely cooperative, the Germans had to divert their own personnel to run the Final Solution there.[12]

Local attitudes toward Jews also had an impact on whether national resistance movements viewed the defense of the Jews as an essential part of their struggle. For example, the Danes expressed their commitment to preserving their democratic values and protecting their fellow citizens by rapidly shepherding most of the Jews residing in their country to nearby Sweden when the Germans tried to deport them in October of 1943.[13] In Belgium the Armée Belge des Partisans (Belgian Partisan Army) sabotaged the bureaucratic machinery for notifying the Jews to report for the first deportations in July 1942. A month earlier the Front d'Indépendance (Independence Front) presided over the creation of the *Comité de Défense des Juifs* (Committee for the Defense of the Jews) to conduct Jewish relief and rescue work in Belgium. This sort of backing played a role in keeping the mortality rate of Jews in Belgium below 45 percent.[14]

Established Jewish leaders had few opportunities to intervene on behalf of their communities because, as a minority, Jews throughout Europe were at the mercy of German military power and native regimes. Consequently, the entreaties of Jewish elites achieved results only when local governments had the capacity to act independently of the Germans. When Jewish councils were under direct German supervision, as in Poland, they had no viable means to prevent the eventual deportation of their communities. Their sincere belief that their compliance would mitigate the harshness of German policy and thereby preserve a remnant of the Jews in the ghettos was completely misguided, failing to take account of the strength of the Nazi resolve to eradicate European Jewry. Jewish officials could play a more effective role in alleviating Jewish suffering when they dealt with regimes that were either satellites or allies of Germany, like Bulgaria and Rumania.[15]

While Jews required the support of either native regimes or resistance movements to survive in any significant numbers, some individuals saved themselves by joining local resistance groups or forming their own partisan bands. Jewish uprisings and resistance movements incurred massive German reprisals, but they also enabled some Jews to escape, hide, inform the outside world about Nazi genocide,[16] and even rescue other Jews. In many countries the level of Jewish participation in the underground was higher than native involvement and disproportionately larger in relation to the size of the Jewish populations there. Zionist groups such as the Hashomer Hatzair (Young Watchmen) of Belgrade and the Dutch Hechalutz (Zionist Pioneers) committed themselves to resistance and rescue efforts. Many Jewish socialists and communists did likewise as a continuation of their previous political activism.[17]

The prospects for Jewish rescue notably improved when external assistance was available. This usually took the form of outside funding, which was used for bribing officials, procuring weapons, producing forged papers, and reimbursing gentiles who sheltered Jews for the expenses incurred in doing so. Diplomatic intervention on behalf of Jews by neutral governments also saved Jewish lives. The accomplishments of Raoul Wallenberg testify to the efficacy of this sort of formal intercession. In 1944 the United States belatedly established the War Refugee Board (WRB) to aid and rescue the victims of Nazism. Fearing the imminent deportation of Hungarian Jewry, the WRB solicited the help of a number of neutral countries to protect this endangered community. Sweden embraced the American proposal and appointed Wallenberg as a special envoy to Hungary whose sole mission was to avert the deportation of Jews. Taking advantage of his diplomatic immunity and money contributed by private organizations like the American Jewish Joint Distribution Committee, Wallenberg issued bogus Swedish "protective passports," rented apartment buildings to serve as Jewish sanctuaries under Swedish protection, and personally whisked hundreds of Hungarian Jews off German transports on the pretext that they were wards of Sweden. Wallenberg's example inspired other neutral embassies and the International Red Cross office in Budapest to protect Jews too. According to some estimates, the rescue campaign launched by Wallenberg may have saved as many as 100,000 Jews.[18]

Finally, a country's location and topography could either facilitate or hinder the rescue of Jews; its distance from or proximity to potential escape routes to safer places contributed to the difficulty or ease of smuggling Jews successfully into such havens. Denmark's proximity to neutral Sweden, for example, allowed the Danes to relocate most of their Jews there. Access to Spain, Switzerland, territories under Italian control, and Mediterranean sea routes to Palestine favored Jewish escape attempts from Vichy France and the countries of the Balkan Peninsula. Certain types of terrain were conducive to concealing groups of fugitives, sneaking them across borders, and mounting guerrilla maneuvers. The sparsely populated and rugged wilderness of eastern Norway, the extensive and thick forests of Belorussia, and the mountainous regions of southern France, Greece, and Yugoslavia served as natural arenas for these kinds of activities.[19]

Germany

In Germany the persecution of Jews was official government policy and had evolved gradually during the years when the Nazi regime attained the height of its popularity and power. Here, unlike conquered or satellite states, the assault on the Jews could not be discredited as a program imposed by a victorious foreign tyrant or enacted to ingratiate a dominant ally. Any German opposition to the persecution of the Jews was interpreted as a form of treason. This does not mean that most Germans shared Hitler's racism and sought the physical annihilation of European Jewry. Instead, they accepted anti-Semitic discrimination as just one plank in the Nazi platform for the restoration of German power. Their support for the Third Reich was predicated on Hitler's overall success in overcoming the civil strife and depression that plagued Germany in the early 1930s and in freeing Germany from the shackles the Treaty of Versailles had clamped on the country's irredentist and military aspirations. When Hitler succeeded in achieving these goals between 1933 and 1941, the suffering of the Jews seemed to be either a necessary or small price to pay for this national revival.[20]

To be sure, Nazi anti-Semitism built on a foundation of ideas that had developed in Germany since the nineteenth century. The emancipation of German Jewry had coincided with the unification of Germany in 1871. During the next forty years many Germans were disoriented and displaced by the problems the rapid wave of industrialization and urbanization that swept the Second Reich brought in its wake. Many critics of this modernization process blamed the loss of Germany's traditional way of life and its attendant socioeconomic ills on the deleterious influence of the recently enfranchised Jews. Extremist parties espousing this viewpoint registered some electoral victories in the 1890s, and a few mainstream parties opportunistically jumped on the anti-Jewish bandwagon, thereby conferring political respectability on anti-Semitism.

Germany's defeat in World War I, the punitive terms of the Versailles treaty, the fall of the Hohenzollern monarchy and the concurrent rise of Germany's first republic, and fear of Russian and domestic communism, broadened the appeal of anti-Semitic demagogues. They attributed these events to German Jews, who had allegedly "stabbed Germany in the back" by promoting the interests of "international Jewry," the Western democracies, and the Soviet Union. The economic crises and political polarization that paralyzed the Weimar Republic lent more credibility to this conspiratorial outlook on the world.[21]

Initially, Hitler dealt with the "Jewish problem" through ostensibly legal and gradual steps, creating the impression that he was more moderate and less violent than the Nazi storm troopers (*Sturmabteilung*, or SA), who sporadically terrorized Jews. From 1933 until 1938, the Third Reich enacted legislation and issued propaganda that led incrementally to the vilification, disenfranchisement, legal identification, segregation, and expropriation of the property of German Jewry.[22] German public opinion clearly preferred orderly discrimination to indiscriminate bloodshed.[23] The SA's *Kristallnacht* (crystal night, or night of broken glass) rampage against Jewish homes, shops, and synagogues in November 1938 marked the first state-sanctioned violence against the Jews, occasioned the first mass internment of Jewish men by the SS, and intensified the confiscation of Jewish wealth.[24] The goal of all these measures was to force German Jews to emigrate, and 330,000 of them did so before the outbreak of war in 1939.[25] After its conquest of Poland, Germany conscripted tens of thousands of German Jews to perform forced labor and considered the possibility of creating Jewish reservations in Poland or Madagascar.[26]

Although the administrative apparatus to carry out the systematic extermination of European Jewry was not formally established until the SS convened a conference of Nazi party and state officials at Wannsee, near Berlin, in January 1942, the bureaucratic preparations for the eventual deportation of German Jews had started the previous year with a ban on their emigration, the mandatory wearing of the Jewish star for identification purposes, and the rescission of their German nationality the moment they left Germany.[27] This last measure reduced them to stateless persons, bereft of the protection of international law, when they were deported.[28] In the last three months of 1941, tens of thousands of German Jews were taken to Lodz, Minsk, or Riga. Train transports to the Polish death camps began in 1942. Some "privileged" and elderly Jews were sent to the "model ghetto" at Theresienstadt, which more often than not served as a way station on the road to the gas chambers further east. In 1943, Germany rounded up Jews still working in German factories and shipped them to the extermination camps. By June, Nazi authorities proclaimed Germany *Judenrein*. Nevertheless, an estimated 25,000 German Jews survived the war. While the period of emigration between 1933 and 1941 enabled 60 percent of German Jewry to flee their homeland, more than 80 percent of the remaining 164,000 German Jews perished in the Holocaust.[29]

Throughout its ordeal, the German Jewish community could do only as much to ameliorate its situation as the Nazi government permitted. The German Jewish leadership formed the Reichsvertretung der Deutschen Juden (Reich Representation of German Jews) in 1933 to tend to the cultural, economic, and spiritual needs of its constituency. The leaders of the Reichsvertretung harbored the illusion that anti-Jewish hostility would wane as the economy improved and believed that some sort of accommodation with the Third Reich might still be achieved. When their hopes were dashed by the enactment of the Nuremberg Laws in 1935, they devoted themselves to promoting mass Jewish emigration consistent with Nazi policy in this period.[30] In 1939, Germany changed the name of the Reichsvertretung to the Reichsvereinigung der Juden in Deutschland (Reich Association for Jews in Germany) and transformed it into an organization that merely implemented governmental orders. Its personnel and the Jewish Order Service (Ordnungsdienst) created by the SS in 1942 assisted in the deportations of German Jews. Armed Jewish resistance proved too costly. In 1942 a group of Jewish communists led by Herbert Baum killed five Germans in Berlin. The Gestapo retaliated by executing 250 Jews, deporting 250, and threatening to murder 250 more for every German killed by Jews in the future.[31]

The German resistance was weak in general and minimally concerned with the plight of the Jews. During the first years of Hitler's rule, the political parties opposed to Nazism were either relentlessly suppressed, like the Social Democratic and Communist parties, or coopted, like the Catholic Center Party.[32] Though the Catholic church and the dissident minority Lutheran Confessing church sometimes challenged Hitler's policies, their resistance arose primarily "out of organizational egoism."[33] Thus, they denounced Nazi racial laws insofar as those laws jeopardized Jewish converts to their denominations and Jewish relatives of their members. Though clerical protest halted the euthanasia program in 1941, an equivalent outcry against the Final Solution never materialized.[34] Traditional German elites representing the army, business, and civil service supported Hitler in 1933 because his political agenda resembled their own anticommunist, conservative, and nationalistic aims. By 1938 some of them feared the consequences of his reckless expansionist policies and resented the erosion of their own authority. Their first plots to overthrow Hitler were undercut by Germany's initial military victories. When German troops subsequently encountered setbacks on the battlefield, these conspirators attempted to assassinate the Führer. But at no time was the rescue of Jews a priority of the resistance, though a few of its members participated in such efforts.[35]

Nevertheless, some Germans did come to the aid of the Jews. Church groups that originally helped only Christians of Jewish descent sometimes extended their protective services to include all Jews. This was true of the Büro Grüber run by Protestant pastor Heinrich Grüber, and the Caritas Catholica, led by Gertrude Luckner. At the end of February 1943, the German wives of Jewish men recently arrested for deportation marched daily in front of the building where their husbands were being held and successfully gained their release.[36] Berlin served as a hiding place for about 5,000 Jews at one time, approximately 1,000 of whom survived the war.[37]

Yet the average German had either become intimidated by the Nazis or inured to the persecution of the Jews. He or she focused on the benefits Hitler had brought Germany before the war and on the outcome of battles during it. Since the government shrouded the Final Solution in secrecy by locating the death camps on foreign soil, rumors about the extermination camps were usually discounted as Allied propaganda. Even many of those whose sympathies were stirred by the plight of the Jews were deterred from acting on those feelings by their suspicions that colleagues, friends, or neighbors might be Nazi informers.[38] It was

difficult and dangerous to smuggle Jews out of a Germany surrounded by other occupied countries and by neutral Switzerland,
which turned back "civilian refugees" seeking sanctuary there beginning in 1942.[39] In short, concern over other matters, disbelief,
fear, obedience to the state, objective obstacles, and plausible rationalizations for inaction prevented the development of extensive Jewish rescue operations in Germany.

Poland

Approximately 3,300,000 Jews lived in Poland before the outbreak
of World War II. It is estimated that over 3,000,000 of them perished in the Holocaust.[40] Several crucial factors contributed to this
staggering 90 percent fatality toll. From the outset of the occupation, German rule in Poland was direct and brutal. The SS and
German police wielded great power throughout Poland despite
the different types of administrative units that the Third Reich
established there. Since the Nazis regarded the Poles as *Untermen-
schen* (subhumans) destined for immediate enslavement and future
liquidation, they did not restrain their oppression of Jews or Poles
in deference to local public opinion. Partitioned by two bordering
enemies, isolated from its Western European defenders, and populated by a large Jewish community, Poland provided Germany
with an ideal environment to initiate its policies of Jewish resettlement and ghettoization between 1939 and 1941. Germany located
extermination camps on Polish soil and rapidly proceeded to
transfer the Jews from nearby ghettos into these camps. Previous
and wartime Polish antagonisms toward Jews delayed the development and limited the extent of organized Polish assistance to the
Jews. Internecine Jewish disputes over how to respond to Nazi persecution also impeded the growth and efficacy of Jewish resistance
movements. When armed Jewish resistance finally materialized in
1943, the majority of Polish Jewry had already been murdered.

The blitzkrieg (lightning war) campaign conducted by Germany in September 1939 devastated Poland and decimated the
ranks of the Polish military, leaving the nation defenseless against
the reign of terror the Germans soon unleashed.[41] For ideological
reasons, the Nazis slated Poland for resettlement along racial lines.
Recapturing territories lost after World War I, the Germans formally incorporated Danzig–West Prussia, the Wartheland, and
German Silesia into the Reich. Dubbed the General Gouverne-

ment der Besetzten Polnischen Gebiete (General Government of the Occupied Polish Territories), central Poland was placed under the jurisdiction of Nazi governor-general Hans Frank. The Nazis tried to colonize designated parts of Poland with German volunteers from the Reich, *Volksdeutschen* (ethnic Germans residing outside the Reich), and selected Poles who qualified for Germanization because they were members of Nazi or German organizations before the war, were married to Germans, raised their children as Germans, or were descended from Germans. While many Poles remained in these areas to serve as slave laborers for the colonists, over 1,000,000 Poles were ruthlessly uprooted and deported to the occupied territories, where they either toiled for the authorities or were eventually conscripted for labor in the Reich. To ensure that the Poles would never revolt, Germany summarily executed members of the Polish elite (clergy, intellectuals, politicians, professionals, and so on) who might potentially lead or participate in such a rebellion.[42]

Simultaneously, Germany started to isolate and persecute Polish Jewry. SS *Einsatzgruppen* received orders on September 21, 1939, to clear the annexed Polish territories of Jews insofar as possible and to concentrate Polish Jews in a few places "located along railway lines."[43] Compounding the hardship of resettlement, groups of Jews from Austria, Czechoslovakia, and Germany were herded along with some of the Polish Jews into a Jewish "reservation" that the Germans planned to create in the Nisko region near Lublin.[44] The formation of Jewish ghettos between 1939 and 1941 completed the segregation of Polish Jews and introduced more systematic methods for exploiting and enervating them. Each ghetto was ordered to establish a Jewish council (*Judenrat*) comprising prominent Jews to administer policies dictated by the Germans. Deaths from shootings, sickness, and starvation in the ghettos accounted for approximately 20 percent of the fatalities suffered by Polish Jewry under the Nazi occupation.[45] During the invasion of the Soviet Union, the *Einsatzgruppen* killed one-third of the 1,500,000 Polish Jews living in the provinces of Poland annexed by Russia in 1939.[46]

With the establishment of the death camps in Poland, Polish Jews became the most immediate and vulnerable targets for mass murder. Chelmno started operating in December 1941. By summer of the next year, Auschwitz, Belzec, Majdanek, Sobibor, and Treblinka were functioning as killing centers. The major deportations from the Polish ghettos occurred throughout 1942. By the end of that year, over 80 percent of the Polish Jews had been sent to the camps. Most of the ghettos were liquidated in the following year, though Lodz was spared this fate until 1944. Altogether, 2,000,000 Polish Jews died in the Nazi extermination camps.[47]

Although gentile Poles faced the same enemy as the Jews, there was little solidarity between the two groups in the first three years of the German occupation. Long-standing historical patterns in the relationships between Poles and Jews contributed to this estrangement. The conspicuous roles of Jews as merchants, money-lenders, estates supervisors, and tax collectors in medieval Poland eventually attracted the hostility of Poles from social classes either aspiring to these positions or suffering under the policies Jewish middlemen enforced for kings and nobles. During the same period, the Catholic church attempted to strengthen its influence in Poland by denouncing the Jews on theological grounds. After the partition of Poland by Austria, Prussia, and Russia at the end of the eighteenth century, the protracted struggle for independence heightened the Catholic component of Polish nationalism and the distrust many Poles felt toward ethnic and religious minorities.[48] Polish suspicions of the loyalties of native Jews during World War I triggered a wave of pogroms in 1918 and 1919, prompting the Entente powers to require the Polish state they created after the war to guarantee the equality of the minorities living within its borders. Resentment over this infringement of Polish sovereignty increased the popularity of the virulently anti-Semitic Endecja (National Democratic Party). Although official antagonism toward the Jews was restrained by Marshal Pilsudski between 1926 and 1935, it was revived by his successors, who enacted a series of discriminatory laws. Before World War II, even "moderate" Polish parties favored emigration as a solution to their country's Jewish problem.[49]

Conditions in Poland after the German and Russian invasions in 1939 exacerbated the animosities between Poles and Jews. The liquidation of Polish elites and the deportation of Poles for servitude in the Reich ostensibly appeared to many Poles to be harsher treatment than the ghettoization of the Jews. Other Poles had profited from taking over abandoned Jewish homes and businesses and did not want the former owners to return and reclaim their property. Until mid-1941, the Poles fought both Germany and Russia. Consequently, they were enraged by the flight of many

Polish Jews into the Soviet occupation zone and by Jewish collaboration with the regime there. To Polish rightists, this "proved" the prewar charge that Jews were part of a Soviet conspiracy, an accusation based on the disproportionate Jewish membership in the Polish communist party. To the Polish underground, the compliance of the Jewish councils with German decrees cast doubts on the value of forging an alliance with the Jews. In any case, the underground was still hampered by its own factional disunity and lack of coordination with the Polish exile government in London. Finally, Germany's military presence and its use of punitive collective reprisals stifled acts of resistance in general and those in behalf of Jews in particular. On October 15, 1941, Germany announced that Poles hiding Jews or abetting their concealment would be put to death.[50]

Though the majority of Poles "remained neutral observers"[51] of the plight of the Jews, a minority either aided the German program of genocide or launched their own anti-Semitic campaigns. Perhaps the most feared and dangerous of these were the gangs of Polish *szmalcowniki* who hunted down Jews hidden by Poles with the intent of blackmailing them and their rescuers or informing on both to obtain cash bounties offered by the Germans for such information. The prospect of being detected by these extortionists probably inhibited many potential rescuers from acting on their sympathies for the Jews. The Polish Blue Police helped the Germans supervise the ghettos, track down escaped Jews, and conduct the deportations to the death camps. In addition to fighting the Germans, members of the right-wing Narodowe Sily Zbrojne (National Armed Forces) attacked both Jewish partisans and the communist underground groups in which many Jewish fugitives found refuge. The anti-Semitic and anticommunist factions of the Polish Home Army (Armia Krajowa, AK) often refused to accept Jewish members and betrayed and battled Jewish partisan groups too.[52]

A minority of Poles tried to protect Jews from being captured and killed by the Germans. Although many managed to help Jews with no outside support, other rescuers relied on the services provided by Zegota (the Council for Aid to Jews) to accomplish their mission of mercy. Formed by concerned Catholic intellectuals and representatives of moderate and leftist Polish parties toward the end of 1942, Zegota located hiding places for Jews and supplied them with food, forged identification papers, and medical care when necessary. Its funding came from the exile government and from Polish and foreign Jewish organizations. Zegota also attempted to stop the rash of blackmailing and informing by condemning these acts and threatening to punish their perpetrators. Initially, Zegota operations were confined to the vicinity of Warsaw, but they eventually expanded to include Cracow, Lvov, Lublin, and Zamość. Unfortunately, its rescue efforts began in 1943, after the major deportations from most of the ghettos. Estimates of the numbers of Jews assisted by Zegota vary widely ranging from several thousand to fifty thousand. Whatever the figure, it does seem clear that tens of thousands of Jews were saved by Polish individuals or networks like Zegota. Moreover, it is equally certain that thousands of Poles were executed or died in concentration camps for trying to help Jews.[53]

The distinctiveness of the Polish Jewish community also restricted the possibilities for cooperating with the Poles in resistance and rescue activities. Polish Jews differed significantly in their occupational and residential patterns from Polish gentiles. Many of them dressed and groomed themselves according to Jewish customs or possessed stereotypical physical features that clearly marked them as Jews. In the 1931 census, 79 percent of Polish Jews listed Yiddish as their mother tongue; another 8 percent listed Hebrew. Only 12 percent considered Polish their native language![54] Polish Jews tended to join and support parties devoted to defending particular Jewish interests like the propagation of Yiddish culture (the General Jewish Labor Bund), the preservation of religious orthodoxy (Agudat Israel), and the settlement of Palestine and the creation of a Jewish state there (the Zionist parties). More assimilated Jews gravitated toward liberal and leftist Polish parties that opposed anti-Semitism.[55] Few Jews had close personal relationships with Poles to whom they could turn for help, and the foundations for Jewish political alliances with most Polish parties had not yet been laid. Such historical barriers served to isolate the Jews from the Poles even before they were segregated behind ghetto walls.[56]

The Jewish councils' responses to Nazi persecution also diminished the prospects for early Polish intervention on behalf of the Jews. *Judenrat* leaders based their compliance with German orders on the assumptions that it might placate the Nazis, make the ghettos economically indispensable to the Germans, and postpone drastic German actions against the ghettos until Allied liber-

ation was imminent. When the Jewish councils suppressed underground Jewish movements or cooperated in preparing lists of Jews
for deportations, they hoped to spare their communities worse
reprisals and save a remnant of the Jewish population by sacrificing a portion of it.[57] Outside the ghettos, however, these strategies
were interpreted as expressions of Jewish servility or collaboration
with the enemy. Moreover, they initially masked the precariousness of the Jewish predicament, since they suggested that the Nazis
could be mollified and were not intent on exterminating the
Jews.[58]

Internal opposition to the accommodationist stance of the
Jewish councils and the political infighting between Jewish groups
advocating resistance hindered the emergence of a unified Jewish
underground. Jewish clandestine activities were often repressed
by the councils. Before attacking the Germans, resistance groups
needed to discredit and undermine the policies pursued by the
councils. Prewar ideological disputes among the Bundists, Communists, and Zionists were complicated by disagreements over the
tactical options available to Jews under the German occupation.
Could armed struggle be viable against the vastly superior German
forces, or would it merely provoke ruthless reprisals in which too
many Jewish casualties would be sustained? If it were undertaken,
should Jews stay in the ghettos and fight the Nazis from there or
flee to the forests to enlist in partisan bands engaging in guerrilla
warfare? These questions were hotly debated by the various factions of the Jewish underground. The mass deportations of 1942
served as the catalyst for the unification of resistance groups in
various ghettos. The formation and consolidation of Jewish defensive alliances like the Jewish Fighting Organizations of Warsaw
and Bialystok paved the way for the revolts against the final evacu-
ations from these ghettos in the spring and summer of 1943.[59]

To comprehend why the Polish underground's support of its
Jewish counterpart was belated and limited, the historical context
described above must be kept in mind. Although the AK did con-
vey information to the government-in-exile about the deportations
and death camps as soon as it knew about them in 1942,[60] it did
not originally seek to ally itself with the Jewish resistance but instead waited to be approached by Jewish groups. Since the primary goal of the AK was to build a secret army capable of rising
against Germany later in the war when the Reich was on the verge
of defeat, the leadership of the AK believed that arming the Jews

would be a wasteful diversion of scarce weapons to a group that had failed to manifest any overt resistance to the Germans up to that point. The Jewish Fighting Organization of Warsaw (ZOB) eventually obtained a few guns from the AK. More military supplies were sent only after the ZOB impressed the AK by staging an attack on German guards in January 1943. Even so, the ZOB's arsenal remained small and inadequate. When the ZOB mounted the Warsaw ghetto uprising in April 1943, the communist People's Guard and some AK units engaged in military support operations and subsequently helped Jews escape from the razed ghetto. The uprising, however, was the final act in the tragedy of the Warsaw Jews. The AK assistance to the Jews was a classic case of too little too late.[61]

The totality of German domination in Poland was undoubtedly the key factor that doomed the Polish Jews. Nevertheless, pro-Polish sources generally exaggerate Polish solidarity with the Jews and minimize Polish anti-Semitism as a cause for the relatively low numbers of rescued Jews, whereas pro-Jewish sources often commit the opposite errors. Although Nazi terror made it more difficult and dangerous to help Jews in Poland than anywhere else in Europe,[62] it still appears that many Poles did not feel obligated to protect the Jews, whom they either disliked or dismissed as aliens.[63]

The Netherlands

Despite the notable history of acceptance of Jews in the Netherlands and the concomitant weakness of anti-Semitism there, its 115,000 Jewish citizens and 25,000 Jewish refugees suffered a proportionally greater loss of lives (between 75 percent and 80 percent) than the Jews in any other occupied country in Western Europe.[64] The primary responsibility for this frightful toll lies with the Germans, who ruled the Netherlands with an iron fist as a protectorate (*Schutzstaat*) under the authority of a *Reichskommissar* and a security chief, directly accountable to Hitler and Himmler respectively. Though only a small minority of the population willingly assisted the Germans, the Dutch governmental bureaucracy and Jewish council engaged in what one historian has termed "reasonable collaboration" to stave off more onerous German reprisals and control.[65] This not only enabled the Nazis to liquidate most of Dutch Jewry with a minimal SS staff but also shrouded

their sinister aims in a deceptive semblance of legitimacy and nor-
mality. Furthermore, Holland's location, population density, and
terrain made escape, hiding, and resistance difficult and dangerous. Concerted Dutch efforts to defend the Jews came either too
prematurely or belatedly to save the majority of them.

The near annihilation of the Jews in Holland constituted a
radical reversal of the country's long national heritage of religious
tolerance and civic equality. Allowed to settle and worship in
many Dutch cities as early as the seventeenth century, Dutch Jews
never became the target of the sort of anti-Jewish riots that sporadically erupted in other European countries. In the 140 years following their emancipation by the invading French revolutionary
army in 1796, they had gained entry into and acceptance by most
sectors of Holland's economic and political life. Political anti-
Semitism exerted little popular appeal among the Dutch in this
period.[66] Honoring its tradition of providing sanctuary to the persecuted, Holland admitted approximately 25,000 Jewish refugees
from Nazi Germany, Austria, and Poland between 1933 and 1940.
Since the domestic unemployment rate was high then, resentment
developed against this influx of aliens and led to Holland's decision in 1939 to intern indigent German Jewish refugees at a camp
in Westerbork in the province of Drente rather than grant them
permanent asylum.[67]

The rapid German victory over the Netherlands in 1940 transformed what had been a secure haven for Jews into a perilous hell.
Holland's borders effectively barricaded most Jews from fleeing to
places where they would be safe from Nazi persecution. Ferrying
across the North Sea to England ceased to be an option once the
Germans seized control of Dutch ports and patrolled the coastal
waters.[68] Reaching occupied Belgium in the south was only the
first hurdle on a tortuous trail that went through occupied and
Vichy France to Spain or Switzerland. The Third Reich itself lay
along the entire length of Holland's eastern frontier. Similarly, the
flat terrain, lack of heavy forestation, and high population density
severely handicapped the efforts of those trying to evade or resist
the Nazis within the country. The intricate network of bridges,
canals, and sluices in Holland could be blocked by the Germans
to isolate communities and restrict travel. The residential concentration of 60 percent of Dutch Jewry in Amsterdam facilitated the
enforcement of Nazi anti-Semitic policies, especially deportations

of Jews. As Raul Hilberg has observed, "It was as though the Dutch Jews had already been placed in a natural trap."[69]

After the German conquest of Holland, Hitler appointed SS General Artur Seyss-Inquart to the position of *Reichskommissar* of the occupied Netherlands. SS influence in Holland was reinforced by SS Commissioner-General of Security Hans Rauter, who took his orders directly from Himmler. This strong SS presence reflected Hitler's view of the Dutch as fellow Aryans whose homeland would someday be merged with Germany once Dutch society was purged of Jewish and other harmful elements. Moreover, Holland's control over the outlets of the Rhine and Maas rivers, its fertile farmlands, fine harbors, and North Sea coast made the country economically and strategically crucial to Germany's war effort.[70]

In contrast to Poland, the persecution of Jews in the Netherlands developed in subtle steps and initially relied more on ostensibly legal discriminatory measures rather than brute force. The Nazis did not want to shock Dutch sensibilities and provoke widespread resistance. Instead, they gradually disenfranchised, impoverished, and isolated the Jews in a period when German domination over Dutch gentiles was still relatively tolerable, thereby dissociating the latter as much as possible from Jewish suffering. At first Seyss-Inquart assured the Dutch that he would not impose an "alien ideology" on Holland. Another occupation official asserted that there was no Jewish problem in the Netherlands. After introducing several minor anti-Semitic laws in the summer of 1940, the Nazis prohibited Jews from holding government jobs and dismissed those already in such positions. Then civil servants were required to fill out forms indicating whether or not their grandparents were Jewish. Jewish businesses were identified for eventual transfer to German owners. This process culminated in the mandatory registration of Jews at the beginning of 1941, which made it easier to bar them during the remainder of that year from most public places, jobs, and social activities. The marking of the Jews was completed in April 1942, when they were compelled to wear a yellow star inscribed with *Jood* (Jew) on their outer clothing.[71]

All these measures to identify Jews and exclude them from Dutch society expedited their subsequent concentration and expulsion from Holland. The concentration process began in 1942 with an order that unemployed Jews report to labor camps and the simultaneous evacuation of Jews from the provinces to predominantly Jewish neighborhoods in Amsterdam. Preceding the deportations, groups of Jews were relocated to the main transit camps at Vugt and Westerbork. From there, the first trains loaded with Jews departed in mid-July for the extermination camps of Auschwitz and Sobibor. Within a year, 77,000 Jews had been deported. In the next fourteen months, 30,000 more Jews embarked on their fatal journey to the same camps or to Bergen-Belsen and Theresienstadt. Only 5,200 of the deported Jews survived. Another 8,000 Jews were arrested and executed by the Germans in Holland for trying to hide.[72]

Some of the blame for this catastrophe rests with the Dutch. After Holland's defeat, the fascistic National Socialist Movement of the Netherlands (Nationaal-Socialistische Beweging der Nederlanden, or NSB) endorsed and disseminated Nazi anti-Semitism. Its 80,000 members served the Germans by filling various political positions, intimidating Jews and informing on them, and assisting in roundups of Jews for deportation. The NSB formed its own version of the Nazi party storm troopers called the Defense Troop (*Weer-Afdeling,* or WA), which terrorized Jews and other political foes. It also created a Dutch branch of the SS (Nederlandse SS) whose recruits fought alongside their German counterparts in Eastern Europe and elsewhere. To most Dutch citizens, the NSB's blatant collaboration with the enemy was considered treason. After the war, the Netherlands convicted over 50,000 people of collaboration.[73]

Hitler, however, preferred to govern the occupied countries in Western Europe through existing governmental channels, and the Dutch civil service played right into his hands. The Secretaries-General, the senior Dutch officials who remained at their posts when the queen and cabinet went into exile, engaged in a form of tactical collaboration. Under the provisions of a 1937 government directive, they were supposed to cooperate with an occupying power if they believed that doing so benefited the general welfare of the Dutch population more than it harmed it. The directive's vagueness left the Secretaries a great deal of discretion in determining whether the overall punitive repercussions for not complying with Nazi orders would be worse than the effects of obeying them. When confronted with the escalating harshness of Nazi policies against the Jews, three key members of the Secretaries-

General often lodged formal protests but then agreed to administer these policies to avoid German reprisals and the further Nazification of Dutch government agencies. Thus, Dutch officials unwittingly lent legitimacy to anti-Semitic laws by tacitly condoning them and supplying native bureaucrats and police to help implement them. Though clearly performed under duress, Dutch participation in the Nazi campaign against the Jews spared the Germans from deploying costly numbers of their own scarce personnel to enforce it. The government-in-exile did not explicitly prohibit Dutch civil servants from carrying out German anti-Jewish decrees until May 1943, when Nazi rule in Holland was becoming unbearably oppressive for gentiles too.[74]

The Jewish council (*Joodsche Raad*) appointed by the Germans pursued a similar strategy of defensive acquiescence. Created by the Nazis in February 1941 to disarm Jews who had defended themselves against WA attacks, the council was led by Jews who had been prominent in the Jewish community before the occupation. These leaders argued that, at best, Jewish compliance with Nazi decrees might mitigate the severity of future German actions against the Jews, and, at worst, fellow Jews would not be as cruel as Germans or Dutch collaborators in administering Nazi policy. The Jewish council relayed each anti-Semitic regulation issued by the Germans to the Jewish community through its newspaper *The Jewish Weekly* (*Het Joodsche Weekblad*), enabling the Germans to communicate directly with the Jews without alarming the Dutch public.[75] The Jewish council inadvertently helped select which Jews were sent to Westerbork for deportation by determining who received exemption permits for the "indispensable" jobs they performed on behalf of the Jewish community. The Germans, however, progressively reduced the number of permits that the council could distribute from 35,000 in July 1942 to none by September 1943. Until then the chance of attaining such exemptions set Jew against Jew in the competitive scramble to gain immunity from deportation. It also preserved the illusion that the Germans would not expel all the Jews.[76] Selected by the Nazis to help administer Westerbork, a few German Jewish inmates diligently prepared transport lists from among the new Dutch Jewish arrivals after choosing which of them would be designated as essential workers.[77]

Not all Jews remained passive in the face of persecution. When WA troops randomly robbed and beat up poorer Jews in

Amsterdam in early 1941, these Jews organized Action Groups (*Knokploegen,* or KPs) to resist the marauders. In one such confrontation, a WA storm trooper was killed, prompting the Germans to retaliate by arresting 425 young Jewish men and banishing them to Mauthausen, where they were worked to death.[78] L. E. Visser, a Jewish judge whom the Germans removed from the presidency of Holland's Supreme Court, steadfastly protested against the Jewish council's conceding to any legal distinctions being made between Dutch gentiles and Jews and pleaded with the Secretaries-General to intercede on behalf of the Jews taken to the concentration camp at Mauthausen in Austria. Visser represented the Jewish Coordinating Committee, whose uncompromising stance against collaboration served as a counterweight to the position adopted by the Jewish council. Unfortunately, he died of coronary failure at the beginning of 1942, but the validity of his message grew more apparent as the reassuring predictions of the Jewish council repeatedly failed to materialize. Once the deportations began, almost 80 percent of the Jews notified to report to Westerbork refused, requiring the Germans to dispatch special pickup squads to capture Jews. Some Jews tried to leave Holland. The Hechalutz ran the most successful of the escape networks and smuggled hundreds of Jews through Belgium into France, Spain, or Switzerland. A few of those saved eventually reached Palestine.[79] Other Jews stayed in Holland and joined the Dutch resistance.[80]

The first overt demonstration of Dutch solidarity with the Jews came too early to actually help them. At the end of February 1941, communist-led workers in Amsterdam mounted a general strike to protest the brutal German raids that netted the Jewish men who were sent to Mauthausen. This manifestation of defiance ended with a German declaration of a state of siege, the killing of seven strikers, and the imprisonment of 100 of the strike leaders. The ruthless suppression of the strike dealt a severe blow to the communist resistance to the Nazis. Moreover, this precedent and the German practice of taking and frequently executing Dutch hostages deterred most of the Dutch from actively opposing Nazi policies over the next two years.[81]

Though the Dutch generally sympathized with the Jews, they remained relatively quiescent until they themselves felt the full brunt of Nazi oppression. Germany tightened its control over the Dutch in the first half of 1943 with detested policies like conscripting Dutch men between the ages of eighteen and thirty-five for labor service in Germany. This sparked Dutch strikes in April and May. The need to assist all those refusing to comply with the new Nazi orders enlarged and unified the fragmented local groups that had organized previously to aid hunted gentile and Jewish "divers" (*onderduikers,* which literally means "people who go underwater"), as such fugitives were called.[82] This entailed overcoming the deep class, political, and religious divisions that had characterized prewar Dutch society.[83] The National Organization for Assistance to Divers (Landelijker Organisatie voor Hulp aan Onderduikers, or LO) did not amalgamate all these groups into a national network until August 1943. By then about 80,000 Jews had been deported. National Action Groups (Landelijke Knokploegen) were formed soon thereafter to counterfeit or steal ration cards and identification papers for divers and those harboring them. The sparsely populated and remote province of Friesland proved to be one of the safest LO sanctuaries because German surveillance there was light. Of the 300,000 people hidden by the LO, 24,000 were Jews, and 16,000 of them survived the war undetected by the Germans. Yet even in the Netherlands the odds of a Jew finding a family willing to conceal him or her were significantly worse than those of a Dutch gentile. Although legally there was no mandatory death penalty for helping Jews, 1,100 members of the LO were executed for their activities.[84]

For the most part, Holland's major Christian churches were outspoken in their opposition to Nazism and intervened to protect the Jews in various ways. Even before the occupation, the Dutch Catholic church and the orthodox Calvinist Reformed churches (Gereformeerde Kerken) banned their members from joining the NSB. The mainstream schismatic orthodox Calvinist Dutch Reformed church (Nederlands Hervormde Kerk) initially appealed to Seyss-Inquart to rescind the racial criteria for civil service appointments and subsequently issued a pastoral epistle enjoining its adherents not to desert the Jews. Catholic and Calvinist churches jointly filed protests with the high commissioner over the impending deportation of Jews in July 1942. Confronted with a German threat to deport baptized Jews if public readings of these protests occurred at Sunday services, the Dutch Reformed church desisted from doing so, but the Catholic church went ahead with the reading, resulting in the arrest of Catholic Jews and the immediate deportation of 100 of them to Auschwitz. In 1943 and 1944, Protestant Jews were sent to Bergen-Belsen or Theresienstadt. The LO originated in 1942 as a Calvinist movement and linked up with Catholic groups in southern Holland in August 1943. Indeed, members of the 8 percent of the population who belonged to the Reformed churches accounted for an estimated 25 percent of the rescues of Dutch Jews.[85]

Substantial numbers of Jews were saved in two other ways. Twelve thousand Jews were married to Dutch gentiles. Few of them severed their relationships with their Jewish mates as Germany encouraged them to do, because this would have doomed their spouses to deportation. Although the Reich interned intermarried Jews in work camps, it did not deport them because it wanted to avoid the outcry this would have provoked among their Dutch relatives.[86] Three thousand more Jews escaped persecution by applying for racial reclassification. Hans Georg Calmeyer, the German official who evaluated such petitions, was not a Nazi and certified many Jews as Aryans on quite flimsy evidence.[87]

Nonetheless, Nazi coercion and determination almost succeeded in making the Netherlands *Judenrein*. Perhaps more Jews could have survived if Dutch and Jewish agencies had complied less with Nazi orders. A fatal combination of circumstances doomed Dutch Jewry: "The Dutch–Jewish catastrophe was in part a consequence of the interactions among efficient and ruthless German implementors on the one hand and indifferent, if not cooperative, Dutch bystanders on the other, including government officials as well as the general public."[88]

France

Statistically, France appears to have been a relatively "safe" country for Jews, especially when compared to the Netherlands or Poland. Of the 350,000 Jews residing there in 1940, over 75,000 were deported, and 2,500 of these survived the war. This constitutes a victimization rate of about 21 percent. However, only 14 percent of the French-born Jewish community perished, while foreign Jews sustained twice that fatality rate.[89]

These figures graphically indicate how Vichy France, the indigenous French government established to negotiate an armistice with Germany in 1940, deliberately abandoned Jewish refugees to their German executioners while trying to protect native Jews from deportation. Although Vichy enjoyed a precarious autonomy between 1940 and 1942, which probably could have been used more effectively to obstruct German persecution of the Jews, it viewed the Jews as an expendable group whose fate could be expediently subordinated to futile attempts to strengthen its position with Germany. Thus, Vichy initiated its own anti-Semitic legislation, provided many of the personnel who herded Jews into transit camps for deportation, and voluntarily deported Jews from territory not occupied by the Germans. French cooperation with the Nazis and indifference toward the persecution of the Jews decreased as the strains of the German occupation and the prospects of Germany's ultimate defeat became greater in 1943 and 1944. This period also witnessed the growth of resistance organizations that sponsored or aided Jewish rescue networks. The dispersion of the Jews in Vichy France, its proximity to other havens from Nazism, and recurring shortages of SS manpower and train cars contributed as much to saving the majority of the Jews in France as did Vichy's reluctance to deport native Jews.[90]

Vichy's authoritarianism and anti-Semitism had firm roots in modern French history. The concurrent democratization and modernization of France during the Third Republic (1875–1940) regularly encountered opposition from traditional elites who had lost influence and power and from social groups displaced and disoriented by cultural and economic change. Conditions in the 1930s—high unemployment, labor strife, the fear of war with Nazi Germany, and the threat of domestic and Soviet communism—enhanced the appeal of authoritarian solutions for France's problems.[91] Anti-Semitism surfaced as a common leitmotiv in the programs of many of the republic's opponents, with Jewish equality and prosperity serving as convenient explanations for everything that reactionaries and fascists found wrong in French society. The Dreyfus affair of the 1890s, the Stavisky scandal of 1934, and the appointment of the Jewish socialist Léon Blum as premier in 1936 seemingly confirmed the Jewish conspiracy theories of right-wing demagogues.[92] Jews also bore part of the brunt of a general animosity toward foreigners in a France inundated by gentile and Jewish refugees fleeing from repressive regimes throughout Europe in the 1930s. Fearing these aliens as competitors for jobs, diluters of French culture, and security risks, France embarked on a program of mass internment of approximately twenty thousand refugees in 1939 and early 1940, thereby preparing more tolerant sectors of the French public for the subsequent betrayal of foreign Jews that Vichy would orchestrate.[93]

The stunning German victory over France in May and June 1940 further eroded the legitimacy of the Third Republic and cata-pulted its right-wing foes into power to negotiate the most lenient peace terms possible with Germany. The new government ac-cepted German annexation of Alsace-Lorraine and military occu-pation of northwestern France in return for French control over the remainder of the country and administrative and legal powers in the occupied zone that did not contravene German military orders there. Because the SS security contingent stationed in the occupied zone was too small to conduct large-scale operations alone, the Nazis sorely needed the assistance of French officials in the implementation of civilian policies, especially those affecting Jews.[94] Vichy leaders justified their collaboration on the grounds that it prevented the entire country from being overrun and might eventually lead to the full restoration of French independence.[95]

Vichy's supporters disagreed among themselves about what shape their anti-Semitic program should take. Led by Marshal Henri Pétain, the conservatives favored discrimination against French Jews and the emigration of foreign Jews as a respectable alternative to Nazi racism; whereas the fascists echoed Nazi calls for the removal of all Jews from France.[96] Without German prod-ding in 1940, the Vichy "moderates" barred native Jews from the civil service and interned foreign Jews in such camps as Gurs and Rivesaltes. In the occupied zone, Vichy officials helped the Ger-mans register Jews and their property and ran the camps at Beaune-la-Ronde, Drancy, and Pithiviers, where Jewish refugees and "troublesome" French Jews were confined. Three thousand inmates died in the camps under Vichy's jurisdiction. When the Germans pressured Vichy in 1941 to escalate its campaign against the Jews, the conservative minister Xavier Vallat conducted a cen-sus of all Jews in the unoccupied zone, "aryanized" their property, and imposed a Jewish Council, the UGIF (Union Générale des Israélites de France), on both zones.

The German incarceration and shooting of a number of re-spected French Jews in December 1941 went beyond Vallat's aim of reducing native Jews to second-class citizens. His protest over this incident and opposition to Nazi proposals for tougher mea-sures against the Jews caused him to be fired and replaced by a more rabid anti-Semite in February 1942. Though Vichy apologists contend that French persecution of the Jews might have pre-empted Germany from introducing harsher policies, it is questionable whether the Nazis could have accomplished so much against the Jews without the steps taken by Vichy.[97]

Although the first transport of Jews left for Auschwitz early in 1942, a shortage of trains halted further deportations until summer. In the interim, Himmler transferred the command of the German police in France from the military to the SS. In June all Jews in the occupied zone were required to wear Jewish stars, a measure Vichy refused to enact because no distinction was made between foreign and native Jews. Nevertheless, SS officials soon learned that Vichy leader Pierre Laval did not object to ridding France of foreign Jews in both zones and would provide French police for this vast undertaking. Descending on Paris in mid-July, French police arrested 13,000 foreign Jews and brutally packed them into a sports arena before moving them to transit camps for eventual deportation.[98] A month later Vichy delivered 7,000 Jews from its zone to Drancy for deportation. By the end of the year, 42,500 Jews from France had been sent to Auschwitz. From then on, for several reasons, the numbers of Jews deported dropped progressively from 22,000 in 1943 to 12,500 in 1944. French support for Vichy ebbed in reaction to the deportations, Germany's occupation of the "free" zone in November 1942, and the conscription of French labor for service in Germany in 1943. Correspondingly, French police cooperation diminished, and organized resistance increased as German rule became more oppressive. Thus, the Nazis now turned to fascist groups like the paramilitary *Milice* (militia) and the anti-Jewish police, the SEC (Sections d'Enquête et Contrôle), to capture and deport French and foreign Jews alike. Finally, 35,000 Jews evaded the Germans by fleeing to the French provinces occupied by Italy in November 1942.[99]

Vichy's initial policy of allowing foreign Jews to emigrate did save some Jewish lives, but far more could have been spared if Vichy had treated emigration as a priority. The south of France provided access to a number of viable land and sea escape routes to Africa, Italy, Palestine, Portugal, Spain, and Switzerland. Vichy delegated the administrative and fiscal responsibility for promoting Jewish emigration to the Jewish refugee assistance organization, HICEM. HICEM's funds and staffing were stretched too thin to handle the paperwork and expenses involved in getting official permission for Jewish refugees to leave France and enter other countries and in arranging and paying for increasingly scarce and costly transportation. Though HICEM helped 24,000 Jews emigrate to safer places, Vichy neither supported it financially nor reduced the amount of red tape required to obtain a French exit visa. Similarly, despite his offer to let Jewish children go to the United States in the fall of 1942, Laval then set difficult preconditions for their release and sabotaged the whole deal in early November when Vichy stopped issuing exit visas in order to stem the depletion of its reservoir of foreign Jews for meeting German deportation quotas.[100]

The reaction of the French Catholic clergy to the persecution of the Jews varied over the course of the war. Since France is a predominantly Catholic country, staunch church opposition to Vichy's treatment of the Jews might have encouraged widespread support for Jewish rescue efforts. Most priests and bishops, however, appreciated Vichy's support of Catholicism and its crusade against traditional church enemies like communists and Jews. Vichy solicited the Vatican's sanction for its anti-Semitic legislation and received assurances that such discrimination against Jews was permissible so long as it was applied justly and mercifully and did not interfere with the sacramental rite of marriage. Yet the roundups in July 1942 shocked and outraged many Catholics and spawned a spate of impassioned denunciations from prominent clergymen. Opposition to the labor conscription further mobilized Catholics to aid fugitives from Vichy.[101] A few Catholic groups like L'Amitié Chrétienne (Christian Friendship) and Father Marie-Bénoit's rescue network in Marseilles distinguished themselves by their tireless efforts to protect thousands of Jews.[102]

The opposition of French Protestant churches to Vichy's Jewish policies was more consistent than that of the Catholic hierarchy. As a small minority with a history of persecution in France, French Protestants were sensitive to the consequences of prejudice and fearful that Vichy might exclude them from public life too. The Protestant CIMADE (Comité d'Inter-Mouvements Auprès des Evacués), which had been established before the war to aid refugees, threw itself into Jewish relief work during the occupation. It criticized poor conditions in the camps, resettled internees in rural areas, smuggled Jews into Switzerland, and hid Jews in safe houses in the Haute-Loire.[103] This rugged and remote region was the site of the village of Le Chambon-sur-Lignon, which was transformed into a haven for five thousand Jews by its spiritual leader Pastor Trocmé and his Huguenot congregants. French Protestant organizations also joined ecumenical efforts to shield Jews from the Germans and their Vichy accomplices.[104]

French secular resistance movements also perceived that Vichy's anti-Semitic program was an attack on the republican or egalitarian values that they represented. Consequently, they, like most underground organizations in Western Europe, condemned the persecution of the Jews in their publications and participated in Jewish rescue operations as one of their clandestine activities. They also welcomed Jews into their ranks, affording them opportunities to help their compatriots and fight their tormentors. Aside from having a common enemy, many of the French and foreign Jews shared the political ideologies of the anti-German nationalists, republicans, socialists, and communists who formed the main resistance organizations. It has been estimated that Jews constituted 20 percent of the membership of such groups as Combat, Franc-Tireur, France Combattante, Libération, and Liberté, even though only 1 percent of the French population was Jewish.[105] The French communists sponsored separate resistance groups for Jewish refugees and printed a Yiddish newspaper to alert foreign Jews to the dangers they faced in Vichy France. Such endeavors on behalf of the Jews followed the same pattern as the resistance itself, becoming more widespread as the disaffection with Vichy grew from mid-1942 until the liberation of France.[106]

Jews in France played a significant role in promoting their own survival. Even the UGIF, the French Jewish Council, functioned primarily as a welfare agency. In this capacity it ran orphanages, concealed Jewish children in safe houses, and even smuggled some of them out of the country in cooperation with officially sanctioned Jewish organizations like the OSE (Organisation de Secours d'Enfants), Jewish Scouts (Éclaireurs Israélites de France), and the Joint Distribution Committee. Some UGIF documents and facilities carelessly fell into enemy hands when the Germans occupied Vichy.[107] In reaction to the summer deportations of 1942, Jewish resistance proliferated and stiffened with the merger of the Toulouse Jewish Army (Armée Juive), the Jewish Scouts, and Zionist youth groups into the Jewish Fighting Organization (Organisation Juive de Combat). The OJC recruited two thousand members who conducted military and espionage missions and hid endangered Jewish children. According to one estimate, such rescue networks saved as many as fifteen thousand children from deportation and death.[108]

Overall, Vichy's collaboration delayed the deportations of French Jews, kept the south of France free of Germans, and allowed emigration from there until late 1942. Yet these opportunities usually translated into actual rescues of Jews primarily because of Germany's logistical problems in carrying out its policies or because of the resolve and resources of French and Jewish relief and resistance groups. Furthermore, Vichy enacted and enforced many of the ordinances that made the Jews in France so vulnerable to the Final Solution. Foreign Jews and French Jews to a lesser extent were the losers in the game of strategic compliance played by Vichy France.[109]

Italy

Of all the countries examined in our study, Italy has the best record of shielding Jews from Nazi Germany. Though Mussolini voluntarily introduced anti-Semitic legislation before the outbreak of the war, he did so for pragmatic reasons and never made the Jewish issue a high priority for his regime. Since the persecution of the Jews alienated most Italians, the enforcement of anti-Jewish measures was inefficient and lax. As an independent ally of the Reich, Italy refused to yield to German requests for the deportation of Jews inside its borders or occupation zones. Indeed, it refused to strike the invidious compromise of delivering foreign Jews to the Nazis for deportation to spare native Jews as Bulgaria and Vichy France had done. When Fascist Italy collapsed in 1943, German troops entered the country and spearheaded a drive to eradicate the Jews with the assistance of Mussolini's resuscitated regime. Seven thousand Jews were killed by the war's end. The 38,000 Jews (85 percent) in Italy who survived owed much to Italian efforts to protect them. Thousands more managed to evade the Germans because of the respite they found in Italian occupation zones. Thus, Italy ranked second only to Denmark in saving Jews during the Holocaust.[110]

Rather than stemming from indigenous feelings of racial hatred, Mussolini's Fascism appealed to Italian desires for territorial expansion, economic recovery, and a strong government capable of ending the social strife that racked Italy after World War I.[111] Since the emancipation of Italian Jewry in 1870, Jewish acculturation and achievement had promoted the acceptance of Jews in Italian society, which, in turn, limited the political viability of anti-

Semitism. Although there was an anti-Semitic fringe in the Fascist Party, its influence was not significant enough to deter a considerable number of Italian Jews from joining the party.[112] Prior to 1938, Mussolini's views on Jews vacillated according to the demands of the moment. He condemned Zionism as unpatriotic but briefly aided the Revisionist Zionists, who shared his aim of driving Great Britain out of the Middle East. While he naturally condemned Jewish involvement in opposition movements like communism and socialism, he praised Jewish support for his regime and the valuable contributions Jews had made to Italy.[113] Though critical of Nazi racism, Mussolini trotted out his anti-Semitism when he wanted to curry favor with Hitler. Impressed with Hitler's diplomatic successes following the formation of the German–Italian Axis in 1936, Mussolini introduced his own anti-Jewish laws in November 1938 to enhance Italy's prestige with Germany in the expectation that it would then back Italian territorial claims that had not been met in the settlement of World War I.[114]

Until 1943 the persecution of the Jews in Italy was less severe than almost anywhere else in Nazi-dominated Europe. Mussolini's ordinances barred Jews from the civil service, military, and Fascist Party, and restricted their ownership of property and types of businesses. Moreover, Jews naturalized after 1918 were stripped of their citizenship, and all foreign Jews were ordered to leave Italy by March 1939. Yet the legal criteria for classifying someone as Jewish were relatively narrow, and special categories of Jews, who eventually numbered close to 2,500, were exempted from the economic and occupational liabilities imposed on their coreligionists. Sympathetic church officials often falsified records, encouraging some 6,000 Italian Jews to convert to Catholicism and benefit from a loophole that spared Jews baptized before October 1938. Another 6,000 availed themselves of opportunities to flee safely from Italy between 1938 and 1941. Lacking enthusiasm for Mussolini's highly unpopular anti-Semitic program, the officials responsible for implementing it often did so in a slipshod manner. This laxity was glaringly apparent in the execution of the order to expel the 10,000 foreign Jews residing in Italy in 1938. Two years after Mussolini's original deadline, 7,000 Jewish refugees, 3,000 of whom were recent arrivals, remained in Italy. These foreigners, however, were subject to internment or enforced confinement in rural villages. Similarly, the conscription of Italian Jews for forced labor in 1942 and 1943 was not rigorously enforced.[115]

As the Final Solution commenced in other Western European countries in 1942, Germany grew impatient with the slow pace and leniency of Italy's campaign against the Jews. Not wanting to offend their most important ally, Nazi officials at first broached this topic gingerly. By early 1943, however, they demanded that Italy adopt the German model for dealing with the Jews in Italy and Italian occupation zones.[116] Aware of the atrocities Germany was committing against the Jews,[117] Mussolini cound not afford the adverse public reaction that introducing the Final Solution into Italy would have provoked. His resistance to German pressure arose from three sources: (1) his personal preference for legal discrimination over violent persecution; (2) deference to the sympathy Italians had for the Jews; and (3) recognition that Germany had become an unpopular ally among most Italians. Italians resented their country's subordinate status in the Axis and were growing weary of the sacrifices they made fighting on Germany's side. The longer the war dragged on, the more they detested the Nazi reign of terror elsewhere and the insulting claim of Nordic supremacy on which it was based. Therefore, refusing to cater to German demands for more ruthless treatment of the Jews became a matter of pride and independence for Italy.[118]

Nowhere was Italian recalcitrance on this issue more evident than in the Italian occupation zones. When Italian troops stationed in the southwestern half of Croatia witnessed the massacres of Serbs and Jews perpetrated by the Croatian *Ustase* police in the summer of 1941, they spontaneously intervened to protect the victims. What started as unauthorized actions on the part of individual Italian soldiers soon became the offical policy of the Italian Foreign Ministry, the Army command in the region, and the Italian civilian government in neighboring Dalmatia. Representatives of these bodies consistently refused German demands in the summer of 1942 to turn the thousands of Jews who had fled into the Italian zone over to Croatia for deportation to German death camps. Even when Mussolini agreed to hand over Croatian Jews living in the zone, the Italian authorities in the area devised means to avert or delay the transfer. Significantly, Mussolini did not reprimand them for thwarting the German plans. Similar subversion of Nazi attempts to deport Jews occurred in the Italian zones of France and Greece.[119]

However, the relative security of Italian Jews came to an end in September 1943, when German troops advanced into Italy, taking control of the northern half of the country, where most of the Jewish population lived. On October 16, German police and military regiments swooped down on the Jews of Rome, arresting over 1,000 of them. Two days later most of these captives were shipped to Auschwitz.[120] Similar raids occurred in other occupied Italian cities that autumn. Renegade fascist militias aided the Germans in these roundups. Mussolini's puppet government at Salò, on Lake Garda, ordered the internment of all Jews as "enemy foreigners" in late 1943. While Mussolini might have calculated that this would keep the Jews under Italian jurisdiction and prevent their deportation, the Germans soon replaced the Italian administration of the concentration camp at Fossoli di Carpi, near Modena, and converted the facility into the main point of departure for transports to the death camps. Italian security forces consisting of the most extreme and opportunistic elements drawn to the Fascist movement assisted the Germans in tracking down and capturing Jews and political enemies. A total of 6,800 Jews were deported to Auschwitz, Bergen-Belsen, and Mauthausen during the German occupation of Italy. Hundreds more perished in executions or from the brutal mistreatment they received in camps and prisons in Italy.[121]

For all its casualties and horrors, the Nazi hunt for Jews in Italy ferreted out only a fraction of its Jewish prey for several reasons. The occupation period in Italy was comparatively short. The Allies liberated central Italy less than a year after Germany entered it. The Nazis were driven out of northern Italy eight months later. Furthermore, Italian Jews were highly assimilated and consequently indistinguishable from Italian gentiles. They had extensive personal and public contacts with the latter, to whom they readily turned when they needed help. Finally, the proximity of the Allied armies in the south and Switzerland in the north provided Jews in Italy with escape routes. Though the Swiss government denied admission to all but designated categories of Jewish refugees until December 1943, it relaxed the enforcement of such regulations after the Salò Republic announced its policy of mass internment for Jews. As many as six thousand Jews found refuge in Switzerland during the German occupation of Italy.[122]

The primary explanation for the survival of most Jews in Italy, however, lies in the widespread aid extended to Jews by many Italians. For example, the Germans expected to catch eight thousand Jews in the "Black Sabbath" raid on Rome, but fell far short of this goal because seven thousand found hiding places among sympathetic Italians. Despite Pope Pius XII's failure to issue an explicit denunciation of the raid, let alone of the Final Solution, the Catholic church concealed hundreds of Jews in the Vatican complex and several thousand more in Roman monasteries and convents during this emergency. Other rescue rings relied heavily on clerical involvement. After Germany occupied the Italian sector of France, the irrepressible Father Marie-Bénoit changed his name to Benedetto and resumed his activities in Rome, where he joined forces with the Jewish relief agency for refugees, DELASEM. From this union sprang a factory for fabricating identity and food-ration cards and a network for distributing them to Jews in hiding. The Benedetto operation ultimately helped 1,500 foreign Jews and 2,500 Italian Jews.[123] Likewise, Padre Ruffino Niccacci sheltered 300 Jewish fugitives in Assisi's religious shrines, convinced a local printer to counterfeit documents for them, and shepherded a group of Jews to safety on the Allied side of the Italian front.[124] Italians and Jews alike flocked to partisan movements in reaction to the German occupation. The Monte San Martino group, led by a Jew, Haim Vito Volterra, liberated the concentration camp at Servigliano in May 1944, saving several hundred Jews interned there.[125]

The Italian experience demonstrated that a country allied to Nazi Germany possessed the freedom to abstain from collaboration in the mass murder of European Jewry. Mussolini passed anti-Semitic laws to please his senior partner, but he originally tempered them according to limits set by his own ambiguous prejudice toward Jews and by what the Italian public and officials would reasonably tolerate. By comparison, Vichy used the latitude it had in formulating Jewish policy and in responding to German demands much more submissively. German coercion and the utter dependence of Mussolini's regime on Germany after its occupation of Italy caused the Holocaust that did occur there. But Italian opposition to the Final Solution, compassion, and active courage saved many Italian Jews who would otherwise have fallen victim to it.

CHAPTER 3

The Acts of Heroism

Aron and his family were herded into the Cracow Ghetto, after which their parents and sister were sent to Auschwitz and he and his brother to a labor camp at Czchow, because they were young and could work. There the Jews were employed in constructing a road. One day the two of them got a pass—probably for their good conduct—and they came to our village, where I saw them again after many years. It was already 1943, and it was clear they would be killed ... I asked them if it wasn't time to escape, but they said, "Not yet." But then they overheard two Germans making preparations for deportation and they escaped. They crossed the river to the forest, and from there they contacted me. It was the summer of 1943.[1]

They came to my place in the evening. My sister had some milk soup and bread ready for them. I gave them some underwear, not new but clean, and some clothes. I also got them new shoes; theirs were completely worn out. They went back to the forest and stayed there until autumn. We helped them with food, and I would bring them our underground newspaper to encourage their hopes for survival. In the winter I arranged a shelter in our barn for Aron—a hole in the ground we clawed out together and in which he stayed all winter long. His brother went to stay somewhere else. From time to time, I would arrange a bath for him; he was covered with lice, and we could do nothing to prevent it. In April or May, when the weather warmed up, he went back to the forest with his brother. They stayed there throughout the next winter because I was afraid to take him in again since I had reasons to fear that people in the village would inform on us. We kept in touch, of course; I kept them informed about events, told them where they might steal something to eat or something to warm themselves, and advised them how to avoid the Germans. That's how they managed to survive until the seventeenth of January 1945, when the Russian Army entered our village. (Stefan, Poland)*

From day to day, the activities of most of the rescuers were more mundane than glamorously heroic. For each dramatic act of rescuing a Jew from incarceration there were months and years of ongoing activities to feed, shelter, and clothe him or her. Many rescuers

*Pseudonym.

49

provided people with these basic necessities while they were hiding elsewhere, as well as keeping them for a short time on their own property, as Stefan did. Also like Stefan, once embarked on their helping course, most (65 percent) persisted on it until liberation, though they did not necessarily maintain sustained contact with the same persons over that time.

Stefan was atypical in not beginning his activities until the summer of 1943; more than 70 percent of our rescuers began in 1942 or earlier. And the year and a half he was involved was somewhat shorter than the average. While about 3 percent of rescuers limited their help to a month or less, the majority (56 percent) participated between two and more than five years. Stefan helped only two people, whereas 65 percent of the rescuers in our sample reported helping more than five people, and 15 percent estimated that they had helped more than 100.

Despite their variety most rescue activities focused on one or more of four tasks: (1) helping Jews sustain life as they were progressively stripped of their rights, segregated, isolated, and incarcerated; (2) helping Jews escape from centers of incarceration; (3) smuggling Jews out of the country; and (4) helping them maintain an underground existence within the national borders. Several rescuers engaged in all four types of activities, while others "specialized" in one of them.

Maintaining contact was one of the earliest forms of help many rescuers provided. They lent sympathetic ears, counseled, brought gifts of food, and provided psychological support. When her Jewish neighbor was confronted with restrictions on shopping and services, a Dutchwoman not only purchased food for her but took her laundry to be done, got medical prescriptions filled, and even secured library books for the family. Several rescuers tried to maintain some semblance of "normalcy" for the Jewish victims, particularly children and the aged. Unable to bear the forced isolation of her former employer's child, a German rescuer insisted on taking the little girl to the park to play with her own children, carefully removing the yellow star on the way. Another German woman agreed to come to her friend's house weekly, ostensibly to continue her violin lessons—the real objective was to assure the friend's aged mother that things were not so bad. Services rendered varied in terms of time, resources, and the degree of risk involved. In agreeing to teach in a Jewish school when Jews were excluded from public schools, a Belgian woman understood that her involvement would be considerable but did not initially perceive it as a very high risk. On the other hand, a French employee at the prefecture who rode her bicycle through the Jewish neighborhoods when this was forbidden to warn the residents of impending arrests limited her involvement to emergencies but perceived the risk as great.

As Jews were forced to evacuate their places of residence, several rescuers stored personal items for them: jewelry, silverware, a prized cabinet, a grand piano, or even food. Such items were sometimes related to the victim's profession—one family kept a suitcase full of models of teeth for a Jewish dentist. Sometimes items were simply valued personal memorabilia: religious objects such as a prayer shawl or phylacteries. One set of stored items put its keepers in considerable jeopardy:

> The people next door, Jewish neighbors, gave us suitcases
> to keep for people who had gone into hiding. We never
> opened them—a big mistake. We never knew what was in
> them. During a search, police came—they opened them
> and found clothes with yellow stars on them. They took
> them away [Dutch rescuer].

Rescuers who stored such items expressed a strong sense of obligation regarding their safekeeping, even after it became clear that their owners would not be returning. An Italian priest agreed to store some valuable gold coins for a Jewish couple who did not return after the war. Considering them a sacred trust, he still had them in his possession forty years later. Shortly before his death, he gave them to the Roman Jewish community, which, in turn, decided to use them to launch a study of Italian rescuers, a fitting tribute, they felt, both to the Jewish couple and the priest.

A few rescuers dared to protest openly. Several Dutch respondents reported participating in the university strikes in Amsterdam after their Jewish professors were discharged. The protesters in our sample suffered no consequences, but they were not successful in reversing the decision.

As Jews were gradually deprived of all forms of employment, some rescuers sought to find them some source of livelihood. When they were discharged from public employment, rescuers tried to find them employment in private enterprises. When they were forbidden to own businesses, some rescuers assumed legal ownership of the businesses while covertly routing profits to their former owners. Some arranged to extend the employment of Jews under varying pretexts, insisting that they were absolutely essential for the production of war matériel. But even for the fortunate few recipients of such benefits, the rewards were of short duration. It was not long before most Jews found themselves with neither possessions nor livelihood and herded into segregated quarters, ghettos, and camps.

Ghettoization took different forms in different countries. In France and Holland, for example, Jews were concentrated in particular residential sections, but there were no enclosures surrounding such areas. In Poland, however, enclosed ghettos were the norm. Here, several million dispossessed, disenfranchised, and impoverished Jews from Poland and other countries under Nazi occupation lived in spaces barely sufficient to house several thousand, without any means of sustenance. Initially, most ghettos were open areas through which public trams from the "Aryan" sectors of the city would sometimes still pass. Eventually, they were sealed by high and impenetrable walls. Forbidden to enter under penalty of death, some rescuers nonetheless tried to fight the overwhelming tide of starvation and disease.

A few Polish rescuers engaged in ongoing social welfare work during the initial stages—providing medical supplies, food and assorted other services. More often, though, help was intermittent. Several Polish rescuers reported simply throwing food over the ghetto walls. Others reported delivering food to persons they knew—putting a yellow armband on as they went in, hiding their food packages under their clothes, and removing the armband as they exited. One was a ten-year-old boy sent by his father; he carried a pistol with instructions to shoot in the event he was caught. One rescuer devised an ingenious scheme to provide employment for the ghetto inmates in Warsaw. He was able to keep a bakery functioning illicitly within the ghetto by smuggling in grain and flour, an arrangement he was able to maintain because his particular employment required legitimate periodic deliveries of uniforms into the ghetto, and because he bribed selected guards. A handful of Polish rescuers reported choosing to live in the ghetto themselves in order to provide help for those they loved. With their "Aryan" documents, they were able to leave the ghetto to procure food and other necessities on a regular basis.

In addition to sustenance, rescuers provided the critical information links between the isolated ghetto inmates and the rest of humanity. They not only carried messages to and from separated family members, but also from ghetto inmates to the outside world. A few Poles in our sample tried to correct the ignorance and overcome the disbelief so pervasive in Western Europe and the United States regarding the plight of the Jews. A member of the Polish underground AK (Armia Krajowa) found himself assuming this role:

In the late summer of 1942 I was carrying 400 pages of microfilmed material approximately the size of two American cigarettes. The report was mounted in a medium-size key. I did not know at the time that this report told precisely what was happening to Jews. It was authored by three individuals—Professor H., who perished in the concentration camp; W., murdered by the Polish Nationalists; and P., who lives in West Germany today. They were all Jews. In September a delegate of the AK called on me. He told me that two Jewish underground organizations, one socialist and the other Poalei Zion, had learned that I was preparing to go to London. They requested my services on their behalf. Would I be willing to deliver the report to London? I said yes. I was taken to the ghetto to see events firsthand. I was not there more than twenty minutes—I became sick at the suffering. It was beyond belief.

He managed to reach London some weeks later, but unfortunately his report suffered the same fate as several others—it was largely dismissed as an exaggeration.

A few Polish rescuers delivered arms to ghetto inmates who were preparing for military action. Money for the purchase of arms was sometimes procured from Jewish sources abroad. One respondent received such funds in London, parachuted into Warsaw, and made his delivery as planned.

Ghettos were not only isolated from the Christian communities but also from other ghettos. Inmates planning resistance tried to coordinate their activities with Jews in other places. Those Jews whose appearance did not immediately betray them would undertake courier activities, and some non-Jews were also recruited in this effort. Although the latter could obviously move more freely, even they faced great difficulties amid the acute uncertainties of life in occupied Poland. An account by a Polish messenger conveys a sense of the obstacles impeding his ostensibly simple task. After receiving instructions from his Warsaw Ghetto contacts in 1940 and memorizing the names and addresses of the various people he was to contact in different towns, he proceeded to fulfill his mission. His first destination was the Bialystok Ghetto. To accomplish this he needed to go to Malkinia and from there arrange illegally to cross the border that divided the General Gouvernement from the part of Poland in which Bialystok was located. Two days later he managed to get to the Bialystok Ghetto but could not locate his first contact. He went on to Grodno, the site of his next contact, but was stopped on the way by a German official demanding to see his documents:

I had none, but I told him I was looking for my family and produced a photo of my little girl. He accepted the explanation. I asked him if I could take the train the rest of the way, but he said it was absolutely prohibited and that if I were found on the train, I would be treated as a saboteur. So I walked to Grodno and found the place I was looking for.

The apartment was filled with fifteen people—young Jewish women and men, some elderly Jews, and some small children. When I entered and asked for B., all of them stiffened with terror. B. identified himself, and I gave him the message while the others listened. The message was that they were to get in touch with other [resistance] organizations in Grodno as well as try to plant their own people in organizations cooperating with the Germans so as to learn their plans. While they listened carefully and quietly, I realized that these people did not trust me very much—and I did not trust them either because I did not know them. Because of their fear, they might not be able to withstand the psychological pressure and someone might inform the German authorities. At the conclusion of the conversation, they asked me not to come again because they were all under scrutiny.

From Grodno I was supposed to go on to Wilno. I heard that on the way there were villages and towns not favorably inclined toward Poles,* and I was warned to be careful in

---

*Wilno was inhabited primarily by Lithuanians who, because of their own nationalistic aspirations, resented Poles.

buying food, seeking shelter, or otherwise asking for help. It was about 180 kilometers from Grodno to Wilno, and because I had hurt my heels and ankles on the walk to Grodno, I went to the train station. The railroad workers at the station, who were Poles, told me that whether I went by train or by foot, I would be taking risks. I asked an elderly German conductor for permission to board the train—he said if I were found on it, I would be shot. I boarded it anyway.

During the train ride, an alarm went off signaling an air raid. At that time Soviet planes were raiding the areas newly occupied by the Germans. As it turned out, this saved me, because the soldiers on board who had wanted to check my documents had to depart quickly for a roll call. In the station at Landwarow, about fifteen to twenty kilometers short of Wilno, German guards and Szualis [Lithuanian guards] were patroling with dogs. I was afraid one would smell me out, but it ended well and the train went on.

When the train stopped, I got out at a station filled with music and light, and amid the noise, I heard two voices speaking Polish. Well, I thought, if they speak Polish, it can't be too bad, so I caught up with them and asked exactly where I was. One said, "How on earth did you get here? There are border guards all over and when they get hold of you. . . . " They showed me the way to follow them, and I found myself at the back of the station—only then did I realize that I was in Wilno.

But how could I find the address I was looking for? I approached a civilian and asked, but he answered in Lithuanian that he did not understand me. So I used German on him—then he got polite and answered my question. I got to the street but could not see the addresses because of the blackout. I lit one match and then another and another but still could not find it. Suddenly I heard someone say in German, "What the hell are you looking for?" I gave him the number and managed to find the apartment.

We made an appointment to meet with some Jews—the core of the *Shomer* [a Zionist group whose literal translation is "watchmen" or "young watchmen"] and the *Chalutz* [Zionist Pioneers] movement in Wilno—who were all hiding in the Dominican cloister in Kolonia Wilenska. Mother Bertranda was the prioress. I met with the twenty Jewish men and women in hiding there several times, communicating my message and making plans.

One of my contacts managed to get two bicycles and we went on together to Troki. From there, we returned to Kolonia, where we informed people about what had happened, and then I went back to Warsaw.

A few rescuers persisted in their efforts to keep Jews alive even after they were removed to concentration camps. A Dutch member of the Red Cross and his mother sent packages of food and medicine to Bergen-Belsen and Theresienstadt. Knowing that the wife and children of a former employee had been marched off to Westerbork without enough clothing, a Dutchwoman determined to do something:

I decided to go to Gestapo headquarters to ask permission to bring some clothes for the kids. The entry room was filled with many people sitting in a row, and they said, "Go away! Don't go in there—the man in there is a monster, a killer." I went in to see him anyway. He asked me, "Are you a friend of these Jews?" I said, "No, I was just a secretary for this family for twelve years." He gave me permission, but I didn't feel safe. I asked my minister if he would come with me to Westerbork and he agreed. There were German soldiers all around, and it was all fenced off. On the way a lady knocked on the window of her big beautiful house and said to us: "You'll never come out if you go in there." She gave us a cup of tea, and we went on our way. I'll never forget it. Mothers were looking for their children, wives were looking for their husbands. Everyone was screaming. When I saw the people, I was paralyzed. Someone ran over to me and said, "What are you doing here?" I said I was looking for X. He said, "You'll never get out of here. Go while you can." I said, "We'll see. I am a Christian." Somehow I found her and delivered the clothes. She was thankful—very thankful. We came out.

Some rescuers were able to delay or abort the very process of extermination by virtue of their official positions. One, a Hungarian Army officer, was assigned a Jewish labor battalion; his instructions were to give them the most dangerous jobs or work them to death. He managed to countermand these orders by getting his group of 200 men assigned to making skis and telephone poles. With adequate food rations and the wood serving as a source of fuel, they were able to survive the freezing winter. The other, a German, was assigned to the Ukraine, where his task was to build and repair locomotives. As he became increasingly aware of what was happening to the Jews in the area, he insisted that only they could provide the skilled labor he needed and thus managed to employ several hundred. Alert to rumors, and through his ongoing connections with leaders of the Jewish community, he was able on two occasions to avert secret SS execution plans for his workers. Once, his activities nearly cost him his life. When some of his employees were arrested despite assurances to the contrary, he brazenly confronted the SS commander:

> I found Dr. P. with a machine gun. I said, "You were lying. Why did you lie to me?" He didn't answer. I said, "I need these people very, very badly—you must let them out." "No," he said, "nobody will get out of here." Then he took his gun out of the holster and put his finger on the trigger. I was thinking, Am I a fool? This is it. It is either him or me. If he shoots, I have to be first or at the same time. He is going with me. I put my finger on the holster of my gun and held it there. I said, "I am going to take these people out. Do you hear me?" He said, "Get them out! Get them out!" I took them and put them in my house.

His audacity so impressed the SS men around him that they were sure he had secret authorization from Berlin, an illusion he did his best to encourage.

Although no single one of the above activities was sufficient to ensure ultimate survival, each was nonetheless important. Rescuers who maintained contacts with Jews gave them hope to go on. Those who provided even minimal physical sustenance made it possible to survive for yet another day. While armed insurrections within the ghettos were uniformly defeated, a few Jews nonetheless managed to escape to continue the struggle on other fronts. Several hundred Jews owe their lives to officials who refused to follow instructions. Regardless of their long-term consequences, such activities communicated to Jews that they were not entirely abandoned.

As it became increasingly apparent that death was inevitable for Jews in ghettos and camps, a small percentage of rescuers in our sample tried to secure their release. Possibilities varied, depending on the degree of incarceration (relatively open or "sealed" ghettos; labor, detention, or concentration camps), region and country, officials who monitored the system, varied plans for the particular sites determined by high-ranking Reich officials in competing bureaucracies, and local officials and overseers.

During the initial stages of ghettoization in Poland, escape was difficult but not consistently impossible. Rescue strategies included a combination of tactics. Access to the potential escapee was, of course, critical. This might require illicit entry into the ghetto or a prearranged meeting in a designated area where selected Poles and Jews could still see each other under severely restricted (and guarded) circumstances, such as workplaces or centers for official transactions. Provision of suitable attire and fictitious identity papers, as well as enough money or goods to bribe the many blackmailers ready at exit points to shout "Jude!" but willing to be muzzled for a price, were also essential. Some Polish rescuers participated in such efforts.

But some Poles arranged escapes even after the ghetto walls were sealed. One engaged in activities of this kind on a regular basis:

> I got a permanent pass to enter the ghetto through the Leszczynski Company. Every day vans pulled out of the ghetto with workers going to the Lesczcznyski workshop in Zabia Street. So you took the ones who were escaping, and put workers' uniforms with the Star of David on them, and took them to the shop. I had an agreement with one of the gatekeepers at the Nowolipki Gate, and when he saw me coming, he always let me through. It used to cost—some vodka, some gift, or something. Everything went for brass. The guards were very greedy because they always sent those tidbits to Germany. When the van pulled into the Leszczynski Company, the escapees got out, took off their rags, and left. It was much harder with children; we couldn't pass them off as workers. So once, when we had to take some young boys out, we made a cage—a box with openwork made of wire. We put the cage on the platform of the van, put the boys in it, and covered it with heaps of uniforms. This way they could breathe.

Walled ghettos were not characteristic of France. Here arrested Jews were either deported to Polish ghettos or sent directly to camps, some of which were on French soil. French rescuers seeking to help Jews escape from camps also had to gain access to the internees. More often than Poles, however, they depended on deceiving or bribing high officials monitoring the system. Working through such persons was somewhat easier in France since Nazi policy in that country differed significantly from the one pursued in Poland. A vivid account of how it worked is given by one Frenchwoman, who describes herself as "really a very shy and timid person":

> I was in Toulouse when I learned this woman had been arrested and that she had probably been taken to du Vernet camp. I heard that there were some possibilities in exceptional cases to get out of the camp. I had a cousin, a very nice guy, who had been a soldier and had escaped from prison. During the first month after his escape, he worked for the Vichy government, dealing with the files of people from the camps. So I took the train and went to Vichy to see him. He told me he would be able to arrange it because he had just helped a policeman, and the policeman owed him someone. He assured me he would take care of it. So I came back to Toulouse, but I could not rest. I told myself that I really couldn't trust the administrative staff. I don't know exactly what got into me, but I decided to go and see the prefect of Toulouse.
>
> When I arrived at headquarters, I was told that he was attending a meeting that would probably be over in a few minutes. I didn't know what the prefect looked like. I had a small amount of money with me and went over to the usher and asked him to point out the prefect to me when he left the meeting. He pointed to this tall man, and I watched him walk up the steps. I followed.
>
> I entered his office without an invitation and simply sat down. I said: "Sir, we are very surprised in Vichy— surprised that you are not following orders here." And then I gave a big speech on the fact that it was not surprising that we lost the war and that there were lots of stories about how orders were not being followed. He asked me what was going on. I said: "What is happening is that the field marshal gave specific instructions that a

certain woman in whom he is particularly interested be
released, but this has not been done." He said, "Okay, it
will be taken care of. Just give me the name of the person."
I said, "No, that's not enough. You are the superior of the
man in charge of the camp. I would like you to call him
and tell him to release the woman." He agreed and called
the man in charge. I said, "I will report back to Vichy what
you have done" and left.

But I was still not satisfied and said to myself, "That's not
enough." So I got on the train again and went to du Vernet
camp. There I was told that instructions had been received
and that the woman would be released. When I saw her she
didn't recognize me at first and thought that I was simply
another person who had been arrested. I signaled to her to
make her understand. A policeman escorted us out of the
camp and even offered us free train tickets. On the way, we
also took out a baby in a basket.

Later people thought that I managed to do this because I
knew the prefect personally, but that was actually just a
rumor. I didn't know it at the time, but I learned later that
the prefect was involved in some resistance activity.

Another Frenchwoman managed to rescue an interned Jewish
doctor with the help of a Jesuit priest ministering to a group of
Gypsies interned in the adjacent camp. Using a subterranean tunnel, and using his helpful Gypsy congregation as lookouts, the
priest entered the Jewish camp regularly, tending to their needs
as best he could. He somehow arranged to gain entrance to the
camp for the French rescuer, who in turn informed the doctor of
a bold rescue attempt being planned for him. The doctor was to
feign an illness requiring surgery, and he would be on the operating table the very moment his deportation was scheduled. The daring plan succeeded. The cooperating surgeon, with his patient on
the operating table, was able to keep the guards from taking him.

Bribes generally took the form of gifts and money—the price
depended on the rank and greed of the grantor. One bribe, paid
by a Dutch group, was rather unusual:

One of the most difficult nights of my life was when we
had a Jewish lady who had escaped from the house of
Corrie ten Boom. Along with some other Jewish people,
she took refuge in a special hiding place we had arranged.

A few days later we got word that Mary was one of the Jewish people who had been caught. She was always very careless, not impressed by the seriousness of the situation. She was standing in front of the window, and somebody recognized her as Jewish. She was sent to the police office—that was always the first place people were taken before being sent on to the camps. We got word and were very worried. Mary knew a lot about the other people in hiding, and we were afraid she would talk. About five of us met to decide what to do.

Somebody, we decided, needed to be willing to take the risk of killing her. We talked and talked. We asked ourselves whether we could ethically do this—murder this woman, for that's what it came down to, in order to save I don't know how many others. After about two or three hours, we called in a minister and asked for his judgment.

Then somebody showed up and said that he had found a policeman who would be willing to release her the next morning when his shift started. The price was finding a hiding place for him and his family. That was a tremendous chance to save her life. So we had to come up with a hiding place for her, the policeman, and his wife and children. We got it fixed.

A more indirect escape ruse was devised by another Dutchman. He was employed as a manager in a quinine factory whose owner collaborated with the Germans. Shipments of quinine were often sent to camps. So he would hide false identification papers in the quinine bottles and seal them. When prisoners found the papers they could be distributed to those attempting escape.

In some cases engineering an escape was relatively simple, but the consequences were not always foreseen. During the early period of ghettoization in one area of Hungary, for example, inmates could be requisitioned to work for the surrounding population at the latter's request. The person making the request would simply write to the appropriate officials asking that a particular individual be released for some critical labor for the day. The petitioner was, of course, responsible for returning the worker at the end of the day. One Hungarian couple agreed to use this procedure in order to help a relative of some friends escape. They duly obtained her work service for the day and instead of returning her, allowed

her to go on her way. They were able to parry the police under
subsequent questioning and deflect any consequences to themselves. But they were surprised to receive a reprimand from the
Jewish ghetto leadership. What they apparently had not foreseen
were the severe reprisals exacted on the remaining ghetto inmates
as a result of any such flight.

As with sustenance activities, escape was insufficient to ensure ultimate survival. Unless they had a safe place to go, Jews would inevitably be rearrested and immediately executed or worse. Hence,
the critical issue was to find them a place of safety. Smuggling
them out of the country was the best way to deal with the problem.

Smuggling operations required an intricate set of steps—es-
tablishing contact with those seeking to be smuggled out of the
country, obtaining or forging the necessary papers, escorting the
victims to the designated places, procuring sufficient funds to pay
for the entire enterprise, as well as finding safe countries willing
to accept the refugees.

Contacts with those seeking to leave the country occurred in
various ways. A German woman with high-level connections began
her smuggling activities in the early thirties. Ever mindful of the
need, she was on a routine shopping errand when she was presented with an unexpected opportunity to help:

> I began my activities in Dresden in 1933, laundering and
> stealing files, but my main job was to get train tickets
> leading to places outside the country.... My husband was
> an official with the Council of German Communities—a
> group with many top-level connections. Because of these
> connections, I was able to get tickets signed by Goering
> himself, the names left blank. People who acted as
> intermediaries would pick up the tickets from me—they
> usually had no idea what they were carrying—and deliver
> them to prearranged places. I would keep my "eyes and
> ears" open all the time to see who needed such help.
>
> One time I had saved a little money in order to have my
> grandmother's antique kitchen cupboard painted, and so I
> went to Wertheim's, to the furniture department, which at
> that time was so charming and which also carried some
> antiques. There was a very nice saleswoman there, and I
> asked her whether she knew anyone who might be able to

paint. I noticed another woman there—my age or perhaps a bit older—who was also looking at things but seemed to be listening to our conversation. When I left the store, this woman approached me and said that she could do the painting. One developed a very keen sense of whom one could trust without exchanging a word, and at that moment I had a feeling that there was something else going on with this woman, so I invited her to have a cup of coffee with me to discuss the matter. She then told me that she was Jewish, and her Jewish husband had left for London, but for reasons she would tell me later, she had stayed behind with her two daughters. I told her to come to my apartment (she had very few so-called racial characteristics) and pretend to do my painting. Her daughters left for Stockholm, and I was able to get a train ticket for her to England through my "source."

The refugees had to be provided with the necessary false papers to display at check points. Obtaining or forging them was a specialized skill several rescuers learned "on the job." A French-woman describes how she eventually mastered the procedure:

I was working in the prefecture at Poitiers, where they issued the required new identification cards. I don't remember anymore who asked me for IDs the first time, but anyway I decided to do it. In the beginning I didn't know how, so I tried all kinds of things. I began by finding out which office at the prefecture was typing cards. I would take my lunch with me, and when everyone was gone, between noon and 2 P.M., I would go into that office, take blank cards, and—using the same typewriter—would fill them in. I would also put on the photograph and the stamp and would also adjust the birthdate, but this wasn't a very good idea, because if anyone checked, the numbers would not correspond with the file books kept in the office. So I decided to steal two of these file books and use those numbers for the IDs since no one would be able to check them out. But later I found that this was too dangerous, and I replaced the books. When I learned that all the papers in the city of Nantes had been destroyed because of the bombing, I used this city as the birthplace since it too could not be checked. Finally I found something much

better. It took me a long time to learn it, because I had to
look around and watch others, and I was also very busy. I
realized that all you needed to get a new ID was an old
one. So I decided to make my cards look old. I would
trample on them to make them look really dirty or wash
them in the laundry. My people could then take these cards
to the appropriate office and ask for new ones.

Escorting refugees to the ships and trains taking them out of
the country was complicated. The passengers had to be fed,
housed, and hidden on the way as well as transported within the
country to embarkation points. Some of them, already trauma-
tized, were terrified. One escort was shocked when the Jewish
woman she was accompanying suddenly became hysterical and
turned to flee. Thinking quickly, she slapped her face to stun her
into silence. Only later did she learn that the Nazi guard at the
train gate was the very one who had arrested the woman a week
earlier. Some of the worst problems revolved around transporting
children. One Jewish child, angered because he could not have
something he wanted, informed his French escort that unless he
got it, he would tell the German guard that "we are Jewish."
Another garrulous little boy would not stop talking; he kept saying, "I guess we must be very important; everyone is hunting for
us."

Yet another incident had its comic overtones:

I was living in Voiron. One day a young lady came to see
me. She told me that she had come on behalf of ORT [the
Jewish Organization for Rehabilitation and Training] and
that she knew I was in touch with some of the people from
that outfit. She said that Rabbi X. wanted to ask for my
help. I answered, "Okay, what kind of help?" Well, they
needed a witness at a civil marriage, and he was asking me
to be the witness. I answered her, "Of course, with
pleasure." After that the rabbi asked me for some other
help—to hide some kids and take some elsewhere. I then
worked with OSE and took some children to Switzerland.
Some contacts from OSE asked me to organize a transport
for the rabbi and his school, about sixty to eighty people,
to Switzerland. What we finally decided was to buy some
furniture, rent a truck, and hide the young people in the
furniture, in cupboards and couches. The truck left with

all the young people, but the rabbi would not consent to be transported in this fashion. So we thought of the idea of bribing a policeman we knew in Voiron so that he would come with a taxi and handcuffs and pretend he was arresting the rabbi and put him in the cab. But at the last minute the policeman got frightened. So the rabbi got into the cab by himself and drove away. Fortunately, nothing happened to him. So he told me, "You see, I told you not to worry. God is with us." He really was an exceptional guy [French rescuer].

Money "greased" the whole enterprise. Outside sources sometimes supplied it—a few rescuers report getting money from Jewish individuals or organizations, particularly the Joint Distribution Committee. Some dipped into their own resources, at times quite heavily. The burden was eased if those to be transported had their own. A French priest tells of his encounter with a Jewish refugee accustomed to pay for everything. "You are the first," he said to the interviewer, "to hear this story":

It's about a couple and their three children. I can see their faces in front of me now. They came to see me in August, a pretty warm day. The man wore a black suit. I received them in my office, the husband and the wife. We talked for a long time, and he asked for my help. I had already been denounced in Vichy for my illegal activities, but I said to them: "Okay, I will take care of you. Tonight, be at this place." Then they stood up to leave. The man put his hands in his pocket and took out a bundle of bills. He offered them to me. I looked at him and said nothing. He put the money back in his pocket and left. Years went by. After the war—I don't remember exactly how long after— we ran into each other one day. He was very glad to see me and invited me to lunch at his house. He was then living close to Paris in a nice house. I was received very well. After lunch the man took me aside and said, "I guess I have to apologize. Do you remember the first time I met you?" I didn't remember exactly, so he told me the story of the money. He said, "Listen to me, Father. We were used to paying for everything. You were helping us, me and my family. You were providing us with the greatest gift of all— our lives. Nothing I have would be mine except for you.

You were the first priest I ever met. You taught me that
priests can help for free."

But smuggling opportunities were limited, depending on the
receptivity of the potential host countries, the terrain, special
skills—particularly in mountainous and highly wooded areas—as
well as on the nature of Nazi control within the particular country.
Sweden and Switzerland offered safe havens for a while but eventually closed their doors. Portugal was also safe, provided one
could reach it through Spain; although an Axis ally, Spain did not
share Germany's obsession with Jews. Italy, another Axis ally, was
also reluctant to enforce anti-Jewish measures, so the southeastern
section of France and Italy itself remained safe as long as they
were occupied by Italians. The Italian-occupied zone in Yugoslavia
(Croatia) was also a good refugee area for a while. Territories under the control of the Soviet Union provided a margin of safety if
one could make it through the shifting borders of battle. In some
cases, Jewish refugees were subsequently interned in Siberia.
Some Jews made the long trek on foot and by railroad across the
Soviet Union to China and to Japan, another Axis ally that did not
share its partner's compulsion. Hungary, too, provided a margin
of safety until 1944. Of course, no route or place was certain for
long in the changing tides of war and politics.

A few Poles and Dutch report successful smuggling efforts,
conducted primarily during the first years of the war. One Dutch
rescuer managed to get a family to Denmark; another reports getting a family to Spain. In 1939 it was still possible to get Jews from
the German zone of Poland to the Soviet zone; Jews themselves
were predominantly involved in organizing this effort, as one Polish rescuer reported. Skiing through the Carpathian Mountains
from Zakopane into Hungary was another pathway. And a Lutheran pastor in Poland managed to secure passage to Canada for
a few hundred Jewish children in 1939. But in our sample, the
largest number of successful smuggling operations is reported by
French rescuers, for reasons largely rooted in their country's proximity to other nations offering safe passage or havens for Jews.

Many rescuers reported smuggling efforts that failed. But,
more frequently than others, Poles told the story of desperate Jews
who allowed themselves to be trapped. Seduced by promises of
exit, they allowed themselves to be lured out of hiding places by
Nazi officials:

After the ghetto liquidation, a devilish idea originated in the Gestapo—they announced that all Jews were to be exchanged for German POWs in England. They were supposed to transport Jews to Sweden and from there to England. I told my friends it was suspicious. I explained to them, like to intelligent people, "Do you really think that the Germans will let the pick of the Jewish intelligentsia out to the West, so that they can tell them what is going on with Jews here?" But I could not convince them. Jews gathered in two hotels—here in Chmielna, now Rutkowskiego Street, the Royal Hotel, and in Dluga, the Polski Hotel. They lived there for about a month, even walking around without armbands. Whole families went there, sitting on the two suitcases they were allowed to bring, waiting for transports. Lawyers, doctors, wealthy merchants—all who had the means to do so came. I watched it the last day. Trucks with trailers pulled up in front of the hotel. Suitcases were loaded on the trailer. We waved to each other—they went away. And no trace of them has ever been found. Nobody knows if they were gunned down in the ghetto's ruins or further away out of Warsaw somewhere. There are even stories that they were taken to Swinoujscie, loaded on some boat, and then simply sunk [Polish rescuer].

Because smuggling opportunities were limited, only one other option remained. Shelters had to be found within the country where Jews could maintain an "underground" existence.

Finding shelters became a major preoccupation for a few rescuers. Sometimes this was part of a coordinated group effort; often it was an individual one. Rural and isolated places were favorite choices, but they were not always available nor accessible. Areas populated by Mediterranean-looking people were safer than those where blond and blue-eyed types prevailed. Heavily forested and mountainous areas were also desirable. In Eastern Europe particularly, the forests became the operating bases for Jewish guerrilla groups that also assumed sheltering functions.

Some forms of organized sheltering occurred in many countries. The Dutch had one of the best-coordinated shelter and hiding networks. Unfortunately, it developed too late to help the majority of Dutch Jews. Organized by the LO (National Organization for Assistance to Divers, which included people forced to seek an underground existence to avoid capture), it developed primarily as a means for helping young men avoid conscripted labor in Germany. Finding hiding places for non-Jews, however, was easier than finding them for Jews.[2] One Dutch searcher reports his keen disappointment when he approached a well-known minister in another town who informed him that under no circumstances would he allow a Jew to cross his threshold. Another managed to persuade some people to take Jews by promising them a smaller-than-normal total of Dutch "divers" (young men seeking to avoid forced labor); being responsible for a smaller number of people was sometimes attractive enough to convince a few.

Most house hunters depended on local liaisons. One Dutchman, a traveling salesman who used his occupation as a subterfuge, usually contacted the church minister first. Accompanied by a local resident who knew the other residents and their political leanings, another Dutch rescuer would make his hunting expeditions at night. He would knock at the door and simply ask whether "divers" were already located there and how many there were. He would also ask to survey the house to determine its sheltering potential. During one of his expeditions he came upon a large and beautiful farmhouse:

> I said to my friend, "We better take a look. It's a big house, and maybe they can take some people there." The farmer greeted us at the door: "What can I do for you?" I said, "I would like to inspect your house and see how many rooms you have. I would like to put a family in here." I could take the house if people were not willing to keep others there. The farmer let us in but was reluctant to have us inspect the house. "What's the problem?" I asked. It turned out that he already had a Jewish family in hiding. I told him I would help by getting a flag from the local doctor showing the name of a contagious disease. "We will put the flag on the front door so that nobody will enter this place." The Germans were scared stiff when they saw those flags.

Rescuers in all countries had special problems placing Jews, and they developed their own techniques for overcoming them. A Belgian woman describes the technique she used:

At the beginning when I used to go and ask for help, I was somewhat apologetic in the sense that I did not want to appear as a "Jew lover." This is connected with the problem of anti-Semitism. I would say, "It isn't that I'm crazy about the Jews or anything like that. But after all, what is happening to them is just too inhuman. You don't need to like them especially or love them. I just personally feel that after what I've seen I must do something." So some people who were unfavorable toward Jews would go along with this. Part of my reason for doing this was to gain their trust, but part of it was fear, too—I felt I had to apologize for identifying with them. In general, this was my approach—except with religious people. With them I talked about Christian charity.

Initial reluctance was sometimes followed by intense commitment. Thus, for example, a Dutch rescuer ruefully recalled the response of a family with four children of their own on being asked to keep a Jewish infant: "This is going too far!" they shouted at her. "We have given money to support and hide Jews and paid for plastic surgery for others. But we don't need a Jewish kid in the house." By the next morning, however, it had all changed. They had spent the night discussing what to do and had already made plans. The woman would pretend to be pregnant, and they would hire a special nursemaid for it in addition to the governess they already had.

Not content with placing her young charges just anywhere, a Frenchwoman demanded the best of circumstances. She was not only determined that her youngsters would lead a normal life and go to school but that they would retain their Jewish identity:

I placed some children in parochial schools, convents, or monasteries. In December 1942 they were of course celebrating Christmas. They put up decorations with the infant Jesus and the manger, prayed, and arranged festivities. Well, the children who were entrusted to them wanted to participate—to go to church and have communion. They even wanted to convert, and the nuns were delighted at the opportunity to convert some of the children. When I heard about it, I went to each one of them and told them that this was not to be done. I acted like the mother of those children, and although I am a Christian myself, I would not allow the nuns, the priests, or the brothers or convert them. The children and the adults might have been angry about what I did, but I had to act like their mother. It worked out in the long run.

Monasteries and convents were frequently sought as shelters. Yet, even here, it was more difficult to place Jews than others. An Italian rescuer, a Dominican brother, was keenly aware of this problem. It was only because he had a letter from the cardinal of Florence asking for protection of Jewish refugees that he was able to persuade convents to take them. As he explains, "Without the cardinal's letter, they would not have done it—they were too afraid of the Germans and the Italian Fascists, who would just come in and start shooting."

Monasteries and convents could also be dangerous, as one Polish rescuer learned:

One of our tenants saw a mother with a baby in the courtyard beside the rubbish bin. He took them home, but couldn't keep them because he had only one room for his wife and two children. He came to me and asked for help. The mother—her husband had already been killed—spoke Polish very badly and couldn't go to work. So I said, "The only thing to do is to leave the baby. Maybe I can place it in Father Baudouin's orphanage in Nowogrodzka Street." They didn't take Jewish children there, but I knew the mother superior and because I had done them a favor at the very beginning of the war, I thought they might agree. I brought the baby to the mother superior, and she said the decision would have to be made by the police. We had to go to the police, the baby, I, and the caretaker of the apartments. When the head of the police yelled at the caretaker, "Whose baby is it?!" he broke down with fear and lost his tongue. By that time there was a whole crowd of people standing there—there were Gestapo, confidential agents, and decent Polish policemen but also many corrupt ones. I knew that unless I thought of something, we would all be arrested. So I said loudly: "What an idea! Everyone on our block knows whose baby it is." Well, the caretaker turned and looked at me with wonder in his eyes. I stared back at him. "It's his," I lied, "but it's an extramarital one. Somebody dumped it with him, and he's afraid of his wife so he won't let on or tell you anything." And that's how we saved the situation.

Sometimes apartments were rented under false names to shelter Jews, a ruse that had better chances of success if the occupant did not look Jewish and spoke the native tongue without accent. In order to overcome the risk posed by accented speech, one rescuer advised his Jewish charge to pretend to stutter. By and large, however, such efforts worked for short periods only; someone would get suspicious, the owner would find out and evict them, and new apartments had to be found repeatedly. Learning that a blacksmith wanted to expel the wife of a friend, one Pole simply threatened him with reprisals from the AK if anything should happen to her, and the blacksmith backed down. Vacated bunkers, cellars, and bombed-out buildings were frequently the only shelters available. Zegota, the only Polish organization designed primarily to help Jews, had few options in placing people and fewer resources; they typically availed themselves of anything at hand.

Although highly vulnerable, the densely forested areas of eastern Poland offered shelter for a small number. Robber gangs as well as partisan guerrilla groups of many stripes and persuasions roamed these areas, some of them all too ready to kill Jews themselves. Jewish partisan groups were also based here, sometimes joining forces with others when they were allowed to. Partisan fighting groups did not normally encumber themselves with women, children, and the old, but Jewish groups did. However, Poles would sometimes act as escorts, guiding Jews to their bases. One such escort described their ordeal:

I remember one day I was escorting a group of Jews to the forest and we went through thick trees. We were met at the station by our Jewish guide. There was quite a big group in the forest, and we had to take small paths, and pass through swamps and marshes. It was soaked with water, and I was totally unprepared. I was wearing a dark suit so as not to be noticed—my best suit—and nice soft suede shoes. On the way we sank in the mud in these swamps up to our chests. And when we finally reached the place, there was a doctor there—Ania was her name, I believe—who asked us if we were hungry. Sure we were hungry. And

what did we see? They took water out of this swamp filled
with frogs, butterflies, and worms. They claimed it was fit
for drinking and they could get no other because it was
impossible to go to the village. Then food came, and what
did they do?! They cooked porridge and noodles right in
melted grease [Polish rescuer].

Forest groups, whether bandits or partisans, had to depend
on the local populace for sustenance. A few respondents, themselves members of partisan groups, report receiving great help
from local people. Others, situated in unfriendly environments,
had a much more difficult time. Partisan Polish groups, who considered themselves a legitimate military arm of the resistance, simply took what they needed, threatening and even executing local
collaborators. Jewish partisan groups did not share a similar status, but they did whatever they had to in order to survive.

Some rescuers in our sample were themselves the victims of
forest groups. One told how he was approached by a group who
had heard that he was harboring a Jew. Hoping to extort money
from him, they harassed him and threatened to kill his "guest,"
but he managed to outwit them. Another Pole complained bitterly
that his household was stripped bare of its belongings by a Jewish
partisan group. Learning that he was actually involved in a Jewish
network, they returned some of his possessions—"but only a fraction," he said. Life in the forests was not pleasant, but it offered
some chance for survival.

The demand for shelters was consistently higher than the supply.
Only a few people were willing to provide them; some would consent for a short period only. The strain was too much for some to
bear, personalities might clash, or a shelter might become unsafe.
There were those, too, who provided shelter for only as long as it
took to exhaust their guests' resources. Ultimately, most rescuers
faced the necessity of providing shelter in their own homes. More
than 90 percent of the rescuers in our sample did so.

Single individuals were preferred, children or adults. Sometimes a married couple would be harbored together; on rare occasions, an entire family might be kept. Many homes served as way
stations for transients moving from one shelter to another. The
most fortunate rescuers and rescued were able to stay in the same
dwelling for the duration; other rescuers, forced to move them-

selves for a variety of reasons, sometimes took their Jewish guests with them. One Polish rescuer reported moving five times, along with the Jewish children he was hiding. Concern about suspicious neighbors, changing financial circumstances, fear of impending arrest, and the destruction of his apartment during the Warsaw uprising were among the reasons for his moves. Another Polish family living in a Ukrainian community fled from their home in fear when signs began to appear in the village threatening death to Poles.

At times rescuers were sheltering several groups of people simultaneously—Allied pilots, Freemasons, young men escaping labor conscription, and members of resistance groups as well as people in need of hiding places because they were hiding Jews. In these cases it was desirable that others be kept ignorant of the presence of Jews, sometimes for the protection of all and sometimes because others could not be trusted. An Italian parish priest was able to deal with this problem quite neatly:

> I had many other people hidden—in fact, during this time fifty men from the British Army were there. Everyone knew what was going on in my house, except about the Jews. The people from the village could be trusted not to inform about the Allied soldiers, but they could not be relied on to support a Jew. Whomever I hid during the war, I forbade from moving around during the day. The house was large and had attics and all kinds of places to hide people, so this was possible. It was also possible for me to keep different people from finding out that others were hidden there. At one time there was another priest in the house. If he had had any idea that there were Jews under the same roof, he'd have gone in his pants.

In a few instances, Germans were quartered in the same residence in which Jews were hiding. A Frenchwoman was keeping several Jewish youngsters in her home when she was forced to take in some German officers:

> I was obliged by the Germans to have some German officers in my home, but I wasn't afraid for the girls. The Germans saw the children, but there wasn't any problem because they were in a boarding school in Marnandes. The children left on Monday morning, came back Wednesday

evening, went back to school on Friday morning, and came back on Saturday evening. So the Germans never suspected anything, nor did they ask me any questions concerning the girls. Girls weren't a problem, but the boys—I was frightened for them.

Seven German officers stayed with a Dutch family for several months, and everything remained quite normal:

We celebrated Christmas with the Jewish people and the Germans. We all sat around on little stools or crates. One played the harmonica, and we all sang together—the Jews, me, and the German soldiers.

In this case the Germans suspected nothing and asked no questions. Another ended in tragedy:

The Germans came and took a look at our house. They told us we had to take in a German couple who were living on the coast. We were worried because they would find out we were keeping Jewish people. They took the living room, bedroom, bathroom, and kitchen upstairs. Slowly they found out the truth. One day we had soup on the kitchen stove. The German woman came downstairs and lifted the lid to see what was in the pot. Willy—the Jewish guy—saw that. He said, "It's not ladylike to lift the lid from the pot." I told him, "Be careful what you say; don't make trouble!" I had the feeling something would happen. I told my husband, "Let's go away, let's find a place," but he said "You're crazy!" But I had a feeling. My husband should have listened to me.

This woman, the German lady, went to the police. She told them we had a Jew in hiding. She said, "I would like to have the Jew taken away from there, but don't do anything to the people." She was referring to us. She thought the police were safe. But the guy she spoke to worked for the NSB, the Nazis. She didn't know that.

It was four o'clock on a clear Sunday afternoon. My husband had just come home from taking our little girl on a sled ride. He was home just ten minutes when the Gestapo came—with a dog. The dog ran upstairs, and there was shooting. My little girl was crying because her Daddy was screaming. I took my little girl and ran out the door.

The dog smelled out the hiding place. My husband
wouldn't say anything, so they set the dog on him. It bit off
his hand. They shot my husband and one of the Jews
[Dutch rescuer].

Providing shelter was the first order of business. Finding a
hiding place in which Jews could disappear in the event of emergencies was the second. Sympathetic family members or neighbors
would sometimes accommodate these temporary needs. One
Dutch policeman hurriedly transported his friends' Jewish guests
to a prison cell during police raids—"the safest place to be until
it was over!"

Most rescuers built some form of hiding place within their
own shelters. Devising the form this might take was one problem;
getting the materials and tools to execute plans was another.
Those living on farms with access to open fields had more natural
resources available to them. Barns, attics, chicken coops, coal cellars, and storehouses were common hiding places. In one isolated
farm area, three boats hidden in the tall grass served as a hiding
place. One family placed a large iron covering over a hideout, on
top of which new hay was put; the only access was through the
horses' stall. As they explained, "Most of the Germans were scared
of the horses and didn't like to approach them." Another lived on
a dead-end country lane that ended on a nature reserve with acres
of open fields. A tunnel was constructed from one of the rooms
in the house, which went through a coal bin, under the back part
of the garden all the way to the reserve—once through the tunnel,
anyone escaping could not be seen from the house. In another
case a hole in the ground led to a tunnel to a nearby house; the
tunnel was covered with soil and equipped with water, food, and
electricity. One similar escape route leading to a neighbor's yard
was used with unexpected consequences. Hearing a policeman approach the front door, the Dutch rescuer quickly warned his Jewish guest to "disappear": "But it so happened that the neighbor
was having a yard tea party. She had all the neighbor ladies there,
and all of a sudden, here was a Son of Abraham! He descended
out of heaven right in the middle of the party!"

Rescuers with more limited space constructed hiding places
in closets, behind fireplaces and bookcases, and in attics and base-
ments. One built double ceilings throughout the entire house.
Those in apartments rented from others had to deal with land-

lords as well as space constraints. A Polish woman found an apartment for herself and seven Jews in the evacuated Jewish section of town; it had no water, no toilet, and no electricity, but it did have two rooms separated from each other in a two-story building. Together they made a bunker under her bed, a hole dug out piece by piece and the soil disposed of in another hole dug expressly for that purpose so as not to arouse the janitor's suspicions. "It was just like a grave," she said.

Assessing a place for its hiding potential became so habitual that some rescuers continued to do so long after the actual need had vanished. "It's ingrained in me," said one. "Even today I still instinctively examine each house with that in mind."

Jewish guests had to be fed. Without ration cards, food could not be bought, and cards were given only to those having proper identification—Jews, of course, had none.

Farming families were generally able to provide themselves and their guests with basic necessities, despite the quotas of produce and meat requisitioned by the German occupiers. Urban dwellers had greater difficulties. Legal rations were rarely sufficient; they amounted to little more than 1,200 calories a day for Poles. The last year in Holland was grueling. Scarce resources reached famine proportions as railroad workers went on strike to sabotage German transports. Rescuers reported making bread from tulip bulbs and pancakes from the pulp of sugar beets. Many Dutch say they weighed less than 100 pounds at the end of the war. Keeping themselves alive was hard enough; providing for their guests presented formidable challenges.

Forgers and thieves were essential to the entire operation. Several rescuers reported making or stealing the coveted ration coupons that were issued weekly or monthly. Some stole them from purses and coats left on benches or coat racks. More adventurous souls, primarily men, stole food from warehouses. A Dutch civil servant recalled standing next to the mayor while he threatened to punish those who stole food provisions the night before. "He didn't know I was one of them," he said with pride.

Rescuers involved in organized network activities would frequently distribute ration cards and money among their charges. They would make their rounds on a weekly basis, sometimes simply leaving the valued packets in mailboxes or on the front steps. They had to be careful, however, not to carry written lists. Young people, particularly young women, often performed this service. A most unusual network was organized by "Grandpa Bakker" and his wife "Aunt Corr." They created a "secret city," which sheltered more than eighty Jews, in a wooded Dutch area. A respondent in our sample was involved in this chain—his particular job was to procure food from the local farmers and black market sources. "Each day I picked up about sixty to seventy loaves of bread, twenty gallons of milk, potatoes, coal, and so on. The farmers were great," he said.

Coupons and money had to be exchanged for food. Shopping, however, was not easy when one had to provide for secret guests. Local tradespeople suspected those who presented more than their legal quota of stamps or bought more than usual amounts. Wary women thus shopped in several different places. Queuing up at three bakers, three vegetable stores, and so on consumed time and sapped energies. Women also became very skilled at creating objects for barter. One respondent made socks from the hairs of her black poodle. After painstakingly reknitting a crocheted bedspread into socks, another respondent traded them to a woman who remade them into a bedspread.

Guests who could earn some money eased the lives of their hosts. Jews of "good appearance" could sometimes manage to find work; their shelterers would sometimes find employment for them. Others sought home employment sewing or knitting, painting buttons, or making cigarettes. Most unusual was the case of a Dutchman who quit his job and began a small business with a Jewish friend making fur caps—they were able to live quite comfortably.

Some Jews had their own resources—money or personal items of value—but rescuers were scrupulous in taking no more than was necessary for sustenance even when their guests offered more. Unable to distribute the large sum of money entrusted to him for rescue purposes, an Italian priest agonized over how he might properly use it:

On September 8, 1943, Italy signed the armistice with the Allies. Jews, who had been hiding out wherever they could outside Italy, came en masse across the border, thinking they were going to meet the Allied troops. Instead the Germans occupied the north, and they were in a worse position than they had been before. Some of these Jewish

people asked help from Cardinal Della Costa (Archbishop
Elia Della Costa of Florence), but due to the position of the
palace in the center of the city, he decided to ask someone
unknown to handle the effort. He asked me.

We formed a committee to settle the refugees coming
from the north in the best possible way. That meant asking
convents to take them in, finding space in garages, in
private homes, and so on. A great deal of money was
needed. The money came from Raffaele Cantoni, an
exceptionally intelligent, generous, courageous man. I don't
know where he got it.

First, he gave me 200,000 lire, then 20,000, and then
500,000 lire—720,000 lire in all, a tremendous sum. He
gave this to me, and I paid the expenses. We were
betrayed, and after a summary interrogation, we were
transferred to prison and each member of the committee
was kept in solitary confinement. I expected to be sent to
death, but through the help of a friend, I was released.

When I got out, I found that all the help had been
stopped and that the others on the committee had all been
deported to Germany. I was now alone, and I still had
400,000 lire. I was told that there were some spies
circulating among the Jews and that my phone was bugged.
I came up with an idea. I let it be known to a few Jews I
knew were unquestionably reliable that every morning I
would be waiting on the Ponte Vecchio, and every
afternoon I'd be in the chapel of Holy Mary in the
cathedral. They were to spread the word that anyone who
needed my help should look for me there. In that way,
when they came, I would ask: "How many of you are there?
How much do you need?" And, in this way, giving this one
2,000, this one 5,000, I distributed all of the 400,000 I had
been asked to.

Money was valuable in procuring services. Getting scarce
goods, however, depended on the black market. "I was a first-class
black marketeer," said one German woman. "I sold diamonds. The
whole German nation dealt in the black market—if they hadn't
done it, they would have starved to death." At one extreme was the
occasional black marketeer, like the Polish peasant woman who
managed to maintain both herself and the Jewish infant she was

keeping through illicit sales of pieces of fruit to ghetto inmates. (Her income ended when the ghetto was liquidated.) At the other was the professional black marketeer who made an occupation of buying and selling illegal goods:

I sold everying I had on the black market and got some sugar from my brother. I started to make candy. Besides Geniek I had two Catholic children with me whose father had died. They helped me make the candy, and my wife sold it. Then Olesz [another Jewish boy] came, a very skinny boy, six years old, Geniek's brother. Olesz got scarlet fever and he died. The doctor came and said: "Mister X., don't make candy anymore because all of Warsaw will get scarlet fever," so I stopped, but then I had no more money, so I sold my apartment with all the furniture. I used most of the money to pay the hospital bill for Geniek who got sick. Then I had nothing left. So I went to my friend who made fur coats to sell on the black market and asked him to let me sell one coat for him. He wanted three hundred zloty for it; I sold it for three hundred fifty. I went back and sold more coats for him and made about one thousand zloty. Then I noticed a woman selling blankets. I said to her, "I see you every day with blankets. Maybe you have more—I could help you sell them." She took me to her house. The basement was filled with blankets, all from the German Army. She had three types of blankets—one was the officer's type, all white wool; the others were cheaper. I made a deal, and in a few days I sold all the blankets to people who made slippers. I began to make a lot of money, too much money, and it became dangerous. I had to vacate my apartment [Polish rescuer].

Although rescue activities encompassed a broad spectrum of behaviors—each with its own attendant set of risks and each requiring its own commitment of time and resources—they are only part of the story. For, as the rescuers themselves make clear, whatever the nature and degree of their involvement, it had far-reaching effects on their lives and relationships: Although they often acted in secret, they did not act in a social vacuum.

CHAPTER 4

The Social Context of Rescue: Trust and Deception

Rescuers lived in a world apart from others, but they were simultaneously embedded in relationships with others. Their activities were secret, but they were not socially isolated. They had families, friends, neighbors, and occupational colleagues. What could they tell their families? Their neighbors? Could they continue routine intimacies with friends? The traditional social conventions did not apply to the new realities.

Rescuers also had to deal with the occupiers, and the enemy wore more than one face. Enemies included Nazis, ordinary German soldiers, indigenous collaborators, and local police. Some were brutal ideologues, many were simply opportunistic, others were equivocal, and a few were even sympathetic. Rescuers were constantly faced with the challenge of discerning these differences.

Several rescuers joined newly formed networks dedicated either to sabotaging the enemy or rescuing Jews, sometimes both. But these networks were made up of individuals whose courage, reliability, and psychological endurance were not always known. How much could be shared? How much needed to be withheld? And how could the bonds of trust essential for their covert activities be strengthened in the face of necessary prudence?

Finally, there were the rescued themselves—a diverse group including children and adults, people of wisdom, character, adaptability, and helpfulness but also the imprudent, weak, stubborn, and helpless. Rescuers had to determine their responsibilities to these assorted individuals and balance them against their responsibilities to themselves and their families. What roles were they to assume? Parent? Friend? Colleague? Savior?

As rescuers interacted with all these groups, they had to consider three primary questions: How much deception was necessary? How much could they trust others? What bearing did their personal feelings of affection or dislike have on their sense of responsibility? They resolved these questions gradually, often unconsciously, in the context of the routine decisions of everyday life.

Many rescuers said they admired and respected the Jews they helped; several even loved them. But they also admit to dislike, anger, and exasperation. Feelings of affection facilitated rescue but did not necessarily determine it. More than half had no prewar acquaintance with any of the Jews they helped. Almost 90 percent helped at least one Jewish stranger.

In relationships with both friends and strangers, rescuers had to define the parameters of their responsibilities. Some indicated no wavering in their course. Others struggled as they tried to balance responsibilities to themselves and their families particularly when they were not always sure that the particular victims they helped were worth the risks.

The relationship between rescuers and victims was colored by how well the latter could adjust to the requirements of their new situations. These varied depending on the circumstances under which the helping act occurred as well as the life-styles of helpers.

Heads of households who kept Jews in their own homes were most content when they were quiet, unobtrusive, helpful, and accommodated generally to the family's life-style. One such ideal couple is described by their rescuer as "always walking in slippers—crocheted slippers—staying in their room all day and coming down only after curfew at eight P.M." Another rescuer who similarly kept a Jewish couple in hiding for more than two years described a variation of this routine:

> We brought meals up, and once in a while I brought my
> baby up. They would play with my baby. They did some
> little chores with me, peeling potatoes and folding laundry.
> She did some crocheting and he would read. He would also
> listen to the news on our hidden radio. During the evening
> when it was dark they would come downstairs with us and
> visit. We made sure all the doors were locked. Before going

to bed, they would go on the balcony to get some fresh air—they would always get a little fresh air before they would go to sleep [Dutch rescuer].

Rescuers in religious households appreciated those who participated in family devotions and Bible readings. Several also expressed admiration for those who maintained their own Jewish traditions, fasting on holy days or wearing the traditional yarmulke. Several reported with pleasure on the animated discussions they had regarding theology and religious beliefs. Some rescuers even attempted to provide their guests with kosher food as long as it was possible.

Religious rescuers were also more likely to insist on proper sexual conduct. Several Dutch Reformed rescuers, for example, would keep either males or females but not both; others would go to great lengths to prepare separate quarters for men and women. This standard of conduct seemed so natural to some rescuers that one Dutchwoman was shocked to learn several years later how often such standards were violated. The young Jewish woman her family had kept told her: "Your father never touched me." "Imagine," the Dutchwoman said. "My father! What an idea!"

Rescuers varied in the range of sexual behaviors they approved or at least tolerated within their households. Opportunities for extramarital sexual relations could pose problems for either the rescued or rescuer. One such problem arose between a heterosexual woman and a homosexual male:

There was a Dutch ballet student who was Jewish, and we hid him with an artist in Amsterdam. The artist, a woman, was heterosexual; the ballet student was a homosexual. They slept in the same bed because if you were hiding somebody, you slept together, so if the Germans appeared, there would be no extra bed. Well, the artist made a lot of sexual advances, and the student came back and said that the situation had to change—he would rather be deported! So we dyed his hair, and we got him in Aryan identity card. From then on he helped us in our work [Dutch rescuer].

Another rescuer came home one night after a round of underground activities to discover her husband in bed with one of the young women she was hiding. Rather than jeopardize her relationship with her husband or evict the young woman, she pretended

not to notice anything. "You are the only one who knows this secret," she told the interviewer. Forty years later, it was still troubling her.

Rescuers hiding people in their own homes universally disliked imprudence, which included any behavior that called attention to the self. Assertiveness, insistence on having some fresh air,
or standing next to the window were all threatening behaviors.
Not all Jews were equally adept at adjusting to the new realities.
Some underestimated the dangers; others did not have the skills
or the temperament to deal with confinement. In such cases some
rescuers would refuse to keep them. One occurrence is described
by a Dutchwoman keeping a Jewish man for whom she found
another place:

> He looked enormously Jewish—a typical, beautiful, gray-
> haired, dignified Jewish person. One day, his wife came to
> us and said, "He absolutely needs an airing. He must get
> out once in a while." So we suggested that he go to the den
> occasionally—we had a beautiful den. But this man was
> absolutely inept at being a hidden person. So this dignified
> gray old man would go out on a brilliant sunny day and
> take an umbrella. He would put up the umbrella so as to
> hide his face, but it was beautiful weather! As a result,
> everybody who passed him took a good look. He brought
> more attention to himself then if he had just walked out.
> We carefully told him that this was not a very smart idea
> and that he had better stay in the garden. We had a garden
> surrounding our house. We told him to walk around the
> house but to be careful when he walked in the front
> because people would see him. So he would walk out of the
> back door very slowly, go to the side of the house slowly,
> and then when he came to the front of the house, he ran.
> Of course, people would stop and wonder what was going
> on.

Rescuers frequently recounted episodes reflecting the incompetence of the rescued. City dwellers would be unable to help with
farm chores; affluent Jews didn't know how to do things with their
hands; skilled tailors had little to offer households in which there
was nothing to sew.

Women more than men were encumbered by keeping additional people in the home. It was they who ultimately bore the

responsibilities of shopping, preparing food, and tending to the needs of their increased households. Carrying out these chores under conditions of wartime scarcity was difficult enough; assuming the extra burdens of additional people sometimes became unbearable. They particularly resented those who were incompetent in performing domestic chores or too ill to do so. "I had to do everything," said one Polish woman. "I had to clean the house, buy the food and prepare it, and take care of her besides."

Dislike for those who were perceived as arrogant, "uppity," or demanding was strong. Assuming the role of appreciative helpee was simply too difficult for some high-status rescued, more accustomed to dispensing favors than receiving them. Men were more often seen this way than women. As one rescuer described the Jewish judge she was keeping: "He just didn't like being told what to do by an ordinary gentile."

In the eyes of several rescuers, the rescued frequently became "childlike" dependents, needing or wanting to be told what to do and how to do it, where to go, and what to say. Rescuers' feelings vacillated between pity, annoyance, resentment, and responsibility. They expressed anger about those who would not listen, who failed to take advice, or who insisted on doing things their own way. Many rescuers—even as they attempt to understand the reasons why—recount stories of Jews who met tragic ends through their failure to heed what they were told:

> She insisted on going back to the ghetto. I warned her not
> to go, but she wanted to see her parents once more. I
> pleaded with her, but she wouldn't listen. That was the last
> time I saw her [Polish rescuer].

While they may acknowledge that they themselves did not foresee in the beginning just what the end would be for Jews, rescuers nonetheless frequently ask: "Why couldn't they see the truth? Why didn't they listen when they had the chance? Jews are supposed to be smart." They also mention occasions when Jews refused to take advantage of offers of help because they did not want to put others at risk.

Like parents, they alternated between chastising, inflicting guilt, bolstering fallen spirits, and imposing responsibilities and taking them. Faced with a melancholy Jewish woman who had just discovered herself to be pregnant, her determined religious rescuer not only insisted that she have the baby but also delivered and provided for it. She also interpreted the meaning of the event to the dispirited woman:

> Hitler is busy destroying the Jewish people but he will never succeed. Your husband planted the seed but the life is from God Almighty. It is a new generation for Him. I shall call you "Blessed Mother" [Dutch rescuer].

Several reported keeping those who yielded to despair from committing suicide or giving themselves up. One rescuer bolted all the doors and ran to the doctor for a tranquilizer when the Jewish woman she was keeping threatened to simply walk away and take the cyanide pill she had managed to acquire. Warned that the house would be searched, a young Jewish man said he would not allow his rescuer to be placed in this danger and prepared to leave. His rescuer put the issue to him clearly and authoritatively:

> I was so angry with him. Can you understand that? I said, "You have been here for over two years. Now you want to give up? Are you crazy? Take off your coat and sit down. Listen to me and listen carefully. On a ship there is one captain. I am the captain, and you have to listen to me. I will find something. I always find something. I have not gone to all this trouble in order to fail. There is only one boss here and I am it. I am in charge of what you can or cannot do" [Dutch rescuer].

The Jew's departure would certainly have relieved the rescuer's burden. If it was voluntary, there might be little reason to feel guilt. But several rescuers would not allow this to happen. To maintain the life of someone targeted for death was itself a consummate statement of autonomy and resistance. Having risked so much, they were not about to acknowledge defeat. The life of the victim no longer belonged only to the victim—it was jointly owned, and death was therefore not a choice he or she could make alone.

Domestic adaptability and quiet appreciative helpfulness were virtues prized by rescuers when the rescued were incorporated into relatively stable households. In more fluid situations, when helping activities occurred outside the family, other virtues were more important and relationships differed.

Christians who worked in conjunction with Jews in rescue efforts valued them for their leadership, resourcefulness, courage, and the ability to withstand torture without revealing secrets. Those who cooperated with Jewish partisan units were impressed by their valor and fighting abilities. The important thing, as one Polish respondent put it, was "to give the Germans 'what for,'" and those who were able to do it were prized. Such relationships tended to be more egalitarian that those in which Jews were sheltered in others' households; in many of these groups Jews assumed leadership roles.

Particularly in Eastern Europe, some rescuers assumed the role of "frontline visible defense" (as one rescuer put it) for groups of isolated Jews to whom they became attached. They would do negotiations with the outside world, find bunkers, rent apartments, buy food, bring information, and the like. These rescuers were often single women, themselves dislocated and uprooted from their families. The groups operated like collectives, pooling resources and deciding jointly how best to maintain themselves.

Several rescuers acknowledged that they became dependent on the Jews they helped. Men with carpentry and other "masculine" skills were particularly appreciated by women who were sole heads of households. Even young people sometimes provided valued skills. One rescuer spoke of learning to depend on the adolescent boy in his household who assumed responsibility for record-keeping chores. Frequently guests provided intellectual stimulation or filled emotional needs not only for the adults but also for their children. In several cases the departure of such people after the war left a significant vacuum.

Relationships between rescuer and rescued were sometimes marked by extraordinary tenderness and love. Some of these attachments predated the rescue; others followed from it. They were not limited to husbands, wives, and sweethearts but included friends, employers, and the old and the very young as well. What distinguishes these relationships is their intensity and the lengths to which rescuers went to satisfy the needs of the rescued.

One German couple, Mr. and Mrs. T., came to love the elderly man, Mr. S., they were hiding "like our own father," and they tried to help him by keeping life as normal as possible for him. These efforts, however, culminated at least once in an event that placed all of them in extreme danger. In the bizarre circumstances that characterized Berlin in the 1940s, Mr. S. was still able to go out on occasion to meet some friends at a café, provided, of course, that he acted with extreme care. During one of those periods when life appeared to be uneventful, Mrs. T. decided to provide him with a special treat—an expedition to the theater. But on the very day of the scheduled event:

> The SS had come looking for him that afternoon.
> Fortunately, he was out at the time, and we were able to tell them that no one was hiding there. When he came back, I didn't want to worry him. So rather than cancel our theater plans, we went ahead as scheduled, and I didn't tell him the SS had been there. That evening, my husband, my daughter, Mr. S., and I went to the theater—Schlusnuss was singing—it was a concert at the Potsdamerplatz. It was sold out. Because there was no room, they set up chairs on the stage, and it was too late to back out. So here was S., with his snow white hair, attractive as the dickens, you know. And there were actors there who still remembered him and they said: "He's just too impertinent—we won't acknowledge him anymore . . . " [German rescuer].

Fortunately, they all survived the occasion, and Mr. S. contin-ued to live with them for two years after the war.

Rescuers who were former employees of the rescued often spoke of them with special regard. They noted their kindnesses, their fairness and their generosity. One Polish woman regarded her former employer with near reverence:

> I came to know him before the war as an excellent man, a man who was very sensitive to the miseries of others. Just as an example—one of his friends was failing in business and lost lots of money. He was badly in debt and attempted suicide. M. F. paid all his debts to help him, to help him start something new. A second case: When he was with his daughter in Krynica, there was a hotel boy, an orphan who played with his daughter. He took an interest in the child. He learned that there was only a granny left, that she lived far away, and that the child had to earn his own living. He contacted the family, took the boy to Warsaw, saw to his schooling, and when he finished, employed him in his own firm. The child had tuberculosis. A third case: He suggested that, together with my daughter, we should spend the holidays on his estate near Radom. I had relatives in the

country and had my own resources. But an acquaintance of mine, from a very poor family, had no means whatsoever; she was a poor ailing girl. I asked him whether it would be possible to take her instead of me, to help her. Willingly! And when the day came, there was a chauffeured car to drive her to the place, and for a whole month she stayed there as one of the family. I had never heard of somebody like this—I knew no one who would be that concerned about other people's problems.

Very close relationships between the families of rescued and rescuer sometimes predated the war and helped explain the rescue act. An Italian man described the Jewish family he and his wife were keeping:

They have always been our friends. They are very good people, darling people. My father did his military service together with Lucia's father when they were twenty years old. When they married, their wives became friends, and when there were children, they became friends and have remained this way. I remember being bound to them from my earliest childhood. We have the same God, we just pray in different ways. We love each other deeply.

In other cases friendships emerged as a consequence of the rescue act. Rescuers tell of how much they learned from their guests or how much they came to admire them:

That was the first time I got a little interested in the Jewish religion; I know more about it now. At that time she was saying *kaddish* [the prayer for the dead], and I didn't even know what it was. She had two children and had lost both of them. She was warmhearted, kindhearted, a very loving person, and strong too. What did I know about Yom Kippur? I even got candles for her, which wasn't very easy. I just respected it [Dutch rescuer].

She had black hair, raven black. Blue eyes. Really a "foxy gal," as they say now. I introduced her to my mother, and my mother said, "Call me Mommy and I'll call you Nina. You will be my children, son and daughter." And Nina and I were friends from the first moment, sort of a mutual confidence. Nina behaved marvelously. She was some girl.

Not easily worried, not losing her nerve. She used to say to me, "You know, Abyszek, if something happens, you will be killed with me." I said to her, "We don't think about it." As concerns her being a woman, there was nothing between us. We were brother and sister. Just as she became a daughter to my mother, she became a sister to me [Polish rescuer].

Some rescuers were already married to Jews before the war; others married during the war or after it. Maintaining such relationships required particular dedication. The rescuers rarely contented themselves with saving the lives of their spouses but exerted efforts on behalf of their families as well. Sometimes this resulted in a sense of obligation to the Jewish community as a whole.

Contracting marriages with Jews posed unique problems. The circumstances and commitment that generally accompanied this effort is suggested in this account by a young Czech military officer:

I met Irina for the first time in a restaurant, on the dance floor. I walked her home after that and remained in contact with her. It was love at first sight. Her parents did not want me even to visit because they were afraid that my contact with them would harm the entire family. By May 1942 they were feeling very threatened, but they had already learned to trust me because I had done many things for them. In 1942, Irina was supposed to be deported. I hid her in my apartment for a while and then in a neighbor's apartment. Irina's father and mother were both arrested. My sister helped to get them out—she got them false identification cards.

But it was not enough to hide her. I had to do something more radical, so I tried to get her out of the country. We contacted a Bulgarian student who helped us get her out of Slovakia. We paid him for his service. She married him so as to get permission from the Bulgarian embassy to travel to Sofia with him. There was a danger that he would fall in love with Irina, but I trusted her and I knew she would continue to love me. But the village in which she and her new husband lived would not accept the civil marriage, so she had to go through a Greek Orthodox marriage. But after this the young man claimed his nuptial rights, so she left the village and went to Sofia. She returned to Slovakia in 1943, and from then on I had to hide her constantly. In order to protect her more effectively, it was best she marry me. So we arranged another baptism—a Roman Catholic baptism—and then I went to the president to try to get an exemption that would permit me to marry her. The baptism did not help—we were just not allowed to marry Jewish people. But I got permission from the bishop; he married us secretly in March 1944.

But even though she now had an identification card as my wife, she was not safe. She could not use the card; it could not protect her. I did not want to leave her alone in the apartment while I was working, so I invited my younger sister to come to Bratyslawa and live with us. My younger sister would answer the door and say Irina was my sister. Officially she was my sister and not my wife.

In some cases, a general feeling of identification with the Jewish community antedated the marriage. One Polish professor, a descendant of nobility, had married a Jewish woman several years before the war. He and his parents had had many Jewish friends, and while still in high school, he found the political orientations of his Zionist friends more compatible with his own than those of the socialists, which he viewed as overly tinged with nationalistic tendencies. He had participated with Jews in their physical defense in a 1905 pogrom in Zytomierz and had already suffered mockery for this activity. At the beginning of the war, he and his wife were living in a luxurious apartment house in Warsaw; all the other apartments were occupied by Jews. Immediately after Poland's capitulation, he volunteered to chair a self-help committee directed primarily to help Jews, for, as he explained, "I felt that they would need the most care." Warned by the Gestapo to divorce his wife in 1941, he refused. That same year, his wife went into the ghetto voluntarily "in order to be with her people," and he chose to go with her. Because of his Aryan status, he was able to provide varied forms of help to Jews.

Sometimes it was the search for a family that prompted the relationship. A young Polish woman who found herself isolated from her warm and protective parents at the outbreak of the war found a substitute family in the home of her Jewish mathematics tutor. She became immediately attached to his beautiful four-year-old sister, whom she describes as being "very beautiful, with green eyes and long hair" and having "very soft skin." Her activities on behalf of the family increased her sense of isolation from others. She wound up marrying her Jewish tutor, whom she divorced in 1953 to marry another Jewish man.

Romantic liaisons were not uncommon consequences of the rescue act itself. A shared sense of danger and isolation from others, as well as physical proximity, often prompted romantic relationships that could not survive under more normal conditions. The suggestion that they helped because of their love for a particular individual, however, affronts some rescuers. A Polish woman who subsequently married one of the Jewish men she hid expressed great bitterness at those who suggested that she undertook her activities out of erotic love, an interpretation that she felt demeaned her.

Particular tenderness is expressed toward children; 70 percent of rescuers were involved with at least one Jewish child twelve years of age or younger. These relationships were frequently among the hardest to relinquish. Rescuers were impressed by the children's courage and intellect and touched by their fear and vulnerability: "He was so isolated from everything, all the fear in his heart and yet so grown-up. My uncle and I had to go way up north on our bikes to get food, and he went right along with us. He was only a child, but he must have had that fear all the time [Dutch rescuer]."

A Dutch farmer described how he carried a young girl on his back over muddy fields about fifteen times to get her away from the house when *razzias* (roundups) were impending and how he comforted her in his arms when she awoke screaming in the night. "I really loved that girl," he said.

Some of the closest attachments formed between single women and children. Their intensity is suggested by the tale of a Polish woman, then approximately twenty years of age.

> I was in Borislaw on August 15, 1942. I went there to buy myself some clothing. I had just come back from the cloister and had no suitable clothing. I went to a special house where I could exchange some things for clothes.
>
> A mother came into the room with a beautiful baby in her arms. He was a lovely boy, a beautiful boy. She started

begging me to take the baby because they were expecting a pogrom that evening. They were the last Jewish people in the town. They needed some engineers and technicians and had permitted some Jews and their families who performed this function to stay alive.

On seeing the baby I immediately wanted to help. I took the baby. The mother didn't give me any clothes for him because she didn't have any. She was very poor. I took a small suitcase and went to my parents' house. There I introduced the baby as an orphan. The baby was absolutely beautiful. He spoke only a few words. Soon after, people would ask him, "Who is your mother?" and although I never told him to do it, he would point at me. He was a very beautiful and clever child.

The neighbors became curious about the situation, and some said it was my own child—that I had been expelled from the cloister because he was illegitimate. But others said, "He must be a Jewish child, because some people do this to help Jews."

I became very frightened and decided to leave. I went to Warsaw where my brother and sister lived. They were working with the underground but they were not very pleased to see me. I had no money and sold the little chain the mother had given me and rented an apartment. Sometimes I would manage to earn some money, but I was always in a hurry to get back to the baby. Sometimes the police confiscated everything, so I came home with nothing.

One time I was arrested on the train. The policeman took my baby and went to examine it. He discovered it was circumcised and said to me, "You are a Jew." I said, "No, I am not a Jew, but this is my baby." They took us to jail. I was able to run away when the policeman was distracted by ten pounds of butter. . . .

I had to move many times. The baby was so emaciated and sickly. He did not have a good diet. When the war ended, I contacted the Red Cross and found out that the mother was alive and lived in Borislaw. In 1945 the mother came. We made contact. We met. I gave her back the child. It is very difficult for me to tell you how I felt then.

Despite their love, rescuers of children reported that they felt a responsibility to return them to their biological parents, even when the children themselves did not want to leave. One Dutch couple related how painful it was when the surviving mother who had experienced the horrors of multiple losses returned to reclaim her children:

> When their mother came back to get them after the war, they didn't want to go. "We have a new mother and father," they said. It was awful. The mother really cried. She said, "I don't have to ask you how you handled my children." Their mother developed cancer and died in 1948. We knew it and she knew. My wife and I wanted to adopt the children. But it was her last wish that the children go to Israel and get a Jewish education. I knew I couldn't give them one. She hoped we weren't insulted. We understood pretty well.

Another rescuer who returned a child to its surviving mother at the war's end told us that it had not occurred to her that the new separation would have its own particular consequences for the child. Only many years later did she learn from the child, then a young woman, that "my leaving was a disaster for her. It was only when she was in analysis that she recognized that the depression she was experiencing was caused by my abandonment of her."

Helping Jews was rarely a one-man or -woman activity. Although rescuers were heavily dependent on others for support, less than half of them (44 percent) belonged to organized resistance groups. About 5 percent belonged to groups whose exclusive concerns were Jews (for example, Zegota and the Jewish Military Union). Approximately 20 percent belonged to groups that included or accommodated helping Jews along with other objectives, such as harboring fugitives, helping homeless children, and intelligence and sabotage. Rescuers who belonged to such groups turned to them frequently for services.

Less dependable were those groups whose primary objective was direct resistance to the enemy. Approximately 20 percent of rescuers belonged to such groups. In some cases they received no help from them; in others, they were occasionally able to create opportunities to use the group's resources to help Jews. One man, in charge of civil resistance in Poland, voluntarily chose to issue a directive through the underground press threatening with death Poles who collaborated with Germans in persecuting Jews. He also informed London on the occasion of the Warsaw ghetto uprising and encouraged the BBC to send the Jewish fighters a message of support, which they did.

This type of support helped create a moral climate in which rescue was encouraged, which sometimes made the difference in shaping the responses of local resistance groups. A Pole who, along with his warrant officers from the Szare Szeregi (Gray Ranks),* reported attacking an SS guardhouse during the Warsaw ghetto uprising did so in response to overt encouragement:

> At the moment when the uprising in the ghetto broke out, the commander of the Home Army, General Bor-Komorowski, issued not an order—but more of a wish—to encourage AK units, to give them moral support, since there was no opportunity to do more. We couldn't ask Home Army units to enter the ghetto with their full military capacity because it would have been useless. The Germans would have destroyed us both. We could only indicate by some actions that we were with them. During the briefing in our Zoliborz division, I volunteered for that action.

In some cases, a tacit understanding, rather than anything explicit, created a climate conducive to rescue. In such circumstances, it was likely to emerge among small groups who shared similar political persuasions. Thus, for a Polish resistance fighter whose local military group included several socialists, helping Jews was a private goal which he and his associates shared, although they received neither directives nor financial support from their group for doing so:

> As early as 1940, I took part in Polish Socialist Party activities, which grew out of the work Cracow socialist circles were involved in. I belonged to the Polish Socialist Party. Later, friends talked me into joining the AK. During the occupation, all antifascist underground organizations

---

*A unit within the AK.

were concerned with helping Jews, both the Army and civilian organizations. I know of many hideouts in and out of Cracow where Jews stayed. My apartment was used to hide both Jews and Poles. Right here in this flat—this room was AK headquarters; the other room belonged to the Polish Socialist Party.

> Interviewer: Do I understand you correctly? Are you telling me that your involvement with helping Jews started within the Polish Socialist Party framework?
> Respondent: Yes.
> Interviewer: Were you sent on this mission by your superiors?
> Respondent: It was not an ordered mission. My family had become involved in this activity. Local party members sent Jews here. Everybody had some contact with Jews. We provided money, new identity cards. There was no financial support from the organization. We paid with our own money [Polish rescuer].

In several cases, rescuers clearly perceived helping Jews as unrelated to the activities or goals of their military groups:

> I helped the resistance as much as I helped the Jews. I always tried to explain to resisters how hard the war was for the Jews. Many of them didn't (and still don't) know what happened to the Jewish people during the war [French rescuer].

> During the occupation, I was with the AK. I cannot say that it was my function to rescue others. A Jewish friend of mine came to my home and asked me for help, and that had nothing to do with my function with the AK. Within the organization, I had something completely different to do. I attended secret medical training [Polish rescuer].

Dual activities—participation in military groups and rescue—sometimes resulted in conflicting loyalties, however. A few rescuers report keeping Jews in quarters designed for participants in resistance activities despite instructions to the contrary. One rescuer risked censure by his group when he used its money to ransom a Jewish man's life:

In late 1943 or early 1944, a substantial sum was entrusted
to me for safekeeping by my underground group. At that
juncture, a young Jewish man, a brother of a member of
the underground, was rounded up along with others on the
street and incarcerated by the German police in the ghetto
camp. His brother, who happened to know me, and his
friends approached me, imploring me to help free the
prisoner and save his life by paying a ransom to the
captors through a trustworthy mediator. I faced an
enormous dilemma. Should I give 50,000 zloty—then a very
large and unusual amount—for the release of the
unfortunate man from dangerous captivity, or should I
deny their request in accordance with my instructions,
which prohibited spending any of the money without
explicit permission from those in authority? Since the
transport that was to carry the prisoner was scheduled to
leave the city the next day—probably for Treblinka or
Auschwitz or some other death camp—and since it would
take at least two days to contact the person who had the
authority to give permission as he was then out of town, I
had to make up my mind quickly. After thinking briefly but
hard, I chose to violate the strict rules rather than lose the
chance to save a life. Within twenty-four hours the poor
chap was freed. To my pleasant surprise and satisfaction, I
received only a pro forma reprimand, but no disciplinary
action was taken against me [Polish rescuer].

Although formally organized networks that either focused on
Jewish rescue or accommodated it provided invaluable help to rescuers, it was at best only a fraction of the support usually needed.
The majority of rescuers (56 percent) did not belong to formal
networks, although some received sporadic help from such
groups. Others worked entirely outside them. Regardless of
whether they were or were not members of formal networks, almost all rescuers depended on informal networks to sustain them
materially and emotionally.

Informal networks were made up first of household members,
usually family members. Sometimes the network was confined to
the nuclear family:

An acquaintance of mine brought Mr. W. and Mrs. S. to us.
We received them most warmly. I asked my daughter to tell
nobody that they were staying with us because the Germans

would have killed us. My daughter was then ten years old. I
was working—with my hands. I went out as a cleaning
woman and I did laundry at night. That's how I earned my
living. My husband had tuberculosis; he worked from time
to time. My daughter helped me both in my work and in
taking care of these people. The two of us took care and
my husband helped us—like soldiers keeping watch. My
husband arranged a hideout in the coal cellar and one in
the closet [Polish rescuer].

Sometimes it extended to parents, aunts, in-laws, and cousins,
friends, and acquaintances:

I met Z. S. at the Association of Independent Socialist
Youth. His wife was Jewish. He lived in Grochow, in
Zamojski Street, and I visited them once. Their house was
used to lodge Jews. It was never empty—always Jews in
hiding. And I met B. J. there and knew he was going to ask
me to help him to take his family out of the ghetto. I found
an advertisement for lodging and rented it for him and his
family—a small house in Wieliszew. His wife went there
with her two children. But after a few months, rumors
started that they were Jews, and they had to leave. So I took
the younger child to live with me, and I found lodging for
the older one with one of my acquaintances. B. J. went to
my cousin in Ozarow and stayed there until the war was
over. My cousin from Ozarow had two sisters, both of them
nuns. So P., who was Mrs. J.'s niece, went to the Baudouin
Shelter, where the nuns were. My parents and my sister
came to accept this—my sister would go to get identity
cards (*Kennkarten*) for me [Polish rescuer].

Sometimes it was a school network:

I was part of "L'École Champagnat," which was opened in
1928 in Budapest. It was considered a foreign
establishment. The Catholic authorities did not recognize it
as a religious institution, and the Hungarian government
considered it a private institution. The school accepted
students from any religion. We managed to get a few
Jewish children out of the Hungarian ghetto. Eight brothers
worked together. The school was placed under the
protection of the Swedish Red Cross. We saved 120 Jews, 70

of them children. The seven other brothers and I were arrested in December 1944 and sentenced to death, but we were liberated within fifty-four days when the Russians arrived [French rescuer in Hungary].

Sometimes it was an intricate network of formal and informal contacts:

I was cooperating with Jewish committees in Marseilles, Nice, Cannes, and Lyons. In 1943 I became president of the Protection Committee for Jews. I worked with my secretary, M. André Joseph Bass, a French Jew—intelligent and courageous—who is still a very good friend. We met people from the synagogue of Nice or from the Organisation UGIF, which was the General Union of French Jews. There was also an Italian Jew in Nice, M. Angelo Donati, who was the director of the Franco Italian Credit Bank. He was devoted to the Jewish cause and also one of my closest friends—until this very day. Our committee met in different places but it was risky. Gradually our committee started to have meetings in our monastery [in Rome]. My religious superiors supported my activities. One day I was told that somebody had complained about my activities in the monastery and that my superior had answered, "Don't worry. If somebody gets arrested with M. B., it won't be you but me."

We constantly received threatening letters. Once a letter arrived asking for 20,000 lire or we would be denounced. Our people were helping Allied escaped prisoners. We were constantly under pressure, and almost every day something happened that we had to face. But we had help from thousands and thousands of people—resistance groups, political parties, religious people, priests, and so on. The Rome police knew what we were doing but didn't bother us. They even sent us some people who needed help [French rescuer].

A Polish rescuer estimated that saving a single Jew required the support of at least ten people: an organizing unit, neighbors, people who would give shelter, and those who were involved in transfers. Approximately this number were involved in the following story of the rescue of a single child:

It started with news brought by E. C., with whom we
worked in the Relief Committee. E. C. reported some
alarming news. Help was immediately needed for an
eleven-year-old girl, Anna. By some miracle she had been
smuggled out of the house while the Gestapo was already
there. The man who owned the place was arrested; he was
sent to Auschwitz, where he died. His wife somehow
escaped with the child. They hid among the willow trees
along the bank of the Vistula. It was imperative that we
take the child away and find a safe place for her, get her an
"authentic" birth certificate, and so on. I immediately
called our reliable friend, S. K. Together we went to Father
M., who was the priest in the Saint Norbert convent. I knew
him from our common illegal work—sending packages to
camps—in which I participated as a representative of the
Democratic Party. Father M. started examining the parish
registers of those born eleven years ago, and—incredible
luck—he came up with just the right person. I'll never
forget the moment—he slapped his thighs with glee. He
had found the name of a maid who had given birth to an
illegitimate child eleven years ago and had subsequently
died. She thus became the mother of our child.

Anna's father wanted her to be converted to Catholicism.
I don't know whether he wanted this out of conviction or
just to save her. I wanted it because as a Roman Catholic
she would be entitled to live. So together with S. K., we
went to the bishop's place with a letter of recommendation.

I found the priest, and while speaking with him, I
noticed his lips were trembling. With the cruelty of which
only the very young are capable, I said to him: "Father, you
must be scared stiff. How can you do missionary work? Do
you imagine that you are in some remote place where
cannibals are waiting to put their teeth into you?" What a
bitch I was! He agreed to perform the ceremony.

Then we had to send the child out of Cracow to some
other place. Dr. S. helped—he signed the document
certifying that someone was to accompany her to the
Kostow orphanage. And Mr. B., who worked for the
Warsaw Relief Committee Branch and was in constant
touch with Cracow Headquarters, accompanied her. She
was taken to a school run by the nuns at Kostowiec [Polish
rescuer].

Doctors were important members of many informal networks. The "good doctor" appears repeatedly in several accounts. He would supply chemicals for dyeing hair, perform plastic surgery, arrange for false or unnecessary surgery, provide prescriptions under a false name, and provide certificates alleging the presence of contagious illnesses. He was also necessary for delivering Jewish babies, treating sick Jews, and arranging for their hospitalization if necessary. Nonetheless there was always an element of risk in approaching anyone for help, and doctors were no exception. Sometimes rescuers depended on exotic skills to determine trustworthiness:

> The woman I was hiding was a graphologist—I would get her many books from the library on the subject. Her son was an asthmatic, and one day he had a awful attack. His mother insisted that I get a sample of the doctor's handwriting before she would allow me to take him there. I found an old prescription with his signature on it. She analyzed it carefully and only then did she allow me to bring the child [Dutch rescuer].

Rescuers thus availed themselves of any and all contacts they had. They presumed on family, friends, colleagues, religious officials, and strangers. If they were heads of households, they used their authority to direct other household members. Sometimes they consulted with them:

> My father's colleague ... asked him to take a Jewish man for a short time only. My mother agreed immediately. But my parents wanted my opinion, and they wanted me to express it because it was a serious matter. Gestapo Headquarters were located right opposite our building. I remember that we sat at the table and discussed it. I agreed immediately [Polish rescuer].

If they had no authority, they tried persuasion. Confronted with a pleading woman with two children, the oldest daughter in a Polish family urged her mother to shelter them:

> Mother said, "I'm scared to death. If they catch us, we will all be killed." I pleaded with her. "They are very poor and have no place to go. Didn't you hear that they killed her husband? She has no family." Mother finally agreed. "Do whatever you like."

If they could not persuade they used deception:

One of the AK girls told us that there were Jewish children hiding in cellars—that they looked like rags, not human beings. She asked us to take care of them. So we decided to take ambulances, wagons, or cabs and tell others that they were Polish children from Zamojszczyzna. Polish children were starved; these were starved. People would not be able to tell the difference. That way those who might have said, "Jewish children, what the heck," would say, "We must help, no question." Polish children would be taken by everybody [Polish rescuer].

And sometimes they threatened:

Our concierge knew. We had to tell her. My brother warned her: "You better pretend not to know anything, because otherwise you'll see heavenly glory. It won't make any difference to you whether you get it from the Gestapo or the AK. Better forget what you know, and don't come here if you don't want to be sorry [Polish rescuer].

Thus, support from others was not simply a matter of circumstances; networks did not suddenly appear. They were the products of the efforts of individuals who deliberately cultivated every contact they could.

Carving out new relationships and roles and redefining old ones vis-à-vis the Jews in their care and neighbors and other members of the community required new skills. The basic issue was whom one could trust and whom one could not. On the surface the world of rescuers was made up of two categories of people, "them" and "us," the latter far easier to identify than the former. "They" were the enemies—Germans and their collaborators who obviously could not be trusted—but it was in the realm of "us" that ambiguity and uncertainty dominated. And, in fact, even the "theys" were not consistently clear.

According to many rescuers in Poland, France, and Holland, their national communities united as never before in common enmity to the occupiers. They said that class, political and ethnic differences largely evaporated in the face of the common threat.

But such unity did not mean a common dedication to rescuing Jews. Moreover, sentiment was insufficient to ensure trustworthiness. Trust involved not only knowing what the person felt, but also that individual's ability to make prudent judgments, steadfastness in the face of personal and family danger, fortitude under psychological pressure and courage to withstand arrest and torture. Trust must emerge from experience and there was no prior experience which prepared rescuers to make such judgments in their new world. As one rescuer put it: "You could not tell the inner man from the outside. People you thought you could trust proved untrustworthy and people you thought you couldn't trust would sometimes turn out to be the very ones who would help you [Dutch rescuer]."

Each rescuer had to determine for him- or herself just how much could safely be shared and how much needed to be withheld. Even minimal self-disclosure could be dangerous. Other people had to be assessed as individuals, not as group members. Rescuers had to remain ever alert to subtle incongruities, to nuances of tone and body posture. An error in assessing the characteristics of any individual could be fatal. Even among those they relied on most, they had to be cautious.

Trust was of paramount importance in relation to those networks on which rescuers depended to carry out their covert activities. Small helping networks that emerged from previously established tightly knit groups with common values were among the most trustworthy. These groups were united by long-standing bonds of friendship, occupation, politics, or religion. Less certain were newly emergent groups—informal or larger organized resistance groups. These included people of varying values and perspectives, many of whom were unknown to each other. Rescuers allude time and again to betrayals and corruption among them. They also speak of those who jeopardized others through their imprudence—heavy drinkers and those who were sexually promiscuous or became too cocky put not only themselves but others at risk.

Rescuers developed a variety of strategies to deal with these problems. One was to parcel out information; no single individual was told more than was absolutely necessary in order to perform a particular function. Pseudonyms were preferred to real names, and the number of people with whom one dealt was kept deliberately small. Whenever possible, messages were delivered by unknown hands. Another strategy was to prepare oneself for the worst. The worst was not necessarily death, but the disclosure of secrets under torture. Several rescuers carried cyanide pills with them, ready for use at the appropriate moment.

These same precautions had to be taken in relation to the rescued. The fact that Jews as a group were universal victims did not mean that all individual Jews could be trusted. Like others, their ranks also included those who succumbed to pressures. Lured by promises of postponed deportations for themselves or their families, or hope of avoiding torture, individual Jews also became informers, betraying rescuers and rescued. Several rescuers relate such incidents. One Polish man became livid as he related his conviction that a Jewish woman, occupying an important coordinator role in rescue, actually lured Jews to particular places only to betray them to the Gestapo. "I cannot prove it," he said, "and when I went to accuse her after the war, she begged me not to say anything." He, among others, had primarily suspicions rather than facts—nonetheless, they were sufficient to make rescuers wary even of Jews themselves.

Precautions also had to be taken with family members not living in the rescuer's household. Approximately a third of rescuers never discussed their activities with any family members. The paramount reason was actually the protection of family members themselves, as well as the rescuer and the rescued. In some cases, family members disapproved, frequently out of concern for the fate of the rescuer. A few were collaborators. In at least one case, family members who were inadvertently informed tried to extort money from the rescuer out of the conviction that the Jews she was keeping were undoubtedly supplying her with huge sums of gold. In another case, however, the disapproving aunt and uncle of a young Polish woman, who called her a "Jewish slave," ultimately also helped, out of affection for her. The behaviors of others in the course of even routine intimacies were too unpredictable to allow rescuers to trust them. One rescuer tells of his brother, quite drunk at the time, who threatened him with exposure. While the rescuer did not take it too seriously, it was nonetheless sufficient to put him on his guard thenceforth.

Family members living in households where Jews were sheltered had to be supportive, at least tacitly. In several cases, spouses or even adolescent children were enthusiastic coparticipants; sometimes they were the original initiators of the activity. But there were also cases in which they tried to remove themselves from the problem. One husband told his wife that she was free to do as she wished, but as for him, he wanted nothing to do with it. But she noted that she was sure he would not betray her.

Living in this social climate, in which trust was essential but dangerous, took its toll. Rescuers had to develop strategies for consolidating feelings of comradeship with others while simultaneously avoiding intimacies that might jeopardize them. Shared festivities provided such opportunities. Several rescuers described evenings of merriment and exuberance when trivial comments would result in peals of laughter:

> We had an enormous amount of fun. That sounds strange, but we had to have it. We gave parties. Somebody said, "I still have one tea bag." All thirty-six of us were going to have a feast with one tea bag. Somebody said, "I'm going to get water." At the end, we didn't even have water anymore. You couldn't buy clothes or anything, so everybody wore each other's dresses and the men wore each other's shirts in order to have the feeling of being dressed up. We had fantastic parties in the dark because there was no electricity. Somebody would say, "I still have a candle." Oh boy! A tea bag, a candle, water! What else do you need? We had a party [Dutch rescuer].

In-jokes, particularly black humor, also helped to bring groups together. The very events that humiliated them and filled them with dread were lampooned and caricatured. Thinking back to the time when a Jewish friend was so frightened at imminent arrest that his body literally quaked with terror, a Polish man recalled apologetically, "I know it was a terrible thing, but we laughed about it for days to come." Pranks served similar purposes. An Italian priest recalled:

> One night Morris' mother and sister had their lights on at ten-thirty, so I stomped up to their room and shouted, "Police! Police! Open up!" We could joke about it. One night we had a party. I had a nice piano, and we all sang— loud, like crazy people, late at night. One of them said, "Do you realize that if you turned us in, you could get a bounty of twenty pounds sterling?"

While having to establish and cement trust with their colleagues in rescue, rescuers' lives were simultaneously dominated by deception; it was the absolute and enduring requirement for saving Jews. Deception was more than lying; it included trickery, subterfuge, and secrecy, striving to avoid notice and creating confusion. It began in hiding the victims from the occupier; eventually it extended to family, friends, and neighbors.

It was not sufficient to hide Jews; they had to become "de-Judaized" or "Aryanized." Physical appearance was the first matter of concern. Hair color and nose shape became obsessions:

> There was a Jewish boy hiding in the neighborhood. One day he came to the house at night to talk to me and said: "My sister needs another house to hide in. Can you take her?" I said, "I don't know. What does she look like? Does she have black hair?" "No," he said, "she is blondish." So we arranged for her to come to the barn at night with her brother so that I might see. I looked at her hair but couldn't see too well with the flashlight. Her hair wasn't black, but it wasn't too blond either. But I said, "Okay, come with me. I'll take you." So I put her on the back of my bike and took her over to our house.
>
> At that time we still had electricity. When she came into our living room, my wife and I were very scared. Her hair was very black. You may ask what difference that makes. Well, if she was a Jewish type, she couldn't walk around. So we thought, "What shall we do now?" So we decided that if we could bleach her hair, she would not look so Jewish.
>
> That night I went to the doctor in our village. He knew what I was doing. He gave me a bottle of peroxide and told me to thin it. My wife put the stuff in her hair with her hands, but her hands became raw because it was much too strong. Miriam put a towel around her head and went to bed. The next morning she came down and knocked on our bedroom door. "Guess what! I'm a redhead," she said. It looked good on her. She had some freckles. So we said, "Today, you can go to church with us because we will say you are our cousin from Amsterdam" [Dutch rescuer].

Some rescuers sought plastic surgeons who might not only transform their features but also "decircumcize" boys and men. Circumcision was unique to Jewish males in several countries and regions, making them particularly vulnerable.

Appearance also included speech. Many of the victims had fled or been deported to foreign lands; others spoke the dominant tongue with unmistakable accents. Subtle mannerisms—a way of using the hands, an inflection, a way of walking—were also dangerous markers. "She just had the Jewish look," said one rescuer, "sad eyes that communicated the message, 'Why was I born?'" "I never realized my very good friends looked Jewish until after the war started," said another. "It was just something I wasn't conscious of." Rescuers had to learn to see not only through their own eyes but through those of others.

Rescuers conspired with Jews in inventing new identities. They would present them as distant family members, evacuees from bombed-out areas, or just old friends. They had to learn these new identities almost as well as the rescued; if questioned, they, too, had to be prepared to give the right answers. They had to be particularly effective in teaching them to Jewish children in their charge. A Dutchwoman reported near calamity when her Jewish child failed to learn her new identity adequately:

> Our children all knew the truth; even the little ones knew what they could or could not say. The funny part was that sometimes the Jewish children didn't know at all.
>
> One day, I found one of the Jewish girls on the tank of one of the Germans who was on the lane where we lived. The Germans were practicing with the tanks. They were very fond of children, so they put a bunch of children on the tank and gave them a ride. One of these children was one of our Jewish children. We stood in agony as we looked out the window. The soldier asked her what her name was. She said, "First my name was Rachel, then it became Marion, and now it's Teresa." She said it very seriously, but fortunately he did not catch on. Maybe it was because of her very blond hair [Dutch rescuer].

Conversely, a Polish Jewish child avoided arrest because she had integrated her new identity very well:

> I was taking care of the child. Her name was Marinka. She was five or six years old when she came to us; she did not understand much of what was going on. But I told her that I was her aunt, her only living relative, and she believed me. We had baptized her with her parents' consent. At that

time she was very pious. Although only a little child, she
felt deeply about her baptism and her new faith. Well, one
day there was some blackmailing, and Marinka was then in
hiding with a few Jews. The police came with the
uniformed Ukrainians, the Black Squadron, as everybody
called them. They dragged everyone off. But Marinka was
on her knees, praying on the bed. A Ukrainian approached
her and said, "You are Jewish." She shouted back, "Jewish
yourself! I am not Jewish. Prove you're not a Jew." This
saved her. He was embarrassed and left her alone [Polish
rescuer].

Once embarked on the fundamental deception involved in
rescuing Jews, dishonesty inevitably began to penetrate other relationships. While family members living elsewhere and neighbors
sometimes knew the truth and were even hiding Jews themselves,
others were deliberately deceived. Parents were discouraged from
visiting, as were friends and neighbors. Several rescuers reported
locking their doors for the first time, offering flimsy excuses to
neighbors about "broken doorknobs" or fears of theft. A brother
of one rescuer was denied the simple courtesy of overnight lodging to keep him from noticing anything; still harder to explain was
another rescuer's refusal of shelter to a sick sister. Pleas of over-
work, inadequate numbers of beds, family illness, or whatever
might serve, had to be convincing enough to deflect the potential
visitor without destroying the relationship.

Unable to rid herself of a suitor who appeared in her apartment at unexpected times, a Polish woman hit on a masterful strategy that won her some disapproval but worked. She managed to
acquire the photograph of a handsome Nazi officer stationed in
the vicinity and hung it over her bed. Her "boyfriend" bothered
her no more. To deceive her neighbors about the impending birth
of a Jewish baby in her home, a Dutchwoman progressively pad-
ded herself with layers of clothing, letting others believe she was
pregnant. None were surprised when a new baby appeared in the
house. In some cases even family members living in the same
household did not know what was going one:

My father-in-law lived with me during the war, but he had
no idea what I was doing. The Jewish girl I was keeping in
our house, he thought was a mute. I told her never to
speak in his presence. When the war was over, I told him

the truth and he was angry, but not for long. "What a
miracle," he said. The only person I could talk to was my
oldest sister, who was in on it. My husband was away—he
was drafted into the Army and was in Germany. The Jewish
woman I was keeping did not know a word of French—
only Yiddish. My own daughter began to have a Yiddish
accent—they told her that in school. I told the woman to
pretend to be a deaf-mute; my daughter knew the truth, but
she also knew she could say nothing [Belgian rescuer].

Some of the most painful aspects of deception were the burdens and dangers it imposed on their own children. Although not
party to the decision making, the children of rescuers were
threatened with parental loss or punishment similar to their parents. A casual remark, a secret shared with a best friend, jeopardized all. To avoid this some rescuers placed their own children
elsewhere; one woman saw her own children for no more than
several months during a period of three years. One Dutch couple
managed to keep their Jewish guests hidden from their own child
under the same roof for several years:

Our little boy never saw them except for one night. School
usually let out at four o'clock. One time, school was let out
early because of an air raid alarm. He came home. She had
just come downstairs with a chamber pot, because that's
what they used upstairs. He came in and said, "Hi, Tante
Johanna!" She wasn't really his aunt, but that's what he
called her. "I haven't seen you in a long time!" It was nearly
three years. She said, "Yes. I'm helping your mother do the
spring cleaning." This was May—the beginning of May. It
didn't bother him at all. He thought it was just normal. But
that's the only time he ever saw her.

The children of rescuers sometimes resented the intrusions
on their privacy and being deprived of their parents' attention.
"Why do we always have to have so many people around?" asked
the younger daughters in one family. Like their parents, they, too,
were forced to endure semi-isolation from friends:

My friend lived right next door, but I could never allow her
to come to the house. When we played, it was either
outside or at her house. I guess that was a little hard on
her mother, because she wondered why it was such a one-

sided thing. I could only confide in one friend. Her parents were definitely "on the right side" and did their own part. But she was the only one I could talk to outside the family [Dutch rescuer].

The overriding principle was to say and know as little as possible. Even separated Jewish family members would not be told of each other's whereabouts. Parents would not be told where their children were hidden, and children would frequently be told that their parents were dead. Several rescuers recount moving stories of how they contrived to bring the children of the rescued to some appointed place to allow parents to glance at them from afar. An embrace could be permitted under special circumstances:

> One day, it was the Jewish woman's birthday. So we decided to have a surprise for her. Her little child was two years old and hiding in another house close to Amsterdam. We made an arrangement for the child to come over to see her mom. It was more than a year since her parents had seen her. On December 16, I will never forget that day, my husband made an arrangement to bring her by train—a two-and-a-half hour ride on the train. We picked her up. She was deaf; she could not speak. She was born deaf and she hardly knew her mom anymore; she had already been in hiding before she was even one year old. There she came—one o'clock. We brought her upstairs to her mom. They hugged, they cried. Such a surprise [Dutch rescuer]!

Yet, if disclosure became necessary, as it sometimes did, and the recipient of the information responded with unexpected approval, new bonds of respect were formed that sometimes lasted a lifetime. One such occurrence is related by a German woman who deceived both her husband and daughter regarding the true identity of the man she was keeping in their home:

> I had told them only that his place was bombed out and that he had no place to live. I didn't tell them that he was Jewish and also a well-known Jew, a man of considerable reputation in the world of commerce. But the time came when I had to tell my husband. "I wonder how he'll react to that?" I thought. I bought some wine, and after we had drunk a little, I told him the truth. He swallowed hard, looked up at me and said, "Well, Paulachen we've managed

to get through so far with him, we'll get him the rest of the way through." Well, after that I knew what kind of husband I had. Life doesn't always give us such situations and opportunities. What a gem!

Deception was easier to maintain in relation to the German occupier, but even here rationships were not without ambiguity. Rescuers expected Germans to behave brutally and cruelly. They knew the enemy and what he could do to them. But several rescuers identified important distinctions, such as that between Nazis and German soldiers—the latter were perceived as less threatening and, on rare occasions, even helpful. A "good German" appears in the accounts of many rescuers—one who would pretend not to see a hiding place, avert his eyes when someone was escaping, and sometimes even provide material goods for the rescuers. Some distinguished between older and younger Germans—the former were perceived as generally less dangerous. Having been socialized in the pre-Hitler era, they appeared to be more susceptible to normal human emotions. There were even occasions when those wearing German uniforms were secretly sympathetic. One rescuer told of a German in Holland who was in charge of validating applications for Aryan identity and known for his lenient interpretations of Aryan identification. Another rescuer told the story of his brother, a member of the SS, who chose death on the Soviet front when he became aware of the extent of Nazi brutality.

Rescuers were careful to consider the individual characters of the occupiers. Such understanding made it possible to fabricate appropriately or to appeal to particular values and emotions to gain some advantage. A Dutchwoman describes how such understanding helped her avoid a search when a young German soldier with "all kinds of weapons hanging on him" appeared at her door at five-thirty in the afternoon:

> He went to the door of the cellar and asked "What's down there?" I said, "You're free to go and look!" I never answered the questions—I always let them make the decisions; that was one trick. From his accent, I knew he was from southern Germany, so I asked him where he was from. He said, "Saxony," so I said, "That's a very beautiful part. Do you have a family?" "Yes." "Do you have children?" "Yes, but I haven't seen them in years." By this time, he was almost in tears. "How come you are doing

this?" I asked. He told me he was being punished. The searchers were punished—the punishment was to leave early in the morning and walk from Leiden to Haarlem—a tremendous distance—and then search houses all day long and then walk back. I invited him to sit down because I knew he was tired, but he refused. In this way I kept him talking, which prevented him from searching next door where some people were hiding [Dutch rescuer].

On occasion, rescuers began to feel some affection for indi-vidual Germans with whom they were forced to have prolonged associations, and had to be careful not to let their guard down in such circumstances. A Polish man reports:

We were forced to take in a German industrialist. He tried to make friends with us, but at first nobody spoke to him. But later we developed a liking for him. It was New Year's Eve or some other occasion, and we had guests. He brought brandy—or was it champagne?—and when he got drunk, he began showering abuses on Hitler, saying that he was waiting for all this to end, to collapse, waiting for all hell to break loose. He reassured us that it was not meant to be a provocation. He said he was against everything that was happening—that he could no longer bear the roundups and the raids, that it made him so sick that he had to take medicine to stand all these antihumanitarian actions. He would show us pictures of his family, but we knew we had to be careful.

Indigenous police forces, the native executors of Nazi rule, were frequently more dangerous than the Germans. They were better able to detect differences in physical appearance and speech patterns and to sniff out fabricated stories. And in their zeal to prove themselves useful to the occupiers, they often outdid them in brutality and efficiency.

Known collaborators were treated warily; rescuers were care-ful not to offend them or arouse their suspicions. But extortionists and blackmailers posed a continuing problem, particularly for Polish rescuers, who mentioned them repeatedly. Known as *szmal-cowniki*, some operated overtly, others covertly. Some would simply accost people on streets or at ghetto exit points and threaten dis-closure unless they received goods or money. Others would send anonymous notes. Sometimes they were neighbors or tradespeople. Polish rescuers refer to them with harsh contempt, labeling them scum, parasites, vermin, and bandits. Most frequently they submitted to the demands, paying whatever was required out of their own resources or from those they were keeping. On rare occasions they would attempt a brazen confrontation with the would-be blackmailers, threatening them with violence or disclosure to the Nazis by virtue of some trumped-up charges. Flight was yet another alternative.

Reflecting back on the deceptions that characterized their lives, rescuers perceive them as part of an acquired mask—a set of behaviors that had little to do with who they really were. Several indicated that they were quite clear that lying and secrecy were wrong but had little doubt that it was the absolutely right thing to do under the circumstances. As one Dutchwoman explained it, "I could lie really well then, but I did not lie to kill, I lied to save." Explaining how she tried to keep her children from succumbing to the new ethos, another woman said: "One of the greatest problems in that period of our lives was on the one hand teaching them to lie in these circumstances, and on the other hand reprimanding them when they lied for other purposes, and understanding the differences between the lies." Several took pride in those instances when they managed to avoid lying technically. Faced with a nosy and untrustworthy neighbor, a woman recalled saying to her: "I wouldn't have a single Jewish person in the house"—she had two of them.

The power that had taken over their lives was awesome and could indeed control much of their behavior—but not all of it. Deception was a fundamental tool for undermining that power; it was a way for the self to assert its own will. Used in the service of saving lives, rescuers had no doubt or hesitancy regarding its appropriateness. Defying the Nazi rules of destruction in whatever way possible was itself a moral victory.

CHAPTER 5

Saving Others: Was It Opportunity or Character?

"I did nothing unusual; anyone would have done the same thing in my place." With these words, a Dutchman who sheltered a Jewish family for two years answers the fundamental question, Why did rescuers do it? As he perceived it, his response was largely a matter of opportunity—of being in the right place at the right time. This rescuer is clearly modest, but if he is correct, rescue can largely be explained as a response to a propitious combination of external circumstances.

Among the circumstances that may have facilitated rescue were:

1. *Information about and comprehension of the need.* Without knowledge and comprehension, no response could be forthcoming. Did rescuers know and comprehend more than nonrescuers?
2. *Risk.* Risk encompasses the likelihood and probable consequences of discovery. Were rescuers less likely to be discovered?
3. *Material resources.* Did rescuers have more of the material resources required for rescue?
4. *A precipitating occasion.* Being asked for help is frequently cited as the critical factor in producing a rescue response. Were rescuers asked for help while others were not?

Information

At its simplest level, knowledge means receiving and registering information. Comprehension involves something more: It requires internal processing of the information, understanding, and interpretation. While these are cognitive processes, they are un-likely to occur without some emotional willingness. Information that is of interest is more likely to be registered and processed than information perceived as irrelevant. Emotional factors also influence interpretation. Instances of observed brutality, for exam-ple, can be explained as deserved or undeserved, or reports of maltreatment can be believed or dismissed as exaggerations.

Having knowledge depends first on the opportunity to ac-quire it. Did rescuers have more opportunities to acquire knowl-edge of the plight of the Jews?

The Nazi occupiers exerted tight control over all forms of me-dia. They characteristically masked their real intentions by a vari-ety of subterfuges, including euphemistic or deceptive language. The full horror of the Final Solution was not apparent from the early measures against Jews. The severity of the restrictions in-creased gradually, usually beginning with social and residential segregation. Furthermore, even once the killings began, knowl-edge of them should have been more common in Eastern Europe, where most of the death camps were located, than elsewhere.

Among the conditions that facilitated acquisition of knowl-edge, the first was geographical proximity. Those who lived among Jews or worked with them would have the greatest opportunity to hear and observe. Those who had Jewish friends would be more likely to be interested in understanding what was going on. Rescu-ers were more favored with respect to such circumstances, but the differences appeared to some degree related to consciousness rather than objective circumstances.

Immediately before the war, Jews were living in the neighbor-hoods of the majority of rescuers and nonrescuers. Although there were significant differences between the two groups in terms of their physical proximity to Jews, awareness (or lack of it) was an important component of these differences. More rescuers (69 per-cent) lived among Jews than did nonrescuers (57 percent for all nonrescuers, 52 percent of bystanders),* but more nonrescuers (13 percent of all nonrescuers, 12 percent of bystanders) than rescuers (4 percent) did not know whether Jews lived in their neighbor-hoods.

*It will be recalled that nonrescuers included actives—people who report being mem-bers of resistance groups or helping Jews but whose accounts have not been authenticated—and bystanders—people who report neither engaging in resistance nor helping Jews.

Awareness was also an important component of the significant differences between rescuers and nonrescuers as to whether they or their spouses had Jewish coworkers. Only a minority of rescuers and nonrescuers worked with Jews immediately before the war, but again rescuers did so in larger percentages (34 percent, as against 17 percent of all nonrescuers and 15 percent of bystanders) and more nonrescuers said they did not know (13 percent of all nonrescuers and 8 percent of bystanders, as against 1 percent of rescuers). More rescuers said their spouses worked with Jews (28 percent, compared with 10 percent of all nonrescuers and 4 percent of bystanders) and more nonrescuers than rescuers did not know (41 percent of all nonrescuers, 32 percent of bystanders, and 19 percent of rescuers).

Awareness that people around them were Jewish may have reflected in part the greater tendency of rescuers to have Jewish friends. Significantly more of them had Jewish friends immediately before the war (59 percent of rescuers, 34 percent of all nonrescuers, and 25 percent of bystanders), and significantly more of their spouses had Jewish friends (46 percent, compared with 25 percent of all nonrescuers and 16 percent of bystanders). (See Table 5.1.) Such friendships were important potential sources of information.

Immediately before the war, then, the majority of rescuers and nonrescuers lived among Jews, but only a minority among all groups worked with them. Rescuers appear to have had more opportunities to acquire information by virtue of the physical proximity of Jews in their neighborhoods and workplaces. This difference, however, may have been more illusory than real, inasmuch as nonrescuers were apparently less conscious of whether Jews were present or not. Rescuers' greater awareness of Jews generally may have been partly due to their greater tendency to have personal friendships with Jews.

However, prewar geographical proximity was not essential to acquiring information. More than 30 percent of rescuers did not live among Jews, more than 40 percent had no Jewish friends, and more than 65 percent had no Jewish coworkers. At best, though prewar proximity and friendships offered some opportunities for gaining knowledge, they were not necessary or sufficient conditions.

In fact, despite differences between rescuers and nonrescuers in living or working with Jews and having Jewish friends, there was little difference in their comprehension of the dire fate awaiting the Jews. Almost all rescuers (99 percent) and nonrescuers (93 percent) said they were either aware of Nazi intentions regarding Jews before the war started or learned about them during the war. While more rescuers than nonrescuers claimed knowing about Hitler's intentions before he came to power (23 percent for rescuers, 16 percent for all nonrescuers, and 15 percent for bystanders), the majority in all groups learned about them during the war itself (Table 5.2). Rescuers and nonrescuers acquired knowledge in similar ways.

German rescuers as well as German nonrescuers who knew about Hitler's intentions early had heard Nazis speak or had observed their behaviors:

> I heard a lecture by Nazis in Breslau in 1929. We knew the Nazis from our student days [German rescuer].

> I saw Jews clobbered in the street weeks before Hitler came to power [German nonrescuer].

Those who lived outside Germany learned about events through the media or from German Jewish refugees:

> We heard about Germany in the press. We had quite a number of Jewish refugees in Poland from Germany and from Czechoslovakia. The outlook was rather grim [Polish nonrescuer].

> We read the newspapers and knew about anti-Semitism in Germany. I remember *Kristallnacht*. It was general knowledge, known to anybody who read the newspapers [Dutch nonrescuer].

> I read about it in the papers constantly [Dutch nonrescuer].

> A lot of German Jews came to our country in the thirties [Dutch rescuer].

> When the Germans occupied Austria, a group of Jews were thrown out of Vienna. Mother wanted to help these people, so she found a refugee in Warsaw who could sew. This person told us what the situation was like in occupied Austria for Jews [Polish rescuer].

While such early information did not necessarily predict mass extermination, it did indicate to rescuers and nonrescuers that

something very special was intended for Jews. As one French rescuer explained: "I knew what was happening to Jews in Germany,
but I did not know what this meant for Jews in France, at least
until 1942." Many respondents say that no single event made them
aware of the plight of Jews; it was rather a series of events.

Most respondents—approximately 76 percent in all groups—
said they learned about Nazi intentions shortly after the Nazi take-
over in their country. One of the earliest directly observed indications was Jews wearing the Star of David. More than 85 percent of
rescuers and nonrescuers alike saw Jews wearing it; there were no
statistical differences among groups. (Among the remainder who
reported never having seen it, most lived in France; the measure
was never extended to the Vichy zone.) The first time they saw this
symbol, a small minority (8 percent of rescuers, 14 percent of all
nonrescuers, and 18 percent of bystanders) regarded it as something of a curiosity or with indifference (Table 5.2):

When I saw a Jew wearing a yellow Star of David, I sort of
laughed about it. My girlfriend and her mother were
wearing it—several people I never even knew were Jewish
[Dutch rescuer].

I thought the star was some kind of pass for them [French
nonrescuer].

When I saw Jews wearing the yellow Star of David, I
thought perhaps they had committed some sort of crime.
Our leaders never told us why they wore the star
[Rumanian nonrescuer].

It meant nothing to me. I was just not interested in Jews
[Polish nonrescuer].

More than 80 percent of rescuers and all other groups (but
significantly more rescuers than bystanders) perceived it as a tragedy for Jews:

It was a disgrace. I felt embittered [German rescuer].

Unjust! Inexplicable [French rescuer].

Uneasiness, pain because of the solidarity I felt for the Jews
[French nonrescuer].

Terrible! Devastating! So cruel [Polish rescuer].

Terrible, terrible! I felt so bad for everybody to see what they were—what it represented and how they must feel [Dutch nonrescuer].

Such feelings were sometimes accompanied by relief that it was not they who were forced to wear it:

I was always glad I wasn't a Jew. They wore the star. Then they started disappearing. It became scary then [Dutch nonrescuer].

I think there was a double feeling—a feeling of compassion for Jews and anger toward the Germans. There was also a feeling of distance from the Jews. There was a part of me that also identified with the aggressor—thank God it's not me. No! Identification with the aggressor is not the right idea. I felt threatened by what they did to Jews [Dutch nonrescuer].

For many Poles it meant that Jews could be murdered at will and also suggested to them their own fate:

I heard that when Jews had to have the yellow Stars of David, then everybody could hit them, kill them, or hurt them in any way [rescuer].

I was very upset. He was a marked man. Everybody could shoot him [nonrescuer].

I was afraid it was going to happen to Poles too. [rescuer].

I thought like everybody else that Jews, as well as Poles, were going to die [nonrescuer].

The particular meaning Poles attributed to the star was the result of the barbarities they had observed directly. Most saw Jews brutalized and killed; most saw the ghettos formed and many saw them burn:

I saw them shoot Jews randomly on the market square in Krosno [nonrescuer].

If they did not wear their yellow armband, they would be beaten mercilessly. I saw this with my own eyes and I will never forget [nonrescuer].

In 1940, as they transported Jews to the ghetto, I lived near the ghetto and saw people begging for bread. I saw them finished off [nonrescuer].

I witnessed mistreatment in the ghetto in Radomsko. We couldn't come too close; we couldn't give them anything to eat. The Jews stretched out their arms—they were hungry—and the Germans beat those arms [nonrescuer].

In 1940 the Germans caught a Jew who had escaped from the ghetto, and they told him to put smoking cigars inside his mouth. They were laughing at him. We could hear the Jew screaming. I was a witness to the liquidation of the ghetto. I saw everything from my window [nonrescuer].

I saw the building of the camps, the smoke from the crematorium [nonrescuer].

I saw in Krasnik how they shot Jews; the Jews dug the ditches and then the Germans shot them [rescuer].

I could smell the smoke from Majdanek; dogs barked; they used them to bite and nip people [rescuer].

I saw Jewish families being taken to be executed in Limanowa. Those Jews had to dig their own ditches—graves. It was horrible; the soil was moving after the execution [rescuer].

Outside Poland, however, respondents were less likely to observe brutal mistreatment of Jews directly. More often, they reported observing single instances of brutality toward Jews—a single shooting, a raid, or a transport or the special treatment of Jewish prisoners if they themselves were imprisoned or visited someone in prison. More rescuers than nonrescuers reported such incidents:

I always had to go to the hall, where I worked for the Central Committee, and that's where I had to go for food. I always got a little more there. I always had to go past there, and I always saw these groups of Jews there—the way they were herded together. They would be picked up later [German rescuer].

In Galicia, April 7, 1942, after my escape from prisoners' camp, I saw ten thousand people killed, Jews and others. I

first saw the Star of David when I was in the Ukraine. From
April 13, 1942, to July 31, 1942, I was a prisoner of war at
Rawa Ruska in the Ukraine. The Germans would kill
hundreds of Jews each day—men, women, children. It was
awful [French rescuer].

I did an autopsy on the first victim. There was no doctor or
nurse, and the prefect designated me to do the autopsy. As
superintendent of police, I knew right away what the
Germans were going to do to the Jews [French rescuer].

In May 1943 I witnessed with my own eyes Jews being
shipped to Westerbork in boxcars. I saw them. I saw it with
my own eyes [Dutch rescuer].

I saw people being picked up. They were kicked and
thrown around, then taken away. I happened to be there.
They brought many Jews together in the concert hall in
Amsterdam. Then they were taken away to the train. I was
there when they took them out of the concert hall and put
them on the train. It was pathetic, indescribable. People
with suitcases—just driven like cattle [Dutch rescuer].

Rescuers and nonrescuers also saw other signs—the posted
ones prohibiting Jews from using facilities, proclamations in the
official press regarding Jews, the removal of belongings from vacated Jewish apartments, the disappearance of a neighbor, and,
finally, the disappearance of those wearing the yellow star:

I saw the signs appear in public places that Jews were not
allowed in swimming pools and restaurants, and they could
not even use park benches [Dutch rescuer].

The only time I saw mistreatment of Jews was the day they
raided my employer's apartment—loading the truck with
all my boss' belongings. What was worse was that it was
Frenchmen who were emptying the apartment—not
Germans [French rescuer].

When Holland surrendered, one of the teachers was
married to a Jew. She and her husband committed
suicide. This stunned me. In my youthful eyes it was
incomprehensible that somebody could do that just out of
the fear of Germans invading. Then there were signs that

Jews could not go to movie theaters and restaurants [Dutch nonrescuer].

Then they started picking on the Jews. They had to wear a star, then they were caught and deported. We knew vaguely about the camps—that the Jews were taken away, but we didn't know for sure. They disappeared and they didn't come back [Dutch nonrescuer].

But neither rescuers nor nonrescuers depended on observations alone for their knowledge. They also heard reports. Rescuers more frequently mentioned hearing them from Jews themselves—neighbors, employers, coworkers, and friends—and experiencing events in a personal way as a result of their interactions with Jews. Nonrescuers, on the other hand, were more likely to refer to "people" telling them, hearing rumors, or knowing vaguely. They were also more likely to have discredited what they heard:

RESCUERS	NONRESCUERS
Friends of ours—the man was Jewish, the woman was Protestant, and the children were considered Jewish by the Nazis. They lived in Rotterdam, and they were put out by the Nazis. They had to leave everything [Dutch].	People found out about it by word of mouth, but it was hard to believe. It was practically unimaginable [French].
First I couldn't go downtown with them. Then I couldn't talk to them [German].	I knew they hated the Jews, but most people didn't put much into that because the statements they made were so ridiculous. People thought it best not to pay attention to it [Dutch].
Our friend made me aware that he would be arrested [French].	I became aware through the BBC. We heard Jews were being arrested and shipped off to Germany. But it was something nobody talked about—the concentration camps. I worked in Germany with a German who had been in a concentration
A close friend was killed in 1940 [French].	
My friend came to ask me for a hiding place [French].	

RESCUERS

In 1942 I had a house that some Jewish friends of mine wanted to buy. I was told I couldn't sell it to them [French].

I couldn't go to the Jewish quarter [Dutch].

I was given Herr Mayer's apartment, and I was supposed to throw him out [German].

The mother of our friend was killed in Ravensbruck. She told us [German].

I was well informed. I knew Jewish people through my work [German].

In 1942 a friend came to tell me that they were going to arrest my neighbor [Belgian].

From the Jews themselves in 1940. They said they were going to be deported [French].

NONRESCUERS

camp in 1934 and was then freed. He described it as "reeducation" and "brainwashing" [Belgian].

I must admit that I knew the Jews were transported, but I didn't have the foggiest idea that they were all being massacred. The rumors were there, but I could not believe they could be such beasts; it was incomprehensible. I heard many stories [German].

We knew vaguely about them—that the Jews were taken away but we didn't know for sure. They disappeared and didn't come back [Dutch].

We lived in the suburbs, where things were very calm and quiet. My mother met a neighbor lady who had spent the night with some friends in the city. They woke up in the middle of the night because of some commotion and looked out the window and saw people going into one of the big department stores, picking up bales of clothing, and throwing them in the river. They sneaked out and went to a police station and notified them. The police said they knew about it, and it was being taken care of. It

NONRESCUERS

> was a clothing store. The
> incident was never in the
> paper. My mother thought it
> was a clothing store that
> belonged to Jews. My
> mother came home with
> that story and thought it was
> just terrible, but she didn't
> know whether or not to
> believe it [German].

Hence, neither knowledge nor comprehension per se distin-guished rescuers from nonrescuers, but rather the credibility and significance of such knowledge. Although rescuers and nonrescu-ers knew similar facts, at some point rescuers began to perceive them in a personal way. At some point information was no longer merely recorded or vaguely apprehended or communicated by supposedly unreliable third persons. At some point, for rescuers, awareness became attention, and attention became focused con-centration on what was happening to particular people in specific contexts. But we might assume that, before making the move from comprehension to action, individuals would consider such factors as the potential risks to themselves and their families and their actual ability to help, especially in terms of financial resources and providing shelter.

Risks

To what degree did risk or the perception of risk influence the decision to rescue?

Objective risk varied considerably, depending on national and regional location, the number of Nazis available to search out defectors, the collaboration of indigeneous police forces and the local population, the vicissitudes of local policy, and the shifting movements of German troops as they advanced or retreated. At any moment a safer area could suddenly become very dangerous; conversely, an area once thick with Germans might become rela-tively safe.

In general, geographically isolated areas were of less strategic value to the Germans, resulting in fewer troops stationed there and lighter patrols. Only a small percentage of rescuers (8 percent) said they lived on isolated farms during the war. But even fewer nonrescuers (less than 2 percent) reported living in such areas.

Geographical location may have shielded a few rescuers from Nazi patrols, but they were nonetheless subject to the potentially prying eyes of neighbors. Of course, neighbors could be a source of help or threat. Most rescuers perceived their neighbors as threatening. Frequently, the threat was very real:

> We started having difficulties with a guy across the street. He pestered my mother: "Mrs. W., this will end up with a hanging." Then we heard that he had been arrested and shot by the Gestapo. My mother said, "Don't you believe it! That son of a bitch will walk out of his grave to persecute us," and indeed, before the week was out, he was back, threatening us as usual with disclosure [Polish rescuer].

> Those houses nearby stood in a row, and there was a huge common yard. Among the lodgers there lived a concierge and his son. I shouldn't tell you this, because it is such a shame that Polish people could do what he did. But he got one woman, who promised him some gold, out of the ghetto. He took her home, and in a few days she was gone. I went to him to ask where she was. He replied, "I don't know. I got up in the morning and she was just not there—the apartment door was open." But somebody told me that after he got the gold, he led her out at night and killed her. And I could say nothing, for such a hoodlum could have done the same to me [Polish rescuer].

But in several cases, neighbors said after the war that they had known all along:

> It was a heavy burden. Imagine how my mother felt! Three meals every day—breakfast, dinner, and supper. Every time before summoning our guests from the hideout, one had to check whether the coast was clear—look from the terrace pretending that the purpose was to fix something or to fetch something from the cellar. Day in, day out! But our neighbor smelled a rat. He lived so close to our place. After the war he told me that he knew. We couldn't see him when he gave food to his pigs, but from there he saw everything [Polish rescuer].

And in fact, among the 65 percent of rescuers who told of their neighbors learning about their activities after the war, more than 70 percent said their neighbors approved. But because such sentiments could not be predicted in advance, safety was better ensured by the absence of neighbors.

Yet few rescuers enjoyed this luxury. More than 85 percent said they had "many neighbors" living nearby during the war, a similar percentage to that of nonrescuers. The majority of rescuers lived in areas of high population density during the war—60 percent in large or medium-size cities, 20 percent in cities with a million or more inhabitants.

One advantage city dwellers had was relative anonymity. Amid the bustle of many strangers, one's activities might not be noticed. This was not the case, however, in small villages, where unusual activities were more likely to be observed and subject to gossip. Yet a significantly larger percentage of rescuers (16 percent, compared with approximately 10 percent of nonrescuers) lived in small villages. When villages were communities sharing similar values regarding rescue, however, neighbors could provide a cover of safety. Le Chambon in France was one such community.[1] Several of the small-village dwellers in our sample lived in Friesland, a largely homogenous Dutch religious community with distinct views about the special favored status of Jews. While rescuers living in this community did not usually disclose their covert activities, several affirmed that their neighbors knew and were sympathetic. To the extent that rescuers benefited from their geographical location, it was not by virtue of isolation from or the absence of neighbors, but rather by virtue of the decency of the neighbors among whom some of them lived.

A household with few people reduced the risk of disclosure; those living alone would have been the safest. However, only 16 percent of rescuers lived alone at the time of their first helping activity. The remaining 84 percent lived in households ranging from one additional person to more than seven; a few in the latter group lived in religious orders and boarding schools. At the outbreak of the war, the distribution of all nonrescuers was similar: Approximately 21 percent lived alone and 79 percent in households ranging from one additional person to more than seven.

Households with children posed a particular threat. Children were more likely to reveal secrets; adults who might be willing to risk their own lives and the lives of other adults would be less

willing to jeopardize unknowing children. Yet 27 percent of rescuers lived in households with at least one child aged ten years or
younger—a percentage similar to that of all nonrescuers (18 percent for all nonrescuers, 19 percent for bystanders). (See Table
5.3.) Thus, the number of people or children in a household does
not explain why some became rescuers and others did not.

Never objectively certain, risk was frequently assessed subjec-
tively—a personal calculus of the probability of disclosure and
punishment perceived differently at times even by people engaged in similar activities in the same areas. The accounts of three
Polish rescuers suggest how varied such perceptions could be. For
one member of Zegota (the Polish group concerned with helping
Jews), involvement with Jews was perceived as inviting the cer-
tainty of death:

> Nobody in Poland, no Army command, civil underground
> authorities, could order anyone or impose on anyone to
> take care of or help the Jews. That would mean sending
> him or her to death. And nobody sent people to death in
> Poland. You could be given an assignment with death as a
> possibility, but you couldn't be sentenced to it.

Another Pole however, was surprised to learn that others regarded saving Jews as more dangerous than general resistance activities:

> There were more Jews hiding in our place than persecuted
> Poles. Poles in the underground seldom came to us. As I
> learned only later, the underground regarded our house as
> not quite safe—they were afraid it might become a trap
> because of the Jews in it.

Yet another Pole perceived the risk in saving Jews as no more
than that involved in having an illegal piece of meat:

> There were only two punishments in the GG [General
> Gouvernement]—the death penalty or a twenty zloty fine.
> So, you know, the punishment was the same either for a
> kilo of meat or for saving a hundred Jews.

Although their subjective perceptions varied, most rescuers
nonetheless perceived helping Jews as very dangerous from the
start. Only 18 percent said they felt no sense of personal risk the
very first time they helped a Jew, and 23 percent perceived

the risk as moderate. But more than half (54 percent) felt that even the very first helping act was accompanied by extreme risk to themselves and to their families.

However, perceived risk was less a calculation of the probabilities of being caught than it was a perception of what would happen to them if they were. In this respect, rescuers had no less reason to be fearful than did nonrescuers. The majority of rescuers (88 percent) experienced no personal harassment at the hands of the Germans as a consequence of their first helping act; neither they nor anyone who helped them was arrested or even questioned. Most (70 percent) of them had never been personally mistreated by the Nazis before their first helping activity. The majority (65 percent), however, had directly observed Nazi mistreatment of others, exclusive of Jews. Hence, they understood that Nazi brutality was not confined to Jews alone and had legitimate fears regarding their own treatment should they be caught. Nonrescuers had no more reason to be fearful. The majority of them (75 percent) never experienced any personal mistreatment at the hands of the Nazis, nor had they witnessed anyone else, other than Jews, being mistreated by them (60 percent). Thus, their direct observation of Nazi brutality with respect to people like themselves was even less than that of rescuers. Therefore, by virtue of personal experience of mistreatment or the mistreatment of others, they had no more apparent reason to be fearful then did rescuers.

On the whole then, objective risk conditions were no less threatening for rescuers than nonrescuers. Indeed, the majority of rescuers perceived the risks—both to themselves and their families—as extreme from the start. What distinguished rescuers from others was their readiness to act despite perceived risks.

Resources

Without resources, however, rescuers could not have undertaken their task. They needed money, appropriate shelters, and help from others. Money was essential to the entire enterprise of rescue. It was needed to purchase food, shelters, forged papers, transportation, and all other basic needs; it was also needed for bribing and silencing blackmailers. Rescuers' and nonrescuers' relative financial situations are suggested by their employment status before and during the war.

Sixty-three percent of rescuers reported being employed immediately before the war; of these, 2 percent were in the military and 9 percent were religious functionaries or intermittently employed (Table 5.4). Among all employed rescuers, 33 percent were at the upper end of the occupational scale; 13 percent were higher executives, proprietors of large concerns, and major professionals; 21 percent were business managers in large concerns, proprietors of medium-size businesses, or lesser professionals and administrators. Approximately 16 percent were at the bottom of the occupational scale; 6 percent were semiskilled workers, 10 percent unskilled (Table 5.5). Approximately half were in the middle levels of the occupational scale. Self-perceptions of their prewar economic status are largely congruent with this occupational distribution. Somewhat more than a fourth (26 percent) said they were either very well or quite well off, 22 percent quite or very poor, and the majority (52 percent) neither (Table 5.6a).

Prewar employment figures for bystanders were similar to those of rescuers. There were no significant differences in prewar occupational distributions between employed rescuers and nonrescuers (Table 5.5). But whereas self-perceptions of economic status were similar for rescuers and all nonrescuers, bystanders as a group did differ from rescuers. Whereas rescuers were represented along the entire continuum from very well off to very poor, bystanders were concentrated in the middle ranges; fewer were very well off, but fewer, also, were very poor (Table 5.6a).

The difference among groups sharpened during the war—this time, however, it was reflected in occupational distributions among the employed but not in self-perceptions of economic status. After the war began, the ranks of employed rescuers increased to 74 percent, primarily because more housewives and students entered the workforce (Table 5.7). There was some slight decrease among those at the top of the occupational ladder and some slight increase among those at the bottom (Table 5.8). Self-perceptions of economic status confirm some general downward mobility. The percentage who perceived themselves as quite or very poor increased to 32 percent (Table 5.6b).

Employment also increased among nonrescuers during the war. Whereas housewives and students entering the workforce accounted for some of the increase, more nonrescuers served with the German military forces (Table 5.7). Occupational distributions among nonrescuers also showed some downward mobility during the war; the ranks of the semiskilled increased substantially among bystanders particularly (from 18 percent before the war to 33 percent during the war). Overall shifts favored employed rescuers. Fewer nonrescuers than rescuers were at the top of the occupational ladder during the war and more were at the bottom (Table 5.8).

But—because of the dominant illegal market and the expropriations of the occupiers—occupational status was less predictive of economic well-being during the war than before. Hence, it is not surprising that nonrescuers perceived their wartime economic status as similar to that of rescuers. Approximately a third of all groups perceived themselves as "quite poor" or "very poor" during the war; approximately half the members of all groups perceived themselves as "neither rich nor poor." There was no significant difference among any groups with respect to such self-ratings (Table 5.6b).

At best, prewar and wartime occupations and economic status favored a few rescuers. But the overall similarity in the range of occupation and economic status among rescuers and nonrescuers suggests that economic resources may have facilitated rescue, but were not a critical factor influencing the decision to rescue. In fact, rescuers included the very poor and the very rich as well as every level in between.

In addition to money, adequate shelters facilitated rescue. Those who owned their own homes would not have prying landlords about. Those who had access to attics and cellars would have better facilities for hiding people than those who did not. Those with larger domiciles could keep people there without major internal discomfort. However, there were no significant differences between rescuers and nonrescuers with respect to living in a house or apartment, owning or renting, or having access to an attic. Forty-eight percent of rescuers, 41 percent of nonrescuers, and 44 percent of bystanders reported living in a house. Approximately 45 percent of rescuers said they owned their house or apartment; 51 percent of all nonrescuers and 50 percent of bystanders made this claim. The majority of all groups had access to an attic: 80 percent of rescuers, 74 percent of all nonrescuers, and 80 percent of bystanders. Significantly more rescuers had access to a cellar (83 percent) than all nonrescuers (69 percent), but the percentage of bystanders having access to a cellar (81 percent) was almost identical to that of rescuers. Rescuers did, however, have a small but significant advantage over bystanders with respect to the number of rooms in their dwellings. Whereas only 40 percent of rescuers reported one to three rooms, 54 percent of bystanders did; whereas 19 percent of rescuers reported seven to nine rooms, only 5 percent of bystanders did. Thus, having a house with many rooms may have facilitated rescue, but it was not a critically determining factor. Rescuers included those with neither attic nor cellar, as well as those living in a single room. More rescuers than bystanders had larger domiciles; with respect to all other conditions, however, they were similar (Table 5.9).

Whereas economic and sheltering capabilities facilitated rescue, a supportive network was in most cases critical to it. Rescuers depended most heavily on informal networks rather than formal ones.

The formal networks were organized resistance groups whose objectives were determined by leaders. Relationships among the members were impersonal and defined by rules and regulations. Fewer than half of rescuers (44 percent) belonged to resistance groups (Table 5.10). Bystanders, by definition, did not belong to such groups. Among actives, by definition nonauthenticated helpers of Jews or participants in resistance, 70 percent belonged to resistance groups. Resistance groups whose objectives included helping Jews provided invaluable services; even those who were not officially concerned with Jews were sometimes helpful. But when the group's objectives did not include helping Jews, membership could also impede rescue since it might interfere with the group's primary objectives by deflecting human and material resources or by increasing the risks of participants. Arms provided to Jewish ghettos, for example, meant fewer arms for the planned Warsaw Uprising; shelters provided to Jews not only meant fewer shelters for fugitive members but also increased members risk. A sense of how rescue could conflict with resistance group activities is captured in this poignant story of an AK member and a Jewish child she found on the street:

> There was a little girl, dirty and in rags. The poor little one was walking. I felt so terribly sorry for her. I asked her, "Where are you from?" And she said, "From the ghetto." She was about eight or nine years old. And at that time we were all in hiding, my group and I. We hid at our printing house in Solna Street—we slept there, ate there, and everything. We had to change quarters constantly—we were

really homeless wanderers. So I brought her there and said that somehow we could help her, since she was blond haired. I said: "Boys, let's take care of her, and we'll manage somehow." And she stayed with us for a little while. We even taught her how to read. But then one of our mates said: "It's too risky. Do you know where she came from?" He kept on talking like this. So I finally agreed that she should leave, but I insisted that we not just abandon her but place her somewhere. So they found a place somewhere; I don't know where [Polish nonrescuer].

More important than formally organized resistance networks were the informal ones rescuers created out of their own contacts with families, friends, and others personally known to them. Relationships among informal networks were not governed by rules and regulations but were rather the product of emergent cooperative processes. Objectives in such groups were not determined by a remote leadership; rather, they emerged in the context of needs as participants defined them.

Nonrescuers had similar opportunities for creating informal networks. Similar percentages of nonrescuers were household heads (27 percent and 26 percent for all nonrescuers and bystanders respectively, 29 percent for rescuers), presumably able to command or convince their households to engage in rescue. Similar percentages report living with others (79 percent and 74 percent for all nonrescuers and bystanders respectively, 84 percent for rescuers). Similar proportions had neighbors nearby and family members living in the same community (53 percent and 55 percent for all nonrescuers and bystanders respectively, 45 percent for rescuers).

What apparently distinguished rescuers from nonrescuers was not access to, or potential for organizing, such informal networks, but rather the sentiments and behaviors of their networks—the types of people who comprised their most intimate contacts. More rescuers had reason to believe that their contacts would support them. More rescuers belonged to formal networks that shared their concerns about Jews. And more rescuers could assume that their families would help them if called on, because of their own activities. Sixty percent of rescuers' families had at least one member involved in rescue or resistance activities compared with 35 percent of nonrescuers' families—a statistically significant difference that becomes even more dramatic when compared with bystanders' families, among whom only 20 percent included such people (Table 5.10).

Were They Asked?

Alert to all instances of human suffering, certain individuals actively seek out the needy and devise means to help them. These are the initiators. Far more commonly, however, a helping response is the result of a specific event or request that compels attention. An abstract awareness of need becomes immediate when someone is asked for help and more immediate still when the asker is the actual victim rather than an intermediary acting on his or her behalf. A specific identifiable human being compels attention, even if only for the moment. Consequences are no longer associated with a conveniently distant group but are now imagined in relation to *this* face, *this* voice, *this* presence. Most rescuers waited to be asked, but many initiated helping on their own.

Approximately one-third (32 percent) of rescuers said they began helping Jews on their own initiative. Initiating took several forms. In some cases it meant organizing a semiformal or formal network, acquiring resources, and seeking out Jews in need:

> I started all alone to find shelter for Jewish people arriving in the southern part of France. I took several of them over the border to Switzerland. To bring people to the border, I needed others. So I contacted people I already knew. At the border I tried to find places for shelter so that I could bring them to Switzerland in the middle of the night. I also had to find people on the other border to keep an eye on the Germans. Most of the Jews did not know me at first. They simply approached me for help. But later I went looking for people who needed help. Those I helped told others about me. I was always very careful to see that I had the right people in my organization—people I could trust. I had my own money and paid my own expenses. Some people in my groups were businesspeople. Some of the rescuers involved in the team were also Jews. Two of my closest associates were Jews. Some people were ready to accept people in their homes and hide them. There were

some young men and girls who were enthusiastic but did not have much money. They helped take people from one place to another [Dutch rescuer in France].

It began in 1941 when I went to Poitiers, where my father-in-law had just died. I rented a little apartment and was looking for work. It was then that I became aware that in the street there were children wearing the yellow star. They were from the concentration camp on the road to Limoges, where they spent every night locked up under the guardianship of the French police. During the day they were supposed to go to Jewish families in the city of Poitiers; these families were supposed to feed them and to be responsible for returning them to the German authorities. But the children were stealing everything they could find on the streets. Many of them came from foreign countries, could not speak French, and were not allowed to talk to anyone and could not find their way. In spite of the fact that it was forbidden, and in spite of the risks, I took ten of them each day into my house. I taught them French, fed them, and we prayed. Their mothers were locked up in the camp and their fathers were working at the Mur de l'Atlantique [German coastal defenses].

I decided to set up my own system. I prepared a plan that I managed to pull off. I went to Chateauroux and took two of the boys with me. A friend, Mr. H., made me aware of the UGIF and the OSE—I had known nothing about them until then. He also introduced me to the Jewish population of Chateauroux and to a variety of other people. When I told them about the Jewish children, they were amazed—they were simply unaware of the great danger. I met Germaine Ribière and convinced her and Dr. Gaston Lévy of the danger. Germaine Ribière contacted Monseigneur Gerlier, who was the bishop of Lyon. Through his work with Les Amitiés Chrétiennes, he gave me the title "social worker" and provided me with the necessary money for my travels and food for the Jewish children I was placing with non-Jewish families [French rescuer].

In some cases it meant the search for a group or individual involved in rescue:

All Germans must have known what was going on with the
Jews. I was a mere housewife, but I had contact all the time
with people who were against Hitler. They told me the
most horrible things—transports, gas chambers, drownings,
gassing in trains—I knew that a huge injustice was taking
place. I felt tense; I couldn't sleep. I decided to go to the
parish minister. I could tell from his sermons that he was
on our side. So when he asked me whether I would help
some hidden Jews, I agreed [German rescuer].

I had a deep friendship with my classmate, a Jewish girl,
very exceptional. During my visit to Frankfurt in Germany,
I had stayed with a Jewish family. I saw some horrible
things. I saw some people coming back from the camps. I
was at the train station at Frankfurt when these people
were coming back. Some had very marked and bruised
faces, swollen legs—hardly a human face anymore. I was
very shocked by this. So, when the war started, I looked for
a way to help. Through Protestant friends—being
Protestant myself—I contacted La Cimade. I had already
been doing some things alone. But I preferred to join an
association, an organization to help people in danger
[French rescuer].

As soon as Zegota, the Council for Aid to Jews, was formed,
I contacted it. I was also in contact with the so-called Jewish
Department as the Chief Command of the Home Army. It
was my own initiative [Polish rescuer].

In several cases it meant offering help to a Jewish friend, acquaintance, or stranger without being asked:

In July 1942 we heard that they were going to start picking
up Jewish boys aged sixteen and up. Mrs. V.'s sister had a
boy of sixteen, and I was very worried about him. Before I
was married I had worked for Dr. V. in Amsterdam as a
dental assistant, and since we had become friends. On
Sunday, July 11, we went to the V.'s to visit and asked them
what Johnny was going to do. She said, "My brother-in-law
says maybe it will be just work camps. Maybe it will be
good for the boy." And I said, "How stupid can he get?! We
know several people who said they are destroying them."
So they said, "What can we do?" I said, "Well, we have a

home—a downstairs bedroom and bathroom. Why don't
you all come over to our place?" We all thought it would
be a matter of three weeks; instead it became nearly three
years [Dutch rescuer].

When I first became aware in 1940 that they were
persecuting the Jews, I contacted my friend, R. R. I said to
her. "R., you can't become an outcast. I'll look after you. I'll
register you at my place, and you'll stay with me." And so I
did. I registered her, and I got her a *Kennkarte,* and she
came to live with me [Polish rescuer].

Most rescuers (67 percent), however, waited to be asked, at
least the first time. Sometimes it was the victim him- or herself
who asked for help; most often, it was an intermediary acting on
the victim's behalf. Only 27 percent of rescuers who began their
helping activities in response to a request said the victim asked;
more than 70 percent were asked by intermediaries. Intermediaries may have included parents:

Four Jews stayed with me from 1942. Two were friends
from secondary school. They had been in touch with my
mother. She arranged to get them out of the Czestochowa
Ghetto and later handed them over to me [Polish rescuer].

A religious functionary:

It was initiated by the Bekennende Kirche [Lutheran
Confessing Church]. One evening, the curate from another
village asked if I would take some Jews for a while. I said,
"Yes, they may come" [German rescuer].

A Jewish acquaintance acting on behalf of other Jews:

Through Leon Poliakov, we met André Bass, who was the
commander of the Action Group Against Deportation. Bass
asked him to save Jews—to go and get them from the Midi
[Southern France]. My husband said, "All I can do for you,
I will" [French rescuer].

A Jewish stranger similarly acting on behalf of others:

It was in the winter of 1942 or 1943. I had a visit from a
young Jewish doctor. Someone must have spoken to him
about me. He contacted me—I didn't ask who sent him.
Really a very charming man. He asked for my help to

rescue eighty Jewish children who were being taken to
Vichy by the Germans. That's how it started [French
rescuer].

A relative:

A niece of mine said: "Tante, can you give some help for a
little while? I have a little Jewish boy. We already have so
many that we need a place for him." "Yes," I said, "for a
while" [Dutch rescuer].

A resistance network contact:

Jo came to our place. She came by bus. The mother of her
sister's husband, who was Aryan, contacted a doctor in
Friesland who was in the organization. They sent Jo to us
[Dutch rescuer].

A teacher:

A high school teacher came to see us one day. He said he
had a German Jewish student who needed help [French
rescuer].

A government official:

A Belgian senator introduced me to Mr. L. S. [French
rescuer].

Or a friend:

My girlfriend came and said to me, "Thea, I have a little
girl. Her father was shot to death, her mother fled with her
brother, and she stuffed her in a closet to hide her." So I
said, "Okay, bring her." She was a little Jewish girl, four
years old [Dutch rescuer].

Once they agreed, rescuers found themselves experiencing
the "foot in the door" phenomenon. Those they helped brought
or sent others. Intermediaries who had received an affirmative answer once came again. Those who were asked would frequently
initiate requests from others. Many rescuers were asked more than
once; several were asked repeatedly.

Did rescuers ever say no? Approximately 15 percent said they
did, on at least one occasion. The reasons varied. Sometimes they
did not trust the person who was asking. A common ruse used by

Germans was to coerce or bribe others to seek out would-be rescuers by asking for help. Sometimes it was a matter of risk:

> I told them that I had to stop for a few months because it
> was too dangerous. The Gestapo was looking for me and I
> had to hide. I reorganized later and started up again with a
> friend [French rescuer].

Some simply put limits on their responsibilities:

> With every new person we accepted, those who were
> already there were threatened. The danger to my family
> would have been disproportionately great. We had taken
> on enough responsibilities already [German rescuer].

> My brother-in-law had married a Jewish girl, and he asked
> me to help his wife and her parents. I refused. It was his
> duty to help them—not mine. He would be having all the
> fun, while I would be having all the responsibility [Polish
> rescuer].

On rare occasions, it was an ideological issue:

> My friend asked me to help his friend's in-laws, who were
> in the ghetto. These were very rich people. I told him I was
> only helping the poor and advised him to go to the people
> who get paid for helping. The rich had ways of getting help
> the poor did not have. The poor were our members and
> party comrades; they were the ones who were primarily
> concerned with fighting for freedom [Polish rescuer].

But most commonly, it was lack of resources:

> A Jewish mother with a nine-year-old child came to rent a
> room, but all were taken. She left and poisoned her child
> and committed suicide out of desperation. Before she
> killed herself, she told people that I had given her humane
> treatment that made her last a few more days. I didn't have
> space for her. I didn't know that she was in such a tragic
> state [Polish rescuer].

> Our house was filled up. We had a small house and we
> couldn't have more [rescuer].

Nonrescuers, too, were asked for help, although significantly
less frequently than rescuers. Approximately 25 percent of all non-

rescuers were asked to help, and approximately 20 percent responded to such requests. (Bystanders, by definition, did not respond to such requests.) What distinguished the responses of active
respondents from most rescuers', however, was that their help
tended to be brief and, in a few cases, was given for payment:

> The Jews were employed in this factory, and a girl whom I
> befriended then asked me to buy her a carp for a holiday
> feast. She wanted to spend this holiday with her parents,
> who were already old. I was afraid to carry it to the factory
> because the *Volksdeutsche* kept an eye on us, watching
> whether we brought in any food. One could not bring
> much at a time, but one could always pretend that one was
> carrying one's lunch. A young boy asked me to bring him
> meat, chops or something. My mother cooked, and I would
> bring it for him. He had nobody else to help him. They
> could not survive on their rations [Polish active
> nonrescuer].

> I had a Jewish friend who was attending first-aid courses
> with me. She came by to see me at dinnertime. She told me
> that she had just escaped. The news distressed me a bit; it
> is not comfortable to share one's bed with some other
> person. Perhaps one could manage one night but hardly
> any longer. I found her another place. When the Jews were
> thrown out of Otwock, a friend asked me to shelter a girl
> for one night. I agreed and next morning I left for work. I
> had to. The girl was very frightened. She asked whether she
> might draw the curtains. I said, "Do what you want." I had
> to leave her alone—I could not do otherwise. After hours, I
> escorted her to others [Polish active nonrescuer].

> A Jew stayed in my flat for three months. It was impossible
> to stretch it any longer. I was single then. I never knew his
> real name—we had never met before. He spent three
> months in my place, and then he went to stay with a
> colleague of mine, S. And that's the last I heard of him
> [Polish active nonrescuer].

> I had a friend who had a Jewish friend. I agreed to take his
> daughter to our house. She was ten years old, a beautiful
> girl. They brought her over. I had her for two weeks but
> she wanted to go back. About three days before the Jewish

uprising, I called her father. The father was pleading with her to stay with me. But she went back [Polish active nonrescuer].

We were very good friends with one Jewish couple—very close friends. I used to keep their baby overnight because they were afraid of being picked up by the Germans. They asked my husband to put the baby on the doorstep of some other good friends who had agreed to adopt it. We went out at night and did it. The couple went into hiding and almost made it; they were discovered a couple of months before the war ended. The baby, I think, made it [Dutch active nonrescuer].

In a few cases, Jews were being sheltered by the active respondent's parents and help was enlisted from time to time. A Polish AK member whose parents were involved describes a most unusual form of help:

During the first evacuation of the ghetto in 1942, the wife and two beautiful daughters of a dentist—a friend of my family—were deported to Treblinka. One of the girls had taught me French during the first year of the occupation. The dentist was of course very worried; he was told they were going to Palestine to be resettled. Outside the ghetto we suspected something different. We knew the trains were going somewhere near Treblinka. The dentist stayed in the ghetto. He wanted to know where the family went. Being a Boy Scout, I volunteered to trace the train. Nowadays, I consider this suicidal. I went to the railway station and asked for a round-trip ticket to Treblinka. They looked at me in disbelief. I actually took the train. I got out at the station and walked to some farmer's house. I can't believe today that I did this. I asked the farmer what was going on. I saw the trains passing by and backing up inside the camp. People in the trains were begging for water, and nobody could approach them because there were Germans with machine guns sitting on top of the trains. I knew I had bad news for the dentist and his son [Polish active nonrescuer].

Like rescuers, actives who were involved in helping Jews were either asked by Jews themselves or by intermediaries acting on their behalf. Although help was extended reluctantly in some of the above cases, respondents did fulfill what was asked of them, entirely or in part. Several actives might even qualify as Yad Vashem rescuers with the appropriate documentation from those they helped. But what distinguishes most actives who did respond from most rescuers is the degree of responsibility assumed and the length of time they persisted at their tasks.

Approximately 10 percent of nonrescuers said they refused help when asked. The reasons they gave for their refusal to help ranged from lack of interest and involvement in other things to feelings of impotence and risk:

> I did not want to get involved in helping Jews. I wanted to help the Polish villagers [Polish nonrescuer].

> A Jewish woman asked me to carry something to another place for her. I couldn't do it because I was too busy [Polish nonrescuer].

> If they asked for help and I could do it, I would; but if I couldn't, I wouldn't. Sometimes people would ask me for something, and then I would say to them, "This is war." I just didn't have the right connections [Belgian nonrescuer].

> We were all busy with just surviving. There was so much misery around, and one just couldn't do anything [Dutch nonrescuer].

> I didn't want to jeopardize the lives of my family [Polish nonrescuer].

> A Jewish man asked me to help a girlfriend of his. I couldn't do it because my neighbor knew her. The Jew I knew because I sold him bricks. I didn't want to risk my family's lives. They would have been better off hiding in a safer place in the villages. I did suggest that to them [Polish nonrescuer].

In view of rescuers' formal and informal networks, which included larger percentages of people sympathetic to rescue activity, it seems understandable that they would be asked for help more frequently than others. In view of the fact, however, that the majority of nonrescuers lived among Jews immediately before the war, and that many of them had Jewish friends, it is not quite clear why more of them were not asked by Jews themselves. One plausible explanation is that they had already communicated, by word, deed, or attitude, that they would not be receptive to such requests. Nonrescuers active in general resistance may have communicated the message that their duties were already sufficient or in some way incompatible with rescue. Bystanders may simply have retreated from their acquaintances, removing themselves from further contacts with Jews—and others—as conditions worsened. Those who had lived among Jews but had not previously befriended them would have little motivation for doing so as the costs of any contacts increased. And it is also possible that other nonrescuers were indeed asked for help and, having refused, may have suppressed such memories. Finally, we cannot discount the possibility that being asked was simply a matter of chance.

Whatever the reason, the absence of requests for help does not fully explain the inaction of nonrescuers in light of the fact that many rescuers initiated help without being asked. And although being asked facilitated responding, even here opportunity may have been foreshadowed by the respondents' communicated receptivity to intermediaries and Jews alike. Thus, external opportunity, including knowledge, risk, material resources, and being asked, did not alone determine who acted to save Jews and who stood by.

CHAPTER 6

The Key to Altruism: Values of Caring

My father said the whole world is one big chain. One little part breaks and the chain is broken and it won't work anymore [Johan].

Rescuers did not simply happen on opportunities for rescue; they actively created, sought, or recognized them where others did not. Their participation was not determined by circumstances but their own personal qualities. Chance sometimes provided rescuers like Johan with an opportunity to help, but it was the values learned from their parents which prompted and sustained their involvement.[1]

Johan was seventeen in 1941 when the Germans drafted him for compulsory labor in Germany. Rather than comply with the order, he decided to evade it and hid in his aunt's house for about three months. Warned that the police had learned of his whereabouts, he sought shelter in a small town sixty miles outside Amsterdam. There he contacted an underground network to help him, and from them he learned about "Grandpa Bakker" and his wife "Aunt Corr." It was through the Bakkers that Johan became involved in helping Jews. Johan's first concern was finding shelter for himself, and he was very grateful when Grandpa Bakker took him in without any questions. The Bakkers were hiding more than eighty Jews on their property, and there were lots of chores to do. After six months he decided to become a formal member of their organization. He remained with the Bakkers until October 1944, when the Germans surrounded the camp and murdered Grandpa Bakker. But Johan, along with most of the Jews in hiding, managed to escape. He went back to his hometown and stayed with his parents until liberation.

Life with Grandpa Bakker was highly risky; a camp with more

than eighty Jews was clearly a dangerous place to be. Although a
fugitive himself, Johan could have asked his underground connections to place him elsewhere. Many Dutch families cooperated in
hiding young Dutchmen like Johan. Asked why he chose to remain, Johan said:

> The main reason was because I was a patriot. I was for my
> country. I was for law and order. The Germans robbed
> people of their freedom. And when they started taking the
> Jewish people, that really lit my fire. They took them like
> sheep, throwing them into trains. I couldn't stand it
> anymore. I really became full of hate because they took
> innocent people—especially when they took little kids.
> That was the worst. They took innocent people and I
> wanted to help.

Patriotism, law and order were among the first reasons Johan
gave for helping Jews—values invoked by numerous groups, including those who have destroyed freedom and persecuted minorities. For Johan, however, these words had special meaning. For
Johan, they were associated with freedom, justice, a fierce egalitarianism, caring for others, and a particular sense of obligation
toward the needy and helpless. The latter, barely implied in the
reasons he gives for his impassioned hatred of Nazis, became
sharply clear when he described the most important things he
learned about life from his parents.

His mother, he said, taught him never to regard others as infe-
riors. "She would never look down on people. She would always
appreciate what people were worth, and it didn't matter whether
they were poor or whatever." And his father, whom he regarded
as his close friend and the most important person in his life, communicated the same message even more strongly.

> He taught me never to forget where you came from; to
> always appreciate anything from anybody. He impressed on
> me never to forget that when you work for yourself and
> have people under you, don't look down on them. Be
> honest and straightforward. See other people as your
> friends. All people are people.

Egalitarianism and the basic universal similarity of all people
also underlay his and his family's attitudes toward Jews. "Jews," he
said, "were just people. We neither looked down on them nor did

we look up to them. We never felt they were any different." Johan's politics and those of his family reflected this outlook. Although neither he nor his parents were politically active, they considered themselves members of the Christian Democratic Union, a political group with democratic principles.

Christianity was also a very important part of Johan's life, but for him it meant primarily caring for the needy. Johan described his parents as very religious. As for himself, he went to church regularly in his youth and attended Bible classes, but he regarded these activities as largely duties. "I was not very religious when I was growing up," he said. "I had to go to church, and I learned the Bible in Bible class. But I thought it was a big drag learning the catechism. I believed in God, though." His grandfather epitomized his religious principles:

> My grandfather was the most religious man I knew. I had more respect for him than for the minister. He practiced what he preached. He visited the sick; he went to the church to get money for poor people. That's the kind of character he was.

In Johan's view, love of country, law and order, politics, and religion converged into fundamental ethical principles characterized by two strands: inclusiveness—a predisposition to regard all people as equals and to apply similar standards of right and wrong to them without regard to social status or ethnicity—and attachment—a belief in the value of personal relationships and caring for the needy. He credited both to his parental home.

As was true for Johan, the basic values and attitudes of rescuers and nonrescuers alike toward Nazis, Jews, religion, and politics anticipated and shaped their wartime activities and behavior toward Jews.

There was a direct connection between hating Nazis and helping Jews. As one rescuer explained it: "I helped Jews because I really hated the Nazis. The more revenge I could take, the better." Helping Jews was a way of resisting an oppressive regime. A few rescued survivors also believed their rescuers were essentially motivated by their hostility toward Nazis:

> He explained it to me in very simple words: "I decided to fight the Germans by saving those persecuted by them. Who were the most persecuted? The Jews."

Anna wanted to fight the hated Germans, and keeping Jews presented the way. She would have helped anyone—not especially Jews.

The overwhelming majority of rescuers and nonrescuers alike were hostile toward Nazis from the start. The dominant motifs among rescuers and nonrescuers to the Nazi takeovers of their countries were despair, impotence, and rage.

Despair was somewhat more characteristic of the French:

We are done for—we'll all be deported to Germany [rescuer].

Heavy heart—very upset [rescuer].

No hope [nonrescuer].

Greatest fright of my life [nonrescuer].

Anger was somewhat more characteristic of the Dutch:

I hated them—every bit of them [rescuer].

I would have loved to kill them all [rescuer].

Very angry, very rebellious [nonrescuer].

More convinced than others of their own invulnerability, many Poles were shocked:

I thought we would be able to stop them fast [rescuer].

I was fooled by our leaders—cheated. I thought we were well prepared and well armed [rescuer].

I thought we would beat them—like most of us [nonrescuer].

I was sure Poland would win [nonrescuer].

I was as stupid as I could be. I was so sure we would be the winners. My idiotic thought was wearing a uniform! First I didn't believe there would be a war. Then I believed strongly that Poland, in alliance with England and France, would be the winner. There was nothing in my mind to doubt the length of the war. It would be very short. We were going to give the Germans a lesson [nonrescuer].

A few hoped for the best—a short occupation followed by defeat:

> I realized that they were powerful, but I was an optimist. I thought God was going to help us [rescuer].

> I didn't think it would last so long [rescuer].

Germans emphasized the need to suppress their feelings:

> I was outraged—but we had to be quiet [rescuer].

> I howled and cried with rage. My husband kept telling me not to cry because there was nothing I could do [rescuer].

But for a significantly larger percent of bystanders (20 percent compared with 7 percent of rescuers), the reactions were qualitatively different (Table 6.1). They expressed greater equivocation, passivity, accommodation—and in one case, exultation:

> I felt some doubt about whether it was right.

> I did not perceive much. I was only seventeen years old. I was not really for the Nazis.

> [I felt] nothing!

> They promised us a lot—economic advantages, contracts. I felt close to them because of my German heritage.

> I had a feeling of triumph.

Acceptance of or accommodation to Nazi authority helps explain why some bystanders engaged neither in general resistance nor in helping Jews. But, for most bystanders, failure to act appeared to have other causes. Despite their hostility toward Nazis, the majority of bystanders were overcome by fear, hopelessness, and uncertainty. These feelings, which encourage self-centeredness and emotional distancing from others, provide fertile soil for passivity. Survival of the self assumes paramount importance. This was the characteristic response of most bystanders. Asked to describe their lives during the war, their stories are brief and overwhelmingly involved with basic survival:

> During the war, we had very bad conditions. We were very poor. My parents couldn't support themselves because they, too, were dislocated from their jobs. Even my grandmother

was no longer able to be self-supporting. She was with us until she died shortly before the war ended.

I was working at odd jobs—I worked at the hospital, where I cleaned and washed patients, helped with the cooking, and also did janitorial work. Because of the food shortage, I would go to villages and try to buy eggs and flour or wheat. Whenever I could, I would bring the peasants stuff from the city, such as needles, which were badly needed, and often oil—for oil lamps. So I spent my time making some sort of a living. My wife did some mending. She used to sew dresses and other items of clothing from drapes or any old clothes that were too big for people. She could cut them and make them into new clothes or make alterations and repairs. We were lucky to have received an old Singer sewing machine, which operated very efficiently, from my grandfather [Polish male].

We were on a dairy farm. We always had enough milk. During the war I learned how to make cheese. We lived rather well. When I worked away from home, I worked for farmers who grew different crops. After a day's work, you didn't get paid in money but in wheat or barley or what have you. So we lived rather well. It was against the rules to take this stuff and use it for your own, but we took chances. My dad wasn't very brave. He never sold any livestock for the black market. Some people did this and got a fair amount of money for it. My dad did sell part of his milk to people coming from Amsterdam. It was tough for a lot of people. We weren't eating rich or throwing any food away, but we lived rather well compared to some people [Dutch male].

I was busy trying to make sure that we had enough food to feed the sixty-eight people residing in the community monastery. We grew our own food because there was a great shortage of food. My responsibility, put on me by the abbot, was to be responsible for the food supply. I had to try to acquire food from the surrounding villages, especially eggs and milk. The civilian population suffered a lot because the Nazis made demands on the entire population. Not just labor and building fortifications, but also materials such as cement, lumber, and so on. In addition, the hardship consisted of constant German surveillance because they feared Allied spies and informers. Sometimes they would be suspicious of our monastery and ask us if we were hiding shot-down Allied pilots. It was scary sometimes during those searches. I did the best I could to carry out my assignment [French male].

Before the war, I was employed at an inn—I helped with the management of the household and the butcher shop. I continued in this work during the war. The butcher was drafted, so I had to help with everything. There was a lot of work to do. I worked from six in the morning until ten at night. I was happy when the work was done. I was not concerned with other affairs. There was continuous work by the hour. My friends and brothers were drafted. My brother was released because of illness. I had no blood relatives at the front [German female].

When war was declared, my mother and I were in the Auvergne. We went back to Orléans, but soon left to live with relatives in Boulogne. In August, we went back to the Auvergne. In October 1940 we returned once again to Orléans, and the month after, I left for Paris without my mother. There I lived in a boardinghouse and studied to get a degree in science. I studied hard and worked on my thesis until 1943.

At the university the atmosphere was more studious than political. Sometimes my friends and I talked about politics. We were against collaboration and criticized the French government's politics and Pétain. I thought about joining the resistance, but fear kept me from doing anything.

In November 1944 I was accepted as a chemist at the Institut de Récherche des Huiles de Palmes. The institute's laboratory was funded by the Centre Nationale de Récherche Scientifique [French female].

Actives and rescuers chose to express their anger. Most actives aimed their hostility directly at their oppressors—sabotaging their machinery, ambushing them if it was necessary and opportune, or engaging them in open battle. More than a third (37 percent) of actives said their resistance was based on their hatred of Nazis. Far fewer rescuers (17 percent) focused on their hatred of Nazis as even one of their reasons for rescuing Jews (Table 6.2). An even smaller percentage of rescued survivors (11 percent) said their rescuers were motivated by their hatred of Nazis (Table 6.2). Thus, hostility toward Nazis accompanied rescue and facilitated it but was not sufficient to explain it.

Whereas hostility toward Nazis could result in passivity or resistance, rescue itself implied some basic acceptance of Jews. As one Polish resistance member explained it: "I wanted to fight the Nazis, but I had no interest in Jews." His perception of Jews' irrelevance had begun early in life, when his parents had emphasized that Jews were rich and shrewd and, above all, how different they were from Poles. The attitudes and experience of this active nonrescuer underscore that how one perceives the victims is an important element in making a decision to help, and that parents play a major role in shaping such perceptions.

In general, victims perceived as attractive and innocent are more likely to receive help than others. Physical attributes, such as beauty and vigor, contribute to a positive perception. A belief in the victim's innocence strengthens the tendency to help him or her. Innocence implies that it is not inherent character flaws but external circumstances that are responsible for someone's victimization. Experimental data suggest that people perceived as lazy[2] or drunk,[3] for example, are less likely to receive help than those who are perceived as industrious and sober. On the whole, children are more readily presumed innocent than are adults. To some extent this may be connected to their physical appearance, for even adults with childlike features are generally perceived as more kindly and attractive than others.[4]

Nazi propaganda portrayed all Jews as genetically flawed in both character and physical appearance. Resistance to this widely disseminated message was more likely if countervailing notions had been taught in the parental home. One would assume that individuals whose parents had emphasized the special attractiveness of Jews would be more likely to perceive them as innocent victims, worthy of help.

In fact, however, rescuers' parents were no different from nonrescuers' parents with respect to communicating positive perceptions of Jews. Where they differed significantly from others was in their greater consciousness of Jews, their less frequent communication of negative Jewish images, and their greater inclination to assess Jews as individuals rather than as group members.

Jews were an unknown group to some parents of both rescuers and nonrescuers. "My parents never even knew Jews existed," said one French rescuer, "until after the war started." For some others "Jewishness" was not distinct enough to warrant special attention. "We didn't know whether people were Jewish or not, and we never talked about it," said several rescuers and nonrescuers alike. Frequently, such comments were accompanied by the statement that "For us, people were just people." Rescuers' parents, however, were significantly more explicitly attentive to Jews than were nonrescuers' parents. Whereas 74 percent of the former had spoken about Jews, only 54 percent of bystanders' (and 59 percent of all nonrescuers') parents had done so.

The majority of rescuers and nonrescuers did recall either some parental experiences with, or statements about, Jews. The differences between them did not lie in expression of positive views, however, but in the absence of negative ones. Recollection of positive parental experiences or relationships with Jews was similar for rescuers and nonrescuers alike (44 percent for rescuers, 38 percent for nonrescuers, 36 percent for bystanders). "We had good Jewish neighbors," "My mother's best friend was a Jew," "My father was able to get credit more easily from the Jewish shopkeeper" are characteristic comments. Similar percentages of rescuers and nonrescuers offered no evaluative comments regarding such experiences; they simply noted that they had Jewish neighbors or had shopped at Jewish stores. But significantly fewer rescuers recalled negative experiences. Whereas only 3 percent of rescuers made comments such as "Mother was cheated by a Jew" or "My father did not like our Jewish neighbors," approximately 10 percent of nonrescuers made such comments.

Several respondents mentioned parental positive stereotypes of Jews as "intelligent," "hardworking," "honest," and "helpful." There were no significant differences between groups on this measure. Negative stereotypes, such as "dishonest," "untrustworthy," "unpatriotic," "cowardly," and "too powerful," however, were significantly less often reported by rescuers (3 percent, compared with 10 percent for all nonrescuers and 16 percent for bystanders). In fact, rescuers' parents made significantly fewer stereotypic comments of any type (12 percent compared with 21 percent for all nonrescuers and 24 percent for bystanders) (see Table 6.3). One of the pernicious consequences of stereotypes—positive or negative—is to obscure and dehumanize the individual, by casting him or her as a "sample specimen" of a prejudged group.[5] Members of the group become mere "statistics, commodities or interchangeable pieces."[6] Thus, because rescuers' parents were less likely to stereotype Jews, rescuers more often learned to judge Jews as individuals and avoid blanket condemnations.

The intensity of feelings also differed between rescuers and nonrescuers' parents who expressed negative views. Rescuers generally contented themselves with one or two negative comments, whereas nonrescuers typically noted three or four:

RESCUERS

Before the war, my father worked for a Jew—the Jew was a dealer. My father didn't say anything special about Jews. Sometimes he used to say—about those he didn't like—that they were misers [Polish].

My father said Jews as businesspeople had excessive influence. The Mannheim department stores were all owned by Jews [German].

I heard about the Dreyfus affair at home. My parents thought he was guilty. Other than the Dreyfus affair, my father didn't talk about Jews very much. He said that Jews had a sense for business [French].

In our district there were very few Jews—only three thousand out of one-half million Poles in the county.

NONRESCUERS

I don't mean this in a bad way, but Jews were considered rather a cowardly people. They would rather talk themselves out of anything than fight. Jews were too smart to fight. Also, anytime that you dealt with a Jew—I hate the word Jew, it sounds so rotten—but if you were buying or selling to them, you knew beforehand that you would be cheated because they were smarter than you. There was a big market in Amsterdam where you could buy anything. It was almost completely Jews. If you were buying a shirt he would say, "Oh, it looks fine," but the shirt wouldn't fit too well. You were pretty dumb if you went there to shop, but the greed of the public led them to those merchants because they were always

RESCUERS

NONRESCUERS

I never heard anything bad about Jews in West Poland—the worst anti-Semitism was in central Poland. The first Polish Jew I met was on an excursion to Warsaw when I was sixteen years old. My brother prepared me. He told me that Jews had a different religion and that I was not to be shocked at their different appearance. He told me that I cannot be a racist—that the worst thing was to be a racist [Polish].

cheaper. But you opened yourself up to some form of cheating, and people would bitch and gripe—but there was no animosity against the Jews because you knew that. If a Jewish guy is in a pushcart and it breaks down—I actually saw this happen—well, Amsterdam people are pretty helpful, and people would try to help him and then the Jewish guy would sit back and he would say, "Let the gentleman go on, he knows what he's doing." And pretty soon everyone is working on his pushcart, and he's standing there watching it. But once they went to Israel, then they became fighters. I wish the hell sometimes we had those Jewish fighters here in this country because they are entirely different. I was surprised—really surprised—that they could do so much with the fighting spirit compared to our experiences before the war. I think it was because they felt they were just tolerated and no more than that [Dutch].

My mother told me that they are strange people who were good businesspeople. Sometimes they could take

NONRESCUERS

advantage of you. They kept
to themselves. My father
told me that they didn't
believe in Christ. They also
showed a great ability for
business. Of course, they
looked quite different from
Poles. They wore special
kinds of clothes and had
beards and sideburns. There
were two hundred tenants
in the apartment house in
which we lived, and there
were two types of people.
The Jewish people's way of
living was different from
ours. It was not a question
of religion, but they didn't
consider themselves Poles.
In gymnasium [high school]
there was probably a
majority of Jews. But this
was a different group. Most
of them were upper class.
They were Poles with a
Jewish face and I accepted
them; I had many friends
among them. In the
apartment house it was
different. They were like
foreigners. They spoke
Polish with an accent
[Polish].

No rescuer reported hearing demonic qualities attributed to
Jews, as these nonrescuers did:

My father told me that they didn't belong with us because
of their religion. It is embodied in their faith that a Jew

may commit any wickedness, but not toward another Jew. This is written in their Bible, in their Talmud [German].

My mother had a good attitude toward Jews. I used to go to a Jewish store. But I was afraid when I saw Jews pray. A Jewish lady comforted me with some candy. But I had heard that when Jews bake matzos, they put children's blood in it [Polish].

And no rescuer suggested that Jews deserved their cruel fate, as this nonrescuer did:

There were practically no Jews in the town we lived in. My father didn't "discuss" Jews, but he had lots of contacts with them because he controlled the movie distribution. He would make some remarks—and they weren't always flattering towards Jews. I think they were always based on fact. I don't think there was much anti-Semitism in Holland. There were some remarks—and I still believe Jews do a lot of things to deserve those remarks—not the general population, but as individuals. Like I said, I have Jewish friends. But to some extent, they have brought the wrath of the world upon themselves, and still do [Dutch].

While most rescuers did not see Jews as a benighted group, neither did they regard them as exalted or uniquely worthy of help. As a few noted explicitly, "I did not help them because they were Jews." Yet, there are some exceptions. A handful of rescued survivors did see their rescuers as having a special feeling for Jews: "She did everything for the love of the Jewish people" said one, while another perceived it as his rescuer's desire to save the Jewish nation. For some Dutch Reformed rescuers, all Jews had special merit regardless of the behaviors or attributes of individuals, for it was bestowed by God himself:

When it came to the Jewish people, we were brought up by a tradition in which we had learned that the Jewish people were the people of the Lord.

The main reason is because we know that they are the chosen people of God. We had to save them. We thought we had to do it—and then you risk everything according to that.

Like I told you, we always liked the Jewish people because the Jewish people are God's people.

The significance of religion in the decision to rescue was not confined to Dutch Reformed rescuers alone. Religion, God, or Christianity was cited by 15 percent of rescuers—Catholics and Protestants of different denominations—as at least one of their reasons for helping Jews. "I did it out of Christian duty," "I know God would have wanted me to," "I am an obedient Christian; the Lord wanted us to rescue those people and we did," are representative comments. An even larger percentage of rescued survivors (26 percent) perceived religion as a primary motive for their rescuers (Table 6.2):

If they hadn't been religious, they wouldn't have rescued any Jews.

My wife for a while was with a family in Friesland—very pious, observant Protestants who thought it was Jesus' command to help Jews.

They were true Christians who took the risk of taking us in.

They were performing a great deed without any ulterior motives, and their goodness was truly rare. I constantly had evidence of their kindness, and I know that it stemmed largely from their deep faith.

Julian was a very good and decent man. He said that Judaism was the origin of all religions and that the Jews were chosen by God as the first people of the world.

He did it because it was the right thing to do according to his religious beliefs.

For rescuers who cited religion as a least one of their reasons for helping, it appeared obvious that Christianity required them to do so. But in actuality interpretations of Christianity are as varied as human beings themselves. As Adorno and his associates found about forty years ago,[7] and others have confirmed since, one's identification with a religious body does not ensure that one will endorse values of tolerance and brotherhood. In fact, several studies suggest an inverse relationship: More intense religiosity is frequently associated with greater prejudice.[8]

That religious affiliation per se did not distinguish between rescuers and nonrescuers is suggested by their similar religious backgrounds. The overwhelming majority in both groups (approximately 90 percent) said they were affiliated with religious institutions while growing up. The majority were Catholic (62 percent of rescuers, 72 percent of nonrescuers), the remainder Protestant (32 and 23 percent respectively) or nonaffiliated. Approximately 45 percent of the respondents in both groups attended a parochial elementary school (Table 6.4). Nor did the parents of rescuers and nonrescuers, or rescuers and nonrescuers themselves, differ in the intensity of their religious commitments. In statistically similar distributions, rescuers and nonrescuers ranked their most influential person, father, and mother as very religious, somewhat religious, not very religious, and not at all religious. Forty-nine percent of rescuers and 43 percent of nonrescuers perceived their mothers as very religious; less than 5 percent in both groups said their mothers were "not at all" religious. Fathers were perceived as less religious generally—approximately 33 percent of rescuers said their fathers were very religious compared with 22 percent of nonrescuers; somewhat more than 10 percent in both groups saw their fathers as "not at all" religious (Table 6.5). In similar percentages, their parents had emphasized church attendance, prayer, and God. Approximately 15 percent in both groups identified religion as a primary value learned from their most influential person or a parent (Table 6.7). In statistically similar distributions, too, rescuers and nonrescuers ranked themselves as very religious, somewhat religious, not very religious, or not at all religious while growing up and before the war (Table 6.6).

Bystanders, however, were significantly less religious than rescuers in their early years, although not immediately before the war (Table 6.6). Their fathers, too, were significantly less religious than the fathers of rescuers (Table 6.5).

At best, however, religiosity was only weakly related to rescue. Overall, rescuers did not differ significantly from bystanders or all nonrescuers with respect to their religious identification, religious education, and their own religiosity or that of their parents.

But rescuers did differ from others in their interpretation of religious teaching and religious commitment, which emphasized the common humanity of all people and therefore supported efforts to help Jews:

My background is Christian Reformed; Israel has a special meaning for me. We have warm feelings for Israel—but that means the whole human race. That is the main principal point.

I have always considered all people regardless of their nationality, ethnic origins or race, religion, and so on, as members of one great family: mankind. This feeling has deep roots in Polish tradition, history, Christian teaching, and the attitudes of my parents and their predecessors.

They taught me about God and respect for human beings— to respect others.

They taught me ethics, being tolerant, honesty, and responsibility—everything that the Catholic religion taught.

Like religion, the meaning of patriotism has varied depending on individual interpretation. Conventional notions of patriotism had little to do with rescue. Only 8 percent of rescuers said that patriotism was even one of their reasons for helping Jews. Only 1 percent of rescued survivors thought patriotism was a motivating force for their rescuers (Table 6.2). In its more conventional sense, patriotism was understood to mean a direct engagement with the enemy. Many participants in general resistance ascribed their activities to patriotic motivations. Forty-four percent of actives said that patriotism was their major motivator (Table 6.2). Conventional patriotic notions thus appeared to be more associated with fighting the enemy than with rescuing Jews.

For a group of Polish rescuers and nonrescuers, patriotism was strongly associated with Polish culture and maintaining Poland's physical existence as a national entity. Some Poles, rescuers and nonrescuers alike, emphasized that they had learned these values in their parental homes:

I learned to love my country—Poland and its people. When we were in Germany, he taught me Polish verses, the history of Poland, and geography [rescuer].

I learned about patriotism and knowledge of Polish history [rescuer].

Patriotism—he instilled in me the need to be a good Pole and a good soldier in the future [rescuer].

She often talked to me about Poland—about the history of Poland. She taught me the greatness of Poland and the beauty of Poland. She taught me to be patriotic. We should always be proud of being Poles and to defend it against all enemies [nonrescuer].

Mother was very patriotic. I was given some kind of love of the country—a pride in wearing the uniform. I would go to national parades with mother and father. She was responsible for my going into the Boy Scouts, and I had a chance to learn about loving my country in scouting. My father always thought I would be loyal if my country needed me [nonrescuer].

My mother was a good Pole. She often remembered her grandfather, a participant in the 1863 uprising, and in this way she developed patriotism in me. From my father I learned a love for the Fatherland—to keep my honor as a Pole—not to be a traitor [nonrescuer].

Honor, fighting, and war are central themes in these statements, confirming Jan Tomasz Gross' characterization of Polish patriotism.[9] Poles, he says, were subjected to a type of "heroic socialization" in which war was glorified as representing a period of heroism and action as contrasted with the routine cunning and greed that characterized peacetime life. This tradition facilitated participation in general resistance but was not particularly conducive to rescue except insofar as it could be considered an act of military cooperation. And in fact, Poles who cited patriotism as one of their reasons for helping Jews often tended to see it in this way. "It was an act of cooperation," said one Polish male who was a member of the Jewish Military Organization (a Jewish fighting group), while another maintained that "some of our Jews were patriots too," since they were also involved in Poland's liberation struggle.

In general, however, patriotism was not emphasized in the parental homes of either rescuers or nonrescuers. Only a small percentage of rescuers and nonrescuers alike (8 and 4 percent, respectively) said they learned patriotism from their most influential parent or role model (Table 6.7a).

Yet rescuers and nonrescuers alike valued patriotism similarly. The majority in both groups (65 and 68 percent, respectively) said they were very patriotic in their youth, and only a small minority in both groups (less than 10 percent) regarded themselves as only slightly or not at all patriotic.

But in the view of more rescuers, patriotism appeared to encompass national acceptance of pluralistic and diverse groups in relationships of equality rather than mere tolerance. This, however, is more apparent from their political affiliations, as well as those of their parents, than from any articulated views about the nature of patriotism itself.

Only 21 percent of rescuers said they belonged to a political party before the war (the Dutch were overrepresented and the French underrepresented in this group). Nonrescuers were similarly apolitical: Eleven percent of all controls and 10 percent of bystanders reported a prewar political affiliation (Table 6.8). As for their parents, similar percentages of rescuers, all nonrescuers, and bystanders reported that at least one parent was politically affiliated before the war (29 percent, 20 percent, and 20 percent, respectively). (See Table 6.9.) On the whole, then, the majority of rescuers and nonrescuers were themselves not very concerned with politics, and the same was true for their parents. Among those who were, rescuers and their parents were more likely to belong to democratic political groups.

Communist and Socialist parties, especially those in which Jews were involved before the war, were helpful in rescue.[10] Communists played a prominent role in many resistance activities. Even among their detractors, several of whom include rescuers and nonrescuers, the virtues of Communists in general resistance were frequently extolled. Nonetheless, only 28 percent of all politically affiliated rescuers in our sample reported being affiliated with the economic left before the war, and almost all of them were Socialists. A similar percentage of rescuers (29 percent) reported that a parent was affiliated with the economic left. There were no significant differences between politically affiliated rescuers and nonrescuers or their parents with respect to identification with the economic left. Nor did politically affiliated rescuers or their parents differ from politically affiliated nonrescuers with respect to membership in parties advocating or tolerating rights for minorities generally and for Jews particularly. However, significantly more affiliated rescuers (80 percent) than affiliated nonrescuers

(31 percent) or bystanders (14 percent) belonged to political parties that embraced democratic pluralism (Table 6.8).[11] Parents of rescuers were similarly more likely than parents of nonrescuers to belong to democratic parties (Table 6.9).

More important, then, than economic ideology, or even attitude toward Jews and minorities, were the respondents' views about democracy or autocracy. Democratic ideologies tend to be associated with egalitarian views, in which others share power as equal members of the larger society. Autocracies may dispense favors to minorities, but in a superior-to-subordinate relationship. Superiors may bestow favors for ideological reasons or out of political expediency, but they are viewed as benevolences, not rights accruing to political equals.

Although the number of politically affiliated respondents was small, and despite the possibility that some may have concealed unpopular political affiliations, the distinction between rescuers and nonrescuers in their emphasis on democratic political values nonetheless suggests that rescuers were more likely than others to endorse egalitarian political views. Hence, for more rescuers, patriotism appeared to connote obligations to Jews as cocitizens.

The core values of rescuers and nonrescuers shaped their attitudes toward Nazis and Jews, religion and politics, and their understanding and interpretation of events, groups, and social institutions. The differences between the basic values and world views of rescuers and nonrescuers can be traced in part to their parents' significantly different views about appropriate standards and the importance of self and others.

Excessive self-interest—self-preoccupation—generally precludes attention to others, reducing not only one's ability to recognize others' needs, but also one's motivation to do so. However much self-interest may guide behavior in routine situations, it is likely to be accentuated under conditions of severe threat. The willingness and ability to transcend oneself under such conditions is usually based on sustained habits of orientation to the world, largely developed early in life.

In recalling the values they learned from their parents, rescuers emphasized values relating to self significantly less frequently than nonrescuers (24 percent compared with 35 percent for all nonrescuers and 40 percent for bystanders). The important difference between them centered on concern with economic compe-

tence—job skills, the values of hard work, and economic prudence—reflected in such recollections as "He taught me how to
farm," "to work hard," "to get a good job," "to be thrifty." While
34 percent of bystanders and 29 percent of all nonrescuers mentioned learning this value, only 19 percent of rescuers did (Table
6.7).

Emphasis on economic competence can be conducive to a materialistic view of life, often fostering a tendency to allow criteria
of economic usefulness to dominate relationships. Less tangible
concerns, feelings, abstract ideas, and moral issues are more likely
to be considered a waste of time. As Bettelheim[12] observed, "The
more man is geared toward achieving 'practical' results, the more
he may view the making of inner decisions that lead to no practical
end as a total waste of energy." That this value may also be associated with a higher degree of conformity and ethnocentrism is suggested by Frenkel-Brunswik, who observed that ethnocentrics are
inclined to view relationships primarily in terms of exchanges of
goods and material benefits.[13]

Altruistic rescue obviously required the abjuring of practical
and instrumental goals. Materialistic considerations played no
role in our rescuers' decisions to help. That it did for many others
who helped Jews is noted in survivor accounts[14] as well as by rescuers in our sample when they speak of others. Several rescuers, however, made a point of saying that the idea of material rewards
never occurred to them. The fact that it did not may well reflect
their early socialization, in which economic factors were generally
considered less important than relationships with others.

Nor was the importance of self in the sense of asserting one's
independence or will emphasized by rescuers' parents, but in this
respect rescuers did not differ significantly from nonrescuers. Few
rescuers or nonrescuers recall a parental emphasis on independence (6 percent and 9 percent, respectively). And only a handful
of rescuers echoed the theme of independence in giving their reasons for rescue, primarily in the form of self-assertion: "I wanted
to do something out of my own authority," or, "I didn't want to
take orders from the Germans." No rescued survivors thought self-
assertion was the reason their rescuers helped.

Others, rather than self, were the primary focus for rescuers.
Rescuers brought to the war a greater receptivity to others' needs
because they had learned from their parents that others were very
important. They had learned the importance not only of human

relationships generally but also of relating to others in specific ways.

The parents of rescuers and nonrescuers were equally concerned with social convention—the fulfillment of prescribed social roles and norms. At least one conventional value (e.g., "to be a good mother and a good wife," "not to drink," "to finish chores") was emphasized in the parental homes of both rescuers and nonrescuers (35 percent for rescuers, 42 percent for all nonrescuers, and 40 percent for bystanders).[15] Matters of propriety—manners, politeness, tidiness, cleanliness, and refraining from the use of obscenities—were emphasized most frequently (21 percent for rescuers, 27 percent for all nonrescuers, and 30 percent for bystanders). Dependability—punctuality, completing chores, keeping one's word, and task perseverance—was stressed somewhat less frequently (16 percent for rescuers, 14 percent for all nonrescuers, and 8 percent for bystanders, Table 6.7). Neither value inhibited focus on others' needs. Dependability was certainly important in rescue activity, and matters of propriety did not conflict with it. Although no rescuers said they helped out of a sense of propriety, many expressed appreciation when the rescued people behaved decorously.

The parents of rescuers, however, were significantly less likely to emphasize obedience. Only 1 percent of rescuers said their parents emphasized obedience as compared with 9 percent of all nonrescuers and 12 percent of bystanders (Table 6.7). Obedience is the hallmark of nonequals; obedience as an end unto itself facilitates adaptation to any type of authority—whether merited or demanded. As Alice Miller observes, parental emphasis on obedience was critically important in preparing Germans for the success of the Nazi regime, paving the way for the necessary submission it required.[16]

Rescue required disobedience, yet obedience sometimes also served its purposes. But this obedience was not blind; rather, it was selective—voluntarily chosen in deference to an accepted authority whose values one shared. Thus, a few rescuers noted that they had helped Jews because their resistance group leadership had ordered it or their minister, spouse, or parent had requested it. Rescue in such cases was consistent with the helper's values, although it was not necessarily a first order of priority. But neither was it a sign of submission to power.

Obedience was invoked by only a handful of rescuers as their major motivation, however. For the overwhelming majority (87 percent) of rescuers, helping Jews was motivated by concerns of *equity* or *care*. Since it is not unusual for individuals who perform helpful deeds to attribute positive motives to themselves, particularly when the costs are high,[17] it is important to note that the overwhelming majority (83%) of rescued survivors also believed that their rescuers were so motivated (Table 6.2).

Equity, as it emerges from the Kantian tradition of Western moral philosophy,[18] includes a concept of fair exchange—reciprocity in sharing valued goods, services, or resources to the mutual benefit of all concerned. It may also refer to a mechanism for a fair allocation of resources and goods generally, as well as fair punishment and fair compensation for those who have been victimized. Finally, it includes notions of fair procedures—procedures that ensure fair exchange, allocation, punishment, and compensation.[19] Fairness is the focal standard of equitable values. What makes things fair, however, is not the results for others but rather the methods that produce them. If all have equal access to the procedures, and if they are applied impartially and universally, then fairness is ensured.

Implicit in the notion of equity is a contractual view of social relationships. People are not asked to abandon self-interest but rather to accede to the fundamental idea that others, like themselves, are entitled to the same. Standards of fairness emerge out of the recognition that societies can function peaceably only when mutual rights to self-interest are recognized. Rationality (reason and thought) rather than emotionality (feelings and subjective reactions) are the basis for equity. Reason serves not only to generate procedural rules but also to evaluate behaviors.

Whereas equity is directed toward the welfare of society as a whole, based on abstract principles of fairness, care is concerned with the welfare of people without necessary regard for fairness.[20] Whereas equity is based on reciprocity, care endorses a willingness to give more than is received. Whereas equity emphasizes fair procedures, care insists on benevolence and kindness. Equity asks that we do our duty in accordance with reason, but care insists that we act out of concern. While equity may be administered blindly— the image of Justice, blindfolded, holding her scales, is apt—care can only be given by a human face. While equity asks that we act out of a sense of self-interest as well as the interests of others, care focuses on the interests of others. Equity is based on honesty, truthfulness, and respect; care, however, can require fraud and deceitfulness. In this sense, care goes beyond what can reasonably and fairly be expected of humans in society, beginning to approach the unreasonable and the unfair.

Overall, rescuers—in significantly higher percentages than nonrescuers (70 percent for rescuers, 56 percent for all nonrescuers, and 57 percent for bystanders)—emphasized learning ethical values and rescuers and nonrescuers alike spoke frequently of parental concerns with aspects of equity. The word *honesty* is highlighted above all others—sometimes with clear reference to property ("She taught me not to steal"; "He taught me never to take anything from anybody—to be very honest") and sometimes in relation to people ("She taught me to be straightforward"; "He taught me never to take advantage of anybody"). They also mention parental emphasis on "truthfulness," "respect," and "fairness." There is no significant difference between rescuers and nonrescuers with respect to parental equity values; approximately 45 percent of rescuers, all nonrescuers, and bystanders mentioned them.

But words and phrases characterizing care—the need to be helpful, hospitable, concerned, and loving—were voiced significantly more often by rescuers as they recalled the values they learned from their parents or other most influential person (44 percent of rescuers, 25 percent of all nonrescuers, and 21 percent of bystanders). Generosity and expansiveness, rather than fairness and reciprocity, were significantly more important to rescuers' than to nonrescuers' parents (Table 6.7):

My mother was a model of Christian faith and love of neighbor.

I learned to live honestly, to study well in school, to respect others, and to have compassion and generosity toward those who were less well treated by life.

I learned generosity, to be open, to help people.

I learned to be good to one's neighbor, honesty, scruples— to be responsible, concerned, and considerate. To work— and work hard. But also to help—to the point of leaving one's work to help one's neighbor.

To be good and caring, to love people. Mother always said to remember to do some good for someone at least once a day.

Equally important, rescuers were significantly more inclusive in noting the groups to whom they felt ethical obligations. In the following comments, more representative of nonrescuers, parental inclusiveness focused on family, friends, elders, church, and country but did not extend further:

She taught me to be honest, pray to God, and be respectful to parents and older people—not to tell lies and not to fight in school.

My father taught me to work hard and not to tell lies—to be neighborly and polite to elders—to go to church and to be a good Catholic—to be good to your family.

My mom taught me to get a good education, to pay attention in school because teachers can be a very great help and because education is vital to getting ahead in life; honesty, fairness, and loyalty to the family as well as friends and elders; and not to curse and to be loyal and supportive of the country.

Rescuers, however, in significantly higher percentages (39 percent compared with 15 percent of all nonrescuers and 13 percent of bystanders) emphasized that ethical values were to be applied universally, that they extended to all human beings (Table 6.7):

They taught me to respect all human beings.

He taught me to respect a man no matter what his origin.

He taught me to love my neighbor—to consider him my equal whatever his nationality or religion. He taught me especially to be tolerant.

I learned logical reasoning. I also learned to be tolerant— not to discriminate against people because of their beliefs or social class.

She taught me to be responsible, honest, to respect older people, to respect all people—not to tease or criticize people of other religions. She taught me to be good.

> My father taught me to love God and my neighbor,
> regardless of their race or religion. He had always had
> something special for the Jewish people. To be more
> precise, my father taught me to love God, to love my
> neighbor, particularly the Jewish people.

What is striking about a large percentage of rescuers is the consistently universalistic orientation, exemplified not only in the values they recall learning from their parents but also in the reasons they give for rescuing Jews. Almost half of all rescuers mention a universalistic obligation as at least one of their reasons for rescue; 29 percent of rescued survivors said their helpers embraced a universalistic ethos often emphasizing care (Table 6.2).

Justice, equality, and respect are the characteristic equity values cited by rescuers in explaining their reasons for helping. The reasoning behind the universal equitable principle, cited by approximately 15 percent of rescuers, was essentially this: Justice demanded that only the guilty be punished. Persecution of the innocent could not be justified. The ethnic identity of the persecuted was irrelevant; what mattered was their innocence. Jews, like themselves and others, belonged to the universal class of humans, all of whom had the right to live and to be free from nonmerited persecution:

> The reason is that every man is equal. We all have the right
> to live. It was plain murder, and I couldn't stand that. I
> would help a Mohammedan just as well as a Jew. We have
> got to live as humans and not as beasts. They were worse
> than beasts.

> These people just had the right to live like other people—
> not just Christian people. Jewish people are the same—all
> people are the same.

> I found it incomprehensible and inadmissible that for
> religious reasons or as a result of a religious choice, Jews
> would be persecuted. It's like saving somebody who is
> drowning. You don't ask them what God they pray to. You
> just go and save them.

> It was unfair that I was safe simply because I was born a
> Protestant. That was the main reason for me. What I did
> was a question of justice. It was a very humble thing

because I was in a privileged situation compared with other people who didn't deserve their situation at all.

I could not comprehend that innocent persons should be persecuted just because of race. We all come from the same God.

Jewish people had as much right to live as I did.

Humane considerations—these people were innocent. I had ascertained that.

It just happened to be Jewish people who were persecuted—it could have been anyone.

All men are equal and are free and equal by right. Consequently I am against all dictatorial systems.

Survivors used essentially the same concepts of justice in describing their rescuers:

She believed that anti-Semitism was poisoning the souls of youth, causing social disorder, and destroying tolerance. [She was] a militant democrat.

She always said that you needed to be an active Christian. I think it was just this feeling of justice and honesty that prompted her.

They believed in humanity and were incredulous that people were being killed simply because of their Jewishness.

They are very noble, very fine people. They felt that people should not be hurt for no reason at all. When they saw injustice, they felt they should do something. To such a degree that had such feelings. Whether it was religion or their sense of justice—they didn't mind paying the price for this.

He did not distinguish between Jews and Gentiles. He felt it was necessary to save every human being other than Nazis. When he saw innocent people persecuted, he decided that it was his mission to help them regardless of the danger to himself and his property.

But for most rescuers and rescued survivors the language of care dominated. *Pity, compassion, concern, affection* made up the vocabulary 76 percent of rescuers and 67 percent of rescued survivors used at least once to express their reasons (Table 6.2):

I was just sorry for them.

I did it out of sympathy and kindness.

I did it out of a feeling of compassion for those who were weaker and who needed help.

We did not want her to get caught—we were sorry for her.

They were good friends—I liked them very much.

In a few cases, the emotional component was intense enough to prepare them not only to die but also to kill:

I liked her very much. When I learned they were exterminating Jews, I decided that even if I had to die, I would help.

Nobody was going to touch those children. I would have killed for them.

Care was not a spectator sport, it compelled action. It meant assuming personal responsibility, not because others required it, but because failure to act meant acquiescence in the consequences:

I could not stand idly by and observe the daily misery that was occurring.

It was unacceptable to watch idly while compatriots perished.

It was necessary. Somebody had to do it.

I knew they were taking them and they wouldn't come back. I didn't think I could live with that knowing that I could have done something.

I saw the Germans shooting people in the street, and I could not sit there doing nothing.

My husband told me that unless we helped, they would be killed. I could not stand that thought. I never would have forgiven myself.

This sense of internal compulsion was characteristically so strong that most rescuers reported rarely reflecting before acting. Asked how long it took them to make their first helping decision, more than 70 percent indicated "minutes." Asked if they consulted with anyone prior to making the decision, 80 percent responded "no one."

Sixteen percent of rescuers said they felt this particular caring obligation toward a lover or valued friend. Asked their reasons for rescue, they simply replied "I liked them"; "They were good people"; "I loved her." More than one-fourth (28 percent) of rescued survivors noted it as a special relationship to them (Table 6.2):

She was fond of us—especially my sister.

He was in love with me.

We were like his two daughters.

He was a good friend.

Yet, rescuers' commitment to caring for others extended well beyond friends or loved ones. Thirty-eight percent of rescuers perceived their caring obligations as universal in application. The suffering of a stranger was as much their responsibility as that of a friend (Table 6.2):

When you see a need, you have to help. Our religion was part of us. We are our brother's keeper. It was very satisfying for us.

Any kind of suffering must be alleviated.

You need to turn to those who suffer and are in pain— direct reaching out to others.

We had to give our help to these people in order to save them. Not because they were Jewish, but because every persecuted human needs some help, just as my father found help when the Turks killed the Armenians. They were our friends and brothers in God.

If you can save somebody's life, that's your duty.

My husband said right after the war started that we had to do something to help our people against the Nazis. It was our Christian duty—we should help as many as we could.

We would have had a house full of Jews if we had had the room.

I think if somebody is in a bad situation, you have to help them.

And, in fact, when asked how many of the people they helped were strangers, more than 90 percent of rescuers replied that at least one was. This universalistic view of their ethical obligations sometimes placed them in a tragic situation in which they needed to make a painful choice. Faced with a house that was already full or a service that could be rendered to only one person, they had to decide which life to save. Some struggled to find a criterion to guide their actions. Should it be the doctor or the judge or the poor and uneducated man or woman whose life promised little more than survival? Should it be the child whose future was as yet unknown or the aged and frail? This "playing God" with people's lives left its mark; choice itself violated the principle of universal responsibility, and feelings of guilt continue to plague some as they reflect on the choices they made.

For most rescuers, then, helping Jews was an expression of ethical principles that extended to all of humanity and, while often reflecting concern with equity and justice, was predominantly rooted in care. While other feelings—such as hatred of Nazis, religion, and patriotism, or even deference to an accepted authority whose values the rescuer shared—influenced them, most rescuers explain their actions as responses to a challenge to their fundamental ethical principles. This sense that ethical principles were at stake distinguished rescuers from their compatriots who participated in resistance activities only. For these resisters, hatred of Nazis and patriotism were most often considered sufficient reasons for their behaviors; for rescuers, however, such reasons were rarely sufficient.

As suggested by the importance of parental values and example, resucers' commitment to actively protect or enhance the well-being of others did not emerge suddenly under the threat of Nazi brutality. As we shall see, more rescuers integrated such values into their lives well before the war began—and remained committed to them long after it ended.

CHAPTER 7

The Roots of Human Attachments

The ethical values of care and inclusiveness that distinguished rescuers were not merely abstract or philosophical preferences. Rather, they reflected a key dimension of rescuers' personalities—the way they characteristically related to others and their sense of commitment to them.[1]

Patterns of attachment to others begin early. John Bowlby believed that they begin in infancy as mothers respond to their infants' need for physical proximity in order to relieve their anxiety and feel secure.[2,3] According to Bowlby, this interaction between mother and child shapes personality and becomes the prototype for all subsequent social interactions. Freud[4] and Erikson[5] had earlier maintained that the infant's relationship with the mother becomes the model for all subsequent relationships, and they had attributed many subsequent personality inadequacies to unsatisfying mother-child relationships. Yet some children are able to overcome apparently inadequate mother-child relationships and develop appropriately. Moreover, in the view of some current researchers, the primacy of mothers as attachment figures may be overestimated. Fathers as well as other adults—aunts, uncles, grandparents, and even strangers—can become satisfactory attachment figures. Even friends can serve this purpose.[6]

Despite such variations, most psychologists agree that a satisfactory early attachment to some individual is important for subsequent intellectual and social development. Trust, security, curios-

We are grateful to Jack Shaffer, whose assistance helped us in writing this chapter.

ity, and self-directedness are among the characteristics associated with satisfactory attachments. That altruism is also a consequence of satisfactory attachments is poignantly illustrated in a study done by Anna Freud and Sophie Dann in 1951.[7] In this case, however, the attachment figures were not parents—or even adults—but other children.

The children Freud and Dann studied were six Jewish three-year-old orphans—three boys and three girls liberated from Theresienstadt in the spring of 1945. Theresienstadt served as a transit camp for individuals on their way to extermination centers. The children had arrived there as infants; their parents had been gassed. It is not clear how they managed to survive; it is likely that no single person cared for them for more than a very short time. Freud and Dann began their study when the children arrived at a residential nursery in England in the summer of 1945.

Initially the children were uncontrollable; they destroyed toys, damaged furniture, and in relationships with adults alternated between indifference and hostility. On the other hand, they were highly attached to each other. They sought each other's company constantly and became very upset if separated even for moments. Wherever one went, another followed. Although they quarreled, they were very sensitive to each other's feelings—they shared their possessions freely, handed food to others before taking it themselves, and looked out for each other's safety. Such kind behaviors were routine; sometimes they bordered on the altruistic. One cold wintry day, for example, two of the children were walking together when one was discovered to have forgotten his gloves. The other gave him his own gloves and did not utter a word of complaint thenceforth.

The children eventually made friends with the nursery staff and began to treat them in similar ways, albeit less intensely. They were sensitive to the staff's feelings and tried to help them with their work. Freud and Dann concluded that the children had suffered no gross impairments as a result of their grisly experiences—they were neither deficient, delinquent, nor psychotic. Thirty-five years later, Dann reported that all six were leading effective adult lives.[8]

Individuals fortunate enough to have experienced warm and satisfactory early attachments are more likely to form satisfactory attachments as adults. Having observed models of responsible caretakers, they are more likely to have learned the skills associated with such roles. Moreover, they are also more likely to have experienced vicariously the rewards of such behaviors. Adults whose behaviors are consistently and dependably responsible communicate the message that such behaviors are self-rewarding, making children more likely to internalize standards of responsibility, caring, and dependability and to adopt them as their own. Our data suggest that this was indeed the case for a significantly larger percentage of rescuers than nonrescuers.

Rescuers described their early family relationships in general and their relationships with their mothers in particular as closer significantly more often than did nonrescuers. Rescuers also felt significantly closer to their fathers than did bystanders.[9] (See Table 7.1.) From such family relationships, more rescuers learned the satisfactions accruing from personal bonds with others.

Significantly more rescuers than nonrescuers accepted the importance of responsibility in maintaining their attachments to people. Additionally, they did not merely restrict this sense of responsibility to their families but also extended it to include the larger community. More rescuers were willing to give more than what they might necessarily receive in return. Once making a commitment, they felt beholden to fulfill it, for letting people down or failing to finish something promised was unseemly, even shameful. Even if others did not fulfill what they had promised, their obligations were not abrogated. If a task was worth starting, it was worth finishing regardless of what others did.

This sense of responsibility toward others emerged in their responses to the Social Responsibility Scale.[10] The scale assesses a person's attitudes about helping others even when there is nothing to be gained. Strong agreement with such statements as "Every person should give some time for the good of the town or country" and "It is the duty of each person to do the best he/she can" contributes to a high social responsibility score, as does strong disagreement with such items as "When I work on a committee, I usually let other people do most of the planning." Rescuers scored significantly higher on this scale than did nonrescuers (Table 7.2).

Feelings of responsibility for others can emerge from internalized standards of appropriate conduct. They may also emerge through empathy—a cognitive or emotional understanding of or sensitivity to others' needs and feelings.[11] Several studies have found adult empathy to be a good predictor of altruistic responses.[12] Rescuers in our study did not differ from nonrescuers with respect to generalized emotional empathy. However, they did differ from nonrescuers with respect to emotional empathy for others' pain.

To assess empathic tendency we used an abbreviated version of the Empathy Scale, which measures the degree of heightened responsiveness to others' emotional experiences.[13] It includes several items relating to different types of emotional empathy: whether it is aroused with respect to people far and near, is experienced in exactly the same way as the other experiences it, and includes heightened responsiveness to others' pleasure as well as pain. Rescuers' scores varied from very high to very low, and were not significantly different overall from the scores of nonrescuers. Rescuers thus did not differ from others with relation to the type of empathy called "emotional contagion"—that is, a general susceptibility to others' moods. Rescuers did not any more than nonrescuers become worried just because others were worried or get upset just because a friend was upset. Nor did they differ from nonrescuers with respect to being moved by others' positive emotional experiences. Demonstrations of affection and pleasure by others affected them similarly to nonrescuers.

What distinguished rescuers from nonrescuers was their tendency to be moved by pain. Sadness and helplessness aroused their empathy. More frequently than others, rescuers were likely to say "I can't feel good if others around me feel sad," "Seeing people cry upsets me," "I get very upset when I see an animal in pain," "It upsets me to see helpless people," and "I get angry when I see someone hurt."[14]

But emotional empathy for pain, however intense, does not necessarily result in a helping response. Rather than attempting to alleviate the pain, one may choose to escape it—by physically removing oneself from the problem, denying it, devaluing the victim, or perhaps contenting oneself with some slight gesture. When personal responsibility for alleviating pain is assumed, however, action on behalf of the victim is more likely. This conjoining of empathy for pain with personal responsibility is reflected in rescuers' greater task perseverance, commitment to fulfill promises once made, willingness to be involved in friends' problems, and acceptance of the obligation to give of their time for the good of the larger community (see Table 7.3). Thus, rescuers were not only more empathic toward others' pain than nonrescuers, but they were also more likely to get and stay involved because of their

general sense of responsibility and tendency to make commitments. (See Prosocial Action Orientation in Table 7.16 for items
on this factor.)

Such feelings, however, were not experienced without ambivalence. Despite their sense of attachment, social responsibility, and
emotional empathy for pain, rescuers were just as likely as nonrescuers to express detachment from others by affirming that "It's
no use worrying about current events or public affairs, I can't do
anything about them anyway," "I have often found that what is
going to happen will happen," and "People would be a lot better
off if they could live far away from other people and never have
anything to do with them" (Table 7.4).[15] Thus, rescuers like nonrescuers inclined toward a degree of self-protection against life's
events through disassociation. However, rescuers maintained their
stronger attachments to others despite this tendency.

Just as rescuers' greater proclivity toward attachment to others emerged early in life, so did their inclusive orientation—their
feelings of connection to diverse people and groups. More frequently than nonrescuers, rescuers reported youthful tendencies
to feel similar to a wider and more diverse range of people.

While they shared with nonrescuers similar perceptions of
their likenesses to the poor, they were significantly more likely
also to perceive their similarities to the rich. While they shared
with nonrescuers similar perceptions of their likeness to other
Christians, they were significantly more likely to perceive their
likeness to Jews and Gypsies. Their sense of shared similarities
with Jews is particularly striking. More than half (54 percent) of
them reported feeling "very like Jews" compared with 21 percent
of all nonrescuers and 18 percent of bystanders. In fact, their sense
of psychological proximity to Jews was no different from what they
felt toward other Christians (Table 7.5). It is probable that the close
and sustained interactions of the rescue experience itself strengthened this perception of psychological proximity to Jews.

The impact of experiences with others on perceptions of similarity is evident in most rescuers' and nonrescuers' (more than 80
percent in both groups) refusal to see any likeness between themselves and Nazis. Moreover, neither rescuers nor nonrescuers were
inclined to attribute similarities to themselves and others unless
they had some experiences on which to base such a judgment. The
majority in both groups refused to say whether they were similar
or different from Turks, saying that they had had no experiences
with them.

However, experiences themselves are filtered through our personal predilections to emphasize likeness or difference. Some people approach others with a predisposition to grant them the benefit of the doubt, to presume that others feel much as they do until they have evidence to the contrary. Others, by contrast, incline toward a presumption of guilt until innocence is shown. They assume that others are not quite like themselves, not quite as good or as worthy. Rescuers were significantly more predisposed to see others as like themselves and to grant them the benefit of the doubt. Nonrescuers were significantly more inclined to emphasize their distinctiveness from others.[16]

Distinctions of class and religion were far less important to rescuers' than to nonrescuers' choice of friends while growing up. Rescuers were significantly more likely to befriend both rich and poor as well as those of different religions. They were not only more likely to befriend Christians of other denominations but were also significantly more likely to befriend Jews than were bystanders (Table 7.6). Moreover, such friendships were a matter of choice, not opportunity. In similar percentages, rescuers and nonrescuers reported having Jewish acquaintances. Almost identical percentages (approximately 58 percent) said they had known Jews while growing up. Similar percentages among all groups said that Jews had attended their elementary schools and gymnasiums (Table 7.7).

As adults, rescuers were more likely to befriend others different from themselves, because external marks of status were less important to them. They were likely to perceive Jews and Gypsies as similar to them because of their general proclivity toward inclusive connections to others. It was not a consequence of their identification with others who were socially marginal or weak.[17]

A small number of rescuers did feel socially marginal, as did a similar percentage of nonrescuers. But the overwhelming majority of rescuers (80 percent) had a sense of belonging to their community, a feeling shared by similar percentages of nonrescuers (82 percent). Just as many rescuers as nonrescuers reported having many, some, few, and no close friends, and just as many perceived their neighbors as very, somewhat, not very, or not at all friendly (Table 7.8).

Neither did rescuers' sense of similarity to outsiders and empathy for the weak and the helpless emerge from their own feel-

ings of personal vulnerability and weakness. Although some rescuers did indeed perceive themselves as bereft of personal power,
this feeling was even more characteristic of nonrescuers. In fact,
more than others, rescuers felt they could control events and
shape their own destinies and were more willing to risk failure.
Rather than regarding themselves as mere pawns, subject to the
power of external authorities, they, in significantly larger percentages than nonrescuers, perceived themselves as actors, capable of
making and implementing plans and willing to accept the consequences.

Their stronger sense of personal efficacy, their feeling that
they could affect events and were responsible for doing do, was
reflected in their scores (compared with those of nonrescuers) on
the Internal/External Locus of Control Scale.[18] Strong agreement
with such statements as "When I make plans, I am certain that I
can make them work," "What happens to me is my own doing,"
and "In my case, getting what I want has little or nothing to do
with luck" are scored as high internal responses. People with an
external locus of control view themselves as at the mercy of external circumstances, buffeted about by events over which they have
little or no control. Strong agreement with such statements as "I
have often found that what is going to happen will happen" or
"Many times I feel that I have little influence over the things that
happen to me" are scored as high external responses. Rescuers
scored significantly higher than all other groups on internal control (Table 7.9).

Rescuers' sense of internal control should not be confused
with a need to control others or lead them. Rescuers sometimes
were leaders and sometimes followers; they sometimes stood their
ground and refused to comply with others, and sometimes they
simply did what others wanted. In this respect they were no different from nonrescuers. In similar distributions rescuers and nonrescuers reported assuming leadership roles with their friends and
going along with what their friends did.

Nor should a sense of internal control be confused with a
sense of self-esteem, a favorable self-evaluation. Rescuers had no
more favorable views of themselves than did nonrescuers. Their
responses to a Self Esteem scale consisting of ten statements
showed that they were just as likely as nonrescuers to feel they had
a number of good qualities and positive attitudes toward them-

selves and just as likely to feel that they had negative qualities and to think ill of themselves.[19] The absence of a connection between self-esteem and altruism should not be surprising. People who are sufficiently content with themselves might feel freer to attend to others' needs, but because of their high self-image might also regard themselves as appropriate recipients of attention and care from others, rather than bestowers. Alternatively, people who think ill of themselves can become so obsessed by their own distress that they barely register others' needs; however, they can just as easily respond to others' needs as a way of enhancing their own self-image. Some rescuers felt they had done nothing of merit in their lives. This, too, should not be surprising, for as William James noted many years ago, people evaluate themselves with respect to their self-expectations.[20] Because of their internal standards, those with high aspirations risk not feeling good about themselves even if they accomplish more than others. As some rescuers noted, "I didn't do enough."

A sense of internal control did allow more rescuers to recognize a choice where others perceived only compliance and to believe they could succeed where others foresaw only failure. This, coupled with their significantly greater attachments to people—their stronger feelings of closeness to others, their greater sense of responsibility toward them, and their heightened empathy for pain—predisposed them to altruistic behavior generally. But it was their inclusiveness—their willingness to see different types of people as essentially similar to themselves and their inclination to befriend others on the basis of personal qualities rather than religion or status—which helps explain why they helped Jews.

How did rescuers get to be such people? A critical influence on their development was the way in which their parents disciplined them.

The extent to which discipline—from teaching to punishing—is a central focus of the parent-child interaction is probably vastly underrated as an influence on development. Some researchers estimate that beginning at age two, children are commonly pressured by parents to change their behaviors on the average of once every six or seven minutes.[21] This means that every few minutes of their waking hours, children and parents engage in an interaction of competing desires and that, most often, children comply with their parents' wishes. The reasons for which compliance is requested and the modes through which it is elicited communicate profound and long-lasting messages about right and wrong and about desirable relationships.

Punitive parental strategies are most commonly associated with aggressive behaviors in children, a phenomenon psychoanalytic theorists explain primarily as the result of repression and displacement. Punishment arouses anger in the recipient. When children cannot express their anger toward those who punish them because they fear either further punishment or the withdrawal of love, they may suppress their anger or transfer it elsewhere, to themselves or to another person.

Parents whose disciplinary techniques are benevolent, particularly those who rely on reasoning, are more likely to have kind and generous children, children who behave helpfully with respect to others. Hoffman, who has done considerable research on discipline and prosocial behaviors, says that inductive reasoning is particularly conducive to altruism.[22] Induction focuses children's attention on the consequences of their behaviors for others, drawing attention to others' feelings, thoughts, and welfare. Children are thus led to understand others cognitively—a skill known as perspective- or role-taking—and are also thus more inclined to develop empathy toward others.

Overall, significantly fewer rescuers recalled any controls imposed on them by the most intimate persons in their early lives. Approximately 33 percent said they were never disciplined by their mothers, compared with 18 percent of all nonrescuers and 19 percent of bystanders. Seventy percent of rescuers reported never having been disciplined by a role model other than a parent, compared with 33 percent of all controls and 22 percent of bystanders. But there were no significant differences among groups with respect to paternal discipline; approximately a third of all respondents said they had never been disciplined by their fathers (Table 7.10).

Perhaps more important, parents of rescuers depended significantly less on physical punishment and significantly more on reasoning (Table 7.11). Significantly fewer rescuers than nonrescuers reported being slapped, spanked, kicked, and beaten with assorted implements and having their hair pulled by their parents. This does not mean, though, that future rescuers were left to misbehave with impunity. Similar percentages of rescuers and nonrescuers recalled being disciplined in response to disobedience; disruptive, impolite behaviors; stealing, lying, or cheating; aggressive behav-

iors, and, most frequently, failure to perform assigned responsibilities (Table 7.12). But an important difference between the groups
lies in how they perceived the punishment they did receive.

As several respondents informed us, discipline tended to be
harsher and more common in their youth and native cultures than
it is today. No one reported liking it, but more rescuers perceived
the parental punishment they received as in some way related to
their behavior. Moreoever, they were more inclined to report punishment as an infrequent rather than a routine response. On the
other hand, significantly more nonrescuers perceived such punishment as gratuitous—a cathartic release of aggression on the
part of the parent and unrelated to their behavior. (See Table
7.13.) Most often, these perceptions had to do with physical punishment, which was sometimes associated with parental drunken-
ness but was usually recalled as a routine and characteristic mode
of behavior:

> He hit me with a wet strap—often with a buckle. He would
> do it for lying—sometimes we didn't know why. Mostly he
> was cross and in a bad humor; then he would find fault
> with something I did months ago [nonrescuer].

> He beat me and yelled at me anytime he was angry. I was
> the weapon's object, even when I hadn't done anything.
> You didn't know if you had done anything or not
> [nonrescuer].

> She beat me with anything she could get in her hands, just
> for anything. She was so hot tempered. When she became
> generous, she preferred to give something to strangers
> rather than to her own children [nonrescuer].

> Father always beat me with a whip. Sometimes he punished
> me because I didn't get food for the horses. But he didn't
> punish as much when he was sober, as when he was drunk
> [nonrescuer].

> Father punched me sometimes, beat me, and also threw me
> out of the house—especially when he was very angry and
> also partly drunk. I seem to remember that he was a very
> moody person. He would punish me for not listening to
> him, for speaking out against him—when he cursed me
> abusively, I used to curse him back. I was very upset with

the way he treated my mother, which sometimes bordered on violence. I sometimes saw her cry, and I knew that something like that might have happened [nonrescuer].

He hit me for any reason at all [nonrescuer].

My father would teach me by kicking me—not for disobedience but because I didn't do his will. He would brag about me outside the house, but at home he was hideous [nonrescuer].

Rescuers were not only less likely to perceive punishment as gratuitous but also more frequently reported physical punishment as an occasional follow-up to a verbal admonishment to desist or to an attempt at reasoning:

Once he gave me a sound thrashing, but that had a special reason—for coming home too late. I was usually punished or admonished only with words [rescuer].

Sometimes she hit us with a small stick, but at first she warned me. I remember once she did this for me taking younger people onto a pond that was covered with ice [rescuer].

When he talked to me and it didn't help, then he would reach for the whip [rescuer].

Generally he used to explain things, but once he beat me for taking money without asking first. My mother used persuasion, explained things. She never hit me. My father used to threaten me with a stirrup but he never hit me [rescuer].

Once he spanked me. He got so carried away—he was so sorry [rescuer].

He had a very strong personality. Discipline was in words— explaining the weaknesses of whatever I had done. He spanked me a couple of times [rescuer].

Thus, it is in their reliance on reasoning, explanations, sug-gestions of ways to remedy the harm done, persuasion, and advice that the parents of rescuers differed most from nonrescuers. Whereas 21 percent of all disciplinary techniques identified by rescuers included reasoning, only 6 percent of behaviors reported by nonrescuers could be so classified (Table 7.11).

Explained is the word most rescuers favored, and some also pointed out the content of such explanations. Parents would tell the child that he or she made "mistakes" or hadn't understood the other point of view. Help, rather than punishment, would some-times follow such explanations:

> She didn't hit but explained everything. Father used to shout when he was in a bad humor. Besides that, he tried to persuade people.

> He would talk to us—he could talk very well. And I would listen to him. I was impressed by what he said.

> My mother talked with me, pointed out mistakes to me.

> She told me when I did something wrong. She never did any punishing or scolding—she tried to make me understand with my mind what I'd done wrong.

> He would discipline me rationally—I am not sure that the word *discipline* applies. Moral questions, interhuman relations—he would say, "It's this way; you are wrong when you consider it that way." When I came home from school full of criticisms of some friend, he would bring up both sides. "Moral education" is the best expression.

> He didn't beat—he used to explain. Sometimes father was upset when we didn't get good grades at school; then he tried to help. Mother sometimes spanked.

Reasoning communicates a message of respect for and trust in children that allows them to feel a sense of personal efficacy and warmth toward others. It is based on a presumption of error rather than a presumption of evil intent. It implies that had chil-dren but known better or understood more, they would not have acted in an inappropriate way. It is a mark of esteem for the lis-tener; an indication of faith in his or her ability to comprehend, develop, and improve.

Parents have power over children; they are not only physically stronger but also have access to material resources they can bestow or withhold. Societal norms generally support their superior posi-tion, affirming their rights to humiliate or insult and simultaneously condemning children who might retaliate. When adults voluntarily abdicate the use of power in favor of explanation, they are modeling appropriate behavior toward the weak on the part of the powerful. Faced with powerless others, children so raised in turn have at their disposal an internal "script"—a store of recollections, dialogues, and activities ready to be activated. They need not depend on innovation or improvisation but rather simply retrieve what is already imprinted on their memories. In such circumstances, too, children are more likely to internalize their parents' standards. Rescuers were significantly more likely to perceive themselves as having personal integrity. They not only saw themselves as more caring and responsible but also as more honest and helpful than nonrescuers (Table 7.14).

In contrast, punishment implies the need to curb some intrinsic wildness or evil intent. Routine gratuitous punishment implies that powerful persons have the right to exert their will arbitrarily. Children who experience such treatment are likely to accept that view of the rights of the powerful over the less powerful. They have little reason to trust others and many reasons to fear them. Having had little influence over their parents' behavior, they are more inclined to feel a sense of helplessness in influencing others generally. More apprehensive, they are less inclined to risk exploring the world. Thus they allow themselves few opportunities to deny their sense of incompetence or to develop the competencies they lack. Human relationships are construed in power terms, superordination and subordination viewed as the inherent social condition of humankind. The best one can do in the face of power is to succumb; but one of the uses of power is to satisfy one's desires. In the context of such relationships, the only restraints on behavior are external ones. "Might makes right" becomes a fundamental law of human relationships.

Supportive and close parental homes propelled many rescuers toward extensive relationships with others, relationships in which ego boundaries were sufficiently broadened so that other people were experienced as part of the self. The family relationship became the prototype for an inclusive view of obligations toward humanity generally. But to suggest that all rescuers developed altruistic and inclusive inclinations because of good family relationships oversimplifies the complex realities. Our statistics inform us that rescuers tended to be of four types, each of which was characterized by clusters of particular experiences, relationships, values, and personality characteristics.[23] Each type has only some of the characteristics significantly associated with rescuers; no type has all of them. This demonstrates that the development of an inclusive altruistic predisposition is not dependent on any single event or experience.

For one group of rescuers, strong and cohesive family bonds were the primary source of their psychological strength and values. Above all, these rescuers perceived their relationships with their families of origin as very close. They felt strongly attached to their fathers as well as their mothers. Parental values emphasized caring for others, dependability, and independence, particularly in the form of self-reliance. Such values were frequently emphasized in a religious context. Both parents inclined toward a strong religious commitment, and rescuers themselves were likely to be characterized by a lifelong religious commitment beginning in childhood. They also tended to choose spouses who shared a similar religious feeling. Rescuers of this type grew up feeling highly potent; they saw themselves as decisive, able to take responsibility, independent, and inclined towards adventurousness and risk taking. They had a positive attitude toward others generally. They made many close friends and tended to see their neighbors as basically good people. While these rescuers were strongly embedded within their own families and communities, they were highly aware of Jews. Their parents were very likely to have spoken to them about Jews, often in the context of their religious culture. While their comments may have been positive or negative, rescuers emerged from this experience with a high consciousness of Jews even if they themselves did not necessarily live among them or know any.

Another group of rescuers developed their extensive orientation primarily through consistently close contacts with Jews. Jews were an integral part of their lives. They lived among them, worked with them, and had close Jewish friends while growing up and in their adult years. Their spouses, too, worked with Jews and had close Jewish friends. Such prolonged experiences with a culture different from their own sensitized them to different points of view and needs. Because of their intimate personal relationships with Jews, they were not only highly aware of events affecting them but were also acutely distressed by them. *Kristallnacht* and anti-Semitism in general pained them greatly, and they were horrified when Jews were forced to wear the yellow star. Relationships within their families of origin varied, as did their feelings of personal potency.

While, for both of these groups of rescuers, a sense of obligation toward others emerged in the context of close personal relationships—family and friends—for others it emerged from a more abstract sense of connectedness. One such group was marked by broad social commitments, an intense sense of personal responsibility for the welfare of society as a whole. They believed they should do whatever they could to affect world events and improve the lives of others. Social involvement was the primary and central value of their lives and the framework that gave it meaning. They derived much of their ego strength from this conviction and, more than others, were likely to have done something unusual before the war to stand up for their beliefs, such as supporting some cause or making some unpopular statements. While their relationships with their families of origin varied from close to distant, they nonetheless credited their most influential parent or person with teaching them the values of care, helpfulness, dependability, and self-reliance. These rescuers were more independent from their families and communities, and their youthful friends were highly likely to have come from various social classes and religions, though not necessarily including Jews. Jews, however, did hover at the peripheries of their social world in their educational experiences. Jews attended their elementary schools, gymnasiums, and universities.

A final group of rescuers, more abstractly connected to others, are the egalitarians. Egalitarian rescuers derived their sense of responsibility to others from their strong feelings of psychological similarity to humankind generally and empathy for persons in pain. Parents of egalitarian rescuers were marked by their strong rejection of ethnocentric views about Jews. Rescuers themselves felt very psychologically similar to outgroups generally (Turks, Gypsies, and Jews) and to different social classes within their own ethnic or religious group. They tended not to be involved in patriotic causes before the war, possibly because it may have suggested to them a narrow chauvinism. What moved them most was others' pain, and they felt a strong responsibility to relieve it. They regarded themselves as having high personal integrity and being helpful, honest, responsible, and willing to stand up for their beliefs. (See Tables 7.15 and 7.16.)

Nonrescuers differed significantly from all these types of rescuers, but they too arrived at their adult values and modes of behavior by varying routes.[24] For one group of nonrescuers, poor family relationships corresponded with a lack of close relationships to family and community and a sense of impotence. For another group, Jews were simply distant objects, physically or socially separated, and basically irrelevant. A third group accepted little in the way of responsibility for others, preferring to keep to themselves and avoiding social involvements generally.[25] Only the fourth type were true ethnocentrics who perceived many people as alien to them, especially outsider groups. (See Tables 7.17, 7.18, 7.19, 7.20, 7.21, and 7.22.)

Involvement, commitment, care, and responsibility are the hallmarks of extensive persons. Disassociation, detachment, and exclusiveness are the hallmarks of constricted persons. Rescuers were marked by extensivity, whereas nonrescuers, and bystanders in particular, were marked by constrictedness, by an ego that perceived most of the world beyond its own boundaries as peripheral. More centered on themselves and their own needs, they were less conscious of others and less concerned with them. With the exception of ethnocentrics, their failure to act was less a reflection of a particular rejection of Jews or other outsiders than it was the expression of a tendency to distance themselves from relationships that imposed burdensome responsibilities on them.

Thus, an examination of the early family lives and personality characteristics of both rescuers and nonrescuers suggests that their respective wartime behavior grew out of their general patterns of relating to others. Those who were inclined toward extensive attachments—feeling commited to and responsible for diverse groups of people—were predisposed to accept feelings of responsibility to Jews, whatever the danger to themselves. Conversely, those who were inclined toward constrictedness—detachment and exclusiveness—were particularly unlikely to reject this behavior when doing so might have exposed them to personal threat.

CHAPTER 8

Concern into Action

My parents were loving and kind. I learned from them to be helpful and considerate. There was a Jewish family living in our apartment building, but I hardly noticed when they left. Later, when I was working in the hospital as a doctor, a Jewish man was brought to the emergency room by his wife. I knew that he would die unless he was treated immediately. But we were not allowed to treat Jews; they could only be treated at the Jewish hospital. I could do nothing.

These are the words of a German nonrescuer, a kind and compassionate woman predisposed by sentiment and the ethics of her profession to help a dangerously ill man but who nonetheless did not do so. Thus, it is clearly not enough—in explaining rescuers' activities—to cite sentiments of caring and compassion. Several nonrescuers shared similar tendencies.

Rescuers' attachments to others and their inclusive view of humanity influenced their interpretations of events and situations and may have inclined them toward benevolent behavior. But the step from inclination to action is a large one. To understand what actually aroused rescuers to act on behalf of Jews, submerging or overriding fundamental considerations regarding their own and their families' survival, we must examine yet another motivational source.

It took a catalyst to translate predisposition into action—an external event that challenged rescuers' highest values. However, such actions were not the consequence of objective external events but rather of the subjective meanings rescuers conferred on them. Rescuers and nonrescuers interpreted the demands on themselves

We are grateful to Janusz Reykowski and Zuzanna Smolenska for their collaboration in developing the concepts and elaborating the case studies which we used in writing this chapter.

differently. Faced with the same knowledge, observation of needs, or requests, only rescuers felt compelled to help.

Based on theoretical proposals developed by Janusz Reykowski, we were able to discern three kinds of catalysts that generally aroused a response. They were able to serve as catalysts because they were congruent with the ways rescuers characteristically made important life decisions. Rescuers who were characteristically *empathically* oriented responded to an external event that aroused or heightened their empathy. Rescuers who were characteristically *normocentrically* oriented responded to an external event which they interpreted as a normative demand of a highly valued social group. Rescuers who characteristically behaved according to their own overarching *principles,* in the main autonomously derived, were moved to respond by an external event which they interpreted as violating these principles.[1]

We propose the above as ideal types, abstractions that reflect reality but are nonetheless rarely found in their pure form in any individual case. Elements of empathy, for example, were sometimes associated with normocentric considerations, and principled behavior was not necessarily devoid of either. Concern with self-enhancement or the fulfillment of personal needs was also apparent in several cases. For example, one rescuer who learned after some months that the woman living with her was Jewish said she was reluctant to ask her to leave because it was the only affectionate relationship she had. In another case, a young man acting as a courier said it gave him a feeling of importance. Some rescuers seemed propelled by a concern with the task itself—the performance of an elaborate set of procedures related to rescue assumed an autonomous life of its own. Demonstrating competence to oneself in carrying out such tasks and taking full responsibility for the results might have been an important motivating consideration for some rescuers. Nor can we ignore suggestions of anticipated postwar rewards. A desire for praise, material goods, and in some cases the avoidance of censure, particularly during the period when an Allied victory was imminent, may well have contributed to the motivation of some rescuers. A few did not begin helping until victory was in sight, and we cannot ignore the possibility that this had some influence on their decision.

Nonetheless, most rescuers were catalyzed into action either by empathy, allegiance to their group or institutional norms, or commitment to principle. As the illustrative profiles of individual rescuers and their situations reveal, the altruistic act of rescue was not a radical departure from previous ways of responding but an extension of characteristic forms of relating to others.

An empathic orientation is centered on the needs of another, on that individual's possible fate. It emerges out of a direct connection with the distressed other. Compassion, sympathy, and pity are its characteristic expressions. The reactions may be emotional or cognitive; frequently they contain elements of both. An empathic reaction aroused more than a third (37 percent) of rescuers to their first helping act.

The impact of a direct encounter with a distressed Jew was sometimes overpowering. Consider, for example, the following episode related by a Polish woman, then approximately thirty-five years of age:

> In 1942, I was on my way home from town and was almost near home when M. came out of the bushes. I looked at him, in striped camp clothing, his head bare, shod in clogs. He might have been about thirty or thirty-two years old. And he begged me, his hands joined like for a prayer—that he had escaped from Majdanek and could I help him? He joined his hands in this way, knelt down in front of me, and said: "You are like the Virgin Mary." It still make me cry. "If I get through and reach Warsaw, I will never forget you."
>
> Well, how could one not have helped such a man? So I took him home, and I fed him because he was hungry. I heated the water so that he could have a bath. Maybe I should not mention this, but I brushed him, rinsed him, gave him a towel to dry himself. Then I dressed him in my husband's underwear, a shirt, and a tie. I had to do it for him because I wasn't sure if he could do it himself. He was shivering, poor soul, and I was shivering too, with emotion. I am very sensitive and emotional.

Despite the striped clothes and the shaven head, the stranger emerged as a human being, the vital connection perhaps being made by his prayerlike gesture. Overcoming what may have been some feelings of aversion and modesty, the respondent took him home to take care of his most basic needs. The interaction terminated quickly. The rescuer gave the man about ten zloty (less than a dollar), and he went on his way.

In the above case, the empathic response was a reaction to a compelling physical display of distress and plea for help from the victim. But cues need not be so visually apparent or forcefully conveyed to arouse an empathic response. The simple recognition of another's danger may prompt an empathic response even when the victim makes no explicit request. A Polish male, thirty-five years of age, responded in an entirely unexpected fashion when he was faced with a strange woman he knew was in danger simply because she looked Jewish:

> In November 1942, I placed an ad in the paper because I was looking for a maid. The third woman I interviewed had a really Jewish appearance. I do not remember our conversation now, but I knew I could not let her out in the street because she would get caught immediately. I checked some references for her because I wanted to make sure she was not involved in any political activity—that was my main concern. I thought to myself, "I am married, have a child, am in trouble myself. I live here unregistered, I trade illegally, I am a reserve officer. How can I let that woman go?" My conscience was telling me that she was sentenced to death because of her appearance. It was the only reason I helped; I couldn't let it happen. If somebody had told me before the interviews that I was going to take a Jewish woman as my maid, I would have said he was a madman.

In both of these episodes, the behavior was impulsive, an immediate reaction to the victim's condition.

Sometimes, however, an empathic motivation took longer to develop. One German rescuer was aroused to action only after he had made some assessment of the social background of the victims:

> In the spring of 1942 I was assigned to Tunisia as a paratrooper. We were to support the safe retreat of Rommel's African troops because the war in Libya was being lost. SS men were gathering up Jews, not to send them away from the area, such as to concentration camps, but for field work at the front.

We had taken a position, facing the Americans, forty kilometers south of Tunis. The Americans, provoked by our troops, made a paratroop attack. Many prisoners were taken. An Italian came to us with a report of spies hidden on a farm between the lines; he claimed that the spies had disclosed our positions to the Americans. I was assigned to direct the assault on the farm. We captured five young Jews; the Italian told us they were Jews. Two were sons of a physician in Tunis. All five were friends—their ages between sixteen and twenty.

The Jews were interrogated; they were very scared. We were monsters to them. They were afraid of anyone wearing a German uniform. The interrogation was conducted by an SS captain. He had been assigned to our unit as it was already customary at that time to assign Nazi Party members to military units. The decision was that these Jews were to be shot because they had been found in the front lines. I was in a leading position (*Regiments-gefechtsführer*), and they were assigned to me.

They were imprisoned in a railroad station. A report was sent to the division but was delayed by enemy action, and so the Jews were put to work digging trenches. A noncomissioned officer from the Hitler Youth came to supervise them during the daytime. They dug graves. The officer held a pistol to the temple of one and threatened to shoot.

In the evening when they came back, quite by chance I entered into a conversation with one of the physician's sons. He spoke German. His father had studied in Germany; they grew up in Sicily but had gone to a German school there. I was told of the threats by the noncommissioned officer. As I had all the documents, I knew that these five men had only come into the present situation by chance, and I knew they were to be shot merely because they had been found in enemy territory. I decided to help them somehow. I told them that I would release them from custody and help them to flee. They were very scared, suspecting we would shoot them during their escape. But I convinced them that I would help them. I provided them with food supplies and gave them a map, explaining the military frontier and how they needed to pass through the lines. I also gave them a pistol. I sent the prison guard away for a while and let them out of the prison. They began their flight in the dark of the evening.

In the instance above, empathy was largely a response to identification with certain surface characteristics—sufficient to lead the rescuer to assume at least some time-limited responsibility for the victims.

In some cases, the character of the empathic response changed. In the following episode the initial response was based on an almost reflexive empathy for a doomed homeless child. Within a short time, however, the rescuer's feeling was transformed into a deeper and more stable empathy, and he began to attend to the child's internal needs—not only present needs but future ones as well.

I think it all started right in the beginning of the war. The Germans bombed Rotterdam pretty badly, and children were sent out. We ended up with a boy about my daughter's age; he was with us for a long time. He was not Jewish. In 1942 a woman came to see us. She said she had heard we had a boy from Rotterdam and asked if we would mind having another. My wife agreed, but then the woman said that the boy was Jewish, and so my wife said she would have to talk it over with me first. When I came home at midnight, we talked about it and I agreed. The little boy, three years old, had asthma and wet the bed. My wife kept saying, "I am so glad we got this boy and not someone else." And then the little boy kept talking about his sister. So I began to snoop around and found out where she was. She was only a year and a half old. I decided that these kids should not be apart, and I brought her home as well.

When the little boy was five years old, someone came from the church to press us to send the boy to Sunday school. We talked about it and decided we had the obligation to save those children, not convert them—we did not have that right. Besides, we would have confused them. This way, they could go back to their mother with their own beliefs and own religion.

The rescuer understood the child's needs for rootedness in continuing relationships, with his sister then and with his mother in the future. He was able to see the world through the eyes and feelings of the child, even though the child himself was unable to articulate this view. The episode is also noteworthy because it did not begin as a result of a direct encounter with the child himself but rather with someone acting on his behalf. The woman making the request did not appear to be a particularly significant figure to the rescuer. She is described neither as a relative nor as a representative of some authoritative group, nor does she provide many details about the child. In this case, direct visible cues were absent, and information alone was sufficient to arouse the rescuer's empathy.[2]

In the case of "Stanislaus" empathic motivations were central and consistent.

Stanislaus was born in 1920 to a poor Polish Roman Catholic family. His mother had come to Warsaw from the countryside, where she worked as a domestic and part-time midwife. His father, who had some high school education, was disabled by an accident when Stanislaus was eight years old and lived on a pension thereafter. He had one brother, four years older than himself. He graduated from high school in 1939 but was unable to resume his studies until after the war, when he completed a degree in the diplomatic-consular department of the Academy of Political Science. During the war, he and his family lived near the Warsaw Ghetto. His helping activities continued over several years:

> The gallery of people changed all the time—it comprised several tens of people. Some obtained help in the form of a bowl of soup, others came for temporary shelter during the roundups. Still others, whom I had never met before, came and stayed with us until some other hideout was found.

The first incident he recalled involved Isidor, a "formerly rich merchant from Gdansk":

> He told me several times how the SS men had drowned his son. He settled in the ghetto and used to visit us at night. The ghetto was situated in Krochmalna Street, and we lived on Chlodna Street, so that between our house and the ghetto there was a kind of *Niemandsland* (no-man's-land). At night it was possible to bring that Jew in, and we treated him very cordially. Commercial transactions began between us. He used to come and say, "Stanislaus, listen" [he had a funny way of speaking], "could you buy that? Might you

bring something else we could sell and make some money?"
I remember that whenever he came at night with his socks
on (he had his socks on regardless of the temperature), he
always checked the pots to see if there was anything to eat.
Naturally, he sat down and ate because he was simply
hungry.

This contact, however, did not last long; Stanislaus says that
he and his mother were almost the witnesses of Isidor's death:

> My mother tried to help in every possible way. I still
> remember how we stood by the barbed wire on the corner
> of Krochmalna and Ciepla Streets—the wire ran in the
> middle of the street. On one side of the wire was that
> unfortunate Isidor, pale as death—and on the other side
> was my mother and me, my mother holding a loaf of bread
> with tears in her eyes. She threw the loaf over the wire, but
> others took it. These were our last moments, the last
> contact.

The daughter of a well-known Jewish antiquarian also used to
come to see them and stay overnight:

> With her, however, we had no trade relationship. Her
> father was unfit for any trade, and so was she. In that case,
> it was purely and solely providing help. She came to us,
> stayed overnight. Very often she went out in the street with
> my mother, and later with me.

But she too suffered a tragic end:

> Their fate was a terrible one. The ghetto border limits were
> changed in the meantime, and we had to move. One day
> she came with her friend whom we did not know—quite
> slim and very pretty, with very Semitic facial features. They
> told us a terrible thing. The Germans had come at night,
> collected all the families, and driven them to the
> Umschlagsplatz* to have them liquidated. The girls hid
> somewhere and later in the evening crossed the barbed
> wire in order to get to us. On the way they were accosted
> by two or three Polish males who pulled them into their
> place, raped them, and threw them out into the street.

*A large temporary concentration point from which people were then sent to their
deaths.

They stayed with us for about one month, and later on they
left one day and never returned; there is no doubt that
they perished.

His mother and he were responsible for the entire household:

My mother did not work, and my father was in the hospital
several times during the occupation. He was a complete
invalid—a living creature, but unable to help with
anything. My brother had moved out; he could not stand
the psychological pressure of living with all those people,
under threat of death twenty-four hours a day. He was
unable to sleep or eat. So there were two people to run the
house—my mother and me.

A total of twenty individuals stayed at Stanislaus's place or at
places he had managed to arrange for them for periods ranging
from several days to several years—an elderly married couple, two
sisters, a young man who had escaped from a concentration camp,
among others.

I made hideouts—not only in my own place but also in
some other places in Warsaw. There were double walls that
were made of bricks at that time, or of material called
Heraklit (cement-and-flax-board). It was three to four
centimeters thick and properly treated. Then it was
covered or painted or wallpaper was put on it—over some
hidden entrance. I made such hideouts in our home and
then in several other places. My first hideouts were very
awkward because I knew nothing about masonry. I laid the
bricks wrong and the whole wall collapsed. But then I got
professional advice from a bricklayer and learned how to
do it right.

He managed to supply food for them out of his own resources
and those of one of the Jews he was keeping:

First of all, the living standard was much lower then. Staple
food was based on groats or the like. My mother did the
shopping, buying in small quantities. Some of the people
we helped were poor as mice; I don't know how they
supported themselves. Professor T. was involved in
underground life, and he had contacts abroad from whom

he got money and that he distributed among those he was in charge of. He contributed, and so when peas or beans were boiled, my mother cooked for all. I worked for an accounting office and made as much as an average Pole earned then; I got an allowance in kind. I contributed my share; sometimes I got an allowance, some peas or the like. But it was partly the professor who supplied the money.

It was not by chance that so many people came to him. Stanislaus had many Jewish friends and acquaintances before the war, and he went to the ghetto often, even after the ghetto walls were sealed. Asked why he went there, he said:

> I had my friends there. Besides, when you went to the ghetto, everybody was buying and selling so that they could sustain themselves. Those people were sentenced to death even more than we were—of simple starvation. If somebody had colossal reserves of cash (I did not know such people), then he might be able to survive. But a workingman, like the man who worked in the slaughterhouse, had to do something to get a piece of bread.

One of the most noteworthy clues to Stanislaus' motivation is his recollection of details regarding almost all the individuals he helped—details not only of their physical appearance but also their psychological condition. He remembers, for example, what Isidor did before the war, how he spoke, what he wore, and what he looked like as he stood on the opposite side of the barbed wire. He remembers his mother with "tears in her eyes." He tells us not only the fate of the two girls before they arrived at his house but is also concerned with what happened to them afterwards. He is mindful of the advantages of the Jew with resources compared with the "workingman" Jew. He tells us about his invalid father and about his brother, who could neither eat nor sleep. He makes few references to himself; sentences that begin with "I" quickly change to focus on others. "I had my friends" in the ghetto, he says, and then begins to describe what life in the ghetto was like from the point of view of those who were there. Stanislaus thus appears particularly capable of centering on others' needs.

Understanding others, taking their perspective, and anticipating their futures may have left Stanislaus little psychological room to consider his own needs. He speaks little of his own wartime deprivations or even his mother's. His understanding of how others felt left him with the feeling of "no choice" regarding his response:

> Can you see it? Two young girls come, one sixteen or seventeen, and they tell you a story that their parents were killed and they were pulled in and raped. What are you supposed to tell them—"Sorry, we are all full already"?

It is reflected in the reasons he gives for his rescue decision:

> Human compassion. When someone comes and says "I escaped from the camp," what is the alternative? One alternative is to push him out and close the door—the other is to pull him into the house and say, "Sit down, relax, wash up. You will be as hungry as we are because we have only this bread."

Attachment to others—his mother particularly and his friends—was very important for Stanislaus. Friendships transcended ethnicity, religion, or social class, and once formed, they were enduring. He was born and brought up in a district inhabited by many Jews, and "the street on which we lived was 80 percent Jewish." Thus, he had lived among Jews, gone to school with them and had many Jewish friends before the war. "I was so involved with Jews," he said, "that I had even learned to speak Yiddish." His Jewish friends and acquaintances included the rich and poor, those of high and low social standing, the assimilated as well as those who were not.

Although Stanislaus described himself as "very independent" while growing up, he does not appear to have high self-esteem. (He scored more than one standard deviation lower than the mean on the Self Esteem scale.) He also revealed a somewhat fatalistic orientation toward life—a sense that external forces control his life (he scored almost one standard deviation lower than the mean on the Internal/External Locus of Control Scale). There is no indication that Stanislaus believed that any external power would protect or even help him; he describes both himself and his parents as not very religious. Although he was a member of the underground, there is no evidence that his activity was in any way connected to or supported by any organization. Not surprisingly, his empathy score was high, almost one standard deviation above the mean.

What Stanislaus also appeared to have was considerable ego strength. Like his brother, he, too, could have chosen to leave the maternal home—to escape the constant strain of witnessing human suffering and the risks entailed by his efforts to alleviate it. He chose instead to stay. It was not that he did not feel fear, however. "I don't want to say that we were not afraid—we were afraid too," and he is sympathetic toward those whose fear immobilized them from taking risks. Stanislaus, however, did not dwell on those risks but rather on the needs of those he helped.

How did such ego strength develop? Although his family was not particularly close while he was growing up, his mother in particular influenced him greatly. Three basic values recur consistently throughout his youth and his mature years: education, the need to care for others, and universal tolerance.

Stanislaus' mother valued education greatly, both as a means to social position and as a worthy end in itself. "She wanted to educate us and give us knowledge so that we would be competitive with others and get a good job and position." But knowledge was also a means for "understanding and interpreting the world," and because of his mother's attitudes, says Stanislaus, "my brother and I learned how to appreciate knowledge." He was "spanked" frequently by both parents when he didn't study hard enough, failed to prepare his lessons, or was "hanging around with bad boys." Although not an exceptional student in his youth, Stanislaus did acquire a master's degree in the diplomatic department of the Academy of Political Science after the war.

Caring for others and respect in its universal sense were both taught by his mother explicitly and by example. "I learned to respect the world from my mother," he said. His mother modeled caring behaviors in many ways. His childhood and adolescence were spent in a household filled with his mother's relatives, who sought her support as they looked for work or studied in the big city. His mother herself worked as a maid and midwife occasionally to earn the money necessary to provide for the boys' education. Stanislaus credits her with initiating his wartime helping activities.

Education, tolerance, and caring remain all-important to Stanislaus today. Asked what he would tell young people if a party with goals similar to those of Nazis came to power today, he replied: "I would tell them two things—about being tolerant and about human relationships, the relationship of one man to an other." Asked to describe the people he most admired during the war, he characterized one as "having knowledge and being wise," the other as being of "good heart, open-hearted, honest, powerful, and a person of strong beliefs." He remains a helpful person to day, regularly extending himself on behalf of the ill and the dis abled. One of the people he is currently very involved with is a Jew: "He is an old and disabled person who lives by himself. I shop for him and I visit him—I take care of his problems. I help him clean his apartment, wash windows, and so on."

Although Stanislaus feels most similar to Catholics and poor people, Jews continue to have a special place in his life. In addition to the fact that he lived in a predominantly Jewish neighbor hood in his youth and had many Jewish friends, his grandmother was born Jewish. As told by his mother, his grandmother gave up her religion and her very wealthy family out of love for his poor Polish Catholic grandfather. Sacrificing all on behalf of people one cares about is something Stanislaus understands, even if the other is an "outsider." Although it is not clear whether he ever knew his grandmother, her values were faithfully transmitted by her daughter to her son.

Unlike an empathic reaction, a normocentric reaction is not rooted in a direct connection with the victim, but rather in a feel ing of obligation to a social reference group with whom the actor identifies and whose explicit and implicit rules he feels obliged to obey. The social group, rather than the victim him- or herself, motivates the behavior. The actor perceives the social group as imposing norms for behavior, and for these rescuers, inaction was considered a violation of the group's code of proper conduct. Feel ings of obligation or duty are frequently coupled with anticipation of guilt or shame if one fails to act.[3] For their first helping act, the majority of rescuers (52 percent) responded to a normocentric expectation.

In some cases, a normocentric response was activated when a person of authority representing the salient social group simply asked the rescuer to help. In the following episode, a very religious German woman, the wife of a parish minister, himself a member of the Bekennende Kirche, responded to a joint request by her husband and a prestigious intermediary:

> I was called to the parish office by my husband. I was then
> expecting my eighth child. The wife of Professor T. was
> there and said she had come on account of two Jews who
> appeared to her as poor animals escaping from the hunt.
> Could they come that very afternoon to stay with me? I said
> yes, but with a heavy heart because of the expected child.
> K. came at midday—she was a bundle of nerves. They
> stayed for three weeks. I was afraid.

Asked for the main reasons why she became involved, she
said: "One cannot refuse someone who is concerned about the
fate of others." The "someone" she was concerned about was not
the Jews but her husband and the professor's wife.

Requests came from various authoritative sources whom rescuers felt obliged to obey: political groups, family members or
friends. Frequently, they came from resistance groups. For example, a Polish member of PLAN (Polska Ludowa Akcja Niepodleg-
losciowa, Polish National Independence Action) found himself
cooperating with Jewish resistance organizations. Asked why he
did it, he responded:

> It was not a personal, individual activity—I had orders
> from the organization. In helping these people, I was
> helping myself since it weakened the Germans. It was an
> act of cooperation, military cooperation.

In several cases, expectations were tacit rather than explicit;
the person knew that others with whom he was closely associated
were helping. Young people living in the parental household were
particularly susceptible to implicit expectations. A Frenchman
who was eighteen years old at the time simply said, "My mother
started . . . I'm not really sure she asked me . . . she told me about
it."

Similar acquiescence to the direction of others also motivated
the actions of "Ilse," a normocentrically motivated German
woman who kept a Jewish couple for four days.

Ilse was born in 1907, the daughter of a German Lutheran
minister. Her mother died when she was eight years old, and she
and her younger sister were then sent to a missionary school in
Basel, Switzerland. When Ilse was twenty-five years old she married a Lutheran minister with whom she lived in a small German
town in a rented parsonage with six rooms and two attics. During

the war, her husband served with the German military, and she along with her three children were living in two rooms in the parsonage. Other renters in the parsonage included a relative and a family with five children.

In the fall of 1944, the young minister of her district asked her to take care of a Jewish couple who were being moved from house to house:

> There would be no food stamps for them. Because a district school of the NSDAP [Nazional Sozialistische Deutsche Arbeiter Partei—the official name of the Nazi party] was in the town, and our parsonage was being observed, I had some concerns. My husband was in the service in Italy, and I was alone with the children. He had been harassed before he became a soldier. When I told the minister of my concerns, he said, "Please keep them at least for a few days." The large, deep cellar of our parsonage was used as an air raid shelter. I wondered what the neighbors would say when they came to the air raid shelter.

Ilse kept the family for four days, and then they left. Although the help was brief, it was nonetheless highly risky. Ilse was German, so she acted not against an external oppressor, as did rescuers from other countries, but against her own national authorities. Hence, the question of why she helped should be preceded by the question of what made her reject those authorities.

Ilse speaks negatively of Nazis. When asked if she felt any similarity to them, she said "not at all." Asked about groups of people toward whom she had strong positive or negative feelings, she repeated "Nazis—negative—rejection." But in fact she supported the Nazis in the beginning "because of their strong opposition to the Communists." What accounts for Ilse's change?

Ilse based her fundamental evaluations on what was happening to her own reference group—her husband and her church. "My husband," she said, "suffered on account of the Nazis and I was there with him." Her rejection of Communists was based on the same type of reason: "My husband suffered on account of the Communists, too," she said. Strongly embedded in her religious community, the daughter and wife of Lutheran ministers, she perceived the NSDAP as "persecuting the church."

Alienation from the larger political system and rejection of official policy stemmed primarily from her identification with the persecuted members of her own group. Overall, she had little awareness of what Nazis did to other nations and groups, including Jews. Asked on what occasion she became aware of what the Nazis intended to do to the Jews, she answered "I don't know." Asked how she felt the first time she saw a Jew wearing the yellow Star of David, she replied, "I never saw it." Nor had she ever heard or seen any forms of mistreatment of Jews other than what she might have heard when hiding the Jewish couple in her house.

"Helping one's neighbor" was an important religious norm for Ilse. The most important things Ilse learned about life from her religious leaders were "acquaintance with the word of God, participation in the church community, respect for other people, complete honesty, helping one's neighbor." How did the concept of "neighbor" develop to include Jews? For Ilse, Jews were rather remote. Before the war she neither knew any Jews nor was aware of any Jews living in her district. But when the minister asked her to hide Jews, she learned that Jews were being transferred from one locality to another by church representatives who were finding shelters for them among trusted church members.

Ilse did not perceive herself as an independent person. Among her childhood friends, "I always went along with what was happening; I never objected to anything." "I am not a leader," she said. She saw her role in life as primarily that of wife and mother. Her subordination to others had its roots in her early years. In talking about what she had learned from a meaningful figure in her childhood, a schoolteacher, she mentioned "consideration of each other, honoring adults, modesty, contentment with what was provided, and subordination." She was very grateful to her mother for teaching her "unconditional obedience, honoring others, including one's peers." From her father, she learned to "believe in God, prayer, and religious participation." This type of upbringing emphasizes obedience to authority.

For Ilse, the relevant authorities were her husband and her church. When the latter applied some degree of pressure, she was able to draw strength from her feelings of belonging to her religious community and the conviction that it was essential to fulfill the group's goals. Thus, her rescue action was taken in response to an authority, and the continuation of the activity depended on the continuing presence and support of the group.

In other cases, however, norms were internalized and the be-

havior assumed more of a voluntary and independent character.
Sometimes, norms were so strongly internalized that the behavior
appeared to be highly independent from any specific authority.
The normative "compass," as it were, existed within the self, and
the obligation to act derived from this self-concept. Approximately a fifth (19 percent) of rescuers were aroused to action by
an internalized norm.

Such an internalized normocentric orientation characterized
a Danish rescuer who began his activities in this way:

> In 1943, on the twenty-ninth of August, we heard that the
> Nazis were going to make a *razzia* and put Danish Jews into
> German concentration camps. Together with friends from
> the police department, we organized a refugee organization
> —it had no name. We ferried by taxi, and even by police
> cars, down to the commercial fishing harbor and arranged
> for people to go over to Sweden. The harbors were
> controlled partly by the German Navy but also by the Coast
> Police—a special department of the Danish police force.
> We had to be rather careful to do our "shipment" from
> places where controllers would not stop fishing boats and
> where we knew German Navy patrol boats would not be
> present. After a week's time, we managed to get all people
> of Jewish extraction out of the country—7,000 of them.

The rescuer did not await a request or approval from an identified authority, but rather independently, albeit in conjunction
with others, organized a ferrying group. Nonetheless, he believed
that Danish society approved the act and his participation
stemmed from a strong identification with the Danish community
and what he believed this community represented:

> The basic morality in this little homogeneous country is
> such that we have been told for generations to be nice to
> your neighbor, be polite, and treat people well. It came
> through during the war. You didn't want anything to
> happen to your neighbors or friends—so you fought for
> them. Denmark is a very lawful society and has law-abiding
> people. People would stop others from doing illegal things;
> even during blackouts, there was no theft. When the Jewish
> people came back to Denmark, they found all their
> property intact; nothing was missing. The Germans didn't

take it, and their neighbors and friends took care of it.
They came back to find their apartments just as they had
left them. It was the only country in which this happened.

His animosity toward Germans was also rooted in this identity:

As a small nation, we always had pressure from Germans
who had tried to advance northward for more than one
thousand years. My grandfather and great-grandfather told
me that we must hate the Germans because someday they
would try to take over. We had an anti-German feeling—
not person to person but nation to nation.

Being Danish meant helping all one's countrymen:

The main reason I did it was because I didn't want
anybody to hurt my friends, my neighbors, my fellow
countrymen, without cause. It was based on good morals
and good traditions.

In general, normocentric motivations were more conducive
to group actions than to strictly individual undertakings. Although
such motivations could lead to extraordinary sacrifices, they were
usually less likely to result in close personal relationships with the
victims. For rescuers like "Dirk," an internalized normocentrically
motivated Dutch rescuer, help was more often perceived as a matter of "duty" rather than sympathy or affection.

Dirk was born in 1911 to a wealthy Dutch Christian Reformed
family, the third oldest of ten children. He graduated from a technical school where he studied engineering. Before the war he
worked as a technical manager in a cotton printing plant and continued working there during the war. In 1936 he married an elementary school teacher with whom he had four children: a daughter born in 1937 and a son in 1938, and two additional children
born during the war, in 1940 and 1943. His family lived in a one-
story house consisting of five rooms with neither loft nor basement. His wife's parents came to live with them during the war.
Dirk joined the Dutch resistance, whose aims he described as "to
sabotage any rule that the Germans issued that did not lead to
open revolt."

In 1942, Dirk's brother-in-law, Ger, came to see him with a
rather unusual problem. Ger, a black market dealer, had been trad-
ing with a Jewish family:

He said to me, "These people [the Jews] will be picked up very soon if they stay where they are. I am afraid that they will be put under pressure to tell with whom they dealt and they will reveal my name. I want them to leave town."

Dirk recalls thinking that it was a "weird request" inasmuch as Ger showed no concern about the Jewish family but only himself. Nonetheless, Dirk promised to do what he could and went to see the Jewish family and said the following:

I am the brother-in-law of so and so. He wants you to get lost. If you ask me, I think he's damned right because if you keep sitting here, they will pick you up and ship you off to Westerbork and wherever the hell else they send you to.

Dirk had already seen how Jews were shipped in boxcars to Germany, allegedly "to work," but as he said, "I knew if you packed eighty people in small boxcars, it was not to work." The couple, however, was unconvinced, and he returned two more times repeating much the same thing on each visit. They finally agreed to leave if Dirk would take their fourteen-year-old daughter; they themselves would go to De Peel in search of shelter.

Dirk agreed and Sara, the daughter, came to stay with them. Dirk warned the parents, however, that they were to "close their mouths and say nothing." When Dirk's fourth child was born, however, the burden became too heavy, and he sought another place for Sara with a Christian Reformed family. The family insisted, however, that Sara's parents were not to be informed where she was, so as to avoid increasing the risk. If the parents learned of her whereabouts, Sara would be returned immediately. On learning of the new arrangement, however, Sara's father became very upset, went looking for her, and finally found her. The result was just as Dirk expected: " . . . that was the end of it. We had her back right away. They sent Sara back to us and we were back at square one."

For a while everything was fine, but then disaster nearly occurred:

It was Friday before Pentecost 1943. It was bedtime, seven o'clock, and my wife and I were looking out the window for our children to summon them inside. We saw a woman coming. We couldn't see too well because the street was directly in the sun's rays, but we saw that it was a woman walking between two girls. And slowly we made out that it was Mrs. Roth, Sara's mother—and she was walking with two girls who were the daughters of the local boss of the Dutch Nazis, who lived only four houses from us across the street.

As it turned out, Sara's mother had escaped from a *razzia* in De Peel and despite her husband's plea that she stay with him, she decided to look for Dirk. Having forgotten his address, she asked these two girls at random. Dirk was very upset and reminded her that he had given her specific instructions not to talk with anyone. Having done this, he now needed to find her a hiding place elsewhere, because all "guests" had to be reported to the local authorities.

He went searching among all his friends for a place to put Mrs. Roth, but could find none willing to take her. The next day he tried his friends at the plant where he worked; again no luck. Finally, a machinery repairman, "notoriously unreliable when it came to making promises and keeping them but completely trustworthy in regard to illegal work," advised him about two sisters who kept boarders. The repairman said:

> They ask no questions and report nothing. Just go there and say you have an aunt from Rotterdam who is still quite upset after the bombing of 1940. You tell them that she needs three weeks rest and that she has lost her voice.

Dirk did as the repairman advised and paid the boarding cost for three weeks, after which, the *razzia* over, Mrs. Roth went back to De Peel.

What prompted Dirk to help? Sara and her parents were not his friends, not even acquaintances. Nor had he met them under conditions in which their abandonment or helplessness was evident. On the contrary, he had to convince them of the danger they were in. Dirk did not comment on how Sara or her parents looked, nor do we have any indication that he was aware of what they felt. This does not mean, of course, that he did not have such an appreciation, but it is not a prominent feature in his story. His tone, on the whole, seems rather brusque—his brother-in-law wants them to "get lost," they are to "close their mouths." The reasons Dirk gave provide the first clue to why he helped but not the only one:

It's not because I have an altruistic personality. It's because I am an obedient Christian. I know that is the reason why I did it. I know it. The Lord wants you to do good work. What good is it to say you love your neighbor if you don't help them. There was never any question about it. The Lord wanted us to rescue those people and we did it. We could not let those people go to their doom.

Religious faith recurs repeatedly throughout his narrative; a faith that not only relied on God as the source of behavioral norms but also as the protector for those who obeyed them. That faith is evident in the following episode.

The family engaged in nightly Bible readings. During the very evening when Mrs. Roth arrived with the two girls, Dirk and his wife interpreted the reading for the night as God's message to them:

We read from the Bible the story of Elisha. When the Syrians were coming to take Elisha, his servant was very afraid and said to Elisha, "My lord, how are we going to survive? They are going to get you." But Elisha said no, and the Lord opened the boy's eyes, and he saw all the Syrians were dead. My wife said, "The Lord sickened his enemies with blindness then and he will do so again." I didn't believe her, but that's what happened. Those girls—the daughters of the local Nazi boss who escorted Mrs. Roth to our house—were also "stricken with blindness." They saw nothing strange in what was happening and never understood what was going on. I know the Lord protected us.

In this view, God wants his servants to help the needy, and in return he protects the just. Obedience to God offered protection if one but succumbed to his will. "I gave it up to the Lord," Dirk said. "It was in God's hands." As his father had taught him, "Trust the Lord."

Dirk had internalized the norms of his religion. "Love thy neighbor" had become so well integrated into his sense of obligations that he was able to act independently in the absence of external pressure, request, or even support from any group with the exception of his family. He felt this obligation even though Sara's parents violated the conditions of their agreement. Strongly embedded in his religious culture and belief system, and supported by his wife, he felt it was incumbent on him to assume personal responsibility. He also understood that outsiders were to be treated graciously. He recalled, for example, the frequent Bible readings in his grandfather's house, to which all were invited:

> At my grandfather's place, when they read the Bible, he invited everybody in. If a Jew happened to drop in, he would ask him to take a seat. He would sit there too. Jews and Catholics were received in our place like everybody else.

After the war he interpreted his responsibilities to include even Nazis. He accepted the organizational task of keeping Nazis from being lynched: "I had a function in the underground to keep order. I had to prevent people from murdering the Nazis."

People with strongly internalized norms can demonstrate considerable autonomy within the parameters allowed by the group or even straining the boundaries of permissible group behaviors. Nonetheless, they are not entirely independent of their groups, for they will stop short of acting in any way that would jeopardize their group membership. Dirk had already shown this capacity for balancing independence with attachment in his relationship to his father, whom he greatly admired:

> I learned many things from my father through his example. I certainly didn't want to become like my father, as much as I admired the man. I wanted desperately to have his approval, but I never quite got it. He wanted me to be a businessman like he was, but I didn't want that. I had too much brain power for that. He wanted me to marry a rich merchant's daughter, but I didn't like that.

The same was true of his political affiliations. While keeping his membership in the Antirevolutionary Party, the party to which his family also belonged, he was nonetheless critical: "The aim, the goal was okay, but they accomplished very little . . . and it was too much in the hands of the power cliques."

Dirk's personality scores reflected fairly high self-esteem (more than one standard deviation above the mean); they were moderately above the mean on social responsibility but lower than average on empathy. Deeply internalized norms that derived from his strong family and religious attachments—conjoined with a moderate sense of independence, self-esteem, and social responsibility that extended to others different from himself—appeared to motivate and sustain him in his rescue activities.

A principled motivation, like a normative one, is rooted in an indirect connection with the victim. The indirect connection, however, does not come about through a social group with whom the actor identifies but is rather mediated by a set of overarching axioms, largely autonomously derived. People with this orientation interpreted the persecution of Jews as a violation of moral precepts, and the main goal of their rescue behavior was to reaffirm and act on their principles. Even when their actions might prove futile, individuals tended to believe that the principles were kept alive as long as there were people who reaffirmed them by their deeds. Somewhat more than a tenth (11 percent) of rescuers were aroused to action by principles.

Rescuers, like most people, had multiple values, any one of which might assume supremacy at a given moment. For some rescuers, however, certain values became central principles around which they characteristically interpreted events and organized their lives. For these people, their principles were fundamental canons of belief whose violation was accompanied by strong moral indignation. They felt compelled to act more out of a sense of these principles than empathy for the victims.

These rescuers most frequently highlighted two kinds of moral principles—the principle of justice (the right of innocent people to be free from persecution) and the principle of care (the obligation to help the needy). Those motivated by the principle of justice tended to exhibit different emotional characteristics than did those who were motivated by the principle of care. They usually had more impersonal relationships with those they assisted and reserved strong emotions (anger and hate) for those who violated the principle of justice they held dear. Rescuers motivated primarily by care, on the other hand, usually focused on the subjective states and reactions of the victims. Kindness toward the victim was the dominant theme, while hate and indignation toward the violators were more transitory. In some cases the rescuer was even ready to extend help to the enemy if he was in pain or danger.

High independence from external opinions and evaluations is the major characteristic of people who share this orientation. Hence, they are more likely to act alone and on their own initiative. If other people are involved, it is mostly for instrumental reasons rather than for psychological support or guidance.

The capacity for such independent action has also been noted in individuals characterized by internalized norms. But principles differ in their origins from internalized norms. While internalized norms can be traced directly back to particular authoritative social groups, those who have a principled motivation appear to a great extent to develop their principles on the basis of their own intellectual and moral efforts. Normocentrically motivated persons refer repeatedly to certain groups or categories of people who espouse the same norms: religious groups, professional groups, friends, or family. Such references are rarely made by people with a principled motivation. To the extent that relationships are mentioned, they are presented as deliberately chosen on the basis of support for the principles to which the subject was previously committed. Adherence to the principles appears to play the primary role in determining the association. Among normocentrically oriented persons, it is the other way around—the reference group with which one is associated appears to be the source of values. As one representative of rescuers who had a principled motivation, we offer "Suzanne," who emphasizes principles of justice.

Suzanne was born in 1909 in Paris to a moderately religious Protestant Calvinist family. Her father was an engineer, her mother a housewife. She had one brother twelve years older than herself. Suzanne completed a university degree in mathematics in 1933. She never married. After her mother's death and her brother's departure from home, she lived with her father in a rented three-room apartment. She worked as a secondary school mathematics teacher in a small town, continuing to work at the same post after the war broke out.

> ... when Marshal Pétain came to power, it was evident that a dictatorship had begun. I knew that one of the first measures would be an indictment against the Jews. I did not react to the first indictment, but when the second statute was published [Xavier Vallat, commissariat general for Jewish Affairs in Vichy, in *La Dépêche de Toulouse* in May 1941], I decided to get involved. I wrote a letter to the three rabbis in my region, and as I remember what I wrote, it said:
>
> Sirs:
> I am very upset that in my country, in the twentieth

century, some citizens are persecuted for their religious or racial conditions. My ancestors, Protestants of Cévennes, have fought for their freedom of belief. I cannot but follow their example and at this time, I will be at your side. Can you put me in touch with some needy French families belonging to your faith so that I may be of help?

One of Suzanne's letters was intercepted, and she was accused of being a provocateur. Undeterred, she continued in her efforts:

About a week later, I received answers thanking me and asking me to provide them with infant clothing as many of the young mothers needed them for their babies. I quickly obtained the required items from the students in the sewing classes who gave me their sewing projects. I also received a letter asking me to get in touch with a Mrs. B. who was in charge of the distribution of clothing. I did so immediately. Through this person, I got in touch with eight Jewish families who needed to be placed in hiding in French homes. Most of the people needing help were intellectuals.

Around May 1942, during a school holiday, I went to Clermont-Ferrand—110 kilometers away—to meet with some refugees. Most of them, without knowing each other, were waiting for me at the train station. The next day I was introduced to several important people of the Rabbinic School—many ladies too. I was given a list of Jewish refugees for whom I would be responsible.

Once having decided on her course of action, Suzanne recruited all the people she knew who could possibly help her. She did not hesitate to use the young girls at her school:

In October 1941 or 1942, at the beginning of the school year, a pamphlet was distributed in my school with a message from the Department of Education and the Pétain government, asking all faculty and students to give a helping hand to French people who were undernourished or impoverished. . . . I informed my directress that I would primarily help the persecuted Jews who were incarcerated in concentration camps. She told me to do as I wished. I then read the circular to my students, aged fifteen and sixteen, and informed them of my own ideas on this matter. Three days later a delegation of students informed me that they too wanted to help. I then organized a corresponding agency between the incarcerated youngsters and my students. Unfortunately that activity did not last too long. All the Jews who were in the French camps were taken to Germany. They disappeared.

Suzanne spent little time, however, mourning failures. She was already busy assisting people detained at a "camp for foreign workers" at Châteauneuf-les-Bains. Again, she took the initiative, writing to the committee in charge to put her in touch with any families who might need help. She was referred to a Jewish family from Rotterdam who apprised her of the situation:

> The daughter of this family informed me by letter that all the men in the camp had been deported to Germany, and that now it would be the women's turn. In order to help the women, I wrote to the Cantal Prefecture asking them to furnish me with a list of all the Help Wanted personnel for domestic work, agricultural work, and so on. The only requirement for being placed was to give a local address, which was not hard for me to get. I then proceeded to place as many people as I could.

Nothing appeared too hard for Suzanne to do. In November 1942 she was asked by one R. V., who was in charge of the Clermont-Ferrand consistory, to accept the responsibility of saving as many children as possible. She was able to place many of them, but wasted little energy describing how she managed to accomplish this complex task:

> I placed the girls fourteen years and over in my school, the boys in the boys' school. The ones who were not able to keep up with the program were put on farms to tend the livestock. The smallest children were placed in boarding school. The parents of most of these children were arrested and taken to concentration camps in Germany.

Suzanne's actions were apparently not responses to direct contact with brutality or suffering; she describes no experiences in which she witnessed mistreatment of Jews or any other people. Her narrative does not center on the psychological states of the people she was helping. This does not mean, of course, that she was unaware of them, but they were not primary concerns for her. Rather she describes her activities as tasks to be done: collect clothing, take care of Jewish children, and find workplaces.

There is also no evidence that previous positive experiences with Jews had evoked in her any particular liking or compassion for Jewish people. Before the war she had very little contact with Jews. None lived in her area; nobody talked about Jews at home. Asked whether Jews went to the school she attended, she replied, "One did not know." Ethnicity, it appears, was an indistinct dimension during her childhood and adolescence. She did, however, have one Jewish friend before the war.

Suzanne's reason for helping was simple: "All men are equal and are born free and equal by right." Pressed by the interviewer to add other reasons, she replied, "There is no other." This is a fundamental conception of the principle of justice—universal in character, it extends to all persons. For Suzanne this principle was rooted in an intellectual world view that made infractions immediately obvious. Fascism, Nazism, and totalitarianism by their very nature violated the principle. "Consequently," she explained, "I am against all dictatorial systems." The Pétain regime was a dictatorship; she recognized its implications immediately and reacted immediately.

Personal relationships played no part in Suzanne's helping activities. Over three years, in various ways, she helped several hundred people, including over a hundred children, all of whom previously unknown to her. In all these cases she initiated helping and actively sought out people to help. She worked independently and was not connected with any resistance group. She did not seem to seek nor need any external reinforcement for her activity; the opinions of others apparently did not interest her. When asked what her neighbors who had found out about her activities felt, she replied, "Don't know." She was remarkably consistent in her action from the moment she made the decision until the end of the war. Stable and sustained task orientation, the impersonal context of helping, independence from external opinions or reinforcement, and engagement in action as long as injustice persisted—all testify to a principled motivation, as did her scores on the personality scales. Empathy is more than two standard deviations below the mean; social responsibility, on the other hand, is one standard deviation above the mean. While Suzanne was capable of acting with considerable self-confidence, it did not result from very high self-esteem; her self-esteem score was only average. This suggests that her ego strength emanated from her principles rather than a sense of self-importance.

How did Suzanne develop into such a person? She describes her family as "very close and very united." Unity came from a convergence of values shared by both parents as well as her brother, twelve years her senior. Both mother and father emphasized above all being a responsible person. It was a value she learned well; "I always finish a task I commit myself to," she said. Her father particularly emphasized the need "to take care of one's neighbor and the duty to be an example to others." She credits her brother with having "taught me to practice and to live a good life." Her brother was a much-decorated hero of the resistance.

Neither parent belonged to any political party. Both shared a Calvinist background, and their religiosity was not expressed in church attendance but rather by frequent readings of the Bible. The effects of their teachings are reflected in Suzanne's assessment of herself as a young adult. She describes herself as being very honest, very independent, very capable of taking responsibility and risks, very helpful, and very ready to assert her convictions. While she too did not see herself as religious, she did see herself as a "very moral person," which she attributed largely to her Protestant upbringing.

While Suzanne attributes much of her morality to her parents, it was not developed out of simple acquiescence to their expectations. She challenged them frequently, and they frequently had to discipline her. Her mother depended primarily on reasoning to convince her daughter of the rightness or wrongness of certain behavior, and when this failed, "she just ignored me." Her father would sometimes slap her in exasperation. Confrontation and disputation also marked her closest friendships. "We argued about everything," she says of her two closest friends, "life, death, religion, and so on." She insisted on screening all behaviors and comments through the prism of her own thinking and autonomously chosen principles. "I never just accepted what others said," she commented. In relationships with her friends, she saw herself as primarily a "leader." It was out of such intense interactions that her sense of self was carved.

Although she did not feel like an outsider with respect to her community, neither did she feel she quite belonged. Part of this, she says, was due to her intense involvement in caring for her father and her similarly intense commitment to her work. It was not because she felt unlike others—she felt very similar to other Protestants in particular and only somewhat less so to Gypsies. (Perhaps the latter represented to her an independence of lifestyle and risk that she admired.) As for Jews, Turks, rich or poor, she said she simply did not know if she felt similar to them. Her sense of universal obligations to others did not stem from feelings of psychological similarity to them but rather from her commitment to the principle that all persons are entitled to be free. She is not a "joiner"; her principles are not expressed through affiliation with groups. But she finds opportunities to express them in whatever setting she finds herself. A mathematics teacher, she does not confine her classroom activities to teaching mathematics, but also uses it "to teach my students about free speech."

Suzanne's ego strength emerged from her intense commitment to principles first learned in her family but sharpened and strengthened through subsequent self-reflection and keen scrutiny. Thus, it is not surprising that she apprised her father of her offer of help to Jews only after she had sent her letter. He approved, of course, but one senses that she would have continued her activities even if he had not.

Another representative of rescuers with a principled motivation is "Louisa," who emphasizes principles of care.

Louisa was born in 1909 to a Dutch Christian Reformed family. Her father was a military officer; her mother, an artistically talented woman, did not work outside the home. Louisa had two sisters, one two years older than herself and the other four years younger. Louisa was an educated woman, having studied at the Sorbonne before the war and later in the United States. At twenty years of age, she left home for Paris where she worked as a writer and journalist. She married a German artist before the war with whom she had two daughters. Divorced in 1940, Louisa married a Dutch agricultural-college graduate who had a nine-year-old son from a previous marriage. She lived with her second husband and three children in Holland on the outskirts of Amsterdam.

Her rescue activities began in 1940 when some Jewish friends asked her to store some valuable items for them. When her friends were forced into a ghetto, she took their three-year-old son and kept him. She and her husband joined the Dutch underground. During the course of the next few years, many Jews and others came to her home for shelter, adults and children. She continued her activities until liberation.

The reasons Louisa gives for her activities are quite different from Suzanne's:

> I cannot give you any reasons. It was not a question of reasoning. Let's put it this way. There were people in need and we helped them.

The "reason" is thus so vague that it cannot even be articulated. Moreover, unlike Suzanne's, it appeared to be highly unpremeditated in character.

> People always ask how we started, but we didn't start. It started. And it started very gradually. We never gave it much thought. We did not wake up one morning and simply say, "We are going to do it."

On the surface, Louisa's focus on "people in need" suggests an empathic motivation, an interpretation that is supported by one other account in her interview, when she describes with great understanding and care the troubles of a Jewish woman who could not bear the stress and almost went mad. But this episode is an exception. Her narrative, which is almost fifteen typewritten pages in length, rarely focuses on the characteristics of those she helped.

Louisa's focus on "people in need" might also reflect a normocentric orientation—an embeddedness in some referent social group. She describes herself as very influenced by religion in her growing-up years. And at one point she makes reference to her Christian identity. While trying to persuade a Jew to accept her offer of help, he turned to her and said, "This has come over our people . . . and we should have to suffer it." She rejected his reasoning:

> Well then, this is something that comes over our people, too. I am a so-called Christian, and all those people who did this to you are Christians too. The people who call themselves Christians do this to you.

She then went on to explain to the interviewer:

> I was consciously aware that I was so ashamed of what other so-called Christians did that I felt I wanted to do the

contrary. I wanted to counterbalance that as much as I could.

But nowhere else does she refer again to religion—nor does she make any single spontaneous comment about God.

The characteristics of the interview cannot comfortably be categorized as those of either empathic or normocentric motivation. A central comment that suggests that the motivation here was principled in character emerges from a conversation she reports between herself and her mother:

> My mother said, "I don't think you have the right to do this. Your responsibility is for the safety of your own children." I said to her that it was more important for our children to have parents who have done what they felt they had to do, even if it costs us our lives. It will be better for them—even if we don't make it. They will know we did what we felt we had to do. This is better than if we think first of our own safety.

What, we may ask, could be more important for children than the lives of their parents? What appears to be at stake here is some fundamental principle—difficult to articulate but nonetheless worth dying for and important enough to leave as a heritage for one's children.

This principle, best described as an ethic of care, is a dominating sense of obligation to help all people out of a spirit of generosity and concern for their welfare. While focus on others' needs is also characteristic of an empathic motivation, the ethic of care is more inclusive. An empathic motivation focuses on specific individuals whose needs assume paramount importance over others. While the ethic of care also emerges out of concrete situations and involvement with others, it is best captured by what Gilligan describes as a concern with minimizing overall harm to all to as large an extent as possible.[4] The interests of individuals may be subordinated to the greater good, as demonstrated in the following incident, when Louisa put her son at risk out of the greater concern for all in her charge:

> We saw a big car in front and knew it was the Germans. It was a big official Ford. Everyone ran out the back door and into the tunnel and disappeared with my husband. But our

children and the Jewish children were taking a nap upstairs. I knew we could not all run. I stayed because I was the last one anyway. I picked up the papers [files on people in hiding] and put them in the sweater that my nine-year-old son was wearing. I said to him—a terrible thing to say—"Try to get out of here quietly and disappear with the papers." He said yes.

Exposing the child to danger appeared to offer the best chances of success in protecting all the people under her care.

This emphasis on coordinating the interests of all, rather than on particular individuals, is evident in yet another of Louisa's reactions during this incident. With the Germans who had arrived at her home was a friend of hers who managed to tell her that he had been arrested and would undoubtedly be killed that evening. Under repeated questioning by the German searchers, she of course denied knowing anything about others' whereabouts. But the reason she gives for such denial is instructive:

I kept denying that I knew anything about it. I had to. I had to rescue all those other people, and I had to rescue my own friend.

"All those other people" included her husband, yet she does not single him out for special treatment. He was submerged in the collective group, which now also included her friend. While the collective to whom she felt responsible at that moment were all those in her house and her newly arrived friend, potentially it included anybody in need:

We helped people who were in need. Who they were was absolutely immaterial to us. It wasn't that we were especially fond of Jewish people. We felt we wanted to help everybody who was in trouble.

Consistent with that view, she began her activities (as she describes it), "the moment the Jews started to get into trouble."

Caring for others had little to do with their intrinsic merit. In fact, Louisa carefully refrained from judging others. She made a point of saying, for example, that the rule observed by her underground group enjoined them "never to judge each other on how much German interrogation we can stand, because they were very cruel. Nobody can judge each other's thresholds for pain." She extended this point of view to others who did nothing during the war:

People often talk harshly about those people who did not help. I don't think that's right. I don't find it such a courageous thing to do. For certain people it is the self-evident thing to do. For other people, it is not evident that they can do it somehow. We have never condemned people, even friends of ours, who did not do it. They couldn't and we could—for whatever reason.

A principled motivation centered on care is very much concerned with the whole context of others' behaviors: If one could stand in the other's shoes, the reasons would be clear. Enlightened empathy mitigates disapproval; understanding replaces evaluation; perspective taking strengthens attachments. Relationship is central to care; judging others jeopardizes relationships.

Relationships based on friendship are of central importance to Louisa. She speaks repeatedly of her "friends"—friends she had before the war, friends she made during the war as well as after the war. It is in the process of befriending that life's satisfactions are best found. When the costs of friendship are high—as they were during the war—the feelings are intensified. It is therefore not entirely surprising that Louisa speaks of those times as having a special kind of beauty: "It was a very beautiful time in the sense of togetherness; we were all for the same thing: to be together."

The importance of relationship and the responsibility to care for others were important features of Louisa's parental home. Her family was a very close one, her mother and father united in an unusual, loving way:

It was the happiest marriage I have ever seen. I have never seen people so much in love until the last moments of their lives.

She describes her mother, the person she regards as most influential in her life, as her "friend":

My mother influenced me mostly by love. She was a warm woman, and we admired her for her wit, her wisdom, and her intelligence. She was our friend and we could confide in her.

Her father, a very religious person, was nonetheless extremely liberal about others' life-styles:

> As a child, I didn't get along with him because he was very strict. He was a very devoutly religious person [who] influenced us greatly without us knowing it with his genuine religion. He was not hypocritical. He was enormously strict for himself and enormously liberal toward other people.

What both parents communicated was an ethic of care and social responsibility that Louisa subsequently adopted for herself:

> They taught me discipline, tolerance, and serving other people when they needed something. It was a general feeling. If somebody was ill or in need, my parents would always help. We were taught to help in whatever way we could. Consideration and tolerance were very important in our family. My mother and father both stressed those feelings. My father would not judge people who lived or felt differently than he did. That point was always made to us.

For Louisa, life lived apart from others has little value (reflected in her low score on the "detachment" measure). Her strong sense of social responsibility is reflected in her high scores on the Social Responsibility Scale and the Prosocial Action Orientation. Thus, Louisa values friendships not because they fulfill self-enhancement needs or because of the unique characteristics of each friend but rather because they offer her the opportunity to express care.

The content of Suzanne's and Louisa's principles may have varied, as did the importance of personal relationships in their lives. Both, however, shared a commitment to principles that did not allow them to rest until the wrong or the "hurt" was somehow set right.

The variation in motivations leading to rescue behavior highlights the important point that the paths to virtue are neither uniform nor standardized. Rather, they represent alternative pathways through which individuals are equipped and disposed to interpret events of moral significance. Different rescuers found different meanings in what was happening to Jews, but once their plight was understood through the prism of the individual's orientation, the necessity to act became compelling.

Most commonly, rescuers were normocentrically oriented. Thus, they were aroused to act by external authorities whose values and standards they had internalized to varying degrees. The majority of rescuers (52 percent) perceived helping Jews as a means of expressing and strengthening their affiliations with their social groups. Those whose group norms were only weakly internalized depended on overt pressure from some authoritative group member to initiate and sustain their activity. (This suggests the potential power authoritative social groups might have galvanized in the service of rescue had more of them chosen to do so.) Those who had internalized their group norms deeply did not require such external pressure.

The empathic orientation was the next most common. An empathic reaction was characteristic of more than a third (37 percent) of rescuers. They had a particular capacity to focus on others' needs and to be moved by their distress. While visible cues were necessary for some, for others merely knowing that others were suffering was sufficient to arouse them. Principled motivations largely autonomously derived were the least common type of motivation. Only 11 percent of rescuers were aroused to action by principles alone.[5]

While in many cases, the motivation appeared to be similar over a number of different helping acts, in several others the motivation for the first helping act was not necessarily the same for the second or third. Nor did the motivation that first aroused the rescuer to action necessarily remain the same during the course of the behavior, even in relation to the same person or people being helped. A normocentric initial motivation sometimes became more empathic as bonds formed between the rescuer and rescued. The same was true for principled rescuers. As one rescuer motivated by the principle of justice explained it, "I began to like the people I was helping and became very distressed at what was happening to them."

What is of final importance is that receptivity to such diverse catalysts did not suddenly emerge in the context of the traumas of the Holocaust. Rather, preparation began long before in the emotions and cognitions through which rescuers normally and routinely related to others and made their decisions. Thus, their responses were less explicit conscious choices than characteristic ways of attending to routine events. Already attuned to conferring meaning on events through their particular moral sensibilities, they depended on familiar patterns to discern the significance of the unprecedented events at hand. To a large extent, then, helping Jews was less a decision made at a critical juncture than a choice prefigured by an established character and way of life. As Iris Murdoch observes, the moral life is not something that is switched on at a particular crisis but is rather something that goes on continually in the small piecemeal habits of living. Hence, "at crucial moments of choice most of the business of choosing is already over."[6] Many rescuers themselves reflected this view, saying that they "had no choice" and that their behavior deserved no special attention, for it was simply an "ordinary" thing to do.

CHAPTER 9

The Enduring Significance
of Altruistic Acts

The war was a traumatic horror, and like other survivors of traumas, rescuers and nonrescuers continued to be haunted by it afterward. Memories were often suppressed only to return with increased intensity as the individuals grew older. Events they did not necessarily fully comprehend during the war itself or even immediately thereafter sometimes assumed new and deeper meanings in their later years. As one rescuer described it: "Sometimes in history you have an eruption of evil that is so archetypal, so demonic, that you can never get it out of your system again . . . but that dawns on you much later in life."

But just as rescuers and nonrescuers differed in their perceptions during the war, they continued to differ in later years. This difference in the lasting significance of wartime events is reflected in their different recollections and interpretations of events. Rescuers' memories and their current behaviors continue to reflect more of the values of inclusive care and characteristics of empathy and personal responsibility than do those of nonrescuers. They concentrate less on their own victimization and speak more of others' pain and others' losses. They derive some comfort and gratification from the knowledge that they were able to help some Jews survive and from an enduring sense of connectedness with those they helped as well as to a larger humanity. They continue today to be more involved in community activities.

Immediately after the war, rescuers and nonrescuers alike were most concerned about restoring some normalcy to their lives. Rescuers and rescued who were together until the war's end generally parted immediately or shortly thereafter. Jews went searching for kin who might have survived; surviving parents or other family members came back to reclaim their children. A few rescuers remained with their rescued for a few months or a few years and sometimes emigrated with them. A few subsequently married those they had helped; some in this group emigrated to Israel together. The vast majority, however, remained where they were and turned their attention to themselves and their own families. The dominant concern of all was the reconstruction of shattered lives. Above all, they had to attend to their own wounds, physical and psychological, as well as those of family members:

> I was home when my brother came from the concentration camp. Mom saw him approaching from afar. "Who is that old man coming?" she asked. It was my twenty-two-year-old brother. You should have seen the boils he had. Mom cried. He was 190 pounds when he left and he was 90 pounds when he came home. He was sent to Germany—he was in hiding but they found him. His brain is damaged in one way or another. He is not crazy but it has damaged him.

> I have a brother who is three years younger than I am. He was in a concentration camp for twenty-two months. It completely broke the man. He is past fifty and completely broken down. He has never overcome the memories of the things he went through.

While rescuers from all countries had to attend to personal and family traumas, Poles in particular suffered grievously at the hands of the Nazis. More Poles reported family deaths and severe damage to themselves—amputated limbs, recurring bouts with ill health, and other permanent disabilities. Several also encountered new threats—actual or potential arrest because of their participation in ideologically suspect underground organizations during the war.

Of the war most rescuers tended to speak little, partly because they were too busy or wanted to forget:

> In those times we didn't talk too much about it. There was a big void. Why did we leave it for so long? I have a few answers. In my country [Holland], the fifties and sixties were a time of rebuilding. Everyone worked hard. There was no unemployment. Everyone was busy with his own

restoration. Second, Jewish people who came back from the concentration camps wanted to forget—they had no household and no children. They wanted to build a new life.

They also wanted to avoid painful confrontations—assorted friends, neighbors, and family members valued before the war were known Nazis or collaborators, while the activities of many others were clouded in ambiguity. Some did not speak because they did not want to present themselves as boastful—like others, they say, who aggrandized themselves undeservedly after the war. And some were not quite certain that their activities would be warmly received by others. "I never speak about it," said one rescuer, "because I know that some people would regard what I did as bad or stupid." Even years later, and even among those who emigrated, it was not necessarily desirable to be perceived as a friend of Jews:

> The Polish American community does not take too well to my special involvement with Jews. When I needed some information from them in Chicago, there was much hostility and gossip—they suspected me of being a Jew. One time I told them that to the best of my knowledge, I wasn't, but if I was, so what? There is still a lot of anti-Semitism among Polish Americans and narrow mindedness. This doesn't mean everybody, but there are a lot.

One Dutch rescuer now living in Canada initially agreed to be interviewed for this study but refused to speak more than five minutes with the interviewer on her arrival. It was all a mistake, she said. She had done nothing unusual during the war; she did not know if she had helped any Jews at all. As her astonished daughter later explained by telephone to the interviewer (who had left), her mother had just been visited by a wartime friend still living in Holland. Her friend had told her that Nazi groups in Holland were searching for those who helped Jews and would often pose as sympathetic inquirers in order to uncover their identity.

Similar fears explain why some rescuers did not attempt to bring Nazis to justice immediately after the war. While a significantly larger percentage of rescuers were involved in this process than were bystanders in particular (18 percent compared with 7 percent)—giving testimony and cooperating in arresting Nazis and their collaborators—the majority refrained from such activities. Several abandoned preliminary efforts only after they became convinced of their futility; they could not locate the people they considered most culpable or they were unable to produce the necessary documentation. A few deliberately excluded themselves because they were horrified by what they perceived as vindictive and excessive retaliations, the product of unrestrained anger and personal vendettas rather than considered weighing of the evidence.

But for most, the reason was their greater concern with the resumption of normalcy, in which jobs and careers were critical issues. Approximately half of all respondents went on to new jobs. All groups experienced some upward mobility, but rescuers continued to maintain a significant occupational advantage. An additional 20 percent among them joined the upper occupational levels (professional, business, and administrative) compared with approximately 14 percent of all nonrescuers and about 11 percent of bystanders (Table 9.1). To some degree these differences may be due to the educational advantage a small number of rescuers had immediately after the war compared with all nonrescuers. While all groups eventually achieved similar levels of education, a larger percentage of rescuers than nonrescuers had completed their university education before the war. Some rescuers were thus in a better position to take advantage of the then expanding economy.

Some part of their success may also be attributable to the networks rescuers had formed or solidified during the war. Several of them tell of work opportunities opened to them by virtue of their wartime associations. Rescued Jews themselves sometimes facilitated such opportunities, offering or finding jobs for those who had helped them. A small percentage of rescuers was recruited by agencies working with displaced persons; such posts in turn led to other opportunities. It is also likely that the personal characteristics of many rescuers, which facilitated rescue, are related to achievement generally. More accustomed to feeling personally potent, rescuers may have applied that sense to the marketplace. More accustomed to diversity in their social relationships, they may have had more developed social skills that facilitated upward mobility. More accustomed to taking risks, they may have ventured to assume them in relation to business and positions of authority.

With the passage of years, as lives returned to some semblance

· of normalcy, rescuers not only continued to remember their wartime experiences but also to reflect on them. Conscious reflection to a large degree mirrored societal reflection. Renewed interest in World War II and the Holocaust as well as the activities of Yad Vashem and our study itself caused them to bring to the surface what were frequently only vague and partially formulated feelings and thoughts. The war continues to remain for them an overwhelming nightmare, but it was not totally bereft of gratifications. Some recall it as the best of times as well as the worst of times—a period when friendships, unity, and a common goal transcended the paltriness of ordinary relationships under more routine circumstances. For them, helping Jews was part of it, not because of any external rewards they may have received, but because in doing so they asserted their humanity at a time when the normative order was destroyed and moral anarchy reigned.

Having behaved in a manner consistent with their values was a source of self-esteem for several:

I am very glad to have done these actions—very proud too.

I'd do exactly the same if the situation recurred. I think about these moments. Everything lives in me. I have good feelings about what I did. I respect myself for doing it. I think I did some good in my life. I didn't do it because I expected something—I wasn't forced to help.

I think that I did what I could—what was possible to do. I knew I was risking my wife's life, but her attitude was very positive. I knew I risked my child's life when a Jewish woman took him for a walk. But I was supported by my wife. She thought what I did was good. I was also supported by my mother and brother.

Rescue allowed them to preserve their sense of integrity and identity. Their image of who they were and what they represented has remained intact:

I did everything from my heart—I didn't think about getting something for it. My father taught me to be this way. I still feel the same way now. I cannot refuse if somebody needs something. That's why I still help people— I'll do it until I don't have the strength to do it anymore.

My nature is the result of being raised by my mother.
She was my role model. She helped a lot of people.

For several, the very idea of any external reward—whether in the form of public appreciation, honors, or monetary compensation—is itself repugnant. What they did, says this group, was just ordinary:

I do not feel I am a hero. I feel that I only did my duty. I am not a hero.

I insist on saying that it was absolutely natural to have done this. You don't have to glorify yourself—considering that we are all children of God and that it is impossible to distinguish between one human and another.

One woman went to great lengths to explain why she rejects the title of "hero" or "Righteous Gentile" (the latter is the label given by Yad Vashem). Labels, she argued, distort the true meaning of events:

We are now called "Righteous Gentiles" or even sometimes "heroes." We very much object to this title, and I can tell you why. One day there was an air raid on the German barracks near our house, some five kilometers away. My husband happened to be there ... When it was over, the barracks were very badly hit. A German soldier came running out with his head practically destroyed. He was bleeding heavily and was obviously in shock. He was running in panic. My husband saw that within minutes he would fall down and bleed to death. So my husband put him on his bicycle—without thinking about it—and brought him to the commandant's house. He put him on the step, rang the bell, waited to see the door open, and left. Later some of our friends and people who were hiding with us heard about it and said: "You are a traitor because you helped the enemy." My husband replied: "No, the moment the man was badly wounded, he was not an enemy anymore but simply a human being in need." As little as we could accept the title of "traitor," so little can we accept the title of "hero" for things we did to help Jewish people. We just helped people who were in need.

Some see themselves not as true actors but rather the instruments of God; hence, any glory belongs to God and not to them:

> The rescue—not only in our family but by many more
> Dutch people—was an act of faith. We were only
> instrumental in saving her. The way I see it, it was not my
> work—it was God's work.

> What I did was my duty as a Christian and as a brother.
> Our feeling about the Jewish people is that God has a
> purpose for them. I always say, "Look at Israel—three
> million people surrounded by forty million enemies—how
> can they exist?"

Even talking about the experience was distasteful to some. The distaste stemmed not only from their sense of not having done anything unusual but also from their view that what they had done paled in comparison with the deeds of real heroes—those who had died for their efforts:

> I admire the people who constantly concerned
> themselves with providing for the A.'s [the people she
> helped] or for others—such as Reverend M. By comparison
> my help is not worth mentioning. There was a minister
> who died in a concentration camp, but he continued to
> appeal to the conscience of the prison personnel until the
> very end.

Some find it difficult to speak because rescue occurred in the context of multiple deaths, memories of those they could not help, as well as times when they themselves had to kill in order to save other lives. Such memories are painful counterpoints to the victories of rescue:

> It is something you cannot plan, this horrible adventure
> with the devil. They came like a tidal wave. When a wave
> comes over a village, you are lucky to be alive and be able
> to save people. You do it—you don't sit down and ask,
> "Can I do it?" It is part of your body—the will is part of
> your body—you feel and you do it. Thank God, my wife,
> family, and I came through. But the poor men and girls
> who were fighting against the Nazis were killed. We lost
> several friends.

My youngest brother was tortured to death by the SS. After the war he was reburied by the Army—they gave him a military funeral. In one year my mother lost a husband and two children.

I did a lot, but there were situations in which I couldn't help at all. I was in such situations a lot. For example, there was this girl, Teresa—she always looked out the window and I would put something in her outstretched hand . . .

In order to help others, I had to liquidate Gestapo agents. It is not a pleasant memory.

What ultimately persuaded one couple to talk was the appearance of neo-Nazis and revisionists who are now denying that the Holocaust ever occurred:

We have not talked about it much with other people because we have always had a terrible fear of giving the impression that we were boasting about it. Even our very close friends did not know. When we got the medal, they were absolutely flabbergasted because they had no idea we had done anything. Of late we have felt we should talk about it because there is so much denial of the Holocaust. I think that's dangerous—especially from the Jewish people's point of view. So now I feel that we should talk about it and not be scared of the judgment of people who say that we are boasting.

What persuaded yet another woman to speak was her perception of the world's need to know that the ethic of caring existed:

It is so important to know that people like my mother, who did not blow up trains or shoot people in the dark, did what she was really cut out to do—to sustain life rather than destroy it. People like her have made such a difference in this world.

The palpable rewards of rescue for some have come from new attachments—sometimes deep friendships for which they are grateful and that they feel have enriched their lives.

We became very close. The woman was older—I was only twenty-three or twenty-four years old—what did I know about anything? I was still too young to really understand, but I became closer to her—she could have just about been my mother. We still keep in touch—we always write to the children. We are still one family.

After the war, we stayed together with these Jewish people. I went with them to Austria. I stayed in a displaced persons camp until I left for Canada in 1948. Then I lost contact with them, but I got their addresses later from someone I knew in Montreal. I started to write, and now we are like a good family. Anything over there—New Year, weddings, bar mitzvahs—we are all over there.

The involvement with rescue strained me—maybe because I was so young. I neglected my studies, but I learned about life. I got to know some fascinating people— Jews. I even got to know one Jew who helped me after the war with specific projects.

Being in close contact with Jewish people enriched my life; I learned about a culture different from my own and made lifetime friends.

We were both pleased to have found true friends.

"Thankfulness" was the way one woman expressed it, suggesting her sense of gratitude for a benefit she had received. The "gift" she received was the knowledge that the family she had helped would be assured of a living future:

After the war was over, we visited each other all the time. On the fifth of May every year, they brought us a gift—a chicken or something. [When] we left the Netherlands in 1950, they gave us a big dinner. After we came back in 1958, they took us to Paris for a trip. I am not proud of what I did, only thankful. We were the most thankful when their one son married a Jewish girl who had also been in hiding. I was proudest when they had a grandson. Don't you think that's nice? That for me was the most thankful moment. They can now perpetuate their family and not be annihilated.

This sense of appreciative attachment to some larger humanity is expressed by yet another woman honored at Yad Vashem. The experience left her with the feeling that she was connected in a vital way with the past and the future by way of a spiritual heritage she would leave for her grandchildren:

> It was a wonderful feeling when I was in Jerusalem to receive a medal. The inscription on it says, "Whoever saves one life, it is as though he saves the whole universe." It is wonderful—I love it. I went into the eternal flame building and was given the honor. It was an unbelievable feeling. I felt the whole floor was filled with faces—I could see the faces. It was an eerie feeling. I thought they were there, and it is up to us to make sure they are not forgotten—that they did not die in vain. I am not Jewish, but I have Jewish feelings in my heart. I saw what happened, and no one can take that away from me. I talk to Jewish people and to non-Jewish people and tell them the same thing I am telling you now. My grandchildren know that my medal from Israel is my treasure. It is my heritage. They know it is for them— they know that it will be there for them. I think they will become better people because they have the background, and it is hard not to be affected. They know what I did. I think they will be better for it. They will have an understanding ...

Some rescuers are embarrassed by the amount of appreciation they have received. "It is too much," said one man who had been to Israel, where he was effusively greeted by a number of those he had helped. They not only pressed gifts upon him but insisted that he stay at their homes and publicly praised him at Yad Vashem ceremonies. His is not a unique experience—several rescuers have been overwhelmed by their reception at Yad Vashem and recall it as one of the high points of their lives. One woman, who accompanied her elderly mother whom she pressed into going, feels it was a fitting conclusion, allowing her to feel that she too is now connected to something larger than herself and her immediate environment:

> Yad Vashem was wonderful—what an experience! We had no idea it existed. One day Emile was visiting with us in Holland and he said, "What do you think about being honored by Yad Vashem?" And he explained what it was. My mother said, "No, no, that's not for me." But I persuaded her: "Mother, you should really do it. You know

how it is. People want to express their gratitude. It's not just for you. It's also an opportunity to say 'thank you' in a tangible way." So she thought about it—she was old, already eighty years of age, but in the end she decided to go. We all went—my brother, myself, and my mother. We had this impressive ceremony—it's a beautiful place, very moving ... wonderful! It's something that sort of rounds off the whole experience. It makes me feel as if I have a place in Israel and I can go there. Part of me is there and I like that idea.

However, rescuers did not necessarily need Yad Vashem or sustained contacts with those helped in order to feel rewarded. One Polish man was simply gratified to learn that the friendship he had valued so highly continues to be meaningful to the young woman he helped:

She left for Sweden to study. She wrote to me: "How could you think, A., that I would ever forget you?" A colleague of mine visited her ... she is married with two grown children, both of them physicians. She told him— she said it formally—that she owed it all to me ... it was a true friendship.

Another Polish man says that he did not even expect any renewed contact with the child he kept for a few weeks. He was touched, and embarrassed, when she returned one day to thank him:

She came to see me here and brought, among other things, her parents' diary. Jews from small towns seldom knew the literary style because they usually spoke their own language. But this diary was written in perfect Polish. Here is the sentence she wanted me to read: "All the gold in the world would not have helped to save the child were it not for the Polish family that profited nothing." She wanted to let me know that. We were embarrassed—we never looked at it from this point of view. She told us that her father used to tell her over and over: "After you go to the United States, you will have to come back to find this family and to thank them." That's what she did. Now her children— although they speak only English and German, not Polish— have become my children's friends. My daughter and her son, who were abroad some time ago, met each other. We were invited to France and the United States, but we have never availed ourselves of these invitations. One should not look for rewards for what one did.

But internal satisfaction and expressions of gratitude are not entirely sufficient for all rescuers. While none expressed regrets, a few did express disappointment. Disappointment is sometimes alluded to obliquely; at others, quite pointedly.

One source of disappointment is a severed relationship. More than 90 percent of all rescuers say they had direct contact with Jews they helped after the war, but not necessarily with all those they helped. Seventy percent say they are still in contact with them. But several long for more contact or more gratifying contacts. Existing relationships are perceived as inadequate in some way—not frequent, close, or appreciative enough. In a few cases contacts were never resumed after the war; sometimes rescuers were blatantly rejected. While several try to understand the reasons, they are nonetheless hurt:

> She [the Jewish girl] underwent a real baptism after the war, and we celebrated the sacrament. On that same day, this picture of the two of us was taken. But finally the time came to part. We decided that she would go to her relatives, see the place and the people. If she was unhappy there, she was to come back to me and I would try to raise her and send her to school. Her next letter arrived a month later [March 24, 1949]—it was her last letter. I did not hear from her again until the article appeared in *Przekroj* [a Polish magazine; its title might best be translated into English as *Potpourri*]. In 1981 we got in touch and she wrote—she even sent me a small package. She is a nurse in Israel—I was very attached to her. Why didn't she write before? I believe one reason is that she had forgotten the language. She spoke English when she phoned. Most certainly she feels Jewish now; I believe that she converted to Judaism—I suppose that's the real reason. But I have nothing against it! I just want her to be . . . honest, good, and a good nurse.

> I met the girls on a regular basis afterward. But the last few years—I don't know if I should say this or not—they

are sort of filled with hate. They are grateful, but they have
said to their foster mother who adopted them officially,
'We don't want to have contacts with non-Jews any more."
That's hatred—so I haven't seen them in the last three
years. They phoned a few times, but if they feel that way, I
would not say a word. It is either there, or it is gone.

We never had contact with this couple. They moved to a
house on our street immediately after the war. We saw
them and were polite, but we were not friends. You can't
expect people to be thankful—it was an impossible burden.
You can't expect them to be thankful all their lives. I am
sure they were happy to be alive.

After the war we found each other again. Their marriage
was already sour; she was somewhat worn out, her nerves
had gone. [When I looked her up] she said, "What is the
use of looking back at the past, at old stories?" Since it is
not my style to be *de trop*, I never tried to approach her
again. I think I heard that she committed suicide—so it
figures. I have forgiven everything, all my grievances, I do
not hold it against her. I do not know how I would act were
I hunted in that way.

That some survivors would seek psychological safety through
withdrawal from a perceived hostile non-Jewish world appears to
be cognitively understood on some level by disappointed rescuers,
but it nonetheless leaves an emotional vacuum and a sense of in-
completeness. Equally distressing for some is the perception that
their sacrifice will be rendered meaningless through collective am-
nesia and the failure to transmit it to posterity. That the general
public might not be aware of rescue events is disappointing
enough; it is a source of deep grief, however, if the children of
those they helped are equally uninformed about the details:

Later, my older son went to Israel and on the twenty-fifth
anniversary of the liberation of Poitiers [1969], he invited
some people to France. Among them was this son of the
Turkish Jewish family. So I asked him: "What does the
liberation of Poitiers mean to you?" "Nothing," he said. I
went out of the room and cried. When I was feeling better,
I came back and tried again. He said that the liberation of
Paris meant a lot to him, but Poitiers, nothing. I was upset

because I had risked my life to warn their parents, and for
their children it no longer meant anything.

Disappointed rescuers generally place the responsibility on
the recipients themselves—a personal failing of specific individuals. But for at least one rescuer, a German soldier who transported a Jewish family to a hiding place during one of the last days
of the war, the failing is viewed as a generalized Jewish characteristic:

I never heard from O. after the war; it would have
pleased me if he had called me. For me the case is closed. I
feel Jews do not want to be reminded of help they received
from their rescuers and do not want to be in contact with
them. I accept this point of view.

Disappointment with the Jewish community was also expressed by one Polish rescuer now living in the United States.
Stung by what she perceives as a widespread attack on Polish culpability for Jewish victimization during the war, she wants Jews to
remove the stain by helping to publicize the positive deeds performed by Poles. She regards her own efforts to write her story as
part of this effort, and she perceives the fact that her writing was
subsidized by her church rather than Jews as a manifestation of
the latter's ingratitude:

Nobody today believes my feeling; the feeling I get when
I hear people say that people did not help Jews. I think
sometimes that the same Jews I helped would perhaps help
me. No, today nobody can understand. I have now a
writer—a Jewish writer—who is helping me tell my story.
His mind is narrow, so in order to help him understand
the events, we went back to Poland last year. You will not
believe this, but my trip was paid by the church. This trip
cost four thousand dollars, and I had no money. So a
friend who also was in the war made a donation to the
church, and the church gave it to me. What a paradox! I
am a Christian; I gave my life to save Jews, but now it is
Christians who are helping me tell the story. Where are the
Jews?

Some rescuers are now in very poor health and in straitened material circumstances. Several have heard or believe that those they helped are now financially prosperous and want them to reciprocate through material assistance:

I did not help for money, it was a usual thing to do. My family wasn't poor—they were noble and aristocratic. They were used to giving to others, not taking. At the war's end, I was in a difficult financial situation and they [the Jews her family hid] were in a good financial situation, but they didn't help me. I am still in a bad financial situation, and I would like to get some help but I don't have the granddaughter's address. She is now living in the United States. His son [who was hidden elsewhere] lives in England. But those whom I helped don't feel grateful in any way. I want some help—but they just don't feel grateful.

A few suggest that such promises to reciprocate were either implied or actually made during the war:

He said he would be grateful unto death. We were robbed and I went to him for help. He was a poor Yid . . . He gave me some money; I don't remember how much. Then he left the country. He wrote in 1966 and sent me the medicine—there is no denying it—but only once and one parcel. And since then he has not written and I cannot find him.

He promised to give me the money from the sale of the house after the war, should he live, but he didn't do it. He sold that house and the land and left. And later, about eight years later, he wrote a letter to our father but sent us nothing. I said, "Maybe he is poor and cannot send anything." Then, later, he sent my father some old things— clothes and the like. He wrote to me asking what he should send. I asked him for twenty dollars—and then the correspondence stopped. I wrote him for two years and he didn't write back. I think he probably got offended about the twenty dollars. That's the way it ended.

Still others are convinced that with proper help they could receive governmental pensions as well as assorted other privileges.

Their expectations raised by virtue of current publicity about rescuers, they resent the failure of those they helped to speak up on
their behalf or take the actions necessary to assure them their due
reward or recognition:

> In 1982 we contacted S. G. when he came to Poland and
> said: "Look S., why don't you set things right concerning
> assistance to the Jews during the occupation. You were
> among those who received help too." "You never asked me
> to settle this for you," he said. "It's not my style," I told
> him. Well, he apologized, made excuses, and promised to
> see to it. Time passed, and nothing happened so I just went
> to the Jewish Institute myself and Xeroxed the statement S.
> G. had made on my behalf. In a job like this, one is
> supposed to get a decoration or some other reward—a
> thank-you letter. I feel that I was wronged; I hold it against
> them. When the war was over, I remained here, and people
> lost their memories. Everybody was free, finally, this
> freedom one had waited for so long. And nobody spoke
> about what had been done. I know of people who knocked
> at different doors, asking their due. They were given
> decorations, rewards, and so forth. As for us, only the B.'s
> gave my wife a golden cross when they were emigrating to
> Israel. They gave me their piano because they were not
> taking it. And that was it. No other rewards, no support.
> Not that we wanted it—I could manage myself. But since
> there is so much talk about—the Warsaw Ghetto, about
> people who were helping Jews—I have a grudge against S.
> G., who never said a word for those who really helped him.
> My wife wrote directly to Yad Vashem and finally the
> replies came to the two of us. But we had to do everything
> ourselves. We had to start it, we had to write. Time passes,
> and in a year or two we shall die without having received
> the satisfaction that is due us.

Such expressions of disappointment are not surprising.
Youthful wartime relationships are the high points of some rescuers' lives, particularly those whose subsequent personal ambi-
tions were thwarted or whose economic circumstances are harsh.
Jews they helped who have emigrated to the United States in particular are presumed to be rich and sometimes still fantasized as
young and strong. Norms of reciprocity, which they suppressed

under wartime conditions, have emerged in the context of supposed possibilities; those they once helped are now expected to
return the favor. Others simply yearn for some external confirmation of the significance of their activities—confirmation that has
less to do with expressions of appreciation than with memory. The
meaning of their activities is trivialized if those they helped or
even their descendants forget. A similar sense of meaninglessness
and futility is shared by those who feel rejected. As for the handful
who express their disappointment in terms of a generalized Jewish
failing, they remind us that even rescuers were not immune to
stereotypic thinking.

Rescuers are not saints but ordinary people who nonetheless
were capable of overcoming their human frailties by virtue of their
caring capacities. No rescuer regrets his or her activity, and most
rescuers feel more than amply rewarded, attesting not only to the
sufficiency of their internal gratifications but also to the continuing warm relationships they enjoy with those they helped as well
as their satisfaction with the expressed appreciation of Yad Vashem and other representatives of the Jewish community.

Whereas most rescuers look back on their wartime experiences with some sense of comfort, this is not the case for the majority of bystanders in particular. The meaning and significance of
those years differ for rescuers and nonrescuers, and it is best captured by their concluding comments, when rescuers and nonrescuers were asked if there was anything else they wished to say.

Most rescuers reaffirmed what they had said previously: They
were still distressed over those who had suffered and died; they
were satisfied they had done something to help; they were pleased
with having learned new things and made new friendships. Several
used the opportunity to reaffirm their values, suggesting the need
for increased humanism in the world and their sensitization towards racism of any kind. One woman emphasized that rather
than dwell on the past she preferred to use her energies toward
needed present reforms. A couple of rescuers made a point of
concluding by emphasizing some humor associated with those
times:

> I just want to conclude with a short story that is a kind
> of a summary of the event. I was sent to Monte Carlo by
> this rabbi to deposit some money with a family. Of course,
> we didn't know the name of the family, but we knew they

were in a hotel, a pretty well-known hotel. As it turned out, there were several hotels bearing this same name, each one of increasingly lower status. So I finally ended up in a small hotel and started to listen behind the different doors to see if I could find the family. Eventually I heard some voices that sounded to me as though they were speaking some kind of Yiddish. So I entered the room and said: "I have come to you on behalf of the rabbi ... " They invited me to sit down but I felt some kind of distrust—hostility— emanating from these people. They asked me: "Do you speak Russian?" "No." "Do you speak German?" "No." This increased their suspicion. So I said: "I am Portuguese Jewish; I am a Sephardic Jew." And then they began to trust me. So you see, I may be the only person during the Nazi occupation who claimed that she was Jewish when she wasn't.

Several nonrescuers, too, concluded on positive themes; particularly those who had been active in some way. One woman, who had in fact sheltered Jews but had not yet been so authenticated, said she was "thrilled" by the interview. Several nonrescuers noted their concerns for helping others and the need for tolerance. And a few went on to note how their postwar attitudes had changed. One, a strongly patriotic French Catholic bystander who described both his parents as distrusting of Jews and Freemasons, concluded with this statement:

Since the end of the war, I have more interactions with Jewish people at my place of work, which eliminated the unfavorable feelings of my former education. I am very much interested in the relations between Christians and Jews. I have Jewish friends whom I visit twice a year while attending the biblical school in Jerusalem. I have participated in the creation of the Christian Institute for Jewish Studies in Jerusalem.

And a Rumanian bystander, whose very poor family she admits initially welcomed the German occupation because it promised improved economic conditions, said that she had subsequently changed her entire world view:

Well, all I can say is that in my late age I found out about Jewish people in World War II. I am very proud that I work for a man who did such a tremendous job for Jews.

If not before or during the war, I am doing a little now even if I didn't do anything earlier in all my life. There is no difference between a black, a Jew, or a Chinese—they are all human. I learned so much so late in my life—so you know, you are never too old to learn something.

But what distinguishes the comments of bystanders in particular is the emphasis on their own impotence and victimization at the hands of external forces. These external forces vary. Some focus on the conditions of the war that left them feeling helpless, permanently deprived, or persecuted:

I take life easier than I did a few years ago when I worked at the school. The damn school upsets you every minute you are in there. In the war we never had any teenage years like my kids have. And the war is very much alive—like it happened yesterday—you have the same feelings, like starvation. I would be working at school and I would relive a certain episode that happened in those years. It changes your life. For the Jews, there was no chance of surviving. For us, there was still a hope because we were not Jewish. But for them, there was no surviving unless they had money or could find a place to hide.

People in apartments in Berlin would sit downstairs and watch visitors who came and report them to the Nazis. They were little guys who pestered the average German to get a loaf of bread or an extra case of beer. Many people offered themselves as spies. Some Germans who were active in doing wrong things were let off too easy—so they don't remember for too long what they did wrong. It is very good you came—I appreciate this. I could say certain things to people who are interested. More and more over the years I have felt that it is up to individual people—not the masses—to go on. But we should not concentrate on the killing of six and a half million.

My sister and brother were bombed out and lost everything. At a family gathering, two archenemies were present. My brother referred to Hitler as a scoundrel. Later my brother was arrested as a result of an anonymous accusation. My brother-in-law covered for him. My brother had to join the party and was later designated a Nazi. Only much later was he able to find employment again as a teacher.

Germans, in particular, focus on the injustice of the "collective guilt" that has been laid upon them—denying they knew anything, asserting they were only obeying orders, and inveighing against the assaults on their national pride by the victors of the war:

> I will say one thing, and that is about collective guilt in Germany—I totally disagree with that. Most people did not know any Jews or knew very few Jews. Concentration camps were known; they were considered hard labor camps. I really don't know of anyone who knew what really went on in these unless they kept it a secret from me—but I doubt it. Collective guilt was proclaimed on the German people— that it was the fault of all the German people . . .

> What I and others of my generation are concerned about is the future, the major political issue between East and West. How will these affect our children and children's children? We have no influence on the developments, except when we vote. The young generation cannot be influenced by us. Their experience is different. One feels helpless. The young people tell us what we did wrong, and we see their political immaturity. In 1933 we had no notion where that would lead, and we do not know now what the future holds. As for collective guilt, I followed orders; I had no choice. The others had the strategic military advantages and won the war. We lack national holidays to celebrate, and German national feelings are still repressed. Much is still not done for the sake of justice. Other countries that have done evil things are not talked about.

Some blame the Western allies, not only for failing to stop Hitler but also for failing to protect their nations against Russia today:

> Why did Hitler happen? Because of the attitudes of the western world, the lack of recognition in the initial stages of the Nazis. People looked the other way at the horrors that were already happening.

> Maybe it is important to mention the outcome of this war. All Eastern Europe was mishandled by the Allies, and

a whole section of Europe is under Russian domination.
This is a definite outcome of it. The leaders were
shortsighted. How could you have eliminated countries in
the twentieth century? It was unbelievable cruelty—
betrayal—injustice for millions of people.

For this man, Jews are to blame for their own victimization:

What puzzles me is the passivity of the Jews who went to
concentration camps. [Although] I know they were peaceful
people who wanted always to stay away from physical
confrontations, in Polish history, you have the tradition of
always resisting enemies—you put your life on the line for
the country.

For yet another, Germany along with England, Italy, and
America share some blame, but the real villians are Communists
and Polish Jews:

Germany is not evil; only the SS is evil. England,
Germany, and Italy and America, too, a little bit, prepared
[the way for] the Second World War. The Treaty of
Versailles was so bad that Germany had to go to war. Then
Germany and Russia made a treaty to oppress Polish
people and the Jewish people in Poland. Then Polish
people and Jewish people died but Russia was not after the
Jews—Russia was after the Poles and Hitler was after the
Jews. The Communists who put the Polish people down
were really Polish Jews. Communists and Polish Jews had a
common interest from a different angle. After liberation
the Communists tried to take over the Flemish and the
French. The first thing they did was take all the Flemish
intellectuals and imprison and torture them, exactly as the
Germans did. I find all this criminal.

For others it is not simply Polish Jews but Jews in general who
are responsible for assorted evils relating to their national destinies, lying about history, and polluting and destroying their national cultures:

Thank God I am a living witness to tell those [Jewish]
people who are lying for history [about the Polish
contribution to Jewish rescue]. Everytime I find out

somebody is lying I will tell them. I am not scared. Nobody can scare me.

I detest politics today, politics and politicians who aren't doing anything. France is dying because of politics. There is much anti-French racism. France is being invaded by foreigners. It is being taken over by Jews.

The situation of Fatherland and Nationality that was offered to youth then is no longer applicable today. All answers and positions rest on that. The destruction of Germany is being continued systematically in a moral realm, through foreign influences, racial mix, and the destruction of the human spirit.

There is of course a qualitative difference between those who focus on their own impotence and those who concentrate on their hatred of "aliens." What they have in common, however, is a self-centration, the absence of any self-blame or assumption of personal responsibility. To them the world is controlled by external malevolent forces that make the rules. These external forces vary: They may be Nazis, Communists, the governments of their nations or other nations, atheists, Jews, "foreigners," or a collective unspecified "they." Innocent people like themselves are neither consulted by nor represented among them. They suffer while the guilty run things in their own self-interest. The forces of selfishness and immorality are all about, and people are essentially helpless in their wake. Mighty others control their destiny and make them act against their will. They are powerless pawns and the principal victims of an unjust world.

The above might be understood as the defensive posture of people attempting to rationalize their wartime behaviors. Censuring and attributing guilt to others help deflect introspection; residual anxieties about actions not taken or nagging doubts about deeds done are not confronted. This may help explain why non-rescuers have been more reluctant to talk about the war to their children; fewer than half say their children know "quite a bit" about their wartime activities as compared with nearly 80 percent of rescuers. Bystanders in particular may feel that their children will not quite approve. There is reason to believe that this would be the case, for among those bystanders who have ventured to speak, only 22 percent say their children strongly approve—a marked contrast with rescuers, among whom 85 percent say their children strongly approve (Table 9.2). As one German rescuer expressed it:

It gives me satisfaction that my son who is now thirty-two can say among his peers, "My parents were not Nazis." He tells me his friends envy him. He always tells them that he had nothing to do with it—it is as much chance as it was chance for my mother to have the kind of parents she had. But they envy him. This age group is very, very conscious of the past—much more than my generation, which tried to forget. They didn't want to remember. I do want to remember. So, if you ask me what the past means to me now, I can say it means many things. My son can be proud—in a way—of his mother. At least, he doesn't have to hide this. I can understand why some of my Jewish friends in America and also in Israel tell me that when they are in Germany, they look at people our age and ask themselves, "What were you at that time? What did you do?" I can't say that I can look freely in everybody's face because I really didn't do much, but I didn't bloody my hands either. I am part of the collective shame of Germany, like everybody else. But in a very, very small way, I did do something—at least I helped one life. Others saved many. I know of cases where people have done fantastic things.

Most rescuers and nonrescuers were content to retreat to their private lives after the war. But consistent with their greater sense of personal responsibility, significantly more rescuers are currently involved in community activities. Equally consistently, they remain more responsive to people in pain and more concerned with diverse groups of people than do nonrescuers.

Significantly larger percentages of rescuers than nonrescuers have participated in community activities during the year preceding our interview with them. Their most common activity was attending to the sick or the aged. The second most common was teaching or counseling others. And in descending order of participation, they had contributed money or goods, given speeches, made telephone calls or collected information on behalf of some cause, and led recreational activities. Rescuers were more likely than nonrescuers to have engaged in four out of these seven activities and more likely than bystanders to have engaged in five of them (Table 9.3). Even controlling for age and sex, rescuers as a group were significantly more helpful than others (Table 9.4). Such differences are even more impressive in view of the significantly poorer health of rescuers today. Approximately 28 percent describe themselves as either in very poor or poor health, compared with 18 percent of all nonrescuers and 13 percent of bystanders. Conversely, only 32 percent of rescuers described themselves as in good or excellent health, compared with 56 percent of nonrescuers (Tables 9.5).

Rescuers are not only more involved in community activities today but extended help to a more diverse group of people after the war. Whereas helpful nonrescuers tended to confine their activities to their families, their church or national communities, and their own age groups, a larger percentage of rescuers extended themselves on behalf of other nationalities or religions, the young and the aged, as well as the disabled and ill:

> I visited the ghetto at Warsaw and the camp at Buchenwald in 1951. I attended a meeting in support of the Rosenbergs who were about to be executed in the United States and in support of some Jewish doctors who were being tried in the Soviet Union. Since retiring I attend many conferences for senior citizen clubs and other conferences concerning Israel. Israel is never far from my mind. Racism continues and the U.S. has taken an ambiguous position on this subject—as have the ecclesiastical authorities.

> I was a volunteer for Saint Vincent de Paul and worked for a local social assistance center. My husband and I have also been active against racism and anti-Semitism.

> I am involved in helping and rehabilitating the sick—I helped open a sanitarium for patients with tuberculosis. I am a member of the Polish Korczak Committee, which concerns itself with orphans and children around the world.

> After the war I was involved in founding an International House at Versailles—a House of Reconciliation. I tried to

have people meet with those who had opposing ideas. I went to India to find out more about Gandhi in 1950. I had lots of international contacts and traveled a great deal.

After the war, I helped French people get resettled in France. I did this from 1945 to 1948. I also helped some Hungarian soldiers. Now I am involved in Catholic missions that send food and clothing to children in Madagascar.

I belonged to several associations. I am now involved in helping the poor in the Sahel in Ethiopia.

My religious activities involve helping people in distress. I attend ecumenical meetings and donate what I can to missions and organizations that help Third World countries.

I helped the politically persecuted of different countries to escape. I also helped during the floods of Polesime, Vajont, Florence.

I helped found an organization to help families and home helpers for seniors in Reims and also to provide health assistance to lepers.

I choose to work in the countryside as a doctor—it is there where I see the real meaning of social activity.

I organized the first marriage counseling service in Italy in 1948.

I helped create the Medical and Educational Institute in 1967. Its purpose is to help predelinquent children. About 100 children are presently involved.

The legacy rescuers leave is thus not communicated by past deeds alone. By their present words and deeds they continue to assure us that there are caring people in the world, people who have retained a basic faith in the value of committed human relationships and a sense of connectedness to humanity. In reflecting on the enduring significance of their wartime actions, they inform us that not all things can be measured in terms of external rewards alone, but that contributing to the quality of life for others is itself a most enduring reward. They acknowledge the reality of evil, of bad people and bad ideologies, but they also tell us that individual effort matters. They assure us that people can shape their own destinies rather than merely stand by as passive witnesses to fate or allow themselves to become nothing more than victimized objects.

CHAPTER 10

Moral Heroism and Extensivity

Rescuers, like nonrescuers, worried both before and during the war about feeding, sheltering, and protecting themselves and their families. What distinguished rescuers was not their lack of concern with self, external approval, or achievement, but rather their capacity for extensive relationships—their stronger sense of attachment to others and their feeling of responsibility for the welfare of others, including those outside their immediate familial or communal circles. While some tried to resist the burdens imposed by such attachments, their sense of personal obligation did not allow them to do so. The help they extended to Jews was rarely the result of a perception of Jews as particularly worthy, but was rather a reflection of their characteristic ways of determining moral values and actions. For some rescuers, helping Jews was a matter of heightened empathy for people in pain. For others, it was due to internalized norms of social groups to whom they were strongly attached. And for a small minority, it was a question of loyalty to overriding autonomous principles rooted in justice or caring.

Although no one developmental course inevitably produces an extensive person, we can provide a composite portrait from the significant differences that distinguish rescuers from nonrescuers.

It begins in close family relationships in which parents model caring behavior and communicate caring values. Parental discipline tends toward leniency; children frequently experience it as almost imperceptible. It includes a heavy dose of reasoning—explanations of why behaviors are inappropriate, often with reference to their consequences for others. Physical punishment is rare; when used, it tends to be a singular event rather than routine. Gratuitous punishment—punishment that serves as a cathartic release of aggression for the parent or is unrelated to the child's behavior—almost never occurs.

249

Simultaneously, however, parents set high standards they expect their children to meet, particularly with regard to caring for others. They implicitly or explicitly communicate the obligation to help others in a spirit of generosity, without concern for external rewards or reciprocity. Parents themselves model such behaviors, not only in relation to their children but also toward other family members and neighbors. Because they are expected to care for and about others while simultaneously being cared for, children are encouraged to develop qualities associated with caring. Dependability, responsibility, and self-reliance are valued because they facilitate taking care of oneself as well as others. Failures are regarded as learning experiences, with the presumption of eventual mastery, rather than inherent deficiencies of character, intellect, or skill.

Out of such benevolent experiences, children learn to trust those around them. Securely rooted in their family relationships, they risk forming intimate relationships outside it. Persuaded that attachment rather than status is the source of basic life gratifications, as they mature they choose friends on the basis of affection rather than social class, religion, or ethnicity. In the context of such diverse relationships, they develop new cognitive and social skills as well as sensitivities. They feel more comfortable dealing with people different from themselves and are readier to emphasize the likenesses that bind them to others than the distinctions that separate them. More open to new experiences, they are more successful in meeting challenges. Each risk they surmount strengthens their abilities to confront further challenges and confirms their sense of potency in affecting external events.

Because of their solid family relationships, such children tend to internalize their parents' values, increasingly incorporating standards for personal integrity and care within their own value systems. While they may articulate such standards as cognitive principles, they experience them viscerally. They provide an organizing framework for their life activities and assessments of right and wrong. Even minor infractions distress them, and fundamental violations threaten them with a sense of chaos.

It is no accident that when the lives of outsiders are threatened, individuals with this orientation are more likely to initiate, or be asked for, help. More sensitive than others to violations that threaten their moral values, they may seek out opportunities to help. Personal relationships with the victims themselves encourage early awareness and empathic reactions. If such relationships do not exist, their social groups, which already embrace norms of inclusive caring, will alert them. Already more accustomed to view social relationships in terms of generosity and care rather than reciprocity, they are less inclined to assess costs in times of grave crisis. Already more deeply and widely attached to others, they find it difficult to refrain from action. Already more inclined to include outsiders in their sphere of concern, they find no reason to exclude them in an emergency. Unable to comprehend or tolerate brutality as anything but destructive of the very fabric that gives their lives order and meaning, they react in much the same way as if caught in a flood—holding back the tide through whatever means possible. Hence, their actions may appear impulsive, without due consideration of consequences. In fact, however, they are merely the extension of a characteristic style of relating developed over the years.

As a consequence of their helping activities, extensive people are more likely to evaluate themselves positively, which further reinforces the original personality characteristics and behaviors that led to helping in the first place. As they continue throughout their lives to help others, they are also more likely to transmit such values to their children.

A prototypical developmental course can also be outlined for those who are resistant to altruism, an orientation more typical of those whose lives have been characterized by constrictedness. Constricted people experience the external world as largely peripheral except insofar as it may be instrumentally useful. More centered on themselves and their own needs, they pay scant attention to others. At best, they reserve their sense of obligation to a small circle from which others are excluded. Whereas extensive individuals are marked by strong attachments and a sense of inclusive obligations, constricted people are marked by detachment and exclusiveness.

The prototypical developmental course of constrictedness emerges from a composite portrait of those characteristics that distinguished bystanders in particular from rescuers. It too begins in early life. Family attachments are weak, and discipline relies heavily on physical punishment, the latter often routine and gratuitous. Reasoning and explaining are infrequent. Family values center on the self and social convention; relationships with others are guarded and generally viewed as commodity exchanges. Stereotypes regarding outsiders are common.

Insecure in their families, such individuals move yet further along the constricted continuum in their relationships with others. Suspicious of others, they are wary of neighbors and peers. Persuaded that others are likely to lack integrity and ask of them more than they will receive in return, they avoid risking attachments by isolating themselves emotionally. As a result, they encounter little in the way of diversity and begin to fear what is unknown. Potential competence is aborted; informational sources are restricted; the repertoire of social skills remains limited. Since they are aware of their own vulnerabilities but do not trust others, constricted individuals insulate themselves yet further so as not to expose themselves to a world perceived as threatening. They find some psychological solace by projecting blame for their unsatisfying condition onto others. Anxious about severing the few social ties they have, however tenuous they may be, they deflect hostilities onto safe targets, notably powerless outsiders.

When a crisis occurs in which the lives of outsiders are at stake, they detach themselves still further from any association with its victims, preferring to know as little as possible about their fate. If they perceive their own interests to be threatened, they may join in devaluing the victims. Under such circumstances they are certainly unlikely to initiate helping voluntarily, are also less likely to be asked for help, and if asked, they are likely to refuse.

If such individuals are subsequently pressed to acknowledge the consequences of their own inaction, either by queries from their children or by repeated public exposure to the victims' fates, they may experience discomfort. If they feel compelled to explain, they are likely to reiterate the themes that have characterized their lives—their own sense of impotence and victimization or the culpability of the victims. Thus they prefer silence except in the context of discourse which will confirm their perspectives and self-worth.

Like all prototypes, however, these two developmental courses are rarely found in pure form in real life. Not all the ingredients identified are essential for the development of one orientation or the other; nor is any orientation an inevitable outcome of any specific precursors, though certain early experiences clearly make one or the other orientation more probable.

Support for this proposition is evident in the statistically significant differences that distinguish rescuers from nonrescuers.

What makes the distinction less than absolute, however, is the fact that neither all rescuers nor all nonrescuers reflected one or the other pattern. Some nonrescuers did not act, despite a generally extensive orientation, whereas some rescuers acted despite a constricted one. Nonetheless, significantly more rescuers were characterized by extensivity and significantly more nonrescuers were characterized by contrictedness. As our statistics inform us, such differences are highly unlikely to be the product of chance. They indicate that these respective orientations help explain an important part of the behaviors of these two groups, although they do not explain all of it. Knowing only whether someone was characterized by an extensive or a constricted orientation enabled us to predict who would be a rescuer or a nonrescuer for 70 percent of the individuals we studied (Tables 7.21 and 7.22). Although this demonstrates the power of these personal orientations in explaining rescue, it also suggests that other ingredients influenced the respective decisions. For some rescuers, risk-taking or self-enhancement needs rather than extensivity may have contributed to the decision. Some nonrescuers might well have become rescuers had their authoritative social groups taken stands on the issue and requested their help.

An extensive orientation not only predisposes people toward altruism but goes beyond it. Individuals capable of highly altruistic behaviors within the confines of their families, or even on behalf of their national communities, may not extend such behaviors toward strangers, particularly members of outsider groups. For example, parents and patriots ready to sacrifice all on behalf of their children or country often closed their doors in the face of supplicant Jews. On the other hand, extensive people who may not routinely engage in community or national affairs nonetheless may rise to acts of altruism in times of grave crisis. Many rescuers did not normally involve themselves in social affairs. Thus, rescue required more than a predisposition to altruism; it required acknowledging responsibilities toward outsiders and being aroused to action under severe conditions. The inclination to act depended largely on rescuers' interpretation of events, which was largely the product of the characteristic ways in which they interpreted their relationships to others.

The importance of relationships in our analysis of what motivated altruistic rescue behavior during the Holocaust contrasts

with the emphasis on autonomy cited by numerous others as the
basis for moral behavior generally[1] and rescue behavior particularly.[2] An outstanding example of this tradition is exemplified in
the well-known Adorno study of the authoritarian personality.[3] It
was a landmark study, not only for its sophisticated application of
Freudian theory, but also for its methodology, which included the
construction of two personality scales used in hundreds of subsequent studies. Although its theoretical and methodological flaws
have become more apparent over the years, it remains an important reference in the study of personality and political ideology.
The comparison is warranted not only because it, too, sought to
explain extreme behavior during the Holocaust in terms of personality factors and formative early experiences and was supported by the same group that sponsored our own (namely the
American Jewish Committee under the leadership of Dr. John
Slawson), but also because its findings and implications both converged with and differed from our own in several important re-
spects.

Concerned with the grave threat that fascist ideology posed
to our traditional values and institutions, the Adorno group constructed two measurement scales. The first, called the E Scale, was
a measure of ethnocentrism, defined as a consistently hostile
frame of mind concerning "aliens" generally. The second scale,
the F Scale, was a measure of personality structures that inclined
individuals toward a fascist ideology. The two scales were found
to be highly correlated—high scorers on ethnocentrism also
scored high on fascism. The scales were administered to more than
2,000 people from varying subpopulations in the United States.
One hundred persons scoring very high and very low on these
respective scales were then selected for clinical in-depth interviews, designed to identify the roots of such propensities.

From this wealth of information, Adorno extracted a typol-
ogy—syndromes of associated personality factors characteristic of
high and low scorers. Although he emphasized that the types were
not absolute and that there were considerable variations, Adorno
concluded that the evidence allowed for some generalizations, particularly in regard to high scorers.

High scorers—those who were ethnocentric and inclined
toward fascism—included six types: "surface resentment," "rough
guy," "crank," "manipulative," "conventional," and "authoritarian," of which the conventional and authoritarian were by far the

most frequent. While differing in some details, these types had parents who were punitive, harsh, and status-driven. As a result they had learned to repress their impulses by imposing or submitting to external constraints, resulting in a weak ego, identification with power, and rejection of the weak. They were conformist, obedient, punitive, moralistically rigid, compulsive, unimaginative, and emotionally constricted. They had a fear of close contacts with other people and difficulty with intimacy. In short, they strongly resembled the extremes of what we have called "constricted" persons.

Low scorers—those who were not ethnocentric and were predisposed toward a democratic ideology—were less clearly typed and less susceptible to generalization. Nonetheless, Adorno identified five low-scoring types: "the rigid," "the protesting," "the easygoing," "the impulsive," and "the genuine liberal." Oddly enough, the authoritarian syndrome was also found among low scorers; those labeled "the rigid" and "the protesting." Because of accidental circumstances and a different resolution of the Oedipus complex, said Adorno and his associates, these more authoritarian types had come to associate themselves with a rejection of ethnocentricism. The ideal type, the one Adorno judged to represent the best balance of superego, ego, and id, was "the genuine liberal."

Above all, the genuine liberal had a strong sense of autonomy and independence; he could not bear interference with his personal convictions nor did he want to interfere with others. His ego was quite developed but he was rarely "narcissistic." He was rational but also emotional. He was antitotalitarian, but consciously so. Strongly aware of himself as an individual, he saw others as individuals and not as examples of some generalization—he was no more a "Jew lover" than a "Jew hater." He was impulsive and had difficulties keeping himself under "control"; he was outspoken. But, although he was emotional, he was not blindly so. His love for others "was not only desire but also compassion," and thus he identified with the underdog, but he was not compulsive about it. In fact, says Adorno, it would be appropriate to call this syndrome "the compassionate." And unlike other low scorers, the genuine liberal was marked by moral courage.

While several of the rescuers in our sample appear to fit this type, the temptation to see all of them in this mold is strong, but it is not supported by our evidence. Nonetheless, we find some striking points of convergence between the *Authoritarian Personality Study* and our own. Rescuers, for example, were much more likely to have had the approving, nonpunitive early parental experiences associated with low ethnocentrism and high democratic potential than were nonrescuers. The benevolent cycle of warm parents, lenient with respect to discipline, and modeling caring behaviors bears many similarities to Adorno's conceptions of the kind of parental home associated with antiethnocentrics and liberals. Our rescuers, like Adorno's antifascists, were more characterized by close relationships with others, empathy for and identification with the underdog, and perceptions of others as individuals rather than as representatives of a type than were nonrescuers. Like Adorno, too, we find different types among our rescuers.

We disagree, however, with some of the interpretations and implications Adorno and his associates drew from their work. One of the primary differences centers on the linkage of moral courage with autonomy and independence.

The Adorno group sought the explanation of human brutality and compassion in an elaborate personality structure that evolved from the critical resolution of the Oedipal conflict. All else ensued from it: sexual relations, religious and political life, and social life in general. With the exception of the genuine liberal, all others, including both high and low ethnocentrics, had resolved this conflict inadequately, resulting in subsequent personality disorders of varying degrees. Thus, the person low in ethnocentrism who is associated with progressive movements (including the struggle for minority rights) but whose personality is similar to that of the authoritarian because of his rigidity is marked by an unhealthy compulsiveness, and his association with liberal causes derives from some external pattern rather than being integrated within his personality. The protesting low ethnocentric also fights injustice, but does so out of neurotic guilt rather than considered rationality. The easygoing low ethnocentric is amiable and gentle but dominated by female images; he is not quite a fully developed adult. The impulsive low ethnocentric sympathizes with everything which is repressed, and while he does not think in stereotypes, it is not really clear that he can think at all. Neither they, nor most certainly their high ethnocentric counterparts, can be reliably depended on to act with moral courage. Moral courage is thus the conspicuous characteristic only of the independent, autonomous, ego-integrated liberal.

While the emphasis on the resolution of the Oedipal conflict as the critical factor in personality development has been largely rejected by mainstream psychologists and modified by some contemporary bearers of the Freudian tradition, the emphasis on autonomous thought as the only real basis for morality continues to enjoy widespread acceptance. The lonely rugged individualist, forsaking home and comfort and charting new paths in pursuit of a personal vision, is our heroic fantasy—perhaps more embraced by men than women but nonetheless a cultural ideal. His spiritual equivalent is the moral hero, arriving at his own conclusions regarding right and wrong after internal struggle, guided primarily by intellect and rationality. It is this vision that underlies much of Western philosophy and psychology.

In a culture that values individualism and rational thought most highly, a morality rooted in autonomy is considered most praiseworthy. Those who behave correctly—ethically, in fact—but do so in compliance with social norms or standards set by individuals or groups close to them or because of empathic arousal are presumed to be in some way morally deficient. That few individuals behave virtuously because of autonomous contemplation of abstract principles—a finding that has been reiterated in numerous studies including Adorno's and our own—has not deterred advocates of independent moral reasoning from advancing it as the most morally admirable style. In some sense, rarity may even confirm its virtue, since it conforms to our cultural notion of the hero as a rather lonely person. But this is also a dispiriting view, for if humankind is dependent on only a few autonomously principled people, then the future is bleak indeed.

Furthermore, the venerators of autonomously principled individuals often fail to acknowledge that such individuals may not in fact extend themselves on behalf of people in distress or danger. Ideology, grand vision, or abstract principles may inure them to the suffering of real people. Fascists, conservatives, democrats, Oliver North and his supporters and detractors, and the killers of kulaks, Mesquito Indians, and fellow Campucheans—all invoke principles in support of their actions, "You ask Hitler," says Ikonnikov to his Bolshevik companion in a German concentration camp, both characters in a novel by Vassily Grossman, "and he'll tell you that even this camp was set up in the name of Good."[4] As Plato knew years ago, says H. J. Forbes, "independence of mind can have more than one outcome; it may promise the philosopher but deliver the tyrant."[5]

Clearly, too, neither empathy nor subscription to normative rules of authoritative social groups is a guarantor of virtue. (Empathic people may not choose to act or may not know how to do so effectively, those who look to others for moral guidance may find themselves bystanders or worse.) They do, however, demonstrate alternative ways of perceiving the responsibilities inherent in our common humanity. Just as there are multiple styles of cognition and affect, so there are multiple styles for arriving at moral decisions. The virtue that may arise out of attachments, care, and affiliations with other people is no less meritorious or reliable than that which arises out of autonomous abstract thought. Those who argue that principled people are less subject to the vagaries of circumstances have little empirical evidence to support this claim. Those who suspect the moral merit of emotional attachments because they are volatile and single out individuals or groups for particular favors might consider Blum's argument that doing something special on behalf of a particularly valued person is morally defective only when it denies the interests of others outside the relationship.[6] Empathy and concern with social norms simply represent alternative but equally profound ways of apprehending moral claims, as Blum, Gilligan,[7] and Noddings[8] have so eloquently argued. According to our study, they are the most common ways. Like principles, they too can inspire heroic moral courage.

If moral decisions arise as much out of affiliation as through autonomous reasoning, we need to cultivate varied forms of moral sensibilities. Our work as well as that of Adorno and many others points to the importance of the parental home. But preparation for social responsibility—preparation that can not only help individuals resist the destructive impulses in society but also empower them to accept the obligation to do so—is not a task that should be reserved for parents alone. It is a community responsibility. In this context we suggest that the school—the social institution that alone commands attendance for a sustained length of time—can play a particularly important role. Schools need to become institutions that not only prepare students for academic competence but also help them to acquire an extensive orientation to others.

Schools need to become caring institutions—institutions in which students, teachers, bus drivers, principals, and all others receive positive affirmation for kindness, empathy, and concern. Participants need opportunities to work and have fun together, develop intimacies, and share successes and pain. Students also need opportunities to consider broad universal principles that relate to justice and care in matters of public concern. Discussions should focus on the logic and values, implications and consequences of public actions, as well as the philosophical heritage that underlies these principles. In short, caring schools will acknowledge diversity on the road to moral concern. They will invoke emotion and intellect in the service of responsibility and caring.

In such settings, young people may come to appreciate, in ways that go beyond words alone, that rootedness in family and local community can be a means toward attachment to a more inclusive group. Citizenship education that focuses on political and legal rights is an important first step in developing the sense of a larger community, but it is not a sufficient one, for such bonds are more susceptible to dissolution than those that bind people together in a shared sense of humanity.[9] More than token gestures are required to achieve the latter. What is required is nothing less than institutionalized structures that promote supportive relationships with the same seriousness as is currently devoted to academic achievement. Above all, rescuers inform us of this important truth.

World War II was a watershed in human history—not only because of subsequent radical political, technological, and social changes but also because it raised so many profound questions about good and evil, about the nature of humans and their capacity to survive as a species. The human potential for destructiveness and indifference that was so manifest then overwhelms us with despair as we view its recurrence around the globe. The naggingly persistent question is, What can ordinary people do?

Rescuers point the way. They were and are "ordinary" people. They were farmers and teachers, entrepreneurs and factory workers, rich and poor, parents and single people, Protestants and Catholics. Most had done nothing extraordinary before the war nor have they done much that is extraordinary since. Most were marked neither by exceptional leadership qualities nor by unconventional behavior. They were not heroes cast in larger-than-life molds. What most distinguished them were their connections with others in relationships of commitment and care. It is out of such relationships that they became aware of what was occurring around them and mustered their human and material resources to relieve the pain. Their involvements with Jews grew out of the ways in which they ordinarily related to other people—their characteristic ways of feeling; their perceptions of who should be obeyed; the rules and examples of conduct they learned from parents, friends, and religious and political associates; and their routine ways of deciding what was wrong and right. They inform us that it is out of the quality of such routine human activities that the human spirit evolves and moral courage is born. They remind us that such courage is not only the province of the independent and the intellectually superior thinkers but that it is available to all through the virtues of connectedness, commitment, and the quality of relationships developed in ordinary human interactions.

They also highlight the important truth that interpretations of events are human inventions, and that what and how we choose to see shape our responses—and thus the future. As W. I. Thomas and D. S. Thomas[10] proposed almost sixty years ago, "Situations defined as real are real in their consequences." If we persist in defining ourselves as doomed, human nature as beyond redemption, and social institutions as beyond reform, then we shall create a future that will inexorably proceed in confirming this view. Rescuers refused to see Jews as guilty or beyond hope and themselves as helpless, despite all the evidence that could be marshaled to the contrary. They made a choice that affirmed the value and meaningfulness of each life in the midst of a diabolical social order that repeatedly denied it. Can we do otherwise?

Methodology

In exploring the sociopsychological factors that contributed to an altruistic behavior such as the rescue of Jews under the conditions of the Holocaust, two basic questions guided our inquiry: (1) Was rescue a matter of opportunity—that is, the consequence of particular facilitating external circumstances? If so, what were they? (2) Was rescue a matter of personal attributes—that is, the consequence of particular values, attitudes, and personality characteristics? If so, what were they?

To find the answers, we interviewed 682 individuals—406 authenticated rescuers, 126 nonrescuers, and 150 rescued survivors—who lived in Nazi-occupied Europe during the war. We developed an interview procedure that recorded our subjects' reconstructions of their prewar and wartime lives as well as their situational and personality characteristics.

The Sample

One of our first concerns was to identify an appropriate sample, one that would be representative of the total population we wished to study and thus allow us to make valid generalizations about the larger population from our findings. Our population consists of rescuers, but only rescuers who behaved altruistically. As we defined it, an altruistic act of rescue was characterized by four criteria: (1) it involved a high risk to the actor, (2) it was accompanied by no external rewards, (3) it was voluntary, and (4) it had to be directed toward helping a Jewish person. While an altruistic behavior is generally defined to include helping anyone, we restricted our definition to helping Jews only as representative of those altruistic behaviors directed toward outsider groups. Identifying the total population of rescuers who met these criteria would have been desirable but was obviously impossible; the search itself would have taken many years. Yad Vashem's list provided us with the best reasonable alternative.

We are grateful to Neil J. Smelser, whose assistance helped us in writing this appendix.

Yad Vashem is a memorial authority in Jerusalem established by the Holocaust Martyrs' and Heroes' Remembrance Law adopted by the Israeli Knesset (Parliament) on August 19, 1953. Its purpose is to commemorate the six million Jews who died at the hands of the Nazis and their collaborators as well as the "Righteous Among the Nations" who risked their lives to save Jews. In fulfillment of the latter purpose, a commission of eighteen members, composed of the chairman of the Yad Vashem Directory and his deputy as well as representatives of assorted other groups and public figures, is appointed to decide who should be so designated. The commission studies all requests for recognition based on evidence provided by survivors as well as other documentary evidence. Each individual member of the commission is assigned a specific case and makes an initial recommendation. The member meets with at least one of the survivors in order to get a firsthand impression of the story. If there are no living survivors or if none can be met in person, a written notarized deposition by relatives or friends is acceptable. In making its final decision, the commission considers all the circumstances related to the rescue story as well as the rescuer's motivation, personal risk, and dedication. Criteria for recognition by Yad Vashem include: (1) the rescuer was motivated by humanitarian considerations alone; (2) the rescuer risked his or her own life; (3) no remuneration of any kind accompanied the rescue act.

Yad Vashem's list, including approximately 6,000 rescuers, is far from complete; the process of authentication is slow and painstaking, and the commission rarely catches up with all submitted names. Moreover, the process by which names are submitted is subject to some degree of chance. Rescued people or friends and families must initiate the process by submitting names; hence identification depends on their knowing about Yad Vashem and being alive to tell the tale and sufficiently motivated and able to act. Despite these shortcomings, Yad Vashem's list has two critical advantages for the purposes of our research: (1) the criteria used for designating rescuers are congruent with the criteria we use to identify an altruistic behavior; (2) people on the list have been authenticated through a painstaking investigation as bona fide rescuers.

Yad Vashem's list, made available to us through the courtesy of Mordecai Paldiel, executive director of Yad Vashem, thus served as the population from which we derived 95 percent of our sample. The other 5 percent consists of persons whose names we obtained from rescued survivors also interviewed by our project. In selecting the latter group, we were guided by the same criteria that characterize Yad Vashem rescuers—and in fact, several among those so identified have now had their names submitted to Yad Vashem.

Having identified our potentially accessible population, our next problem was to select a representative sample—one that would best capture all the salient characteristics of Yad Vashem's total list. Statistical random sampling is the best means for ensuring representativeness, but pragmatic considerations did not allow us to choose a random sample. Several rescuers had died; addresses were no longer accurate for some others; and still others lived in places too remote to be accessible to our interviewers.

We used two criteria in selecting rescuers from the list—that they be geographically accessible and that they come from a number of different countries. We used the latter criterion because we wanted to study rescue activities in a variety of wartime conditions (varying for example in degree of Nazi control, accessibility of resistance networks, and prewar anti-Semitism and Jewish assimilation). Most respondents were drawn from Poland, France, the Netherlands, and Germany—but we also included a few from Italy, Norway, Denmark, Belgium, and the Ukraine. We assembled a fairly representative sample—one that is highly diversified in terms of age, socioeconomic class, and country of origin as well as assorted other factors. Of the 406 rescuers, 231 serve as the basis for our statistical calculations, while the other 175 provide informational background for supplementary purposes. Most of the latter were interviewed by us before the formal launching of the Altruistic Personality Project; a few are rescuers interviewed by others whose accounts became available to S. P. Oliner when he assumed the directorship of the Institute for Righteous Acts. Unlike the interviews conducted specifically for this project, these earlier interviews are primarily qualitative in character and nonstandardized—for these reasons we used them in our qualitative analyses only.

Our objective, of course, was to study rescuers, but in order to make any claims regarding what distinguished rescuers, we needed a group of nonrescuers with whom to make comparisons. Rescuers had behaved differently from others; our assumption was that situational and personality factors leading to such behaviors were also different. If rescuers and nonrescuers turned out to be the same with respect to given factors, we could infer that the latter were not particularly important in the rescue decision; conversely, if they were found to be different, we could infer the reverse. Hence, our second concern was to identify and select a sample of nonrescuers.

We defined a nonrescuer as a person neither on Yad Vashem's list nor verified by our project as an authenticated rescuer living in Nazi-occupied Europe during the war. Ideally, this group—called a control group—should have been a random sample from the universe of nonrescuers—practical reality again made this impossible. We chose instead to try to obtain a matched sample of nonrescuers—matched with rescuers on age, sex, education, and geographic location during the years of the war. We were successful in matching our sample in the sense that there are no statistically significant differences between rescuers and nonrescuers in relation to all the above variables with the exception of age. The mean average age of rescuers is four years older than that of nonrescuers. We addressed this issue by holding age constant in our statistical anlaysis through a process called analysis of covariance. This procedure allows us to judge whether the particular variable in question is age related and whether group differences occur independently of age. Our total sample of nonrescuers includes 126 respondents.

In interviewing the nonrescuers, it became apparent that there were some differences within the sample with respect to helping behavior. This became clear when respondents were asked to answer the question, Did you do anything out of the ordinary during the war to help other people or resist the Nazis? On the basis of their responses, we were able to identify the following types: (1) People who claim to have been members of general resistance groups as well as people who claim to have helped Jews—sometimes both. Although we have no particular reason to doubt either of these claims, in both cases they are self-reported and noncorroborated. These individuals we termed "actives." (2) People who simply said no in response to the question—claiming neither membership in resistance groups nor having helped Jews. These individuals we termed "bystanders." Our sample includes 53 active controls and 73 bystanders.

At one point we considered eliminating all "actives" from the sample, on the grounds that the occasional self-reported helpers of Jews and those who resisted the Nazis might share common characteristics with authenticated rescuers; eliminating them would sharpen the differences between rescuers and the remaining group of bystanders. However, we decided to retain the "actives" as members of the control group, on the grounds that there might be important differences between authenticated rescuers and all other groups. In our statistical analyses, however, we did separate and make comparisons among rescuers and all nonrescuers, as well as rescuers and bystanders. Most of our tables are based on these two types of comparisons.

Yet one other group participated in our research—a sample of 150 rescued survivors, a few of whom were interviewed prior to the formal beginning of the project. Others were interviewed after 1982, identified through a massive letter campaign (6,500 letters) to American and Canadian rabbis requesting names of such people from among their congregants. Data from survivors were used primarily to compare the motivations they attribute to their rescuers with those given by the rescuers in our sample. The survivors were also helpful in providing insights into potentially salient situational and personality factors of rescuers.

The Questionnaire

Each rescuer and nonrescuer in our sample was interviewed in his or her native language by means of a questionnaire developed specifically for the project. English was used with respondents currently living in the United States or Canada. The questions asked and the scales we used were developed on the basis of preliminary hypotheses about the determinants of altruistic behavior that were largely but not entirely elicited from the work of other researchers.

The interview schedule consisted of approximately 450 items; 75 percent were "forced choice" answers, the remainder were open-ended. In addition each respondent was asked to describe his or her wartime activities in detail. The questionnaire administered to nonrescuers was much the same as that given to rescuers, except that instead of being asked to describe their rescue activity and its setting, the nonrescuers were asked to describe their particular activities and lives during the war.

The interview questionnaire consisted of six sections. In Section A we asked about the characteristics of the family household in which respondents lived during their early years and the relationships among family members. In Section B we explored parental education, occupation, politics, and religiosity as well as parental values, attitudes, and disciplinary techniques. The same questions were asked for any other person who was identified as the most significant role model for the respondent. In Section C we focused on the respondent's childhood and adolescent years—education, religiosity, friendship patterns, as well as self-attributed personality characteristics, including independence, self-confidence, leadership, patriotism, and honesty. In Section D we focused on the five years immediately preceding the war—marital status, occupation, work colleagues, politics, religiosity, sense of community, psychological closeness to various groups of people, and any unusual activities in which the respondent may have participated during this time. If the respondent was married before the war, we asked several questions relating to the spouse's occupation, religion, politics, and friendships. Section E concentrated on the immediate prewar and war years—employment, attitudes toward Nazis, whether Jews lived in the neighborhood, and awareness of Nazi intentions toward Jews. All respondents were asked to describe their wartime lives: where they lived for most of the war, their wartime households, any mistreatment they themselves may have experienced at the hands of the Nazis or any mistreatment of others, including Jews, they may have heard about or observed. Rescuers and actives were also asked specific questions about their activities—whom they helped, resistance groups they belonged to, who asked them to help, and their relationship to those who asked them. Section F focused on the years after the war, including the present. Here we probed relationships with children and personal or community helping activities in which respondents engaged during the last year. This section also included forty-two personality items comprising four psychological scales: (1) the Social Responsibility Scale, developed by Berkowitz and Lutterman (1968); (2) the Internal/External Locus of Control Scale, developed by Rotter (1966) and modified by Gurin, Gurin, and Morrison (1978); (3) the Self Esteem Scale, developed by Rosenberg (1965); and (4) an Empathy Scale, developed by Mehrabian and Epstein (1972) and modified subsequently by Midlarsky (1981).

The questionnaire described above is the final one we developed only after having already completed 110 interviews (107 rescuers, 3 active non-rescuers) using a slightly different form. This earlier version was similar in most ways to the revised form but was modified to include some new questions and exclude some others that proved not to be particularly useful.

The varying sample sizes reported in our tables are to a large degree the consequence of a merging process. Where questions were identical in both questionnaires, the full sample size is reflected. In cases where sample sizes reported for rescuers are less than 200, it generally reflects omissions in the first questionnaire. Another source of variation in sample sizes reported was incomplete gathering or recording of data. On a few occasions, respondents declined to answer certain questions; on other occasions an interviewer neglected to ask questions. Yet other variations are due to the nature of the questions themselves—some questions are contingent on affirmative answers to preceding ones. Thus, for example, the presence of data regarding occupational status depended on whether the person reported being employed.

Because our research design is ex post facto—that is, the presumed causes of behavior are studied *after* the behavior has taken place rather than before—the cause-and-effect relationship is blurred. Put more formally, the dependent variable (effect) is a person engaged in rescue activity; the independent variables (possible causes) are the various situational, attitudinal, personality, and socialization factors we have identified. But the rescue act itself may have affected the presumably independent variables over time. The fact that rescuers behaved as they did may have affected their subsequent attitudes, their sense of responsibility, their notions of justice and care, and indeed the accuracy of memory about the act itself. We attempted to minimize the biasing impact of this dynamic process by asking several questions relating to the same independent variable in a variety of contexts throughout the interview. Thus, for example, when we inquired about the religiosity of our respondents, we asked them about their religious education in elementary school, gymnasium, and university; their religiosity while growing up, immediately before the war and after the war; as well as the religiosity of their parents. We did the same with regard to several other variables that were of particular interest to us.

Data Collection

Collecting the data required the cooperation of an international team knowledgeable about the issues and methods of our study. Data collection in the United States was coordinated and supervised by S. P. Oliner. Data collection in respective European countries was coordinated and supervised by associates designated for that purpose. Our European associates included Professor Janusz Reykowski (social psychologist at the Polish Academy of Science, and international scholar who has written broadly on prosocial behavior and altruism), Dr. Zuzanna Smolenska (a child development specialist also at the Polish Academy of Science), Professor Jürgen Falter (political scientist at the Freie Universität, Berlin, a specialist in the rise of Nazism), Professor André Kaspi (a historian and international relations expert at the Sorbonne), Professor Richard Van Dyck (a psychiatrist at the University of Leiden), Dr. Michele Sarfatti and Professor Luisella Mortara Ottolenghi (both historians at the Centro di Documentazione Ebraica Contemporanea in Milan), and Susan Schwartz (a clinical psychologist and marriage, family, and child counselor in Oslo).

Coordinators selected the interviewers and sometimes conducted interviews themselves. Most of the interviewers held a Ph.D. or were in the process of obtaining one. Some received interview training in this country, mainly in sessions at the Survey Research Center at the University of Michigan and at the Survey Research Center at the University of California at Berkeley. S. P. Oliner also trained some bilingual interviewers in Europe.

Interviewees were contacted by letter and phone. In setting up the appointment, interviewers requested that no one else be present during the interview, so that respondents' answers and reports be as unconstrained as possible; in almost all cases this request was honored. The interviews themselves were long, ranging from three to eight hours, depending mainly on how talkative or how easily fatigued the respondent was.

Interviewers began the interview by describing the purposes of the study and informing respondents that their answers would be taped. The following statement was read to respondents at the beginning of the interview:

> Let me begin by introducing myself. My name is———, and I
> am an interviewer for the International Study of Attitudes during
> World War II. I want to thank you for consenting to be part of
> this study.
>
> The purpose of this study is to find out what people did in
> World War II and how the war affected the lives of people who

experienced it. We want to compare the attitudes, situations, and activities of people who were engaged in resistance and rescue and people who just made it through the war. We are particularly interested in people's unusual experiences during the war.

I am going to ask you a number of questions about your life. I'll begin by asking you some questions about your life when you were growing up and before the war. After that we will talk about what happened to you during the war. And we will follow that with some questions about your life today. You will have as much time as you need to tell me about your activities during the war.

Many of the questions I will ask you will have a fixed set of answers like the one on this page (hand respondent booklet). All you need to do is to choose the answer that comes closest to the way you feel—you don't need to explain your answers unless I ask you for further information. I want to assure you that your answers are completely confidential. Also, this interview is voluntary. If there is a question that you would rather not answer, please let me know and we will move on to the next question. Please don't hesitate to ask me to repeat a question or tell me when you don't understand a question. If you should need to rest briefly in the middle of the interview, please let me know.

In order to make sure that I do not miss anything, I'll leave the tape on as we speak. I will also be taking notes as you talk.

We also obtained from each respondent written permission to use information obtained for scholarly purposes, without revealing his or her name.

We cannot know the extent to which disclosure of purpose and taping affected subsequent responses. There were times when interviewees asked the interviewers to turn off the tape, and these requests were always honored. In general, however, respondents appeared to be largely unaffected by the disclosure of purpose and the presence of the tape. A few asked that we send them copies of the transcribed tapes when completed, which we did.

Considering the passage of time and the possibility of memory lapses due to the advanced age of many of our respondents, we were particularly concerned about information distortion. The exact effects of such distortion are impossible to determine. We assume, though, that memories of events like rescuing should survive better than other memories, since those events were fraught with danger and of great personal significance. Furthermore, while older people experience declines in information processing capacities, they continue to retain a large store of information, much of which relates to events that occurred in the distant past.[1]

The interviews did have a ring of authenticity about them. Accounts are replete with names, places, and dates and graphic descriptions of people, relationships, objects, and events. Many rescuers recalled in minute detail, for example, how they forged papers and what they used to dye hair.

Another possible source of distortion lies in the "halo effect"—namely that the rescuer may, over time, come to bend and assimilate many of his or her perceptions, opinions, and judgments around the positive image of being a "hero." If this occurs, it can affect not only the memory of the rescuing event but also many of the factors—sense of values, social relationships, even physical circumstances—considered to be causally prior to the rescue act. The investigators were apprehensive about this matter in the initial phase of interviewing, but the interviews themselves tended to disabuse them of their apprehension. While there were a few reports that might be suspected of manifesting self-aggrandizement, the vast majority of respondents tended to present themselves and their actions in ordinary, nonheroic terms.

Mention must also be made of another aspect of the interviews that attests to the vividness of recall; their affective tone. These interviews were by no means neutral experiences. Nearly all those interviewed were clearly moved. Some wept openly, and others expressed concern that the interview itself would revive emotions—even nightmares—that had been buried or scarred over by time. Interviewers also reported that many respondents reached out to them in affectively positive ways. Almost all the interviewers experienced warm hospitality; many were asked to return for another visit. One respondent, learning that her interviewer was a working mother, offered to take care of her child when she needed help. Some of these reactions might be read as appreciation for attention given to older and sometimes lonely people, but we suspect that the emotionality was also an intrinsic part of the process of exciting these profound memories. Many of the reported memories appeared to be especially vivid to the respondent because of the powerful affect associated with them.

We had two additional sources of independent information as checks on accuracy. In several cases we conducted interviews with individuals whom the interviewed rescuers had saved; the stories tended to be consistent except for some differences in detail. In a few cases, too, we had access to the Yad Vashem files on verified rescuers—and again these accounts tended to match those given during our interviews, with the exception of some details.

As a further check, each interviewer was asked to evaluate the interview, whether respondents' understanding of the questions as well as their memory appeared to be poor, fair, good, or excellent, and whether the respondent was very cooperative, cooperative, and mildly cooperative. Interviewers also described the setting of the interview—whether the respondents were alone and any problems of communication, as well as the respondents' emotional state during the interview.

Coding and Analyses

Tapes and completed questionnaires were sent to the Altruistic Personality Project headquarters at Humboldt State University, where they were subsequently translated and transcribed. There were in fact two stages in our translation process—the translation of the interview schedules from English to the native language of the interviewee and the translation of the recorded interviews into English. Our translators were proficient in both languages—most were native speakers who had lived in the United States for several years, and most were university graduates. University associates in the respective countries in which our interviews were conducted supervised the translation of the interview schedule. As a check on the quality of the translations, we asked two translators of the same language to do independent translations of a few identical interviews using both tapes and interviewer notes. Resultant differences centered less on meaning than on style and syntax.

The closed-ended questions were, of course, precoded and simply entered into the computer for purposes of statistical computation and analysis. The responses to the open-ended questions had to be assessed and coded into a number of standard categories in order to make the responses comparable. For any given question we conducted an initial impressionistic scan to locate identifiable clusters of responses. For example, for question B32—which asks, "What were the most important things you learned about life from your father?"—we discovered that many of the responses could be grouped under the headings of equity, care, propriety, religiosity, patriotism, independence, and so on. After identifying these categories, we asked raters to read the protocols "blind" (that is, without knowing whether the respondent had engaged in rescuer activities) and code the responses according to the categories supplied. We used the method of inter-rater reliability as a means to test the effectiveness of this method of coding. Convergence among raters ranged from 75 to 95 percent for all such codings.

The statistical methods used to assess the differences between rescuers and others were chi-squares on all variables, factor analysis, one-way analysis of variance, and discriminant analysis. A probability level of .05 was accepted as the level of significance. This means that the probability of finding a particular difference between rescuer and nonrescuer samples if there were no true differences among the larger populations of compared groups is five times in 100 samples. Many of the findings are statistically significant at well below this probability level, at the .001 level and better.

Our final summary statistical analysis involved a comprehensive factor analysis and discriminant function analysis based on the 247 revised questionnaires only, because these were the most complete for all relevant variables. This analysis serves as the basis for the discussion in our final chapter of the central overarching construct called "extensivity" and its two associated constructs, "inclusiveness" and "attachment."

We selected from the interviews a set of basic variables thought to have direct relationships to the two central constructs "inclusiveness" and "attachment," including situation, personality, attitude, and value variables. Wherever possible, variables were combined to create synthesized variables by either a simple linear summation of scores on the variables being combined or a factor analysis of a set of variables and creation of factor scores for each set. Both of these procedures create more reliable variables that provide more accurate measures of the qualities under scrutiny with minimal loss of detail. Twenty-seven synthesized variables were created out of more than 100 single variables, following the operations outlined in Table 7.16. Analyses of variance were conducted on each of the new variables, comparing rescuers with nonrescuers, with age and sex as controlled covariates. The synthesized variables were then entered into a matrix for factor analysis. Factor scores were calculated and analyses of variance were conducted for all group combinations (rescuers compared with all nonrescuers, rescuers compared with active nonrescuers, rescuers compared with bystanders), with age and sex as controlled covariates. Tests of statistical significance indicated that the groups differed on all factors. We concluded with a discriminant function analysis to determine how well these factors could predict group membership—that is, how well they could determine whether respondents were rescuers, actives, or bystanders. Predictions obtained were well above the chance level for all groups.

We conclude this discussion of our research methods with a word of caution. Our statistical procedures were rigorous and powerful, allowing us to speak with considerable confidence about aggregate differences among groups and about the personality factors, values and attitudes, and situational conditions associated with rescue behavior in general. But such analyses cannot identify the particular situational or personality factors influencing any one individual's decision to rescue or not to rescue. Each individual act must be regarded as a unique event shaped by many discrete factors. An individual may have possessed all the personality and attitudinal characteristics we find correlated with acts of rescue, and yet, because of high risk or lack of resources, did not carry out a rescue. In another situation an act of rescue might have been easily accomplished because of little or no risk and many resources, but was not attempted because of the individual's particular values or personality characteristics. Each identified contributing factor makes a rescue action more likely, but we cannot specify the exact combination necessary or sufficient to precipitate one on the part of a particular individual in a particular set of circumstances.

APPENDIX B

Tables

Significance values of .05 or less indicate significant differences between the groups at the .05 criterial level. NS denotes that differences between the groups are not significant at the .05 criterial level. All factor scores are on a standardized scale having a total group mean of 0 and a standard deviation of 1.00. ANOVA scores that are not based on factor analyses are presented in their unstandardized form.

(*Continued*)

TABLE 5.1 *Potential Sources of Information: Jewish Contacts*

	Yes (%)	No (%)	Don't Know (%)	Significance (chi-square)
a. Rescuers vs. Nonrescuers				
Jews lived in prewar neighborhood				
Rescuers (*n* = 223)	69.1	26.9	4.0	
Nonrescuers (*n* = 126)	57.1	30.2	12.7	.005
Had Jewish coworkers				
Rescuers (*n* = 97)	34.0	64.9	1.0	
Nonrescuers (*n* = 83)	16.9	69.9	13.3	.0005
Had Jewish friends before war				
Rescuers (*n* = 119)	58.8	39.5	1.7	
Nonrescuers (*n* = 115)	33.9	60.0	6.1	.0004
Spouse had Jewish coworkers				
Rescuers (*n* = 72)	27.8	52.8	19.4	
Nonrescuers (*n* = 42)	9.5	50.0	40.5	.01
Spouse had Jewish friends				
Rescuers (*n* = 143)	46.2	49.0	4.9	
Nonrescuers (*n* = 53)	24.5	50.9	24.5	.0001
b. Rescuers vs. Bystanders				
Jews lived in prewar neighborhood				
Rescuers (*n* = 223)	69.1	26.9	4.0	
Bystanders (*n* = 73)	52.1	35.6	12.3	.006
Had Jewish coworkers				
Rescuers (*n* = 97)	34.0	64.9	1.0	
Bystanders (*n* = 52)	15.4	76.9	7.7	.008
Had Jewish friends before war				
Rescuers (*n* = 119)	58.8	39.5	1.7	
Bystanders (*n* = 68)	25.0	70.6	4.4	.0000
Spouse had Jewish coworkers				
Rescuers (*n* = 72)	27.8	52.8	19.4	
Bystanders (*n* = 25)	4.0	64.0	32.0	.03
Spouse had Jewish friends				
Rescuers (*n* = 143)	46.2	49.0	4.9	
Bystanders (*n* = 32)	15.6	68.8	15.6	.002

TABLE 5.2   *Knowledge of Events*

a. Rescuers vs. Nonrescuers

	Rescuers (%)	Nonrescuers (%)	Significance (chi-square)
Awareness of Nazi intentions toward Jews	(*n* = 207)	(*n* = 117)	
Before Nazi takeover	23.2	16.2	
During Nazi takeover	75.8	76.9	
After liberation[a]	1.0	6.8	.01
Saw Jews wearing yellow star	(*n* = 207)	(*n* = 112)	
Yes	86.0	88.4	
No	14.0	11.6	NS
Reactions to yellow star first time saw it	(*n* = 172)	(*n* = 93)	
Empathic	91.9	86.0	
Didn't understand/nothing	8.1	14.0	NS

b. Rescuers vs. Bystanders

	Rescuers (%)	Bystanders (%)	Significance (chi-square)
Awareness of Nazi intentions toward Jews	(*n* = 207)	(*n* = 67)	
Before Nazi takeover	23.2	14.9	
During Nazi takeover	75.8	76.1	
After liberation[a]	1.0	9.0	.01
Saw Jews wearing yellow star	(*n* = 207)	(*n* = 66)	
Yes	86.0	92.4	
No	14.0	7.6	NS
Reactions to yellow star first time saw it	(*n* = 172)	(*n* = 56)	
Empathic	91.9	82.2	
Didn't understand/nothing	8.1	17.9	.05

[a]Those who responded "after liberation" said they did not know the full extent of Nazi intentions regarding Jews until after the war.

TABLE 5.3 *Risk*

a. Rescuers vs. Nonrescuers

	Rescuers (%)	Nonrescuers (%)	Significance (chi-square)
Size of town lived in for longest period during war	(n = 214)	(n = 115)	
Farm	7.5	1.7	
Village	16.4	9.6	
Small city	15.9	17.4	
Medium-size city	5.6	13.0	
Large city	54.7	58.3	.01
Many neighbors living nearby during war	(n = 119)	(n = 106)	
Yes	86.3	87.7	
No	13.7	12.3	NS
Numbers of others living in household in 1939	(n = 226)	(n = 126)	
None	15.9	20.6	
1–2	31.4	32.5	
3–4	32.3	30.2	
5–6	14.2	12.7	
7 plus	6.2	4.0	NS
Children 10 years or younger living in household in 1939			
None	73.5	82.5	
One or more	26.5	17.5	NS

b. Rescuers vs. Bystanders

	Rescuers (%)	Bystanders (%)	Significance (chi-square)
Size of town lived in for longest period during war	(n = 214)	(n = 65)	
Farm	7.5	1.5	
Village	16.4	9.2	
Small city	15.9	26.2	
Medium-size city	5.6	15.4	
Large city	54.7	47.7	.007
Many neighbors living nearby during war	(n = 117)	(n = 61)	
Yes	86.3	90.2	
No	13.7	9.8	NS

(*Continued*)

TABLE 5.3 *Risk (Continued)*

b. *Rescuers vs. Bystanders*

	Rescuers (%)	Bystanders (%)	Significance (chi-square)
Number of others living in household in 1939	(n = 226)	(n = 73)	
None	15.9	26.0	
1–2	31.4	23.3	
3–4	32.3	32.9	
5–6	14.2	11.0	
7 plus	6.2	6.8	NS
Children 10 years or younger living in household in 1939			
None	73.5	80.8	
One or more	26.5	19.2	NS

TABLE 5.4 *Work Status Before War*

a. *Rescuers vs. Nonrescuers*

	Rescuers (n = 215) (%)	Nonrescuers (n = 122) (%)	Significance (chi-square)
Employed	52.6	45.9	
Military	1.9	2.5	
Student	18.1	33.6	
Housewife	14.0	9.8	
Other[a]	8.8	7.4	
Unemployed	4.7	0.8	.02

b. *Rescuers vs. Bystanders*

	Rescuers (n = 215) (%)	Bystanders (n = 72) (%)	Significance (chi-square)
Employed	52.6	44.4	
Military	1.9	4.2	
Student	18.1	31.9	
Housewife	14.0	9.7	
Other[a]	8.8	8.3	
Unemployed	4.7	1.4	NS

[a]"Other" includes members of the clergy as well as those intermittently employed. Percentages of employed cited in the narrative include employed, military, and "other."

TABLE 5.5　*Occupational Status Before War*[a]

a. Rescuers vs. Nonrescuers

	Rescuers (n = 135) (%)	Nonrescuers (n = 68) (%)	Significance (chi-square)
Professional	12.6	4.4	
Business	20.7	20.6	
Administrative	14.1	7.4	
Clerical	20.7	20.6	
Skilled	15.6	17.6	
Semiskilled	5.9	19.1	
Unskilled	10.4	10.3	NS

b. Rescuers vs. Bystanders

	Rescuers (n = 135) (%)	Bystanders (n = 40) (%)	Significance (chi-square)
Professional	12.6	5.0	
Business	20.7	22.5	
Administrative	14.1	5.0	
Clerical	20.7	22.5	
Skilled	15.6	20.0	
Semiskilled	5.9	17.5	
Unskilled	10.4	7.5	NS

[a]Includes employed, military, and "other."

TABLE 5.6 *Self-Perceptions of Economic Status*

	Very Well Off (%)	Quite Well Off (%)	Neither Rich Nor Poor (%)	Quite Poor (%)	Very Poor (%)	Significance (chi-square)
a. Prewar						
Rescuers (n = 218)	4.6	21.6	51.8	15.1	6.9	
Nonrescuers (n = 123)	4.1	16.3	61.8	16.3	1.6	NS
Rescuers (n = 218)	4.6	21.6	51.8	15.1	6.9	
Bystanders (n = 72)	0.0	16.7	66.7	16.7	0.0	.02
b. During War						
Rescuers (n = 116)	0.9	19.0	48.3	25.0	6.9	
Nonrescuers (n = 111)	1.8	15.3	53.2	21.6	8.1	NS
Rescuers (n = 116)	0.9	19.0	48.3	25.0	6.9	
Bystanders (n = 65)	0.0	12.3	53.8	29.2	4.6	NS

TABLE 5.7   *Work Status During War*

a. Rescuers vs. Nonrescuers

	Rescuers (n = 181) (%)	Nonrescuers (n = 121) (%)	Significance (chi-square)
Employed	60.8	53.7	
Military[a]	4.4	12.7	
Student	7.2	13.2	
Housewife	10.5	8.3	
Other[b]	8.8	9.9	
Unemployed	8.3	2.5	.01

b. Rescuers vs. Bystanders

	Rescuers (n = 181) (%)	Bystanders (n = 73) (%)	Significance (chi-square)
Employed	60.8	49.3	
Military[a]	4.4	17.8	
Student	7.2	13.7	
Housewife	10.5	9.6	
Other[b]	8.8	8.2	
Unemployed	8.3	1.4	.002

[a]Military were those serving in the German armed forces.

[b]"Other" includes members of the clergy as well as those intermittently employed. Percentages of employed cited in narrative include employed, military, and "other."

TABLE 5.8 *Occupational Status During War*[a]

a. Rescuers vs. Nonrescuers

	Rescuers (n = 135) (%)	Nonrescuers (n = 88) (%)	Significance (chi-square)
Professional	11.2	5.7	
Business	18.6	15.9	
Administrative	14.1	3.4	
Clerical	21.5	28.4	
Skilled	11.9	11.4	
Semiskilled	9.7	23.9	
Unskilled	13.4	11.4	.02

b. Rescuers vs. Bystanders

	Rescuers (n = 135) (%)	Bystanders (n = 52) (%)	Significance (chi-square)
Professional	11.2	5.8	
Business	18.6	17.3	
Administrative	14.1	2.0	
Clerical	21.5	19.3	
Skilled	11.9	11.6	
Semiskilled	9.7	32.7	
Unskilled	13.4	11.6	.01

[a]Includes employed, military, and "other."

TABLE 5.9 *Sheltering Potential*

a. Rescuers vs. Nonrescuers

	Rescuers (%)	Nonrescuers (%)	Significance (chi-square)
Lived in house, apartment, or other during war	(*n* = 216)	(*n* = 114)	
House	48.1	41.2	
Apartment	47.2	49.1	
Other	4.6	9.6	NS
Own, rent, or other	(*n* = 103)	(*n* = 51)	
Own	44.7	51.0	
Rent	38.0	31.4	
Other	16.5	17.6	NS
Attic in dwelling	(*n* = 204)	(*n* = 105)	
Yes	80.4	74.3	
No	19.6	25.7	NS
Cellar in dwelling	(*n* = 208)	(*n* = 108)	
Yes	82.7	69.4	
No	17.3	30.6	.006
Number of rooms in dwelling	(*n* = 208)	(*n* = 105)	
1–3	39.9	47.6	
4–6	36.5	35.2	
7–9	18.8	12.4	
10 plus	4.8	4.8	NS

b. Rescuers vs. Bystanders

	Rescuers (%)	Bystanders (%)	Significance (chi-square)
Lived in house, apartment, or other during war	(*n* = 216)	(*n* = 64)	
House	48.1	43.8	
Apartment	47.2	45.3	
Other	4.6	10.9	NS
Own, rent, or other	(*n* = 103)	(*n* = 30)	
Own	44.7	50.0	
Rent	38.8	26.7	
Other	16.5	23.3	NS
Attic in dwelling	(*n* = 204)	(*n* = 60)	
Yes	80.4	80.0	
No	19.6	20.0	NS
Cellar in dwelling	(*n* = 208)	(*n* = 63)	
Yes	82.7	81.0	
No	17.3	19.0	NS

(*Continued*)

TABLE 5.9   *Sheltering Potential (Continued)*

b. Rescuers vs. Bystanders

	Rescuers (%)	Bystanders (%)	Significance (chi-square)
Number of rooms in dwelling	$(n = 208)$	$(n = 59)$	
1–3	39.9	54.2	
4–6	36.5	35.6	
7–9	18.8	5.1	
10 plus	4.8	5.1	.005

TABLE 5.10   *Networks: Potential Sources of Information, Being Asked for Help,*
and Recruiting Others to Help

	Yes (%)	No (%)	Significance (chi-square)
a. Rescuers vs. Nonrescuers			
Respondent member of resistance group			
Rescuers (*n* = 222)	43.7	56.3	
Nonrescuers (*n* = 123)	28.5	76.5	.007
Respondent head of household			
Rescuers (*n* = 226)	29.2	70.8	
Nonrescuers (*n* = 126)	27.0	73.0	NS
Other persons living in household			
Rescuers (*n* = 226)	84.1	15.9	
Nonrescuers (*n* = 126)	79.4	20.6	NS
Other family members in community			
Rescuers (*n* = 211)	45.0	55.0	
Nonrescuers (*n* = 113)	53.1	46.9	NS
Family members involved in helping Jews or resistance			
Rescuers (*n* = 183)	59.6	40.4	
Nonrescuers (*n* = 113)	35.4	64.6	.0000
b. Rescuers vs. Bystanders			
Respondent member of resistance group			
Rescuer (*n* = 222)	43.7	56.3	
Bystanders (*n* = 73)	0.0	100.0	.0000
Respondent head of household			
Rescuer (*n* = 226)	29.2	70.8	
Bystanders (*n* = 73)	26.0	74.0	NS
Other persons living in household			
Rescuers (*n* = 226)	84.1	15.9	
Bystanders (*n* = 73)	74.0	26.0	NS
Other family members in community			
Rescuers (*n* = 211)	45.0	42.9	
Bystanders (*n* = 63)	55.0	57.1	NS
Family members involved in helping Jews or resistance			
Rescuers (*n* = 183)	59.6	40.4	
Bystanders (*n* = 64)	20.3	79.7	.0000

TABLE 6.1 *Attitudes Toward Nazis*
(How did you feel about Nazis taking power in your country?)

	Negative (%)	Accommo-dating (%)	Other[a] (%)	Significance (chi-square)
a. Rescuers vs. Nonrescuers				
Rescuers (n = 123)	82.1	7.3	10.6	
Nonrescuers (n = 119)	72.3	12.6	15.1	NS
b. Rescuers vs. Bystanders				
Rescuers (n = 123)	82.1	7.3	10.6	
Bystanders (n = 71)	66.2	19.7	14.1	.02

[a]"Other" responses focused primarily on comments regarding Nazi power without any indication of feelings.

TABLE 6.2   *Reasons Given for Activity*[a]
(Can you summarize for me the main reasons you became involved?)

a. Rescuers vs. Actives

	Rescuers (n = 222) (%)	Actives (n = 43) (%)	Significance (chi-square)
Religion	15.3	0.0	.01
Patriotism	8.1	44.2	.0000
Hatred of Nazis	16.7	37.2	.004
External approval	2.7	0.0	NS
Ethical	86.5	34.9	.0000
Equity	19.4	14.0	NS
Care	76.1	23.3	.0000
Friend	15.8	0.0	.01
Jews	3.6	0.0	NS
Universal ethical	49.5	20.9	.001
Universal equity	14.9	7.0	NS
Universal care	38.3	14.0	.003

b. Rescuers vs. Rescued Survivors[b]

	Rescuers (n = 222) (%)	Rescued Survivors (n = 93) (%)
Self-centered motives (money, desire to convert to Christianity, exploitation)	0.0	5.4
Religion	15.3	25.8
Patriotism	8.1	1.1
Hatred of Nazis	16.7	10.8
External approval	2.7	0.0
Ethical	86.5	82.8
Equity	19.4	25.8
Care	76.1	66.7
Friends, lovers, relations	15.8	28.0
Jews	3.6	2.2
Universal ethical	49.5	29.1
Universal equity	14.9	6.5
Universal care	38.3	23.7

[a]Respondents frequently gave more than one reason for their activities. Each reason received one tally in the appropriate category. If the respondent repeated the same type of reason more than once (e.g., "I did it because I am an obedient Christian; God would have wanted me to do it"), it was recorded as one tally in the appropriate category for that respondent.

[b]Reasons here refer to those rescued survivors attribute to people who helped them. Coding followed the same procedures as described in note a above.

TABLE 6.3　*Parental Attitudes Toward Jews*

a. Rescuers vs. Nonrescuers

	Rescuers (n = 216) (%)	Nonrescuers (n = 117) (%)	Significance (chi-square)
Neither parent discussed	25.9	41.0	.007
Stereotypes mentioned	11.6	21.4	.02
Positive	4.2	5.1	NS
Neutral	4.2	6.8	NS
Negative	2.8	10.2	.008
Other comments			
Positive	44.4	37.6	NS
Neutral	39.8	29.9	NS
Negative	2.8	9.4	.01

b. Rescuers vs. Bystanders

	Rescuers (n = 216) (%)	Bystanders (n = 67) (%)	Significance (chi-square)
Neither parent discussed	25.9	46.3	.002
Stereotypes mentioned	11.6	23.9	.02
Positive	4.2	7.5	NS
Neutral	4.2	10.4	NS
Negative	2.8	16.4	.0001
Other comments			
Positive	44.4	35.8	NS
Neutral	39.8	25.4	.04
Negative	2.8	10.4	.02

TABLE 6.4   *Religious Affiliation and Education*

	Catholic (%)	Protestant (%)	Non-sectarian (%)	Other (%)	Significance (chi-square)
a. Rescuers vs. Nonrescuers					
Affiliation while growing up					
Rescuers					
(n = 224)	61.6	32.1	4.9	1.3	
Nonrescuers					
(n = 123)	72.4	22.8	4.1	.8	NS
Type of elementary school					
Rescuers					
(n = 203)	25.6	20.2	52.7	1.5	
Nonrescuers					
(n = 123)	35.8	9.8	51.2	3.3	.02
Type of gymnasium					
Rescuers					
(n = 153)	26.1	14.4	56.9	2.6	
Nonrescuers					
(n = 90)	28.9	3.3	62.2	5.6	.03
b. Rescuers vs. Bystanders					
Affiliation while growing up					
Rescuers					
(n = 224)	61.6	32.1	4.9	1.3	
Bystanders					
(n = 73)	72.6	23.3	4.1	0.0	NS
Type of elementary school					
Rescuers					
(n = 203)	25.6	20.2	52.7	1.5	
Bystanders					
(n = 71	33.8	9.9	53.8	2.8	NS
Type of gymnasium					
Rescuers					
(n = 153)	26.1	14.4	56.9	2.6	
Bystanders					
(n = 47)	29.8	2.1	63.8	4.3	NS

TABLE 6.5 *Parental Religiosity*

	Very (%)	Somewhat (%)	Not Very (%)	Not At All (%)	Significance (chi-square)
a. Rescuers vs. Nonrescuers					
MOTHER					
Rescuers (n = 164)	49.4	36.0	9.8	4.9	
Nonrescuers (n = 111)	43.2	43.2	9.0	4.5	NS
FATHER					
Rescuers (n = 140)	32.9	31.4	25.0	10.7	
Nonrescuers (n = 106)	21.7	40.6	24.5	13.2	NS
b. Rescuers vs. Bystanders					
MOTHER					
Rescuers (n = 164)	49.4	36.0	9.8	4.9	
Bystanders (n = 66)	43.9	43.9	4.5	7.6	NS
FATHER					
Rescuers (n = 140)	32.9	31.4	25.0	10.7	
Bystanders (n = 61)	16.4	47.5	18.0	18.0	.02

TABLE 6.6   *Religiosity Growing Up, Before War, Today: Self*

	Very (%)	Somewhat (%)	Not Very (%)	Not At All (%)	Significance (chi-square)
a. Rescuers vs. Nonrescuers					
GROWING UP					
Rescuers					
(n = 210)	38.6	34.8	18.6	8.1	
Nonrescuers					
(n = 120)	25.0	46.7	19.2	9.2	NS
BEFORE WAR					
Rescuers					
(n = 119)	31.1	37.8	19.3	11.8	
Nonrescuers					
(n = 120)	21.7	42.5	24.2	11.7	NS
TODAY					
Rescuers					
(n = 206)	40.3	32.5	11.7	15.5	
Nonrescuers					
(n = 103)	25.2	45.6	18.4	10.7	.01
b. Rescuers vs. Bystanders					
GROWING UP					
Rescuers					
(n = 210)	38.6	34.8	18.6	8.1	
Bystanders					
(n = 71)	21.1	54.9	12.7	11.3	.008
BEFORE WAR					
Rescuers					
(n = 119)	31.1	37.8	19.3	11.8	
Bystanders					
(n = 72)	23.6	47.2	15.3	13.9	NS
TODAY					
Rescuers					
(n = 206)	40.3	32.5	11.7	15.5	
Bystanders					
(n = 65)	27.7	49.2	15.4	7.7	NS

TABLE 6.7   *Values: Most Influential Parent/Role Model*[a]

a. Rescuers vs. Nonrescuers

	Rescuers (n = 219) (%)	Nonrescuers (n = 118) (%)	Significance (chi-square)
Religion	15.5	16.9	NS
Patriotism	8.2	4.2	NS
Values relating to self	24.2	34.7	.05
Economic competence	19.2	28.8	.05
Independence	6.4	8.5	NS
Conventional	35.2	41.5	NS
Propriety	21.0	27.1	NS
Dependability	16.0	13.6	NS
Obedience	1.4	8.5	.003
Ethical	70.3	55.9	.01
Equity	43.8	45.8	NS
Care	43.8	24.6	.0007
Universal ethical	39.3	15.3	.0000
Equity	14.2	7.6	NS
Care	28.3	8.5	.0000

b. Rescuers vs. Bystanders

	Rescuers (n = 219) (%)	Bystanders (n = 67) (%)	Significance (chi-square)
Religion	15.5	22.4	NS
Patriotism	8.2	4.5	NS
Values relating to self	24.2	39.4	.01
Economic competence	19.2	34.3	.01
Independence	6.4	7.5	NS
Conventional	35.2	40.3	NS
Propriety	21.0	29.9	NS
Dependability	16.0	7.5	NS
Obedience	1.4	11.9	.0004
Ethical	70.3	56.7	.05
Equity	43.8	47.8	NS
Care	43.8	20.9	.001
Universal ethical	39.3	13.4	.0002
Equity	14.2	10.4	NS
Care	28.3	4.5	.0001

[a]Respondents characteristically noted multiple values they learned from their most influential parent or role model. Each value noted was recorded as one tally in the appropriate category. If the respondent repeated the same value more than once (e.g., "My mother taught me to care for people and help them"), it was recorded as a single tally in the appropriate category for that respondent.

TABLE 6.8   *Political Affiliations: Self*

a. Rescuers vs. Nonrescuers

	Rescuers (%)	Nonrescuers (%)	Significance (chi-square)
Belong to political party before war?	(*n* = 209)	(*n* = 121)	
Yes	21.1	10.8	
No	79.0	89.3	NS
Type of political affiliation[a]	(*n* = 40)	(*n* = 13)	
Economic left	27.5	30.8	NS
Democratic	80.0	30.8	001
Tolerant of minorities	80.0	69.3	NS
Tolerant of Jews	77.5	69.3	NS

b. Rescuers vs. Bystanders

	Rescuers (%)	Bystanders (%)	Significance (chi-square)
Belong to political party before war?	(*n* = 209)	(*n* = 71)	
Yes	21.1	9.9	
No	79.0	90.2	.05
Type of political affiliation[a]	(*n* = 40)	(*n* = 7)	
Economic left	27.5	14.2	NS
Democratic	80.0	14.3	.001
Tolerant of minorities	80.0	57.2	NS
Tolerant of Jews	77.5	57.2	NS

[a]Each party identified was coded with respect to its economic orientation (whether socialist, capitalist or mixed), subscription to autocratic or democratic principles, attitudes toward minorities generally and attitudes toward Jews. For specific examples see Chap. 6, Fn. 11.

TABLE 6.9   *Parents' Political Affiliations*

a. Rescuers vs. Nonrescuers

	Rescuers (%)	Nonrescuers (%)	Significance (chi-square)
Father or mother belong to political party before war?	(n = 195)	(n = 111)	
Yes	28.8	19.9	
No	71.3	80.2	NS
Type of political affiliation[a]	(n = 56)	(n = 22)	
Economic left	28.6	13.7	NS
Democratic	78.6	54.6	.05
Tolerant of minorities	87.5	72.8	NS
Tolerant of Jews	85.8	68.2	NS

b. Rescuers vs. Bystanders

	Rescuers (%)	Bystanders (%)	Significance (chi-square)
Father or mother belong to political party before war?	(n = 195)	(n = 61)	
Yes	28.8	19.7	
No	71.5	80.4	NS
Type of political affiliation[a]	(n = 56)	(n = 12)	
Economic left	28.6	16.7	NS
Democratic	78.6	66.7	NS
Tolerant of minorities	87.5	75.0	NS
Tolerant of Jews	85.8	83.4	NS

[a]Each party identified was coded with respect to its economic orientation (whether socialist, capitalist, or mixed) subscription to autocratic or democratic principles, attitudes toward minorities generally, and attitudes toward Jews. For specific examples, see Chap. 6, Fn. 11.

TABLE 6.10   *Father's Education*

a. Rescuers vs. Nonrescuers

	Rescuers ($n = 150$) (%)	Nonrescuers ($n = 114$) (%)	Significance (chi-square)
Self-taught or elementary school only	48.7	59.7	
Attended gymnasium but not university	29.4	24.6	
Attended university	22.0	15.8	NS

b. Rescuers vs. Bystanders

	Rescuers ($n = 150$) (%)	Bystanders ($n = 66$) (%)	Significance (chi-square)
Self-taught or elementary school only	48.7	60.6	
Attended gymnasium but not university	29.4	25.8	
Attended university	22.0	13.7	NS

TABLE 6.11   *Father's Occupational Status*

a. *Rescuers vs. Nonrescuers*

	Rescuers ($n = 198$) (%)	Nonrescuers ($n = 116$) (%)	Significance (chi-square)
Professional	12.6	12.1	
Business	15.2	11.2	
Administrative	18.7	18.1	
Clerical	15.2	22.4	
Skilled	23.2	23.3	
Semiskilled	7.6	10.3	
Unskilled	7.6	2.6	NS

b. *Rescuers vs. Bystanders*

	Rescuers ($n = 198$) (%)	Bystanders ($n = 69$) (%)	Significance (chi-square)
Professional	12.6	8.7	
Business	15.2	7.2	
Administrative	18.7	24.6	
Clerical	15.2	21.7	
Skilled	23.2	26.1	
Semiskilled	7.6	8.7	
Unskilled	7.6	2.9	NS

TABLE 7.1 *Family Closeness*

	Very (%)	Somewhat (%)	Not Very (%)	Not At All (%)	Significance (chi-square)
a. Rescuers vs. Nonrescuers					
Closeness of family					
Rescuers					
(*n* = 222)	78.4	15.5	4.5	1.4	
Nonrescuers					
(*n* = 122)	55.7	32.8	7.4	4.1	.0002
Closeness to mother					
Rescuers					
(*n* = 118)	67.8	28.0	4.2	0.0	
Nonrescuers					
(*n* = 116)	53.4	31.0	12.1	3.4	.01
Closeness to father					
Rescuers					
(*n* = 110)	53.6	34.5	7.3	4.5	
Nonrescuers					
(*n* = 110)	40.9	34.5	18.2	6.4	NS
Closeness to most influential person other than mother or father[a]					
Rescuers					
(*n* = 33)	75.8	21.2	3.0	0.0	
Nonrescuers					
(*n* = 32)	43.8	46.9	3.1	6.3	.04
b. Rescuers vs. Bystanders					
Closeness of family					
Rescuers					
(*n* = 222)	78.4	15.8	4.5	1.4	
Bystanders					
(*n* = 69)	52.2	31.9	10.1	5.8	.0003
Closeness to mother					
Rescuers					
(*n* = 118)	67.8	28.0	4.2	0.0	
Bystanders					
(*n* = 69)	55.1	29.0	11.6	4.3	.02

(Continued)

TABLE 7.1   *Family Closeness (Continued)*

	Very (%)	Somewhat (%)	Not Very (%)	Not At All (%)	Significance (chi-square)
b. Rescuers vs. Bystanders					
Closeness to father					
Rescuers					
(n = 110)	53.6	34.5	7.3	4.5	
Bystanders					
(n = 65)	33.8	35.4	20.0	10.8	.01
Closeness to most influential person other than mother or father[a]					
Rescuers					
(n = 33)	75.8	21.2	3.0	0.0	
Bystanders					
(n = 18)	44.4	38.9	5.6	11.1	NS

[a]The small *ns* in this category reflect the fact that only a small percentage of respondents identified someone other than a parent as having the most influence on them when they were growing up.

TABLE 7.2   *ANOVA: Social Responsibility Scale[a]*

a. Rescuers vs. Nonrescuers

MEANS[b]
   Total population: 25.90
   Cell means, rescuers: 26.17
   Cell means, nonrescuers: 25.43

SOURCE OF VARIATION	Sum of Squares	df	Mean Square	F	Significance of F
COVARIATES	14.245	2	7.122	0.729	
Sex	6.415	1	6.415	0.657	0.418
Age	9.105	1	9.105	0.932	0.335
MAIN EFFECTS	55.749	1	55.749	5.705	0.017[c]

b. Rescuers vs. Bystanders

MEANS
   Total population: 25.86
   Cell means, rescuers: 26.17
   Cell means, bystanders: 24.90

SOURCE OF VARIATION	Sum of Squares	df	Mean Square	F	Significance of F
COVARIATES	10.634	2	5.317	0.546	
Sex	4.854	1	4.854	0.498	0.481
Age	6.289	1	6.289	0.646	0.422
MAIN EFFECTS	99.758	1	99.758	10.245	0.002[d]

[a]The Social Responsibility Scale consists of eight items assessing an individual's attitudes toward helping others even when there is nothing to be gained.

[b]A higher score indicates a stronger sense of social responsibility.

[c]The main effects show that rescuers had a significantly stronger sense of social responsibility than did all nonrescuers independently of sex and age.

[d]The main effects show that rescuers had a significantly stronger sense of social responsibility than did bystanders independently of sex and age.

TABLE 7.3   *ANOVA: Prosocial Action Orientation*[a]

a. Rescuers vs. Nonrescuers

MEANS[b]
    Total population: 0.00
    Cell means, rescuers: 0.14
    Cell means, nonrescuers: −0.14

SOURCE OF VARIATION	Sum of Squares	df	Mean Square	F	Significance of F
COVARIATES	9.107	2	4.553	6.171	
Sex	9.068	1	9.068	12.288	0.001[c]
Age	0.034	1	0.034	0.046	0.830
MAIN EFFECTS	3.907	1	3.907	5.294	0.022[d]

b. Rescuers vs. Bystanders

MEANS
    Total population: −0.01
    Cell means, rescuers: 0.14
    Cell means, bystanders: −0.26

SOURCE OF VARIATION	Sum of Squares	df	Mean Square	F	Significance of F
COVARIATES	7.859	2	3.930	5.590	
Sex	7.858	1	7.858	11.179	0.001[c]
Age	0.038	1	0.038	0.054	0.816
MAIN EFFECTS	6.589	1	6.589	9.373	0.003[e]

[a]The Prosocial Action Orientation factor consists of twelve intercorrelated variables assessing the degree to which individuals are likely to help others based on their emotional empathic response to pain and feelings of social responsibility. Individual items comprising the factor and factor loadings are given in Table 7.16, Prosocial Action Orientation.

[b]A higher score means a greater inclination toward helping based on strong emotional empathy towards pain and social responsibility.

[c]Covariates show that a prosocial action orientation is significantly related to sex.

[d]The main effects show that rescuers were significantly different from all nonrescuers independently of sex and age.

[e]The main effects indicate that rescuers were significantly different from bystanders independently of sex and age.

TABLE 7.4 *ANOVA: Detachment Factor*[a]

a. Rescuers vs. Nonrescuers

MEANS[b]

Total population:	0.00				
Cell means, rescuers:	−0.04				
Cell means, nonrescuers:	0.04				

SOURCE OF VARIATION	Sum of Squares	df	Mean Square	F	Significance of F
COVARIATES[c]	1.607	2	0.803	1.203	
Sex	1.264	1	1.264	1.892	0.170
Age	0.523	1	0.523	0.783	0.377
MAIN EFFECTS[d]	0.622	1	0.622	0.932	0.335

b. Rescuers vs. Bystanders

MEANS

Total population:	0.00				
Cell means, rescuers:	−0.04				
Cell means, bystanders:	0.06				

SOURCE OF VARIATION	Sum of Squares	df	Mean Square	F	Significance of F
COVARIATES[c]	1.325	2	0.663	0.938	
Sex	1.006	1	1.006	1.424	0.234
Age	0.414	1	0.414	0.585	0.445
MAIN EFFECTS[e]	0.650	1	0.650	0.920	0.339

[a]The Detachment Scale, consisting of eight intercorrelated variables, assesses the degree to which individuals are inclined to disassociate themselves from others. Individual items comprising this scale and factor loadings are given in Table 7.16, Detachment Factor.

[b]A higher score indicates a stronger sense of detachment.

[c]Covariates show that detachment was unrelated to sex or age.

[d]The main effects show that rescuers did not differ significantly from controls with respect to detachment independently of sex and age.

[e]The main effects show that rescuers did not differ significantly from bystanders with respect to detachment independently of sex and age.

TABLE 7.5   *Feelings of Similarity to Diverse Groups*

	Very Like (%)	Somewhat Like (%)	Not Very Like (%)	Not At All Like (%)	Significance (chi-square)
a. Rescuers vs. Nonrescuers					
Rich					
Rescuers ($n = 105$)	23.8	13.3	34.3	28.6	
Nonrescuers ($n = 111$)	9.0	26.1	21.6	43.2	.0004
Poor					
Rescuers ($n = 104$)	42.3	33.7	16.3	7.7	
Nonrescuers ($n = 110$)	32.7	32.7	21.8	12.7	NS
Catholics					
Rescuers ($n = 104$)	51.0	23.1	12.5	13.5	
Nonrescuers ($n = 109$)	55.0	26.6	8.3	10.1	NS
Protestants					
Rescuers ($n = 89$)	49.4	31.5	9.0	10.1	
Nonrescuers ($n = 92$)	37.0	35.9	13.0	14.1	NS
Turks[a]					
Rescuers ($n = 37$)	16.2	10.8	18.9	54.1	
Nonrescuers ($n = 48$)	12.5	18.8	12.5	56.3	NS
Jews					
Rescuers ($n = 90$)	54.4	20.0	8.9	16.7	
Nonrescuers ($n = 95$)	21.1	34.7	18.9	25.3	.0001
Gypsies					
Rescuers ($n = 78$)	20.5	15.4	25.6	38.5	
Nonrescuers ($n = 85$)	5.9	10.6	17.6	65.9	.002
Nazis					
Rescuers ($n = 88$)	5.7	3.4	5.7	85.2	
Nonrescuers ($n = 88$)	1.1	5.7	5.7	87.5	NS

TABLE 7.5   *Feelings of Similarity to Diverse Groups*

	Very Like (%)	Somewhat Like (%)	Not Very Like (%)	Not At All Like (%)	Significance (chi-square)
b. Rescuers vs. Bystanders					
Rich					
Rescuers ($n = 105$)	23.8	13.3	34.3	28.6	
Bystanders ($n = 64$)	7.8	28.1	20.3	43.8	.001
Poor					
Rescuers ($n = 104$)	42.3	33.7	16.3	7.7	
Bystanders ($n = 66$)	25.8	40.9	16.7	16.7	NS
Catholics					
Rescuers ($n = 104$)	51.0	23.1	12.5	13.5	
Bystanders ($n = 65$)	53.8	26.2	7.7	12.3	NS
Protestants					
Rescuers ($n = 89$)	49.4	31.5	40.0	10.1	
Bystanders ($n = 53$)	34.0	35.8	35.0	17.0	NS
Turks[a]					
Rescuers ($n = 37$)	16.2	10.8	18.9	54.1	
Bystanders ($n = 28$)	14.3	10.7	7.1	67.9	NS
Jews					
Rescuers ($n = 90$)	54.4	20.0	8.9	16.7	
Bystanders ($n = 55$)	18.2	30.9	16.4	34.5	.0003
Gypsies					
Rescuers ($n = 78$)	20.5	15.4	25.6	38.5	
Bystanders ($n = 48$)	8.3	4.2	10.4	77.1	.0005
Nazis					
Rescuers ($n = 88$)	5.7	3.4	5.7	85.2	
Bystanders ($n = 54$)	1.9	9.3	5.6	83.3	NS

[a]Most respondents refused to answer this question, saying they "didn't know any."

TABLE 7.6 *Variety of Friendships*

	Yes (%)	No (%)	Don't Know (%)	Significance (chi-square)
a. Rescuers vs. Nonrescuers				
While growing up, did you have close friends different from you in social class?				
Rescuers ($n = 109$)	62.2	37.8	0.00	
Nonrescuers ($n = 108$)	45.4	54.6	0.00	.01
While growing up, did you have close friends different from you in religion?				
Rescuers ($n = 109$)	65.1	34.9	0.00	
Nonrescuers ($n = 107$)	41.1	58.9	0.00	.0007
While growing up, did you have any close Jewish friends?				
Rescuers ($n = 205$)	45.9	52.2	2.0	
Nonrescuers ($n = 113$)	34.5	61.9	3.5	NS
Did you have any Jewish friends before the war?				
Rescuers ($n = 119$)	58.8	39.5	11.7	
Nonrescuers ($n = 115$)	33.9	60.0	6.1	.0004
b. Rescuers vs. Bystanders				
While growing up, did you have close friends different from you in social class?				
Rescuers ($n = 109$)	62.2	37.8	0.0	
Bystanders ($n = 64$)	35.9	64.1	0.0	.002
While growing up, did you have close friends different from you in religion?				
Rescuers ($n = 109$)	65.1	34.9	0.0	
Bystanders ($n = 67$)	35.8	64.2	0.0	.0003
While growing up, did you have any close Jewish friends?				
Rescuers ($n = 205$)	45.9	52.2	2.0	
Bystanders ($n = 66$)	22.7	74.2	3.0	.003
Did you have any Jewish friends before the war?				
Rescuers ($n = 119$)	58.8	39.5	1.7	
Bystanders ($n = 68$)	25.0	70.6	4.4	.0001

TABLE 7.7 *Opportunities for Making Jewish Friends While Growing Up*

	Yes (%)	No (%)	Don't Know (%)	Significance (chi-square)
a. Rescuers vs. Nonrescuers				
Know any Jews while growing up?				
Rescuers ($n = 111$)	57.7	41.4	0.9	
Nonrescuers ($n = 84$)	58.3	36.9	4.8	NS
Did Jews attend your elementary school?				
Rescuers ($n = 205$)	40.0	46.3	13.7	
Nonrescuers ($n = 123$)	39.8	40.7	19.5	NS
Did Jews attend your gymnasium?				
Rescuers ($n = 150$)	57.3	27.3	15.3	
Nonrescuers ($n = 90$)	53.3	27.8	18.9	NS
b. Rescuers vs. Bystanders				
Know any Jews while growing up?				
Rescuers ($n = 111$)	57.7	41.4	0.9	
Bystanders ($n = 55$)	58.2	38.2	3.6	NS
Did Jews attend your elementary school?				
Rescuers ($n = 205$)	40.0	46.3	13.7	
Bystanders ($n = 71$)	33.8	46.5	19.7	NS
Did Jews attend your gymnasium?				
Rescuers ($n = 150$)	57.3	27.3	15.3	
Bystanders ($n = 47$)	51.1	29.8	19.1	NS

TABLE 7.8 *Marginality*

a. Rescuers vs. Nonrescuers

Sense of belonging in community	Belonging	Outsider	Other		Significance (chi-square)
Rescuers					
(n = 215)	80.0	14.4	5.6		
Nonrescuers					
(n = 124)	81.5	12.9	5.6		NS

Close friends when growing up	Many	Some	Few	None	
Rescuers					
(n = 224)	38.8	35.3	19.6	6.3	
Nonrescuers					
(n = 124)	29.0	37.9	25.8	7.3	NS

Perceptions of neighbors when growing up	Very Friendly	Somewhat Friendly	Not Very Friendly	Not At All Friendly	
Rescuers					
(n = 197)	53.8	35.5	7.1	3.6	
Nonrescuers					
(n = 112)	46.4	39.3	8.0	6.3	NS

b. Rescuers vs. Bystanders

Sense of belonging in community	Belonging	Outsider	Other		Significance (chi-square)
Rescuers					
(n = 215)	80.0	14.4	5.6		
Bystanders					
(n = 72)	83.3	11.1	5.6		NS

Close friends when growing up	Many	Some	Few	None	
Rescuers					
(n = 224)	38.8	35.3	19.6	6.3	
Bystanders					
(n = 73)	24.7	45.2	23.3	6.8	NS

Perception of neighbors when growing up	Very Friendly	Somewhat Friendly	Not Very Friendly	Not At All Friendly	
Rescuers					
(n = 197)	53.8	35.5	7.1	3.6	
Bystanders					
(n = 63)	41.3	54.0	3.2	1.6	NS

TABLE 7.9 *ANOVA: Internal/External Locus of Control Scale*[a]

a. Rescuers vs. Nonrescuers

MEANS[b]

Total population:	13.23			
Cell means, rescuers:	13.47			
Cell means, nonrescuers:	12.81			

SOURCE OF VARIATION	Sum of Squares	df	Mean Square	F	Significance of F
COVARIATES[c]	1.435	2	0.718	0.122	
Sex	0.478	1	0.478	0.081	0.775
Age	1.076	1	1.076	0.183	0.669
MAIN EFFECTS	35.186	1	35.186	5.992	0.015[d]

b. Rescuers vs. Bystanders

MEANS

Total population:	13.21			
Cell means, rescuers:	13.47			
Cell means, bystanders:	12.40			

SOURCE OF VARIATION	Sum of Squares	df	Mean Square	F	Significance of F
COVARIATES[c]	1.444	2	0.722	0.118	
Sex	1.148	1	1.148	0.188	0.665
Age	0.354	1	0.354	0.058	0.810
MAIN EFFECTS	65.388	1	65.388	10.711	0.001[e]

[a]The Internal/External Locus of Control Scale measures the extent to which individuals view themselves as able to affect external events through their own efforts.

[b]A higher score indicates a stronger sense of internal control; that is, a stronger sense of being able to affect external events through one's own efforts.

[c]The covariates show that a sense of internal control is unrelated to sex or age.

[d]The main effects show that rescuers had a significantly stronger sense of internal control than did all nonrescuers independently of sex and age.

[e]The main effects show that rescuers had a significantly stronger sense of internal control that did bystanders independently of sex and age.

TABLE 7.10   *Respondents' Perceptions of Ever Having Received Discipline*

	Yes (%)	No (%)	Significance (chi-square)
a. Rescuers vs. Nonrescuers			
Father			
Rescuers ($n = 108$)	60.2	39.8	
Nonrescuers ($n = 110$)	67.3	32.7	NS
Mother			
Rescuers ($n = 117$)	67.5	32.5	
Nonrescuers ($n = 116$)	81.9	18.1	.01
Other			
Rescuers ($n = 34$)	29.4	70.6	
Nonrescuers ($n = 33$)	66.7	33.3	.005
Father, mother, other combined			
Rescuers ($n = 259$)	59.5	40.5	
Nonrescuers ($n = 259$)	73.7	26.3	.001
b. Rescuers vs. Bystanders			
Father			
Rescuers ($n = 108$)	60.2	39.8	
Bystanders ($n = 64$)	68.8	31.3	NS
Mother			
Rescuers ($n = 117$)	67.5	32.5	
Bystanders ($n = 68$)	80.9	19.1	NS
Other			
Rescuers ($n = 34$)	29.4	70.6	
Bystanders ($n = 18$)	77.8	22.2	.002
Father, mother, other combined			
Rescuers ($n = 259$)	59.5	40.5	
Bystanders ($n = 150$)	75.3	24.7	.01

TABLE 7.11   *Type of Discipline*[a]

	Physical Punishment (%)	Verbal (%)	Reasoning (%)	Miscellaneous (%)	Significance (chi-square)
Rescuers (*n* = 192)	32	33	21	14	
Nonrescuers (*n* = 240)	40	37	06	18	.001
Rescuers (*n* = 192)	32	33	21	14	
Bystanders (*n* = 144)	39	40	06	15	.01

[a]Responses are for father, mother, and "other" combined. The *n* refers to the number of incidents of discipline reported. Each subject could report from zero to four incidents. If more than one incident was reported in a type of discipline, it was counted as one incident in that type.

TABLE 7.12   *Behaviors Related to Punishment*[a]

a. Rescuers vs. Nonrescuers

	Rescuers (*n* = 146) (%)	Nonrescuers (*n* = 119) (%)	Significance (chi-square)
Failure to carry out responsibilities	.39	.36	
Aggressive behavior	.05	.08	
Disobedience	.30	.26	
Impolite behaviors	.19	.24	
Immoral behaviors	.06	.07	NS

b. Rescuers vs. Bystanders

	Rescuers (*n* = 146) (%)	Bystanders (*n* = 114) (%)	Significance (chi-square)
Failure to carry out responsibilities	.39	.31	
Aggressive behavior	.05	.11	
Disobedience	.30	.25	
Impolite behaviors	.19	.24	
Immoral behaviors	.06	.10	NS

[a]Responses include those given for mother, father, and other significant role model.

Tables

TABLE 7.13   *Perceptions of Discipline as Gratuitous*[a]

	Gratuitous Perception Noted (%)	No Gratuitous Perception Noted (%)	Significance (chi-square)
Rescuers			
($n = 116$)[b]	0.9	99.1	
Nonrescuers			
($n = 145$)	7.6	92.4	.01
Rescuers			
($n = 116$)	0.9	99.1	
Bystanders			
($n = 78$)	9.0	91.0	.01

[a]"Gratuitous" refers to perceptions of discipline as unrelated to the respondent's behavior.
[b]The *ns* reflect codable pooled responses in relation to mother, father, and other significant role model.

TABLE 7.14   *ANOVA: Personal Integrity*[a]

a. Rescuers vs. Nonrescuers

MEANS[b]
Total population: .00
Cell means, rescuers: .16
Cell means, nonrescuers: −.16

SOURCE OF VARIATION	Sum of Squares	df	Mean Square	F	Significance of F
COVARIATES	4.145	2	2.072	4.453	
Sex	3.871	1	3.871	8.318	0.004[c]
Age	0.077	1	0.077	0.166	0.684
MAIN EFFECTS	5.739	1	5.739	12.332	0.001[d]

b. Rescuers vs. Bystanders

MEANS
Total population: .01
Cell means, rescuers: .16
Cell means, bystanders: −.26

SOURCE OF VARIATION	Sum of Squares	df	Mean Square	F	Significance of F
COVARIATES	1.894	2	0.947	2.156	
Sex	1.830	1	1.830	4.166	0.043[c]
Age	0.025	1	0.025	0.058	0.810
MAIN EFFECTS	7.762	1	7.762	17.673	0.001[e]

[a]Personal Integrity, consisting of four intercorrelated variables, assesses the degree to which individuals attribute to themselves qualities of honesty and helpfulness. Individual items comprising this factor and factor loadings are given in Table 7.16, Personal Integrity.

[b]A higher score indicates a stronger self-attribution of personal integrity.

[c]Covariates indicate that sex is significantly related to feelings of personal integrity.

[d]The main effects show that rescuers considered themselves to have higher personal integrity than nonrescuers independently of sex and age.

[e]The main effects show that rescuers considered themselves to have higher personal integrity than bystanders independently of sex and age.

TABLE 7.15   *Summary Factor Analysis: Extensivity (Varimax Rotated Factor Matrix After Rotation with Kaiser Normalization)*[a]

	Strong Family Attachments	Jewish Friends	Broad Social Commitments	Egalitarians
1. Belonged to political party	.03894	.16388	.14499	−.09529
2. Close friends	.37855	.16657	.26511	−.09250
3. Community helping today	.34737	.14318	.36106	−.00405
4. Defended country before war	.09483	.10135	.19835	−.40412
5. Detachment	−.04723	.05542	−.50735	−.16891
6. Empathy for Jews	.10562	.39081	.13351	.20939
7. Equity	−.04178	.09738	−.00410	−.19020
8. Ethnocentrism	.16976	.19515	.00590	−.55867
9. Family closeness	.66626	−.01963	−.00388	.15355
10. Feel similar to socio-econ. levels within group	.17483	.15887	−.07342	.37759
11. Feel similar to "outgroup"	−.03636	.11800	.16983	.44544
12. Jewish coworkers	.07144	.58117	−.13660	.01975
13. Jewish friends	−.05848	.72503	.08798	−.00027
14. Jews in neighborhood	−.05113	.31092	.14352	.07199
15. Jews at school	−.10200	.10041	.61016	.04766
16. Parents talked about Jews	.45430	.09718	.11290	−.26016
17. Patriotism	.11370	.24709	.09315	−.04831
18. Perception of neighbors	.29680	−.05087	−.17226	.08677
19. Personal helping today	.08933	−.19724	.21571	.10514
20. Personal integrity	.25477	.14930	.07758	.38346
21. Personal potency	.34151	.14561	.21960	−.04402
22. Prosocial action orientation	.08045	.17777	.09328	.47280
23. Religiosity	.33616	−.09469	.00123	.12021
24. Self-esteem[b]	−.22733	−.17801	−.01771	−.00328
25. Social responsibility	.30494	−.04072	.30121	−.00603
26. Stand up for beliefs	−.00005	.07926	.41065	−.05955
27. Variety of friendships	.20424	.20985	.59810	−.00944

[a]Descriptions of the construction of each variable are given in Table 7.16.
[b]A lower score indicates higher self-esteem.

TABLE 7.16 *Construction of the 27 Variables Used in the Summary Factor Analysis*

Synthesized Variable	Items
1. Belonged to political party	This is a single item relating to whether respondent belonged to a political party before the war (D15).
2. Close friends	This is a single item relating to the extent to which respondent had close friends while growing up (C11).
3. Community helping today	This is one of two factors which emerged in relation to postwar helping behavior:

	Loadings	*Item*
	(F10e) .75	During past year, how often have you given speeches or lectures or written letters on behalf of an issue or cause?
	(F10f) .73	During past year, how often have you investigated, collected, or prepared information on behalf of an issue or cause?
	(F10d) .67	During past year, how often have you made telephone calls on behalf of a group or cause or helped raise money for a group or cause?
	(F10c) .52	During past year, how often have you taught children or adults or counseled anyone about jobs or personal problems?
	(F10a) .48	During past year, how often have you led recreational activities for children or adults?
	(F8) .48	Are you now or have you recently been involved in helping activities in your community, such as volunteer work with charities, schools, churches, and so on?
	(F7) .41	After the war, did you ever do anything unusual to help someone?
	(F9) .40	Of the people listed, what kinds of people have you given help to in the last year or so?—Stranger (loaded on personal help also)
	(F10g) .36	During past year, how often have you contributed money or goods to some cause?
	(F10b) .35	During past year, how often have you helped feed the sick or the aged or visited the ill?

(Continued)

TABLE 7.16   *Construction of the 27 Variables Used
in the Summary Factor Analysis (Continued)*

Synthesized Variable	Items
4. Defended country before war	This is a single item that asked if the respondent had ever done anything unusual to defend or support his country before the war (D19).
5. Detachment	This factor was one of three that emerged from a factor analysis of 42 personality items relating to feelings at present time. High scores show detachment from events and persons; they are on the whole self-satisfied.

	Loadings	*Item*
	(F14:14).58	It's no use worrying about current events or public affairs. I can't do anything about them anyway.
	(F14:5) .47	I have often found that what's going to happen will happen.
	(F14:9) .45	I take a positive attitude about myself (also loads with self-esteem).
	(F14:30).37	People would be a lot better off if they would live far away from other people and never have anything to do with them.
	(F14:1) .37	Letting people down is not so bad, because you can't do good all the time for everybody.
	(F14:15).37	When I work on a committee I usually let other people do the planning.
	(F14:42).33	On the whole I am satisfied with myself (also loads on self-esteem).
	(F14:19).30	Children sometimes cry for no reason.
	(F14:38).27	I get irritated rather than sympathetic when I see someone cry.

Synthesized Variable	Items
6. Empathy for Jews	This variable is a summation of the following variables: D23 Distressed at *Kristallnacht* D23a Distressed at anti-Semitism in country. E8 Distressed at seeing Jews wear the yellow star.
7. Equity	This variable is a single item derived from the values passed on to the respondents by most influential role model (B12, B22, B32).

TABLE 7.16 *Construction of the 27 Variables Used in the Summary Factor Analysis (Continued)*

Synthesized Variable	Items
8. Ethnocentrism	This variable is an item summation based on classification of what respondents were told about Jews by pooled responses from mother, father, and significant others. It includes measures relating to *stereotypes* and *differentiated* status of Jews (B14a, B24a, B34a).
9. Family closeness	This variable measures closeness of family members and is a summation of the following variables:

A14 Closeness of family members when growing up.
B11 Closeness to significant other role model.
B21 Closeness to mother when growing up.
B31 Closeness to father when growing up.

| 10. Feelings of similarity to different socioeconomic levels within group | This is one of two factors that emerged from responses to items relating to feelings of similarity to assorted groups before the war: |

Loadings	Item
(D21a) .53	Rich people
(D21c) .46	Catholics
(D21b) .44	Poor people

| 11. Feelings of similarity to "out group" members | This is one of two factors that emerged from responses to items relating to feelings of similarity to assorted groups before the war: |

Loadings	Item
(D21e) .88	Turks
(D21g) .69	Gypsies
(D21f) .61	Jews
(D21d) .44	Protestants

| 12. Jewish coworkers | This variable is a summation of the following variables: |

(D11b) Had Jewish colleagues/coworkers at job
(D3b) Spouse had Jewish colleagues/coworkers at job

| 13. Jewish friends | This variable is a summation of the following variables: |

(C16) Had close Jewish friends while growing up.
(C17) Knew Jews while growing up.
(D4) Spouse had Jewish friends before the war.
(D12) Had Jewish friends before the war.

(Continued)

TABLE 7.16   *Construction of the 27 Variables Used
in the Summary Factor Analysis (Continued)*

Synthesized Variable	Items
14. Jews in neighborhood	This is a single item relating to whether Jews lived in the neighborhood before the war (E4).
15. Jews at school	This variable is a summation of the following variables: (C2a) Jews attended elementary school. (C3b) Jews attended gymnasium. (C5b) Jews attended university.
16. Parents talked about Jews	This variable is an item summation of whether mother, father, or significant other ever discussed Jews (B14, B24, B34).
17. Patriotism	This variable is a single item derived from the values passed on to the respondents by most influential role model (B12, B22, B32).
18. Perception of neighbors	This is a single item relating to perception of neighbors as friendly and helpful while growing up (A16).
19. Personal helping today	This is one of two factors which emerged in relation to postwar helping behaviors:

Loadings	Item
(F9).67	Helped friend during past year
.62	Helped neighbor during past year
.53	Helped relative during past year
.48	Helped stranger during past year (also on community helping factor)

Synthesized Variable	Items
20. Personal integrity	This is one of two factors which emerged from self-attributed personal qualities when respondents grew up:

Loadings	Item
(C18:a).47	Honest
(C18:h).46	Helpful
(C18:d).45	Able to take responsibility (also on personal potency factor)
(C18:i) .36	Willing to stand up for beliefs

Synthesized Variable	Items
21. Personal potency	This is one of two factors that emerged from self-attributed personal qualities when respondents grew up:

Loadings	Item
(C18:f) .76	Able to make decisions
(C18:c).58	Independent
(C18:g).53	Adventurous
(C18:e).52	Willing to take chances
(C18:d).45	Able to take responsibility
(C18:b).38	Self-confident

TABLE 7.16 *Construction of the 27 Variables Used
in the Summary Factor Analysis (Continued)*

Synthesized Variable	Items
22. Prosocial action orientation	This was one of three factors that emerged from a factor analysis of 42 personality items relating to present time. High scorers show strong empathic feelings towards others in distress and personal standards for persistence and follow-through on what they undertake:

Loadings	Item
(F14:7) .59	I can't feel good if others around me feel sad.
(F14:36).59	Seeing people cry upsets me.
(F14:8) .54	The feelings of people in books affect me.
(F14:10).52	I get very upset when I see an animal in pain.
(F14:35).52	If it's worth starting, it's worth finishing.
(F14:28).51	I feel very bad when I have failed to finish something I promised I would do.
(F14:12).51	It upsets me to see helpless people.
(F14:21).51	I get angry when I see someone hurt.
(F14:26).50	The words of a song can move me deeply.
(F14:3) .47	I feel I'm a person of worth at least on an equal basis with others (loads also on self-esteem).
(F14:2) .42	I get very involved with my friends' problems.
(F14:29).40	Every person should give time for the good of the country.

Synthesized Variable	Items
23. Religiosity	This is a factor relating to religiosity of self, parents, and spouse:

Loadings	Item
(D14) .86	Religiosity before the war
(C9) .74	Religiosity while growing up
(F12a).72	Religiosity today
(B29) .62	Father's religiosity
(B19) .57	Mother's religiosity
(D9) .38	Spouse's religiosity before the war

(Continued)

TABLE 7.16   *Construction of the 27 Variables Used
in the Summary Factor Analysis (Continued)*

Synthesized Variable	Items
24. Self-esteem	This factor was one of three that emerged from a factor analysis of 42 personality items relating to feelings at present time. High scores mean low self-esteem:

Loadings		Item
(F14:40)	.60	I certainly feel useless at times.
(F14:6)	.58	At times, I think I am no good at all.
(F14:9)	−.54	I take a positive attitude about myself.
(F14:42)	−.53	On the whole, I am satisfied with myself.
(F14:33)	.53	I feel I do not have much to be proud of.
(F14:24)	.50	I wish I could have more respect for myself.
(F14:27)	.49	All in all, I am inclined to feel I am a failure.
(F14:17)	−.47	I feel that I have a number of good qualities.
(F14:16)	.39	Many times, I feel that I have little influence over things that happen to me.

Synthesized Variable	Items
25. Social responsibility	This variable is a summation of the variables of values of *care, dependability,* and *independence,* which were derived from values passed on to the respondents by most influential role model (B12, B22, B32).
26. Stand up for beliefs	This variable is a single item in which respondents indicated whether they had ever done anything unusual to stand up for their beliefs before the war (D17).
27. Variety of friendships	This variable is a summation of the following variables: C14 had friends of different religion while growing up. C15 had friends different from social class while growing up.

TABLE 7.17 *ANOVA: Attachment to Family Factor*[a]

a. Rescuers vs. Nonrescuers

MEANS
Total population:	.00
Cell means, rescuers:	.17
Cell means, nonrescuers:	−.17

SOURCE OF VARIATION	Sum of Squares	df	Mean Square	F	Significance of F
COVARIATES	5.651	2	2.826	4.467	
Sex	5.046	1	5.046	7.978	.005[b]
Age	1.098	1	1.098	1.736	NS
MAIN EFFECTS	7.169	1	7.169	11.333	.001[c]

b. Rescuers vs. Bystanders

MEANS
Total population:	.02
Cell means, rescuers:	.17
Cell means, bystanders:	−.23

SOURCE OF VARIATION	Sum of Squares	df	Mean Square	F	Significance of F
COVARIATES	8.569	2	4.285	6.641	
Sex	8.071	1	8.071	12.511	.001[b]
Age	.811	1	.811	1.256	NS
MAIN EFFECTS	7.979	1	7.979	12.367	.001[d]

[a]This factor indicates the degree to which individuals were attached to their families and communities. (See Table 7.15 for factor loadings.)

[b]Covariates show that the attachment to family factor is significantly related to sex.

[c]The main effects show that the attachment to family factor is significantly higher for rescuers than for all nonrescuers independently of sex and age.

[d]The main effects show that the attachment to family factor is significantly higher for rescuers than for bystanders independently of sex and age.

TABLE 7.18   *ANOVA: Attachment to Jewish Friends Factor*[a]

a. Rescuers vs. Nonrescuers

MEANS

Total population:	.00
Cell means, rescuers:	.27
Cell means, nonrescuers:	−.27

SOURCE OF VARIATION	Sum of Squares	df	Mean Square	F	Significance of F
COVARIATES	15.065	2	7.533	12.386	
Sex	.242	1	.242	.397	NS
Age	14.142	1	14.142	23.254	.001[b]
MAIN EFFECTS	9.763	1	9.763	16.054	.001[c]

b. Rescuers vs. Bystanders

MEANS

Total population:	.05
Cell means, rescuers:	.27
Cell means, bystanders:	−.32

SOURCE OF VARIATION	Sum of Squares	df	Mean Square	F	Significance of F
COVARIATES	12.877	2	6.438	10.935	
Sex	.151	1	.151	.257	NS
Age	12.474	1	12.474	21.186	.001[b]
MAIN EFFECTS	9.611	1	9.611	16.323	.001[d]

[a]This factor indicates the degree to which individuals were personally involved with Jews. (See Table 7.15 for factor loadings.)

[b]Covariates show that the attachment to Jewish friends factor is significantly related to age.

[c]The main effects show that the attachment to Jewish friends factor is significantly higher for rescuers than for all nonrescuers independently of age and sex.

[d]The main effects show that the attachment to Jewish friends factor is significantly higher for rescuers than for bystanders independently of age and sex.

TABLE 7.19   *ANOVA: Broad Social Commitment Factor*[a]

a. Rescuers vs. Nonrescuers

MEANS
Total population: .00
Cell means, rescuers: .06
Cell means, nonrescuers: −.06

SOURCE OF VARIATION	Sum of Squares	df	Mean Square	F	Significance of F
COVARIATES	7.379	2	3.690	5.693	
Sex	.613	1	.613	.946	NS
Age	6.177	1	6.177	9.530	.002[b]
MAIN EFFECTS	3.657	1	3.657	5.643	.018[c]

b. Rescuers vs. Bystanders

MEANS
Total population: −.03
Cell means, rescuers: .06
Cell means, bystanders: −.18

SOURCE OF VARIATION	Sum of Squares	df	Mean Square	F	Significance of F
COVARIATES	4.390	2	2.195	3.357	
Sex	.221	1	.221	.339	NS
Age	4.017	1	4.017	6.144	.014[b]
MAIN EFFECTS	5.463	1	5.463	8.356	.004[d]

[a]This factor indicates the degree to which individuals felt committed to and accepted responsibilities for the welfare of society as a whole. (See Table 7.15 for factor loadings.)

[b]Covariates show that the broad social commitment factor is significantly related to age.

[c]The main effects show that the broad social commitment factor is significantly higher for rescuers than for all nonrescuers independently of age and sex.

[d]The main effects show that the broad social commitment factor is significantly higher for rescuers than for bystanders independently of age and sex.

TABLE 7.20   *ANOVA: Egalitarian Factor*[a]

a. Rescuers vs. Nonrescuers

MEANS
    Total population: .00
      Cell means, rescuers: .19
      Cell means, nonrescuers: − .19

SOURCE OF VARIATION	Sum of Squares	df	Mean Square	F	Significance of F
COVARIATES	18.636	2	9.318	16.689	
Sex	16.424	1	16.424	29.415	.001[b]
Age	.957	1	.957	1.714	NS
MAIN EFFECTS	5.781	1	5.781	10.353	.001[c]

b. Rescuers vs. Bystanders

MEANS
    Total population: − .02
      Cell means, rescuers: .19
      Cell means, bystanders: − .37

SOURCE OF VARIATIONS	Sum of Squares	df	Mean Square	F	Significance of F
COVARIATES	17.996	2	8.998	15.088	
Sex	16.310	1	16.310	27.351	.001[b]
Age	1.032	1	1.032	1.730	NS
MAIN EFFECTS	10.377	1	10.377	17.402	.001[d]

[a]This factor indicates the degree to which individuals perceived others as similar to themselves. (See Table 7.15 for factor loadings.)

[b]Covariates show that the egalitarian factor is significantly related to sex.

[c]The main effects show that the egalitarian factor is significantly higher for rescuers as compared with all non-rescuers independently of sex and age.

[d]The main effects show that the egalitarian factor is significantly higher for rescuers as compared with bystanders independently of sex and age.

TABLE 7.21   *Discriminant Analysis: Extensivity Factors*
Rescuers vs. Nonrescuers

GROUP MEANS

Group	Family-Based	Jewish Friends	Broad Social Commitments	Egalitarian
Rescuers	.16852	.26645	.05989	.18814
Nonrescuers	−.16989	−.26861	−.06038	−.18967

GROUP STANDARD DEVIATIONS

Group	Family-Based	Jewish Friends	Broad Social Commitments	Egalitarian
Rescuers	.83348	.85977	.86164	.63973
Nonrescuers	.77889	.72435	.79095	.90962
Total	.82278	.83766	.82771	.80672

CLASSIFICATION RESULTS

Actual Group	No. of Cases	Predicted Group Membership Rescuers	Nonrescuers
Rescuers	124	85	39
		(68.5%)	(31.5%)
Nonrescuers	123	34	89
		(27.6%)	(72.4%)

PERCENTAGE OF GROUPED CASES CORRECTLY CLASSIFIED: 70.45[a]

[a]Means significantly above chance.

TABLE 7.22 *Discriminant Analysis: Extensivity Factors Rescuers vs. Bystanders*

GROUP MEANS

Group	Family-Based	Jewish Friends	Broad Social Commitments	Egalitarians
Rescuers	.16852	.26645	.05989	.18814
Bystanders	−.22733	−.32136	−.18204	−.36569
Total	−.02976	.02183	.04863	−.01709

GROUP STANDARD DEVIATIONS

Group	Family-Based	Jewish Friends	Broad Social Commitments	Egalitarians
Rescuers	.83348	.85977	.86164	.63973
Bystanders	.81999	.63818	.76400	1.04772
Total	.83310	.84835	.83337	.85556

CLASSIFICATION RESULTS

Actual Group	No. of Cases	Predicted Group Membership Rescuers	Bystanders
Rescuers	124	90 (72.6%)	34 (27.4%)
Bystanders	73	19 (26.0%)	54 (74.0%)

PERCENTAGE OF GROUPED CASES CORRECTLY CLASSIFIED: 73.10[a]

[a]Means significantly above chance.

TABLE 9.1   *Occupational Status After the War*

a. Rescuers vs. Nonrescuers

	Rescuers (n = 91) (%)	Nonrescuers (n = 91) (%)	Significance (chi-square)
Professional	17.6	8.8	
Business	23.1	16.5	
Administrative	23.1	13.2	
Clerical	22.0	30.8	
Skilled	6.6	14.3	
Semiskilled	3.3	9.9	
Unskilled	4.4	6.6	.05

b. Rescuers vs. Bystanders

	Rescuers (n = 91) (%)	Bystanders (n = 57) (%)	Significance (chi-square)
Professional	17.6	8.8	
Business	23.1	17.5	
Administrative	23.1	10.5	
Clerical	22.0	22.8	
Skilled	6.6	19.3	
Semiskilled	3.3	14.0	
Unskilled	4.4	7.0	.02

TABLE 9.2 *Children's Knowledge and Feelings About Respondents' Wartime Activi*

a. Children's Knowledge

	Quite A Bit (%)	Some (%)	Very Little (%)	Nothing At All (%)	Signifi- cance (chi- square)
Rescuers (n = 164)	78.7	13.4	6.7	1.2	
Nonrescuers (n = 80)	48.7	27.5	20.0	3.7	.0000
Rescuers (n = 164)	78.7	13.4	6.7	1.2	
Bystanders (n = 47)	44.7	31.9	17.0	6.4	.0001

b. Children's Feelings

	Strongly Approve (%)	Some- what Approve (%)	Neither approve nor Dis- approve (%)	Some Dis- approval (%)	Strongly Dis- approve (%)	Don't Know (%)	Signifi cance (chi- square
Rescuers (n = 156)	85.3	8.3	2.6	0.0	0.6	3.2	
Nonrescuers (n = 73)	41.1	12.3	24.7	4.1	2.7	15.1	.0000
Rescuers (n = 156)	85.3	8.3	2.6	0.0	0.6	3.2	
Bystanders (n = 47)	22.0	14.6	36.6	4.9	2.4	19.5	.0000

TABLE 9.3   *Help Given in Past Year*

	Very Often (%)	Often (%)	Few Times (%)	Once (%)	Never (%)	Significance (chi-square)
a. Rescuers vs. Nonrescuers						
Led recreational activities for children or adults						
Rescuers (n = 96)	9.4	4.2	9.4	1.0	76.0	
Nonrescuers (n = 108)	1.9	3.7	12.0	5.6	76.9	NS
Helped feed the sick or the aged or visited the ill						
Rescuers (n = 96)	27.1	15.6	16.7	1.0	39.6	
Nonrescuers (n = 109)	9.2	11.9	28.4	7.3	43.1	.001
Taught children or adults or counseled anyone about jobs or personal problems						
Rescuers (n = 99)	19.2	9.1	17.2	2.0	52.5	
Nonrescuers (n = 107)	8.4	9.3	25.2	7.5	49.5	.05
Made telephone calls on behalf of a group or cause or helped raise money for a group or cause						
Rescuers (n = 96)	11.5	9.4	16.7	0.0	62.5	
Nonrescuers (n = 107)	6.5	6.5	8.4	6.5	72.0	.02
Given speeches or lectures or written letters on behalf of an issue or cause						
Rescuers (n = 98)	13.3	9.2	12.2	2.0	63.3	
Nonrescuers (n = 106)	1.9	6.6	8.5	7.5	75.5	.006
Investigated, collected or prepared information on behalf of an issue or cause						
Rescuers (n = 96)	11.5	8.3	8.3	2.1	69.8	
Nonrescuers (n = 104)	3.8	3.8	11.5	5.8	75.5	NS
Contributed money or goods to some cause						
Rescuers (n = 97)	16.5	14.4	22.7	6.2	40.2	
Nonrescuers (n = 106)	16.0	14.2	37.7	4.7	27.4	NS

(Continued)

TABLE 9.3 *Help Given in Past Year (Continued)*

	Very Often (%)	Often (%)	Few Times (%)	Once (%)	Never (%)	Significance (chi-square)
b. Rescuers vs. Bystanders						
Led recreational activities for children or adults						
Rescuers ($n = 96$)	9.4	4.2	9.4	1.0	76.0	
Bystanders ($n = 64$)	0.0	0.0	7.8	6.3	85.9	.01
Helped feed the sick or the aged or visited the ill						
Rescuers ($n = 96$)	27.1	15.6	16.7	1.0	39.6	
Bystanders ($n = 64$)	4.7	9.4	34.4	1.6	50.0	.001
Taught children or adults or counseled anyone about jobs or personal problems						
Rescuers ($n = 99$)	19.2	9.1	17.2	2.0	52.5	
Bystanders ($n = 63$)	3.2	9.5	22.2	11.1	54.0	.007
Made telephone calls on behalf of a group or cause or helped raise money for a group or cause						
Rescuers ($n = 96$)	11.5	9.4	16.7	0.0	62.5	
Bystanders ($n = 63$)	1.6	6.3	7.9	4.8	79.4	.008
Given speeches or lectures or written letters on behalf of an issue or cause						
Rescuers ($n = 98$)	13.3	9.2	12.2	2.0	63.3	
Bystanders ($n = 63$)	0.0	1.6	6.3	7.9	84.1	.0009
Investigated, collected or prepared information on behalf of an issue or cause						
Rescuers ($n = 96$)	11.5	8.3	8.3	2.1	69.8	
Bystanders ($n = 63$)	4.8	0.0	11.1	4.8	79.4	NS
Contributed money or goods to some cause						
Rescuers ($n = 97$)	16.5	14.4	22.7	6.2	40.2	
Bystanders ($n = 63$)	17.5	14.3	39.7	7.9	20.6	NS

TABLE 9.4   *ANOVA: Community Helping Factor*[a]

a. Rescuers vs. Nonrescuers

MEANS

Total population:	.00
Cell means, rescuers:	.15
Cell means, nonrescuers:	−.15

SOURCE OF VARIATION	Sum of Squares	df	Mean Square	F	Significance of F
COVARIATES	1.626	2	0.813	1.262	
Sex	1.568	1	1.568	2.434	0.120
Age	0.007	1	0.007	0.001	0.916
MAIN EFFECTS	6.705	1	6.705	10.405	0.001[c]

b. Rescuers vs. Bystanders

MEANS

Total population:	−.03
Cell means, rescuers:	.15
Cell means, bystanders:	−.32

SOURCE OF VARIATIONS	Sum of Squares	df	Mean Square	F	Significance of F
COVARIATES	2.404	2	1.202	2.028	
Sex	2.368	1	2.368	3.997	0.047[b]
Age	0.087	1	0.087	0.146	0.720
MAIN EFFECTS	11.277	1	11.277	19.032	0.001[d]

[a]The community helping factor consists of 9 items reflecting community activities during the past year. (See Table 7.16, Community Helping Today for factor loadings.)

[b]Covariates show that the community helping factor is significantly related to sex when rescuers are compared with bystanders only.

[c]The main effects show that the community helping factor is significantly higher for rescuers than for all nonrescuers independently of sex and age.

[d]The main effects show that the community helping factor is significantly higher for rescuers than for bystanders independently of sex and age.

TABLE 9.5   *Health Today*

	Excellent (%)	Good (%)	Fair (%)	Poor (%)	Very Poor (%)	Significance (chi-square)
Rescuers $n = 120$)	5.8	25.8	40.0	20.8	7.5	
Nonrescuers ($n = 120$)	18.1	37.5	26.7	11.7	5.8	.002
Rescuers ($n = 120$)	5.8	25.8	40.0	20.8	7.5	
Bystanders ($n = 72$)	16.7	40.3	30.6	9.7	2.8	.005

Questionnaire

Section A: Growing Up

A1   I would like to begin by asking you some questions about you and your family when you were growing up. First of all, when were you born, in which month and what year?

A2   Where were you born, in which town and which country?

A3   Where did you grow up, in which town and which country? INT: IF RESPONDENT INDICATES SEVERAL PLACES, ASK FOR THE PLACE OF LONGEST RESIDENCE.

A4   (RB., page 1) Please look at page 1 of the Respondent Booklet. Did you live in a large city, a middle city, a small city, a village, or did you live on an isolated farm when you were growing up?

A5   What was the approximate size of the population?

A6   Now, I would like you to think of your home when you were 10 years old. That would be in 19——. Were your father and mother both living in your home when you were 10?

A7   Did you have any older brothers or sisters living with you when you were 10?

A7a   How many older brothers?

A7b   How many older sisters?

A7c   How much older than you was the oldest child in your family?

A8   Did you have any younger brothers or sisters living with you when you were 10?

A8a   How many younger brothers?

A8b   How many younger sisters?

A8c   How much younger than you was the youngest child in your family?

A9   Was anyone else living in your household when you were 10? For example, did you have any aunts or uncles or boarders living with you?

A9a   Who were these people? INT.: PROBE FOR THESE PEOPLE'S RELATIONSHIP TO R.

A10   In what country was your father born?

A11

> INT.: IF R'S FATHER WAS REPORTED NOT LIVING IN THE HOUSEHOLD, GO TO A12.

(RB, page 2) Please turn to page 2 of the Respondent Booklet. What did your father do while you were growing up? Was he employed, unemployed, retired, in the military, or what?

A11a   Specifically, what kind of work did your father do? INT.: PROBE FOR SPECIFICS: *TITLE* OF POSITION, *OWNER* OR *NON-OWNER* OF BUSINESS OR FARM, PRINCIPAL *PRODUCT* OF BUSINESS OR FARM, *SIZE* OF BUSINESS OR FARM.

A12   In what country was your mother born?

A13

> INT.: IF R'S MOTHER WAS REPORTED AS NOT LIVING IN THE HOUSEHOLD, GO TO A14.

(RB, page 2) Please turn to page 2 of the Respondent Booklet again. What did your mother do while you were growing up? Was she employed, unemployed, retired, a housewife, or what?

A13a   Specifically, what kind of work did your mother do? INT.: PROBE FOR SPECIFICS: *TITLE* OF POSITION, *OWNER* OR *NON-OWNER* OF BUSINESS OR FARM, PRINCIPAL *PRODUCT* OF BUSINESS OR FARM, *SIZE* OF BUSINESS OR FARM.

A14   (RB., page 3) Please turn to page 3 of the Respondent Book. How would you describe the relationship between the members of your family when you were growing up. In general, would you say your family was very close, somewhat close, not very close or not at all close?

A15   (RB.,page 4) Please turn to page 4 of the Respondent Book. When you were growing up, was your family very well off financially, quite well off, neither rich nor poor, quite poor, or very poor?

A16   (RB.,page 5) Please look at page 5 of the Respondent Booklet. How would you describe your neighbors when you were growing up? Were they, in general, very friendly and helpful, somewhat friendly and helpful, not very friendly and helpful, or not at all friendly and helpful?

Section B: Role Models

B1   Now I would like to ask you some questions about certain people that you knew when you were growing up. First of all, who was the *one* person who had the *most influence* on you when you were growing up? That is, who taught you most about life? INT.: PROBE FOR RELATIONSHIP TO R.

B2   What was (OTHER'S) sex? [Asked if respondent's answer did not indicate sex.]

B3   Did (OTHER) live in your household when you were 10 years old?

B4   (RB, page 2) Please turn to page 2 of the Respondent Booklet. What did (OTHER) do when you were 10 years old? Was he/she employed, unemployed, retired, disabled, a student, (housewife), (in the military), or what?

B4a   What kind of work did (OTHER) do? INT.: PROBE FOR SPECIF-ICS: *TITLE* OF POSITION OR MILITARY RANK, *OWNER* OR *NON-OWNER* OF BUSINESS OR FARM, PRINCIPAL *PRODUCT* OF BUSINESS OR FARM, *SIZE* OF BUSINESS OR FARM.

B5   Did (OTHER) attend elementary school?

B5a   Could (OTHER) read and write?

B6   Did (OTHER) attend gymnasium, high school, or lycée?

B6a   Did (OTHER) graduate from gymnasium, high school, or lycée?

B7   Did (OTHER) attend university?

B7a   Did (OTHER) graduate from university?

B8   What was (OTHER'S) religious affiliation? Was he/she a Protestant, a Catholic, or did he/she belong to some other religion?

B8a   What Protestant denomination?

B9   (RB, page 6) Please turn to page 6 of the Respondent Booklet.

Was (OTHER) very religious, somewhat religious, not very religious, or not religious at all?

B10   Did (OTHER) belong to a political party when you were growing up?

B10a   What party did (OTHER) belong to?

B10b   Was (OTHER) politically active when you were growing up? For example, was he/she an officer in the party or did he/she attend political meetings?

B11   (RB, page 3) Please turn to page 3 of the Respondent Booklet. How close did you feel to (OTHER) when you were growing up? Would you say that you were very close, somewhat close, not very close, or not at all close?

B12   What were the most important things you learned about life from (OTHER)?

B13   Did (OTHER) ever discipline you? That is, did he/she ever tell you that you did something wrong or keep you from having things that you wanted, or did he/she ever scold you or strap you?

B13a   How did (OTHER) discipline you?

B13b   What kinds of things did (OTHER) discipline you for?

B14   Did (OTHER) ever talk to you about Jews?

B14a   What did (OTHER) tell you about Jews?

B15

> INT.: IF R'S MOTHER WAS NOT LISTED AS LIVING IN THE HOUSEHOLD IN A6, THEN GO TO B25, PAGE 13.

I'd like to ask you some questions about your mother. First, did your mother attend elementary school?

B15a   Could your mother read and write?

B16   Did your mother attend gymnasium, high school, or lycée?

B16a   Did your mother graduate from gymnasium, high school, or lycée?

B17   Did your mother attend university?

B17a   Did your mother graduate from university?

B18   What was your mother's religious affiliation? Was she a Protestant, a Catholic, or did she belong to some other religion?

B18a   What Protestant denomination?

B19   (RB, page 6) Please turn to page 6 of the Respondent Booklet. Was your mother very religious, somewhat religious, not very religious, or not at all religious?

B20   Did your mother belong to a political party when you were growing up?

B20a   What party did your mother belong to?

B20b   Was your mother politically active when you were growing up? For example, was she an officer in the party or did she attend political meetings?

B21   (RB, page 3) Please turn to page 3 of the Respondent Booklet. How close did you feel to your mother when you were growing up? Would you say that you were very close, somewhat close, not very close, or not at all close?

B22   What were the most important things you learned about life from your mother?

B23   Did your mother ever discipline you? That is, did your mother ever tell you that you did something wrong or keep you from having things that you wanted, or did she ever scold you or strap you?

B23a   How did your mother discipline you?

B23b   What kinds of things did your mother discipline you for?

B24   Did your mother ever talk to you about Jews?

B24a   What did your mother tell you about Jews?

B25

> INT.: IF R'S FATHER WAS NOT LISTED AS LIVING IN THE HOUSEHOLD IN A6, THEN GO TO C1, PAGE 17.

I'd like to ask you some questions about your father. First, did your father attend elementary school?

B25a   Could your father read and write?

B26   Did your father attend gymnasium, high school, or lycée?

B26a   Did your father graduate from gymnasium, high school, or lycée?

B27   Did your father attend university?

B27a   Did your father graduate from university?

B28   What was your father's religious affiliation? Was he a Protestant, a Catholic, or did he belong to some other religion?

B28a   What Protestant denomination?

B29   (RB, page 6) Please turn to page 6 of the Respondent Booklet. Was your father very religious, somewhat religious, not very religious, or not religious at all?

B30   Did your father belong to a political party while you were growing up?

B30a   What party did your father belong to?

B30b   Was your father politically active when you were growing up? For example, was he an officer in the party or did he attend political meetings?

B31   (RB, page 3) Please turn to page 3 of the Respondent Booklet. How close did you feel to your father when you were growing up? Would you say that you were very close, somewhat close, not very close, or not at all close?

B32   What were the most important things you learned about life from your father?

B33   Did your father ever discipline you? That is, did he ever tell you that you did something wrong or keep you from having things that you wanted, or did he ever scold you or strap you?

B33a   How did your father discipline you?

B33b   What kinds of things did your father discipline you for?

B34   Did your father ever talk to you about Jews?

B34a   What did your father tell you about Jews?

Section C: Self

C1   Now I'd like to ask some questions about *you* during the time you were growing up. Did you attend elementary school?

C1a   Did you learn to read and write?

C2   What kind of elementary school did you attend? Was it Protestant, Catholic, nonsectarian, or something else?

C2a   Did any Jews attend your elementary school?

C2b   Were there many Jewish students, some Jewish students, or a few Jewish students attending your elementary school?

C3   Did you attend gymnasium or high school or lycée?

C3a   What kind of gymnasium did you attend? Was it Protestant, Catholic, nonsectarian, or something else?

C3b   Did any Jews attend your gymnasium?

C3c   Were there many Jewish students, some Jewish students, or a few Jewish students attending your gymnasium?

C4   Did you graduate from gymnasium?

C4a   In what year did you graduate?

C5   Did you attend university?

C5a   What was your major field of study at the university?

C5b   Did any Jews attend your university?

C5c   Were there many Jewish students, some Jewish students, or a few Jewish students attending your university?

C6   Did you graduate from the university?

C6a   In what year did you graduate?

C7   Did you ever apprentice in a trade?

C7a   Did you complete the apprenticeship?

C8   What was your religious affiliation during the time you were growing up? Were you a Protestant, a Catholic, did you belong to some other religion, or what?

C8a   What Protestant denomination?

C9   (RB, page 6) Please turn to page 6 of the Respondent Booklet. How religious were you when you were growing up, were you very religious, somewhat religious, not very religious, or not religious at all?

C10   What were the most important things you learned about life from your religious leaders?

C11   During the time you were growing up, did you have many close friends, some close friends, a few close friends, or didn't you have any close friends at all?

C12   When you were with your close friends, were you usually a leader, usually a follower, or what?

C13   Among your circle of friends, did you always go along with what was happening or did you sometimes object to some things?

C13a   What sort of things did you object to?

C14   Were any of your close friends different from you in terms of religion?

C15   Were any of your close friends different from you in social class?

C16   Were any of your close friends Jewish?

C17   Did you know any Jews during the time you were growing up?

C18   (RB, page 7) Please turn to page 7 of the Respondent Booklet. Now I would like to name some personal qualities. For each quality listed on page 7, I'd like to know if you thought that you had the quality very much, somewhat, not very much, or not at all *when you were growing up.*

	Very	Some	Not Very	Not At All
a. Honesty				
b. Self-confidence				
c. Independence				
d. Able to take responsibility				
e. Willing to take chances				
f. Able to make decisions				
g. Adventurous				
h. Helpful to others				
i. Willing to stand up for beliefs				
j. Patriotic				

Section D: Prewar

D1   Now, I would like to ask you questions about *the 5 or so years immediately preceding the war.* First of all, where were you living at that time?
INT.: IF R INDICATES SEVERAL PLACES, ASK FOR THE PLACE IMMEDIATELY PRECEDING THE OUTBREAK OF WAR.

D2   Were you married before 1945?

D2a   In what year were you married?

D3   (RB, page 2) Please turn to page 2 of the Respondent Booklet. What did your husband/wife do immediately before the war. Was he/she employed, unemployed, disabled, student, (housewife), (in the military), or what?

D3a   What kind of work did your husband/wife do before the war? INT.: PROBE FOR SPECIFICS: *TITLE* OF POSITION OR MILITARY RANK, *OWNER* OR *NONOWNER* OF BUSINESS OR FARM, PRINCIPAL *PRODUCT* OF BUSINESS OR FARM, *SIZE* OF BUSINESS OR FARM.

D3b   Did your husband/wife have any Jewish colleagues or coworkers in his/her job?

D4   Did your husband/wife have any Jewish friends before the war?

D5   Did your husband/wife attend elementary school?

D5a   Could your husband/wife read and write?

D6   Did your husband/wife attend gymnasium, high school, or lycée?

D6a   Did your husband/wife graduate from gymnasium, high school, or lycée?

D7   Did your husband/wife attend university?

D7a   Did your husband/wife graduate from university?

D8   What was your husband/wife's religious affiliation? Was he/she a Protestant, a Catholic, or did he/she belong to some other religion?

D8a   What Protestant denomination?

D9   (RB, page 6) Please turn to page 6 of the Respondent Booklet. Before the war, was your husband/wife very religious, somewhat religious, not very religious, or not religious at all?

D10   Did your husband/wife belong to a political party before the war?

D10a   What party did your husband/wife belong to?

D10b   Was your husband/wife politically active before the war? For example, was he/she an officer in the party or did he/she attend political meetings?

D11   (RB, page 2) Please turn to page 2 of the Respondent Booklet.

What did you do immediately before the war? Were you employed, unemployed, student, housewife, in the military, or what?

D11a   What kind of work did you do before the war? INT.: PROBE FOR SPECIFICS: *TITLE* OF POSITION OR MILITARY RANK, *OWNER* OR *NONOWNER* OF BUSINESS OR FARM, PRINCIPAL *PRODUCT* OF BUSINESS OR FARM, *SIZE* OF BUSINESS OR FARM.

D11b   Did you have any Jewish colleagues or coworkers in your job?

D12   Did you have any Jewish friends before the war?

D13   (RB, page 4) Please turn to page 4 of the Respondent Booklet. Before the war, were you very well off financially, quite well off, neither rich nor poor, quite poor, or very poor?

D14   (RB, page 6) Please turn to page 6 of the Respondent Booklet. Before the war, were you very religious, somewhat religious, not very religious, or not at all religious?

D15   Did you belong to a political party before the war?

D15a   What party did you belong to?

D15b   Were you politically active before the war?

D16   Thinking back to the place you lived in the 5 years or so before the war, did you have a sense of belonging in your community, did you feel like an outsider, or what?

D16a   (RB, page 8) Please turn to page 8 of the Respondent Booklet. In which ways did you feel like an outsider. INT.: READ LIST AND CHECK ALL THAT APPLY.
        a. Political beliefs
        b. Educational background
        c. Ethnic background
        d. Social class background
        e. Income
        f. Life-style
        g. Occupation or business
        h. Religious beliefs

D17   Now I would like to ask you to think about things that you may have done that were out of the ordinary, either while you were growing up or before the war.
            First of all, at any time in your life before the war, did you ever do anything unusual to stand up for your beliefs? For exam-

ple, did you ever fight someone for something you believed in, or did you lose friends for standing up for what you believed in?

D17a   What sort of things did you do?

D18   At any time in your life before the war, did you ever do anything unusual to help other people? For example, did you work as a volunteer in your community or in a hospital, or did you take a child into your home?

D18a   What sort of things did you do?

D19   At any time in your life before the war, did you ever do anything unusual to defend or support your country? For example, were you active in any kind of political youth or student group?

D19a   What sort of things did you do?

D20   At any time in your life before the war, did you ever do anything unusual that was risky or adventurous?

D20a   What sort of things did you do?

D21   (RB, page 9) Please turn to page 9 of the Respondent Booklet. People sometimes think of others as being *like or unlike* themselves. I'm going to read you this list of different groups of people. I would like you to think back to the time before the war. For each group of people, I'd like you to tell me what you thought of those people before the war. In general, did you think the people were very much like you, somewhat like you, not very much like you, or not like you at all?

	Very Like	Somewhat Like	Not Very Like	Not At All Like	Don't Know
a. Rich people					
b. Poor people					
c. Catholics					
d. Protestants					
e. Turks					
f. Jews					
g. Gypsies					
h. Nazis					

D22   Before the war, was there any group of people that you had strong positive or negative feelings about?

D22a   Would you please tell me which group(s) you had strong feelings
        about and what you felt about them?

D23

> INT.: IF R LIVED IN GERMANY BEFORE THE WAR, ASK:
> Thinking back to the time before the war, were you distressed
> by the *Kristallnacht* events, were you unaware of them, or
> didn't you have any feelings about them one way or the other?

D23a

> INT.: IF R DID NOT LIVE IN GERMANY BEFORE THE WAR,
> ASK:
> Thinking back to the time before the war, were you distressed
> by the anti-Semitism in your country, were you unaware of it,
> or didn't you have any feelings about it one way or the other?

Section E: War Years

E1   Now I would like to ask you questions about your experiences
        during the war. First of all, was your work during the war the
        same as or different from your work just before the war?

E1a   (RB, page 2) Please turn to page 2 of the Respondent Booklet.
        During the war, were you employed, unemployed, a housewife,
        in the military, or what?

E1b   Specifically, what kind of work did you do during the war? INT.:
        PROBE FOR SPECIFICS: *TITLE* OF POSITION OR MILITARY
        RANK, *OWNER* OR *NONOWNER* OF BUSINESS OR FARM,
        PRINCIPAL *PRODUCT* OF BUSINESS OR FARM, *SIZE* OF BUSI-
        NESS OR FARM.

E2

> INT.: IF R WAS NOT MARRIED BEFORE 1945, GO TO E3.

        Was your husband's/wife's work during the war the same as or
        different from his/her work just before the war?

E2a   (RB, page 2) Please turn to page 2 of the Respondent Booklet.
        During the war was your husband/wife employed, unemployed,
        a housewife, in the military, or what?

E2b   Specifically, what kind of work did your husband/wife do during
        the year? INT.: PROBE FOR SPECIFICS: *TITLE* OF POSITION
        OR MILITARY RANK, *OWNER* OR *NONOWNER* OF BUSINESS

OR FARM, PRINCIPAL *PRODUCT* OF BUSINESS OR FARM, *SIZE* OF BUSINESS OR FARM.

E3   Where were you living when the war broke out in your country? Which town and which country?

E4   Before the war, did any Jews live in your neighborhood?

E6   How did you feel about the Nazis taking power in your country? Can you tell me in your own words?

E7   On what occasion did you become aware of what the Nazis intended to do to the Jews?

E8   How did you feel the first time you saw a Jew wearing the yellow Star of David?

      INT.: THIS IS A MAJOR DECISION POINT; PROCEED CAREFULLY!

E9

> INT.: IF R IS AN IDENTIFIED RESCUER, SAY THE FOLLOWING: Please tell me in your own words about your rescue activity. Because your story is so important, I will be taking notes as you talk. I will also be recording your story so as not to miss anything. INT.: RECORD MAIN RESCUE/RESISTANCE EVENTS BELOW.

E9a

> INT.: IF R IS NOT AN IDENTIFIED RESCUER, THAT IS, IF R IS ANYONE ELSE BUT AN IDENTIFIED RESCUER, ASK: Did you do anything out of the ordinary during the war to help other people or resist the Nazis?
> Please tell me in your own words about your (helping/resistance) activities during the war. Your story is important, so I will be taking notes as you talk. I will also be recording your story so as not to miss anything. INT.: RECORD MAIN HELPING/RESISTANCE EVENTS BELOW.

E9b

> INT.: IF R IS NOT AN IDENTIFIED RESCUER OR WAS NOT INVOLVED WITH RESISTANCE, SAY THE FOLLOWING: Please tell me in your own words what you did during the war. Your story is important, so I will be taking notes as you talk. I will also be recording your story so as not to miss anything. INT.: RECORD ANY NOTABLE EVENTS BELOW.

> INT.: IF R IS NOT AN IDENTIFIED RESCUER OR DID NOT
> ENGAGE IN ANY HELPING OR RESISTANCE ACTIVITY,
> GO TO E40.

E10   When did these activities that you just told me about first start?
       Do you remember the month and year?

E11   When did these activities finally end?

E12   During the war, did you ever discuss these activities with mem-
       bers of your family?

E12a   In general, did these family members approve or disapprove of
       your activities?

E13   During the war, did you ever discuss these activities with your
       close friends?

E13a   In general, did these friends approve or disapprove of your activ-
       ities?

E14   During the war, did you ever discuss these activities with your
       neighbors?

E14a   In general, did these neighbors approve or disapprove of your
       activities?

E15   Were you ever a member of a resistance group?

E15a   What was the name of the group?

E16   Overall, about how many people do you think you helped, di-
       rectly or indirectly, during the war?

       Is this number exact or approximate?

E17   How many, if any, people did you *directly* help during this period.
       That is, how many, if any, people did you personally help or have
       personal contact with?

       Is this number exact or approximate?

E18   How many, if any, of the people that you directly helped were
       close friends?

       Is this number exact or approximate?

E19   How many, if any, of these close friends were Jews?

       Is this number exact or approximate?

E20   Not counting your close friends, about how many of the people that you directly helped were acquaintances?

E20a   About how many of these acquaintances were Jews?

E21   About how many of the people that you directly helped were strangers to you?

E21a   About how many of these strangers were Jews?

E22   About how many of the people that you directly helped were children under 12 years of age?

E22a   About how many of these children were Jews?

E23

> INT.: IF R IS AN IDENTIFIED RESCUER OR HAS OTHER-
> WISE INDICATED THAT HE/SHE DID HELP JEWS, SAY:
>
> Now I would like to ask you some specific questions about the
> *very first time* that you became involved in helping a Jewish
> person. I may go over some of the information that you have
> already given me, but this is important, and I want to get it
> right.
>
> Please describe briefly, in one or two sentences, what hap-
> pened the *very first time* you became involved in helping a Jew-
> ish person.
>
> Was this your first involvement of any kind in a helping or
> resistance activity?

E23a

> INT.: IF R IS NOT AN IDENTIFIED RESCUER AND HAS
> NOT OTHERWISE INDICATED THAT HE/SHE HELPED A
> JEWISH PERSON, SAY:
>
> Now I would like to ask you some specific questions about the
> *very first time* that you became involved in helping someone or
> resisting the Nazis. I may go over some of the information that
> you have already given me, but this is important, and I want
> to get it right.
>
> Please describe briefly, in one or two sentences, what hap-
> pened the *very first time* you became involved in helping some-
> one or in resisting the Nazis.

E24   How many people did you help at this time?

Is this number exact or approximate?

E25   How many, if any, of these people were children under 12 years of age?

E26   Who were the people that you helped your first time? Were they relatives, friends, neighbors, strangers, or what? INT.: PROBE FOR RELATIONSHIP TO R.

E27   How did you become involved in this first activity? Did you initiate it yourself or did someone ask for your help?

E27a   Who asked you to give this help? INT.: PROBE FOR RELATIONSHIP TO R.

E28   (RB, page 10) Please turn to page 10 of the Respondent Booklet. How long did it take you to make your decision to help? Did you make your decision in a few minutes, several hours, a few days, several weeks, or what?

E29   Did you consult with anyone before you made your decision?

E29a   Whom did you consult?

        INT.: FOR EACH PERSON CONSULTED, DETERMINE RELATIONSHIP TO R AND WHETHER THE PERSON ENCOURAGED OR DISCOURAGED THE ACTION.

E30   Had you or someone you cared about ever been unjustly treated by the Nazis before you became involved in this first activity?

E30a   Would you please describe (this/these) for me?

E31   Had you witnessed or heard about mistreatment of Jews by the Nazis before you became involved in this first activity?

E31a   Would you please describe (this/these) for me?

E32   (RB, page 11) Please turn to page 11 of the Respondent Booklet. How much risk did you think you would be taking at the time that you made your decision? Did you think that you would be taking extreme risk, moderate risk, slight risk, or no risk at all?

E33   How much risk did you think you were putting members of your family in at the time that you made your decision: extreme risk, moderate risk, slight risk, or no risk at all?

E34   Did you expect any payment or reward for this first activity?

E34a   Would you please describe this for me?

E35   Did you carry out your first activity alone or with others?

E35a How many others did you work with?
Is this number exact or approximate?

E35b Who were the people that you worked with?

E36 Were you ever given material assistance in carrying out your activity? For example, did other people supply you with food, ration coupons, or false papers?

E36a What kind of assistance were you given?

E37 During your first activity, were you, or was anyone who helped you, searched, detained, or arrested? Was anyone who helped you executed?

E37a How many times did this happen during your first activity?

Is this number exact or approximate?

E38 Would you please describe (this/these) for me?

E39 Now, can you summarize for me the main reasons why you became involved in this first activity?

E39a Are there any other reasons?

E40 Was there ever a time during the war that you were asked to help somebody and *had to say no?*

E40a Were any of the people to whom you had to say *no Jewish?*

E41

> Now I would like to ask you some questions about the first time that you were asked to help a Jewish person and you had to say no. INT.: GO TO QUESTION E43.

E42 Now I would like to ask you some questions about the first time that you were asked to help somebody and you had to say no.

E43 Could you briefly describe this first time for me?

E44 How many people were you asked to help at this time?

E45 Who were the people that you were asked to help? Were they friends, neighbors, strangers, or what? INT.: PROBE FOR RELATIONSHIP TO R.

E46 Who asked you to give this help? INT.: PROBE FOR RELATIONSHIP TO R.

E47 (RB, page 10) Please turn to page 10 of the Respondent Booklet. How long did it take you to make this decision? Did you make the decision not to become involved in a few minutes, several days, a few hours, several weeks, or what?

E48   Did you consult with anyone before you made this decision not to help?

E48a   Whom did you consult with? INT.: FOR EACH PERSON CON-SULTED, DETERMINE RELATIONSHIP TO R AND WHETHER THE PERSON ENCOURAGED OR DISCOURAGED THE AC-TION.

E49   Had you or someone you cared about ever been unjustly treated by the Nazis before the time you made your decision?

E49a   Would you please describe (this/these) for me?

E50   Had you witnessed or heard about mistreatment of Jews by the Nazis before the time that you made your decision?

E50a   Would you please describe (this/these) for me?

E51   (RB, page 11) Please turn to page 11 of the Respondent Booklet. How much risk did you think you would be taking at the time that you made this decision? Did you think that you would be taking extreme risk, moderate risk, slight risk, or no risk at all?

E52   To how much risk did you think you would be exposing members of your family at the time that you made your decision: extreme risk, moderate risk, slight risk, or no risk at all?

E53   Would you have received any payment or reward for this activity?

E53a   Would you please describe (this/these) for me?

E54   Would you have had to do this activity alone or with others?

E55   Can you tell me in your own words the reasons for your decision; that is, why you had to say no?

E56   Were there any times, other than those you may have already told me about, when you, personally, were mistreated by the Nazis?

E56a   Would you please describe (this/these) for me?

E57   Were there any times, other than those you may have already told me about, when you witnessed or heard about mistreatment of Jews by the Nazis?

E57a   Would you please describe (this/these) for me?

E58 Were there any times, other than those you may have already told me about, when you witnessed anyone else being mistreated by the Nazis?

E58a Would you please describe (this/these) for me?

E59 Did your father or mother or any of your brothers or sisters engage in any kind of helping or resistance activities during the war?

E59a Would you briefly tell me about (this/these)? INT.: PROBE TO DETERMINE IF HELP WAS GIVEN TO JEWS.

E60 During the war, was there a leader or two whom you particularly admired?

E60a Who were they? What were the things that you admired about them:

E61 Now I'd like to ask you about other parts of your life during the war. First of all, where did you live for the longest period during the war? Which town and which country?

E62 Was that a large city, a middle city, a small city, a village, or an isolated farm?

E63 What was the approximate size of the population?

E64 Did you have many neighbors living nearby?

E65 Did you live in a house, an apartment, or what?

E65a Did you own your home, pay rent, or what?

E66 How many rooms were in your (house/apartment), not counting bathrooms?

E67 Was there a cellar?

E68 Was there an attic?

E69

> INT.: IF R IS AN IDENTIFIED RESCUER OR HAS TOLD YOU ABOUT ANY RESCUE OR RESISTANCE ACTIVITY, SAY: Now I would like to make a list of the people who were living in your house *at the time that your helping activity first began.* Please begin with the first name of the oldest person. INT.: RECORD THIS INFORMATION ON THE TABLE BELOW.

E69a

> INT.: IF R HAS NOT TOLD YOU A STORY ABOUT RESCUE
> OR RESISTANCE ACTIVITY, SAY: Now I would like to make
> a list of the people who were living in your house *when the war
> broke out in your country*. Please begin with the first name of the
> oldest person.

Name	Relation to R	Sex	Age	Head

E69b   INT.: FOR EACH PERSON NAMED, DETERMINE AND NOTE
ABOVE:

(PERSON'S) relationship to R.
(PERSON'S) sex.
(PERSON'S) age.

E69c   INT.: THEN ASK:

Who was the head of your household? That is, who was the main
breadwinner or wage earner? INT.: MARK A 1 IN THE HEAD
COLUMN FOR THIS PERSON.

E70   During the war, was your household very well off financially,
quite well off, neither rich nor poor, quite poor, or very poor?

E71   Other than members of your family who were living with you
during the war, were there any other relatives living in your community or town?

E71a   How many different families of your relatives lived in your community or town?

Section F: Today

F1   Now I would like to ask you some questions about your life after the war, including your life today. First of all, were you involved in bringing Nazis or Nazi collaborators to justice after the war?

F1a   In what ways?

F2   Was your work after the war the same as or different from your work during the war?

F2a   What was your work after the war?

F3   Was your husband/wife's work after the war the same as or different from his/her work during the war?

F3a   What was your husband/wife's work after the war?

F4   Do you have any children?

F4a   How much do your children know about your life during the war? Do they know quite a bit, some, very little, or nothing at all?

F4b   Do you believe that your children have been influenced in any way by what they know about your life during the war?

F4c   In what way(s)?

F5   (RB, page 12) Please turn to page 12 of Respondent Booklet. Overall, do you think that your children strongly approve, somewhat approve, somewhat disapprove, or strongly disapprove of your wartime activities?

F6   What would you tell young people if a party with goals similar to those of the Nazis came to power today? INT.: PROBE FOR RECOMMENDATIONS OF ACTION IN SUPPORT OF OR AGAINST THE NAZIS.

F7   Now I would like to ask you some questions about things that you might have done to help or assist others since the war.

      First of all, after the war, did you ever do anything unusual to help someone?

F7a   Would you please describe (this/these)?

F8   Are you now or have you recently been involved in helping activities in your community, such as volunteer work with charities, schools, churches, or anything of that sort?

F8a   Would you please describe (this/these)? INT.: PROBE FOR TYPE OF HELP AND HOW OFTEN HELP IS/WAS GIVEN.

F9   (RB, page 13) Please turn to page 13 of the Respondent Booklet. Of the people listed here, what kinds of people have you given help to in the last year or so? INT.: CHECK AS MANY AS APPLY:

Relative
Friend
Neighbor
Stranger

F10   (RB, page 14) Please turn to page 14 of the Respondent Booklet. During the past year, how much, if any, have you done of the following activities: very often, often, a few times, once or never.

	Very Often	Often	Few Times	Once	Never
a. Led recreational activities for children or adults					
b. Helped feed the sick or the aged or visited the ill					
c. Taught children or adults or counseled anyone about jobs or personal problems					
d. Made telephone calls on behalf of a group or cause or helped raise money for a group or cause					
e. Gave speeches or lectures or wrote letters on behalf of an issue or cause					
f. Investigated, collected or prepared information on behalf of an issue or cause					
g. Contributed money or goods to some cause					

F11   INT: ASK ONLY IF R HAS INDICATED SOME HELPING BE-HAVIOR WITHIN THE PAST YEAR.

About how many hours a month do you or did you spend on these activities?

F12   What is your religious affiliation today? Are you a Protestant, a Catholic, or do you belong to some other religion?

F12a   Do you consider yourself very religious somewhat religious, not very religious, or not at all religious?

F13　　How would you describe your health today? Would you say that you were in excellent health, good health, fair health, poor health, or very poor health?

.
.
.

F15

> INT.: IF R IS AN IDENTIFIED RESCUER, CONTINUE WITH R1.
>
> IF R IS NOT AN IDENTIFIED RESCUER BUT HAS TOLD YOU ABOUT OTHER HELPING/RESISTANCE ACTIVITIES, GO TO O1.
>
> IF R HAS NOT TOLD YOU ABOUT ANY RESCUE OR RE-SISTANCE ACTIVITY, GO TO G1.

Section R: Identified Rescuers Only

R1　　After the war, did your neighbors find out that you rescued Jews?

R1a　　In general, did your neighbors aprove or disapprove of your rescue activities?

R2　　Do your present neighbors know that you rescued Jews during the war?

R2a　　In general, do your present neighbors approve or disapprove of your rescue activities?

R3　　If they did know, do you think they would approve or disapprove?

R4　　Have you received any compensation or public recognition for your rescue activities?

R4a　　What kind of compensation or recognition did you receive?

R5　　Have you spoken about your rescue activities in any public place?

R5a　　About how many times have you spoken about your activities?

R6　　Did you have contact with (any of) the person(s) you rescued after the war?

R6a　　Are you still in contact with them?

R7   Do you know the names and addresses of any of the people that you rescued?

R7a Can you give these to me?

     INT.: GO TO G1.

Section O: Active Controls Only

O1   After the war, did your neighbors find out about your helping/ resistance activities?

O1a In general, did your neighbors approve or disapprove of your activities?

O2   Do your present neighbors know about your helping/resistance activities during the war?

O2a In general, do your present neighbors approve or disapprove of your activities?

O3   If they did know, do you think they would approve or disapprove?

O4   Have you received any compensation or public recognition for your helping/resistance activities?

O4a What kind of compensation or recognition did you receive?

O5   Have you spoken about your helping/resistance activities in any public place?

O5a About how many times have you spoken about your activities?

O6   Did you have contact with (any of) the person(s) you helped after the war?

O6a Are you still in contact with them?

O7   Do you know the names and addresses of any of the people that you helped?

O7a Can you give these to me?

G1   Is there anything else you would like to tell me?

G1a What else would you like to tell me?

G2   INT.: INTERVIEW ENDS. NOTE EXACT TIME HERE (HOURS, MINUTES).

G3   Do you have any records of things that you did in your life *before the war*? For example, do you have any photographs, letters, awards, or medals for things that you did in your life before the war?

G3a   INT.: INSPECT AND MAKE NOTE OF ANY MATERIALS THAT ARE RELATED TO R'S REPORTS OF UNUSUAL COURA-GEOUS, HELPING, PATRIOTIC, OR RISKY ACTIVITIES WHILE GROWING UP OR BEFORE THE WAR.

G4   Do you have any records of things that you did during the war? For example, do you have any photographs, letters, awards, or medals for things that you did during the war?

G4a   INT.: INSPECT AND MAKE NOTE OF ANY MATERIALS THAT ARE RELATED TO R'S REPORTS OF HIS/HER ACTIVITIES DURING THE WAR.

      INT.: PLEASE THANK R FOR HIS/HER ASSISTANCE.

Section T: Interviewer Observations

T1   The interview was conducted by:
      Int. in R's native language
      Int. in English
      Int. with a translator

T1a   What was the relationship of the translator to R?

T1b   What effect, if any did the translator have on R's responses? For example, did you feel that the translator was leading or "answer-ing for" R in any way?

T2   Was anyone else present during the interview?

T2a   Who were they and what affect did they have on R's responses?

T3   Generally, R's understanding of the questions was:
      Excellent
      Good
      Fair
      Poor

T4   Generally, R's memory or recall was:
      Excellent
      Good
      Fair
      Poor

T5   Generally, R was:
Very cooperative
Somewhat cooperative
Not very cooperative
Not at all cooperative

T6   Please give a brief description of the interview situation including any problems of understanding or recall, R's emotional state during the interview, anything that struck you as particularly unique about R, and your overall assessment of the quality of R's responses.

Notes

Foreword

1. Sigmund Freud, *Civilization and Its Discontents* (New York: W. W. Norton, 1961), 58.

2. Zohar III 80B, Soncino edition.

3. Yosef H. Yerushalmi, *Zakhor* (Seattle: University of Washington Press, 1982), p. 99.

4. Camus as quoted in Matthew I. Spetter, *Man the Reluctant Brother* (New York: Fieldston Press, 1967), 31.

Preface

1. Shmulek's story is told in a personal memoir by Samuel P. Oliner, *Restless Memories: Recollections of the Holocaust Years* (Berkeley, Calif.: Judah L. Magnes Memorial Museum, 1986).

2. Quoted in Philip Friedman, *Their Brothers' Keepers* (New York: Holocaust Library, 1978).

CHAPTER 1   Why Risk One's Life?

1. Charles Patterson, "Yad Vashem Conference: 35 Educators Learn How to Teach the Holocaust," *Jewish World* (October 14–20, 1983). Also communicated by M. Paldiel to S. P. Oliner in a personal interview (Summer 1984).

2. Historian Philip Friedman (*Their Brothers' Keepers* [New York: Holocaust Library, 1978]) estimates that of the approximately two million Jews who survived, one million received active assistance from the Christian population; allowing for the fact that some people engaged in multiple rescues and that a single rescue in some cases involved multiple people, this suggests an average of one non-Jewish helper for each Jew helped.

3. For an interesting historical look at the construct and its advent on the American scene in particular, see Louis J. Budd, "Altruism Arrives in America," *American Quarterly* 8 (1956): 40–52. Pointing to the obsolescence of the idea by the mid-1950s is the short, anonymous comment about the article that accompanies it; Louis Budd, it says, "rediscovers a forgotten aspect of social thought in the late Nineteenth Century," 40.

4. Pitirim A. Sorokin, *The Reconstruction of Humanity* (Boston: Beacon Press, 1948); *Altruistic Love* (Boston: Beacon Press, 1950); *Explorations in Altruistic*

Love and Behavior (Boston: Beacon Press, 1950); *Forms and Techniques of Altruistic and Spiritual Growth* (Boston: Beacon Press, 1954).

5. Auguste Comte, *System of Positive Polity* (New York: Ben Franklin, 1973).

6. The proposition that human behavior can be motivated by self-transcendence has still not penetrated mainstream psychology. In a well-reasoned and detailed analysis, Michael and Lise Wallach (*Psychology's Sanction for Selfishness: The Error of Egoism in Theory and Therapy* [San Francisco: W. H. Freeman, 1983]) argue that the underlying assumption within many current psychological orientations is that self-interest is the only determinant of human behavior; current clinical practice, they assert, legitimates it. Traditional therapeutic techniques focus on clients learning to concentrate on seeking their own interests; the Wallachs argue that psychological health could be advanced by appealing to the client's sense of serving others.

7. R. N. Bellah, ed., *Emile Durkheim: On Morality and Society* (Chicago: University of Chicago Press, 1973).

8. Lauren G. Wispé, "Positive Forms of Social Behavior: An Overview," *Journal of Social Issues* 28, no. 3 (1972): 1–20; Pitirim A. Sorokin, *The Reconstruction of Humanity.*

9. Garrett Hardin, *The Limits of Altruism: An Ecologist's View of Survival* (Bloomington: Indiana University Press, 1977).

10. Lawrence A. Blum, *Friendship, Altruism and Morality* (London: Routledge & Kegan Paul, 1980); Joseph Katz, "Altruism and Sympathy: Their History in Philosophy and Some Implications for Psychology," *Journal of Social Issues* 28 no. 3 (1972): 59–70.

11. Elizabeth Midlarsky, "Competence and Helping: Notes Towards a Model," in *Development and Maintenance of Prosocial Behavior: International Perspectives on Positive Morality,* ed. E. Staub et al. (New York: Plenum Press, 1984), 291–308.

12. Daniel Bar-Tal, Ruth Sharabany, and Amiram Raviv, "Cognitive Basis of the Development of Altruistic Behavior," in *Cooperation and Helping Behavior: Theories and Research,* ed. Valerian J. Derlega and Janusz Grzelak (New York: Academic Press, 1982); J. Philippe Rushton, *Altruism, Socialization and Society* (Englewood Cliffs, N.J.: Prentice-Hall, 1980).

13. Robert B. Cialdini, Douglas T. Kenrick, and Donald J. Baumann, "Effects of Mood on Prosocial Behavior in Children and Adults," in *The Development of Prosocial Behavior,* ed. Nancy Eisenberg (New York: Academic Press, 1982), 339–357; Jacqueline R. Macaulay and Leonard Berkowitz, "Overview," in *Altruism and Helping Behavior,* ed. J. Macaulay and L. Berkowitz (New York: Academic Press, 1970).

14. Dennis Krebs, "Empathy and Altruism," *Journal of Personality and Social Psychology* 32, no. 6 (1975): 1134–1146.

15. Daniel Bar-Tal, *Prosocial Behavior: Theory and Research* (New York: John Wiley & Sons, 1976).

16. Shalom H. Schwartz and Judith A. Howard, "Internalized Values as Motivators of Altruism," in *Development and Maintenance of Prosocial Behavior: International Perspectives on Positive Morality,* ed. E. Staub et al. (New York: Plenum Press, 1984), 229–256.

17. Shalom H. Schwartz and Judith A. Howard, "Helping and Cooperation: A Self-Based Motivational Model," in *Cooperation and Helping Behavior: Theories*

and Research, ed. Valerian J. Derlega and Janusz Grzelak (New York: Academic Press, 1982), 328–352.

18. Daniel Bar-Tal and Amiram Raviv, "A Cognitive-Learning Model of Helping Behavior Development: Possible Implications and Applications," in *The Development of Prosocial Behavior,* ed. Nancy Eisenberg (New York: Academic Press, 1982), 199–216.

19. For an excellent review of research relating to the rescue of Jews, see Lawrence Baron, "The Holocaust and Human Decency: A Review of Research on the Rescue of Jews in Nazi-Occupied Europe," *Humboldt Journal of Social Relations* 13, nos. 1–2 (1985/86): 237–251.

20. Friedman, *Their Brothers' Keepers;* Wladyslaw Bartoszewski and Zofia Lewin, eds., *The Samaritans: Heroes of the Holocaust* (New York: Twayne Publishers, 1970); K. Iranek-Osmecki, *He Who Saves One Life* (New York: Crown, 1971); T. Berenstein and A. Rutkowski, "O Ratowaniu Żydów Przez Polaków W Okreśie Okupacji Hitlerowskie"; (Polish rescue of Jews during the occupation), *Biuletyn Żydowskiego Instytutu Historycznego* 35 (1960): 3–46; E. Chodziński, "Pomoc Żydom Udzielana Przez Konspiracyjne Biuro Fałszywych Dokumentów W Okresie Okupacji Hitlerowskiej" (Help offered to Jews during the occupation by the underground office of illegal documents), *Biuletyn Żydowskiego Instytutu Historycznego* 75 (1970): 129–132; H. D. Leuner, *When Compassion Was a Crime: Germany's Silent Heroes: 1933–1945* (London: Oswald Wolf, 1966); K. Grossman, *Die Unbesungenen Helden* (The unsung heroes) (Berlin-Grunewald: Arani Verlag, 1961); Yehuda Bauer, *A History of The Holocaust* (New York: Franklin Watts, 1982), 279–302; *Rescue Attempts During the Holocaust,* Proceedings of the Second Yad Vashem International Historical Conference, Jerusalem, 8–11 April 1974 (New York: Ktav Publishing House, 1978); Peter Hellman, *Avenue of the Righteous* (New York: Bantam Books, 1981).

21. Bartoszewski and Lewin, *The Samaritans;* Iranek-Osmecki, *He Who Saves One Life;* Nechama Tec, *When Light Pierced the Darkness: Christian Rescue of Jews in Nazi-Occupied Poland* (New York: Oxford University Press, 1986); Louis De Jong, "Help to People in Hiding," *Delta: A Review of Arts, Life, and Thought in the Netherlands* 8, no. 19 (Spring 1965): 37–39; J. Presser, *The Destruction of The Dutch Jews* (New York: E. P. Dutton, 1969); W. Warmbrunn, *The Dutch Under German Occupation 1940–1945* (Stanford, Calif.: Stanford University Press, 1963).

22. Frederick B. Chary, *The Bulgarian Jews and the Final Solution, 1940–1944* (Pittsburgh, Pa.: University of Pittsburgh, 1972).

23. Harold Flender, *Rescue in Denmark* (New York: Manor Books, 1964); Leni Yahil, *The Rescue of Danish Jewry: Test of a Democracy,* trans. Morris Gradel (Philadelphia: Jewish Publication Society, 1969).

24. S. Zuccotti, *The Italians and the Holocaust: Persecution, Rescue, and Survival* (New York: Basic Books, 1987); Mae Briskin, "Rescue Italian Style," *Jewish Monthly* (May 1986): 20–25.

25. Ezra Mendelsohn, *The Jews of East Central Europe Between the World Wars* (Bloomington: Indiana University Press, 1983); S. Ettinger, "Jews and Non-Jews in Eastern and Central Europe Between the Wars: An Outline," in *Jews and Non-Jews in Eastern Europe 1918–1945,* ed. Bela Vago and George L. Mosse (New York: Halsted Press, 1974), 1–19; Lucy S. Dawidowicz, *The Golden Tradition: Jewish Life and Thought in Eastern Europe* (Boston: Beacon Press, 1972); Nora Levin, *The Holocaust: The Destruction of European Jewry*

1933–1945 (New York: Schocken Books, 1973); R. Hilberg, *The Destruction of the European Jews* (New York: Holmes and Meier, 1985), II. Approximately half of Rumania's Jewish population perished, most of them before 1942.

26. Yitzhak Arad, "The 'Final Solution' in Lithuania in the Light of German Documentation," Yad Vashem Studies 11 (1976): 234–272. More than 90 percent of Lithuania's Jews perished.

27. Warmbrunn, *The Dutch Under German Occupation.*

28. Michael R. Marrus and Robert O. Paxton, *Vichy France and the Jews* (New York: Schocken Books, 1983); Philip Paul Hallie, *Lest Innocent Blood Be Shed: The Story of Le Chambon and How Goodness Happened There* (New York: Harper & Row, 1979); Armin F. C. Boyens, "The Ecumenical Community and the Holocaust," *Annals of the American Academy of Political and Social Sciences* 450 (July 1980): 143–147; Emile C. Fabre, ed., *God's Underground* (St. Louis, Mo.: Bethany, 1970); Sam Waagenar, *The Pope's Jews* (La Salle, Ill.: Alcove, 1974); Francois Le Boucher, *The Incredible Mission of Father Bénoit,* trans. J. F. Bernard (Garden City, N.Y.: Doubleday, 1969); H. D. Leuner, *When Compassion Was a Crime: Germany's Silent Heroes 1933–1945* (London: Oswald Wolf, 1966).

29. Douglas Huneke, *The Moses of Rovno* (New York: Dodd, Mead & Co. 1985).

30. Thomas Keneally, *Schindler's List* (New York: Simon & Schuster, 1982).

31. Per Anger, *With Raoul Wallenberg in Budapest: Memories of the War Years in Hungary,* trans. D. M. Paul and M. Paul (New York: Holocaust Library, 1981); John Bierman, *Righteous Gentile: The Story of Raoul Wallenberg* (New York: Viking, 1981); Harvey Rosenfeld, *Raoul Wallenberg: Angel of Rescue—Heroism and Torment in the Gulag* (Buffalo, N.Y.: Prometheus Books, 1982); Frederick E. Werbell and Thurston Clarke, *Lost Hero: The Mystery of Raoul Wallenberg* (New York: McGraw-Hill, 1982).

32. David Knout, *Contribution à l'histoire de la Résistance juive en France 1940–1944* (Paris: Éditions du Centre, 1947); David Diamant, *Les Juifs dans la résistance française 1940–1944* (Paris: Roger Maria, 1971).

33. S., Krakowski, *War of the Doomed: Jewish Armed Resistance in Poland, 1942–1944* (New York: Holmes and Meier, 1983); Meyer Barkai, ed., *The Fighting Ghettos* (Philadelphia: Lippincott, 1962).

34. Warmbrunn, *The Dutch Under German Occupation;* L. Steinberg, *Not as a Lamb: The Jews Against Hitler,* trans. M. Hunter (Farnborough, England: Saxon House, 1974).

35. Amy Latour, *The Jewish Resistance in France (1940–1944),* trans. Irene R. Ilton (New York: Holocaust Library, 1981).

36. J. Kermish, "The Activities of the Council of Aid to Jews ("Zegota") in Occupied Poland," in *Rescue Attempts During the Holocaust,* Proceedings of the Second Yad Vashem International Historical Conference, Jerusalem, 8–11 April 1974 (New York: Ktav Publishing House, 1978), 379–382.

37. Amy Latour, *The Jewish Resistance in France.*

38. W. Laqueur, *The Terrible Secret: Suppression of the Truth About Hitler's 'Final Solution'* (New York: Penguin, 1982).

39. Werner T. Angress, "The German Jews, 1933–1939," in *The Holocaust: Ideology, Bureaucracy and Genocide,* ed. H. Friedlander and S. Milton (Millwood, N.Y.: Kraus International Publications, 1980, 69–82); Yerahmiel Cohen,

"French Jewry's Dilemma on the Orientation of Its Leadership (From Polemics to Conciliation: 1942–1944)," *Yad Vashem Studies* 14 (1981): 167–204.

40. Marie Syrkin, *Blessed Is the Match: The Story of Jewish Resistance* (Philadelphia: Jewish Publication Society, 1976); Reuben Ainsztein, *Jewish Resistance in Nazi-Occupied Eastern Europe* (New York: Barnes & Noble, 1975); Steinberg, *Not As a Lamb.*

41. Sarah Gordon, *Hitler, Germans and the "Jewish Question"* (Princeton, N.J.: Princeton University Press, 1984).

42. Manfred Wolfson, "Zum Widerstand gegen Hitler: Umriss eines Gruppenporträts Deutscher Retter von Juden," in *Tradition und Neubeginn* (Munich: Heymann, 1975), 391–407.

43. Frances Henry, *Victims and Neighbors: A Small Town in Germany Remembered* (South Hadley, Mass.: Bergin and Garvey, 1984).

44. Tec, *When Light Pierced the Darkness.*

45. E. O. Wilson, *Sociobiology: The New Synthesis* (Cambridge, Mass.: Harvard University Press, 1975).

46. Jaak Panksepp, "The Psychobiology of Prosocial Behaviors: Separation Distress, Play, and Altruism," in *Altruism and Aggression: Biological and Social Origins,* ed. Carolyn Zahn-Waxler, E. Mark Cummings, Ronald Iannotti (New York: Cambridge University Press, 1986), 19–57.

47. Jane Goodall (*In the Shadow of Man* [Boston: Houghton Mifflin, 1971]), for example, observed that among the chimpanzees she studied, parents vary considerably in dealing with and modeling behaviors, and their offspring learn many of such skills from parental tutelage.

48. M. L. Hoffman, "Empathy, Role Taking, Guilt and Development of Altruistic Motives," in *Moral Development and Behavior: Theory, Research and Social Issues,* ed. T. Lickona (New York: Holt, Rinehart & Winston, 1976), 124–143.

49. P. H. Wolff, "The Biology of Morals from a Psychological Perspective," in *Morality as a Biological Phenomenon,* ed. G. S. Stent (Berlin: Dahlem Konferenzen, 1978), 93–103.

50. S. Freud, "The Psychopathology of Everyday Life," vol. 6 of *The Standard Edition of the Complete Psychological Works of Sigmund Freud,* ed. J. Strachey (London: Hogarth Press, 1960); "The Ego and the Id," vol. 19 of *The Standard Edition of the Complete Psychological Works of Sigmund Freud,* ed. J. Strachey (London: Hogarth Press, 1961).

51. H. R. R. Holt, "A Review of Some of Freud's Biological Assumptions and their Influence on his Theories," in *Psychoanalysis and Current Biological Thought,* ed. N. S. Greenfield and W. C. Lewis (Madison: University of Wisconsin Press, 1965), 93–124; H. R. R. Holt, "Drive or Wish? A Reconsideration of the Psychoanalytic Theory of Motivation," in *Psychology Versus Metapsychology: Psychoanalytic Essays in Memory of George S. Klein—Psychological Issues* no. 36, ed. M. M. Gill and P. S. Holzman (New York: International Universities Press, 1976), 158–197; Wallach and Wallach, *Psychology's Sanction for Selfishness,* chaps. 2, 3.

52. Jean Piaget, *The Moral Judgment of the Child* (Glencoe, Ill.: Free Press, 1948).

53. L. Kohlberg, "Stage and Sequence: The Cognitive-Developmental Approach to Socialization," in *Handbook of Socialization Theory and Research,* ed. D. A. Goslin (New York: Rand McNally, 1969), 347–480.

54. Nancy Eisenberg-Berg and Michael Hand, "The Relationship of Preschoolers' Reasoning About Prosocial Moral Conflicts to Prosocial Behavior," *Child Development* 50 (1979): 356–363; Daniel Bar-Tal, Amiram Raviv, and T. Leiser, "The Development of Altruistic Behavior: Empirical Evidence," *Developmental Psychology* 16 (1980): 516–524; Augusto Blasi, "Bridging Moral Cognition and Moral Action: A Critical Review of the Literature," *Psychological Bulletin* 88 (1980): 1–45.

55. Nancy Eisenberg, "The Development of Reasoning Regarding Prosocial Behavior," in *The Development of Prosocial Behavior,* ed. Nancy Eisenberg (New York: Academic Press, 1982), 219–246; Robert Coles, "How Do You Measure a Child's Level of Morality?" *Learning* (July/August 1981): 70–72.

56. Iris Murdoch, *The Sovereignty of Good* (London: Routledge & Kegan Paul, 1970), 1–2; E. L. Simpson ("Moral Development Research: A Case of Scientific Cultural Bias," *Human Development* 17 [1974]: 81–106) maintains that the cognitive approach is biased toward Western societies while C. Gilligan (*In a Different Voice: Psychological Theory and Women's Development* [Cambridge, Mass.: Harvard University Press, 1982]) proposes that it is also biased in favor of males. Studies by N. Eisenberg (*Altruistic Emotion, Cognition and Behavior* [Hillsdale, N.J.: Lawrence Erlbaum 1986], chaps. 7, 8, 9) suggest that prosocial behavior may be associated with a different type of reasoning, which she calls prosocial moral reasoning. Whereas Kohlberg's moral reasoning stages are based on considerations of justice, prosocial moral reasoning stages are based on considerations of responsibility and caring. Like Kohlberg, she finds this type of reasoning to be age and stage related, and several of her studies point to an association between prosocial moral reasoning and prosocial behavior.

57. O. H. Mowrer, *Learning Theory and the Symbolic Processes* (New York: John Wiley & Sons, 1960).

58. B. F. Skinner, *Science and Human Behavior* (New York: Macmillan, 1974).

59. Bernice L. Neugarten ("Adult Personality: Toward a Psychology of the Life Cycle," in *Middle Age and Aging: A Reader in Social Psychology,* ed. Bernice L. Neugarten [Chicago: University of Chicago Press, 1968], 137–147) was among the first to point out that personality theorists had concentrated their attention on the first "two sevenths" of life, largely ignoring the last "five sevenths." It is only in recent years that psychologists have begun to respond to the need she noted almost thirty years ago—the need to systematically accumulate evidence on the changes that take place between early adulthood and the middle years and those that take place between the middle years and old age.

60. Paul B. Baltes and Hayne W. Reese ("The Life-Span Perspective in Developmental Psychology," in *Developmental Psychology: An Advanced Textbook,* ed. Marc H. Bornstein and Michael E. Lamb, [Hillsdale, N.J.: Lawrence Erlbaum, 1984], 493–532) propose that life-span research is not so much new in its principles as in its emphasis. They identify six substantive, theoretical, and methodological principles that characterize and coordinate the life-span perspective. The first principle is that "development is a life-long process. No single period in the life span can claim general primacy for the origin and occurrence of important and interesting developmental changes." The second principle is that developmental courses can vary greatly among individuals. The third principle relates to "intra-individual plasticity"—that is, the developmental course of an individual can vary de-

pending on his or her life experiences. The fourth principle is "that evolution (phylogeny) and individual development (ontogeny) are intricately related." This means that genetic and cultural evolution regulate individual development in part and that individual development is affected by biocultural change. The fifth principle relates to the recognition of various interacting influences on individual development. And the sixth principle acknowledges that development needs to be understood within a cross- and interdisciplinary context of knowledge, 523.

61. E. L. Kelly, "Consistency of the Adult Personality," *American Psychologist* 10 (1955): 659–681.

62. Ibid.

63. Ilene C. Siegler, "Psychological Aspects of the Duke Longitudinal Studies," in *Longitudinal Studies of Adult Psychological Development,* ed. K. Warner Schaie (New York: Guilford Press, 1983).

64. Robert R. McCrae and Paul T. Costa, Jr., *Emerging Lives, Enduring Dispositions* (Boston: Little, Brown & Co., 1984).

CHAPTER 2   The Historical Context of Rescue

1. The model used here is based largely on the one formulated by Helen Fein, *Accounting for Genocide: National Responses and Jewish Victimization during the Holocaust* (New York: Free Press, 1979), 31–49.

2. The issue of when and by whom the orders for the Final Solution were issued is still a subject of historical controversy. For overviews of this debate, see Ian Kershaw, *The Nazi Dictatorship: Problems and Pespectives of Interpretation* (Baltimore, Md.: Edward Arnold, 1985), 82–105, and Saul Friedlaender, "Introduction," in Gerald Fleming, *Hitler and the Final Solution* (Berkeley and Los Angeles: University of California Press, 1984), vii–xxxvi.

3. George M. Kren and Leon Rappoport, *The Holocaust and the Crisis of Human Behavior* (New York and London: Holmes and Meier, 1980), 87–93.

4. The classifications of types of German rule used here represent a synthesis of typologies employed by Fein, *Accounting for Genocide,* 38–40; Raul Hilberg, *The Destruction of the European Jews,* vol. 2 (New York and London: Holmes and Meier, 1985); and Gordon Wright, *The Ordeal of Total War 1939–1945* (New York: Harper & Row, 1968), 107–143.

5. Hilberg, *The Destruction,* vol. 2, 609–638.

6. Harold Flender, *Rescue in Denmark* (New York: Manor Books, 1964), 52.

7. Leonard Gross, *The Last Jews in Berlin* (New York: Simon & Schuster, 1982).

8. Ezra Mendelsohn, *The Jews of East Central Europe between the World Wars* (Bloomington: Indiana University Press, 1983); S. Ettinger, "Jews and Non-Jews in Eastern and Central Europe Between the Wars: An Outline," in *Jews and Non-Jews in Eastern Europe 1918–1945,* ed. Bela Vago and George L. Mosse (New York: Halsted Press, 1974), 1–19; Lucy Dawidowicz, *The Golden Tradition: Jewish Life and Thought in Eastern Europe* (Boston: Beacon Press, 1972), 5–90.

9. Nora Levin, *The Holocaust: The Destruction of European Jewry 1933–1945* (New York: Schocken Books, 1973), 561–596; Hilberg, *The Destruction,* vol. 2, 758–796.

10. Yitzhak Arad, "The 'Final Solution' in Lithuania in the Light of German Documentation," *Yad Vashem Studies* 11 (1976), 234–272.

11. Frederick B. Chary, *The Bulgarian Jews and the Final Solution, 1940–1944* (Pittsburgh: University of Pittsburgh, 1972).

12. Fein, *Accounting for Genocide*, 152–155.

13. Leni Yahil, *The Rescue of Danish Jewry: Test of a Democracy*, trans. Morris Gradel (Philadelphia: Jewish Publication Society, 1969).

14. Fein, *Accounting for Genocide*, 155–158.

15. Lucjan Dobroszycki, "Jewish Elites Under German Rule," in *The Holocaust: Ideology, Bureaucracy, and Genocide*, ed. Henry Friedlander and Sybil Milton (Millwood, N.Y.: Kraus International Publications, 1980), 221–230; Wilhelm Schlesinger, "On a Reappraisal of the *Shtadlan* During the Holocaust: the Activity and Correspondence of Dr. Wilhelm Filderman on Behalf of Roumania's Jews," *Centerpoint: A Journal of Interdisciplinary Studies* 4, no. 1 (Fall 1980), 113–121. For opposing interpretations of the role played by the Jewish councils, see Raul Hilberg, "The Ghetto as a Form of Government," *Annals of the American Academy of Political and Social Science*, 450 (July 1980), 98–112; Isaiah Trunk, *Judenrat: The Jewish Councils in Eastern Europe Under Nazi Occupation*, trans. J. Robinson (New York: Stein & Day, 1977).

16. Erich Kulka, "Attempts by Jewish Escapees to Stop Mass Extermination," *Jewish Social Studies* 47, nos. 3–4 (Summer/Fall 1985), 295–306; Walter Laqueur, *The Terrible Secret: Suppression of the Truth About Hitler's "Final Solution"* (New York: Penguin, 1982).

17. Reuben Ainsztein, *Jewish Resistance in Nazi-Occupied Eastern Europe* (New York: Barnes & Noble, 1975); Lucien Steinberg, *Not as a Lamb: The Jews Against Hitler*, trans. Marion Hunter (Farnborough, England: Saxon House, 1974); Marie Syrkin, *Blessed Is the Match: The Story of Jewish Resistance* (Philadelphia: Jewish Publication Society, 1976); *They Fought Back: The Story of the Jewish Resistance in Nazi Europe*, ed. Yuri Suhl (New York: Schocken Books, 1975).

18. Per Anger, *With Raoul Wallenberg in Budapest*, trans. David M. Paul and Margarita Paul (New York: Holocaust Library, 1981); Yehuda Bauer, *American Jewry and the Holocaust: The American Joint Distribution Committee* (Detroit: Wayne State University Press, 1981); John Bierman, *Righteous Gentile* (New York: Viking Press, 1981); Eleanore Lester, *Wallenberg: The Man in the Iron Web* (Englewood Cliffs, N.J.: Prentice-Hall, 1982); Kati Marton, *Wallenberg* (New York: Random House, 1982); Harvey Rosenfeld, *Raoul Wallenberg: Angel of Rescue* (Buffalo, N.Y.: Prometheus Books, 1982).

19. Fein, *Accounting for Genocide*, 49, 344–347.

20. Sebastian Haffner, *The Meaning of Hitler*, trans. Ewald Osers (New York: Macmillan, 1979), 25–72. For a synopsis and evaluation of interpretations on the bases and extent of Hitler's power, see Kershaw, *The Nazi Dictatorship*, 18–81, 130–148.

21. Richard S. Levy, *The Downfall of the Anti-Semitic Political Parties in Imperial Germany* (New Haven, Conn.: Yale University Press, 1975); Paul Massing, *Rehearsal for Destruction: A Study of the Political Anti-Semitism in Imperial Germany* (New York: Harper & Bros., 1949); George L. Mosse, *The Crisis of German Ideology* (New York: Grosset & Dunlap, 1964); George L. Mosse, *Toward the Final Solution: A History of European Racism* (New York: Howard Fertig, 1978); Peter Pulzer, *The Rise of Political Anti-Semitism in Germany and Austria* (New York: John Wiley & Sons, 1964); Fritz Stern, *The Politics of Cultural Despair* (Berkeley and Los Angeles: University of California Press, 1961); Uriel Tal,

Christians and Jews in Germany: Religion, Politics, and Ideology in the Second Reich, 1870–1914 (Ithaca, N.Y.: Cornell University Press, 1975).

22. Uwe Dietrich Adam, *Judenpolitik im Dritten Reich* (Düsseldorf: Droste Verlag, 1972); C. C. Aronsfeld, *The Text of the Holocaust: A Study of the Nazis' Extermination Propaganda: 1919–1945* (Marblehead, Mass.: Micah Publications, 1985); Gilmer W. Blackburn, *Education in the Third Reich: Race and History in Nazi Textbooks* (Albany: State University of New York Press, 1984); Karl A. Schleunes, *The Twisted Road to Auschwitz: Nazi Policy Toward German Jews* (Urbana: University of Illinois Press, 1970).

23. Sarah Gordon, *Hitler, Germans, and the "Jewish Question"* (Princeton: Princeton University Press, 1984), 165–295; Frances Henry, *Victims and Neighbors: A Small Town in Germany Remembered* (South Hadley, Mass.: Bergin and Garvey, 1984), 91–120; Ian Kershaw, *Popular Opinion and Political Dissent in the Third Reich: Bavaria 1933–1945* (Oxford, England: Oxford University Press, 1983); Lawrence D. Stokes, "The German People and the Destruction of the European Jews," *Central European History* 6, no. 2 (June 1973): 167–192.

24. Rita Thalmann and Emmanuel Feinermann, *Crystal Night: 9–10 November 1938,* trans. Gilles Cremonesi (New York: Coward, McCann and Geoghegan, 1974). Heinz Höhne, *The Order of the Death's Head* (New York: Coward, McCann & Geoghegan, 1970); Robert Lewis Koehl, *The Black Corps: The Structure and Power Struggles of the Nazi SS* (Madison: University of Wisconsin Press, 1983); Helmut Krausnick and Martin Broszat, *Anatomy of the SS-State* (New York: Walter and Co., 1968); Gerald Reitlinger, *The SS: Alibi of a Nation: 1922–1945* (New York: Viking Press, 1957).

25. Herbert A Strauss, "Jewish Emigration from Germany—Nazi Policies and Jewish Responses," *Leo Baeck Institute Year Book* 25–26 (1980/1981): 313–361, 343–409.

26. Philip Friedman, "The Lublin Reservation and the Madagascar Plan," *YIVO Annual of Jewish Social Science* 8 (1953): 151–177; Jonny Moser, "Nisko: The First Experiment in Deportation," *Simon Wiesenthal Center Annual* 2 (1985): 1–30; Leni Yahil, "Madagascar—Phantom of a Solution for the Jewish Question," in *Jews and Non-Jews in Eastern Europe, 1918–1945,* ed. Bela Vago and George L. Mosse (New York: Halsted Press, 1974) 315–334.

27. Yehuda Bauer, "Genocide: Was It The Nazis' Original Plan?" *Annals of the American Academy of Political and Social Science,* 450 (July 1980): 35–45; Christopher R. Browning, "A Reply to Martin Broszat Regarding the Origins of the Final Solution," *Simon Wiesenthal Center Annual* vol. 1 (1984): 113–132.

28. Richard Rubenstein, *The Cunning of History: The Holocaust and the American Future* (New York: Harper & Row, 1975), 1–21.

29. Hilberg, *The Destruction,* vol. 2, 416–481; Strauss, "Jewish Emigration from Germany," 316–337. Unfortunately, many of those who fled to other countries were subsequently captured by the Nazis when Germany occupied those countries.

30. Werner T. Angress, "The German Jews, 1933–1939," in *The Holocaust: Ideology, Bureaucracy and Genocide,* ed. H. Friedlander and S. Milton (Millwood, N.Y.: Kraus International Publications, 1980) 69–82; Lucy S. Dawidowicz, *The War Against the Jews 1933–1945* (New York: Holt, Rinehart & Winston, 1975), 169–196.

31. Levin, *The Holocaust,* 185–193, 465–495.

32. *The Path to Dictatorship 1918–1933: Ten Essays,* trans. John Conway (New York:

Anchor Books, 1966), 50–152; Peter Hoffmann, "Problems of Resistance in National Socialist Germany," in *The German Church Struggle and the Holocaust,* ed. Franklin H. Littell and Hubert G. Locke (Detroit, Mich.: Wayne State University Press, 1974), 97–103.

33. William Sheridan Allen, "Objective and Subjective Inhibitants in the German Resistance," in *The German Church Struggle and the Holocaust,* ed. Franklin H. Littell and Hubert G. Locke (Detroit, Mich.: Wayne State University Press, 1974) 121.

34. John S. Conway, *The Nazi Persecution of the Churches* (London: Weidenfeld and Nicolson, 1968); Richard Gutteridge, *The German Evangelical Church and the Jews, 1879–1950* (Oxford: Blackwell, 1976); Ernst Christian Helmreich, *The German Churches Under Hitler: Background to Struggle* (Detroit: Wayne State University Press, 1978); Franklin H. Littell, *The German Phoenix* (Garden City, N.Y.: Doubleday, 1960); Guenter Lewy, *The Catholic Church and Nazi Germany* (New York: Holt, Rinehart & Winston, 1964); Gordon C. Zahn, *German Catholics and Hitler's Wars* (New York: Sheed and Ward, 1962).

35. The best history of the German resistance is Peter Hoffmann, *The History of the German Resistance, 1933–1945* (Cambridge, Mass.: MIT Press, 1978). See also Eberhard Zeller, *The Flame of Freedom: The German Struggle Against Hitler,* trans. R. P. Heller and D. Masters (Coral Gables, Fla.: University of Miami Press, 1969); Cristof Dipper, "Der Deutsche Widerstand und das Judentum," *Geschichte und Gesellschaft, 9,* no. 3 (1983): 349–380.

36. H. D. Leuner, *When Compassion Was a Crime: Germany's Silent Heroes 1933–1945* (London: Oswald Wolf, 1966).

37. Gross, *The Last Jews in Berlin;* Jochen Köhler, *Klettern in der Grossstadt; Volkstümliche Geschichte vom Überleben in Berlin, 1933–1945* (Berlin: Das Arsenal, 1979); Manfred Wolfson, "Zum Widerstand gegen Hitler: Umriss eines Gruppenporträts deutscher Retter von Juden," *Tradition und Neubeginn* (Munich: Heymann, 1975), 391–407. For accounts of German rescuers, see Saul Friedlaender, *Kurt Gerstein: The Ambiguity of Good* (New York: Knopf, 1969); Pierre Joffroy, *A Spy for God: The Ordeal of Kurt Gerstein,* trans. Norman Denny (New York: Grosset & Dunlap, 1970); Douglas K. Huneke, *The Moses of Rovno* (New York: Dodd, Mead & Co., 1985); Thomas Keneally, *Schindler's List* (New York: Simon & Schuster, 1982).

38. Laqueur, *The Terrible Secret,* 17–40; Milton Mayer, *They Thought They Were Free: The Germans 1933–1945* (Chicago: University of Chicago Press, 1966), 71–173.

39. Alfred Haesler, *The Lifeboat Is Full: Switzerland and the Refugees, 1933–1945* (New York: Funk & Wagnalls, 1969).

40. Dawidowicz, *The War Against the Jews,* 394–397, 403; Levin, *The Holocaust,* 715–718. Estimates of the extent of casualties suffered by the Jews in Poland and in other countries vary. For a discussion of the problems in calculating these statistics, see Helen Fein, "Reviewing the Toll: Jewish Dead, Losses and Victims of the Holocaust," *Shoah* 2, vol. 2 (Spring 1981): 20–27.

41. Nicholas Bethell, *The War Hitler Won: The Fall of Poland, September 1939* (New York: Holt, Rinehart & Winston, 1972).

42. Jan Tomasz Gross, *Polish Society Under German Occupation: The Generalgouvernement 1939–1944* (Princeton, N.J.: Princeton University Press, 1979), 29–91, 195–198; Richard C. Lukas, *The Forgotten Holocaust: The Poles Under German Occupation 1939–1944* (Lexington: University Press of Kentucky, 1986), 1–

39. For an overview of how the Nazis envisaged the reorganization of Eastern Europe, see Ihor Kamenetsky, *Secret Nazi Plans for Eastern Europe: A Study of Lebensraum Policies* (New Haven, Conn.: College and University Press, 1961.)

43. *Documents on the Holocaust*, Yitzhak Arad, Yisrael Gutman, and Abraham Margaliot, eds., (Jerusalem: Yad Vashem, 1981), 173–178.

44. Moser, "Nisko," 1–21; Gross, *Polish Society Under German Occupation*, 59–68.

45. Dawidowicz, *The War Against the Jews*, 197–241; Yisrael Gutman, *The Jews of Warsaw 1939–1943: Ghetto, Underground, Revolt* (Bloomington: Indiana University Press, 1982), 48–116; Hilberg, *The Destruction*, vol. 1, 215–269; Trunk, *Judenrat*, 1–171.

46. Christopher R. Browning, "Nazi Resettlement Policy and the Search for a Solution to the Jewish Question, 1939–1941," *German Studies Review* 9, vol. 3 (October 1986): 497–519; Hilberg, *The Destruction*, vol. 1, 274–368.

47. Yitzhak Arad, *Belzec, Sobibor, Treblinka: The Operation Reinhard Camps* (Bloomington: Indiana University Press, 1987), 1–178; Hilberg, *The Destruction*, vol. 2, 482–542, vol. 3, 863–989; Wolfgang Scheffler, "The Forgotten Part of the 'Final Solution': The Liquidation of the Ghettos," *Simon Wiesenthal Center Annual*, 2 (1985) 31–47.

48. Celia S. Heller, *On the Edge of Destruction: Jews of Poland Between the Two World Wars* (New York: Schocken Books, 1980), 14–45; Frank Golczewski, *Polnisch-Jüdische Beziehungen, 1881–1922* (Wiesbaden: Franz Steiner Verlag, 1981).

49. Heller, *On the Edge of Destruction*, 47–139; Lukas, *The Forgotten Holocaust*, 121–126; Joseph Marcus, *Social and Political History of the Jews in Poland 1919–1939* (New York: Mouton Publishers, 1983), Edward D. Wynot, Jr., "'A Necessary Cruelty': The Emergence of Official Anti-Semitism in Poland," *The American Historial Review* 76, no. 4 (October 1971): 1035–1058.

50. Lukas, *The Forgotten Holocaust*, 40–60, 126–130; Gutman, *The Jews of Warsaw*, 27–36, 55–61.

51. Gross, *Polish Society Under German Occupation*, 184.

52. Ibid., 117–144; Lukas, *The Forgotten Holocaust*, 76–83, 117–120; Joseph Kermish, "The Activities of the Council for Aid to Jews ("Zegota") in Occupied Poland," in *Rescue Attempts During the Holocaust*, Proceedings of the Second Yad Vashem International Historical Conference, Jerusalem, 8–11 April 1974 (New York: Ktav Publishing House, 1978), 379–382.

53. Wladyslaw Bartoszewski and Zofia Lewin, *The Samaritans, Heroes of the Holocaust* (New York: Twayne Publishers, 1970); Kazimierz Iranek-Osmecki, *He Who Saves One Life: A Documented Story of the Poles Who Struggled to Save the Jews During World War II*, vol. 2 (New York: Crown, 1971; Kermish, "The Activities of the Council, of Aid" 367–398; Lukas *The Forgotten Holocaust*, 147–151; Nechama Tec, *When Light Pierced the Darkness: Christian Rescue of Jews in Nazi-Occupied Poland* (New York: Oxford University Press, 1986).

54. Heller, *On the Edge of Destruction*, 64–76.

55. Ibid., 144–293; Bernard K. Johnpoll, *The Politics of Futility: The General Jewish Workers Bund of Poland, 1917–1943* (Ithaca, N.Y.: Cornell University Press, 1967); Marcus, *Social and Political History*, 260–436; Ezra Mendelsohn, "The Dilemma of Jewish Politics in Poland: Four Responses," in *Jews and Non-Jews in Eastern Europe 1918–1945*, ed. Bela Vago and George L. Mosse (New York: Halsted Press, 1974), 203–219.

56. Tec, *When Light Pierced the Darkness,* 37–39, 127–128; Lukas, *The Forgotten Holocaust,* 144–145.

57. Dawidowicz, *The War Against the Jews,* 223–241, 279–310; Hilberg, "The Ghetto," 98–112; Trunk, *Judenrat,* 259–547; Leonard Tushnet, *The Pavement of Hell* (New York: St. Martin's Press, 1972); Aharon Weiss, "Jewish Leadership in Occupied Poland", *Yad Vashem Studies* 12 (1977): 335–366.

58. Lukas, *The Forgotten Holocaust,* 127, 171; Laqueur, *The Terrible Secret,* 123–128.

59. Meyer Barkai, ed., *The Fighting Ghettos,* (Philadelphia: Lippincott, 1962); Schmuel Krakowski, *War of the Doomed: Jewish Armed Resistance in Poland, 1942–1944* (New York: Holmes and Meier, 1983); Ber Mark, *Uprising in the Warsaw Ghetto* (New York: Schocken Books, 1975).

60. Laqueur, pp. 101–121.

61. Gutman, *The Jews of Warsaw,* 250–267, 401–430; Lukas, *The Forgotten Holocaust,* 152–181.

62. Lukas, *The Forgotten Holocaust,* 121.

63. Gutman, *The Jews of Warsaw,* 252.

64. Joods Historisch Museum, ed., *Documents of the Persecution of the Dutch Jewry 1940–1945,* (Amsterdam: Polak and Van Gennep, 1979), 174; Henry Mason, "Testing Human Bonds Within Nations: Jews in the Occupied Netherlands," *Political Science Quarterly* 99, no. 2 (Summer 1984): 316. We have used Mason's statistics, which are based on the definitive history of the German occupation of the Netherlands by Louis De Jong, *Het Koninkrijk der Nederlanden in de Tweede Wereldoorlog,* 10 vols. (The Hague: Staatsuitgeverij, 1969–1982).

65. Werner Warmbrunn, *The Dutch Under German Occupation 1940–1945* (Stanford, Calif.: Stanford University Press, 1963), 272–275. For a description of the spectrum of native reactions to German occupation of countries during World War II, see Werner Rings, *Life With the Enemy: Collaboration and Resistance in Hitler's Europe 1939–1945* (Garden City, N.Y.: Doubleday, 1982).

66. Judith C. E. Belinfante, *Joods Historisch Museum* (Haarlem: Joh. Enschede en Zonen Grafische Inrichting, 1978), 62–83.

67. Bob Moore, "Jewish Refugees in the Netherlands 1933–1940: The Structure and Pattern of Immigration from Nazi Germany," *Leo Baeck Institute Year Book* 29 (1984): 73–101; Dan Michman, "The Committee for Jewish Refugees in Holland (1933–1940)," *Yad Vashem Studies* 14 (1981): 205–232.

68. Jacob Presser, *The Destruction of the Dutch Jews* (New York: E. P. Dutton, 1969), 7–9.

69. Hilberg, *The Destruction,* 570; Leni Yahil, "Methods of Persecution: A Comparison of the 'Final Solution' in Holland and Denmark," *Scripta Hierosolymitana* 23 (1972): 283.

70. Warmbrunn, 21–33; Konrad Kwiet, *Reichskommissariat Niederlande* (Stuttgart: Deutsche Verlags Anstalt, 1968).

71. Presser, *The Destruction,* 7–94; Mason, "Testing Human Bonds," 317–325.

72. Presser, *The Destruction,* 94–213; Fein, *Accounting,* 262–289; Laqueur, *The Terrible Secret,* 149–156; Mason, "Testing Human Bonds," 316, 325–337.

73. Warmbrunn, *The Dutch Under German Occupation,* 83–96; For a sense of how NSB were ostracized, see the novel by Evert Hartman, *War Without Friends,* trans. Patricia Crampton (New York: Crown, 1982).

74. Gerhard Hirschfeld, *Fremdherrschaft und Kollaboration: Die Niederlande unter Deutscher Besatzung, 1940–1945* (Stuttgart: Deutsche Verlagsanstalt, 1984); Presser, *The Destruction*, 238–277; Rings, *Life With the Enemy*, 323–325.

75. Yahil, "Methods," 290–291.

76. Presser, *The Destruction*, 45–277.

77. Jacob Boas, *Boulevard des Misères: The Story of Transit Camp Westerbork* (Hamden, Conn.: Archon, 1985).

78. Warmbrunn, *The Dutch Under German Occupation*, 106–107; Steinberg, *Not as a Lamb*, 157–158.

79. Joseph Michman, "The Controversial Stand of the Joodse Raad in the Netherlands: Lodewijk Visser's Struggle," *Yad Vashem Studies* 10 (1974): 9–68; Haim Avni, "The Zionist Underground in Holland and France and the Escape to Spain," in *Rescue Attempts During the Holocaust*, 555–590; Presser, *The Destruction*, 278–296; Syrkin, *Blessed Is the Match*, 277–290.

80. For an example of Jewish involvement in the Dutch resistance, see Leesha Rose, *The Tulips Are Red* (New York: A. S. Barnes and Co., 1978).

81. Henry L. Mason, *Mass Demonstrations Against Foreign Regimes* (New Orleans: Tulane Studies in Political Science, 1966), 4–7, 20–22, 35–36, 47–48, 60–61, 72–76; B. A. Sijes, *De Februari-Staking* (The Hague: Martinus Nijhoff, 1954).

82. Warmbrunn, *The Dutch Under German Occupation*, 112–118.

83. This process of political and social separatism is described as *Verzuiling*, or "pillarization," by Dutch political scientists. See John P. Williams, "Netherlands' Foreign Policy as a Reflection of its Political System," in *Papers from the First Interdisciplinary Conference on Netherlandic Studies*, ed. William H. Fletcher (Lanham, Md.: University Press of America, 1985), 191–196.

84. Louis De Jong, "Help to People in Hiding," *Delta: A Review of Arts, Life, and Thought in the Netherlands*, 8, no. 19 (Spring 1965): 37–79; Presser, *The Destruction*, 381–405; Warmbrunn, *The Dutch Under German Occupation*, 185–196.

85. Pieter De Jong, "Responses of the Churches in the Netherlands to the Nazi Occupation," in *Human Responses to the Holocaust: Perpetrators and Victims—Bystanders and Resisters*, ed., Michael D. Ryan (New York and Toronto: Edwin Mellen Press, 1981), 121–143; David Blumenthal, "Religious Jews and Christians in the Holocaust; A Review Essay: *The Holocaust and Halakha* and *The Hiding Place*," in *Emory Studies on the Holocaust: An Interfaith Inquiry* (Atlanta, Ga.: Emory University, 1985), 80–88; Warmbrunn, *The Dutch Under German Occupation*, 156–164.

86. Presser, *The Destruction*, 115–116, 195–202, 313–316, 377–380; Mason, "Testing Human Bonds," 317–318.

87. Presser, *The Destruction*, 297–311.

88. Mason, "Testing Human Bonds," 316.

89. M. R. Marrus and R. O. Paxton, *Vichy France and the Jews* (New York: Schocken Books, 1983), 343–344. Marrus and Paxton based their figures on the list of deported Jews compiled by Serge Klarsfeld, *Memorial to the Jews Deported from France, 1942–1944* (New York: Beate Klarsfeld Foundation, 1983).

90. Marrus and Paxton, *Vichy France*, 345–372.

91. William Buthman, *The Rise of Integral Nationalism in France* (New York: Co-

lumbia University Press, 1939); Robert Soucy, *Fascism in France: The Case of Maurice Barrès* (Berkeley and Los Angeles: University of California Press, 1972); Zeev Sternhell, *La Droite révolutionnaire, 1885–1914: Les origines françaises du fascisme* (Paris: Editions du Seuil, 1978); Eugen Weber, "France," *The European Right: A Historical Profile*, ed. Hans Rogger and Eugen Weber (Berkeley and Los Angeles: University of California Press, 1965), 71–121; Eugen Weber, *Action Française* (Stanford, Calif.: Stanford University Press, 1962); Eugen Weber, *The Nationalist Revival in France* (Berkeley and Los Angeles: University of California Press, 1959).

92. Jean-Denis Bredin, *The Affair: The Case of Alfred Dreyfus*, trans. Jeffrey Mehlman (New York: Braziller, 1986); Robert F. Byrnes, *Anti-Semitism in Modern France: The Prologue to the Dreyfus Affair* (New York: Howard Fertig, 1969); Nicholas Halasz, *Captain Dreyfus: The Story of a Mass Hysteria* (New York: Simon & Schuster, 1955); Robert L. Hoffman, *More Than a Trial: The Struggle Over Captain Dreyfus* (New York: Free Press, 1980); Michael Marrus, *The Politics of Assimilation* (New York: Oxford University Press, 1971). For a popularized summary of modern French anti-Semitism, see Erna Paris, *Unhealed Wounds: France and the Klaus Barbie Affair* (New York: Grove Press, 1985), 47–58. For background on the Jewish community in France, see Paula Hyman, *From Dreyfus to Vichy: The Remaking of French Jewry, 1906–1939* (New York: Columbia University Press, 1979).

93. Marrus and Paxton, *Vichy France*, 34–71. For the response of French Jewry to the crises of the 1930s, see David H. Weinberg, *A Community on Trial: The Jews of Paris in the 1930's* (Chicago: Univeristy of Chicago Press, 1977).

94. Hilberg, *The Destruction*, vol. 2, 609–614; Robert O. Paxton, *Vichy France: Old Guard and New Order, 1940–1944* (New York: Knopf, 1972).

95. Stanley Hoffmann, *Decline or Renewal? France Since the 1930s* (New York: Viking Press, 1974), 26–44.

96. Ibid., 3–25; Bertram M. Gordon, *Collaborationism in France during the Second World War* (Ithaca, N.Y.: Cornell University Press, 1980), 326–346.

97. Marrus and Paxton, *Vichy France*, 3–21, 75–176, 252–255.

98. Ibid., 217–255; Claude Levy and Paul Tillard, *Betrayal at the Vel d'Hiv* (New York: Hill and Wang, 1969).

99. Marrus and Paxton, *Vichy France*, 255–339; Gordon, *Collaborationism in France*, 166–194.

100. Leon Poliakov and Jacques Sabille, *Jews Under the Italian Occupation* (Paris: Éditions du Centre, 1955); Marrus and Paxton, *Vichy France*, 112–115, 161–164, 247–248, 265–269; David S. Wyman, *The Abandonment of the Jews: America and the Holocaust 1941–1945* (New York: Pantheon Books, 1984), 30–37.

101. Louis Allen, "Jews and Catholics," in *Vichy France and the Resistance: Culture and Ideology*, ed. Roderick Kedward and Roger Austin (Totowa, N.J.: Barnes & Noble, 1985), 73–87; Bill Halls, "Catholicism Under Vichy: A Study in Diversity and Ambiguity," in *Vichy France and the Resistance*, 133–146; Marrus and Paxton, *Vichy France*, 197–203, 270–279.

102. Fernande Le Boucher, *Incredible Mission*, trans. J. F. Bernard (Garden City, N.Y.: Doubleday, 1969); Philip Friedman, *Their Brothers' Keepers* (New York: Schocken Books, 1978), 49–59.

103. Marrus and Paxton, *Vichy France*, 203–207, 239, 267; Emile C. Fabre, ed., *God's Underground*, (St. Louis, Mo.: Bethany, 1970).

104. Philip P. Hallie, *Lest Innocent Blood Be Shed: The Story of Le Chambon and How*

Goodness Happened There (New York: Harper & Row, 1979); Armin F. C. Boyens, "The Ecumenical Community and the Holocaust," *Annals of the American Academy of Political and Social Science*, 450 (July 1980): 143–147; H. R. Kedward, *Resistance in Vichy France: A Study of Ideas and Motivation in the Southern Zone 1940–1942* (New York: Oxford University Press, 1978), 180–184; *The Courage to Care: Rescuers of Jews During the Holocaust* (New York: New York University Press, 1986), 99–119.

105. David Knout, *Contribution à l'histoire de la Résistance juive en France 1940–1944* (Paris: Éditions du Centre, 1947); David Diamant, *Les Juifs dans la Résistance française 1940–1944* (Paris: Roger Maria, 1971).

106. Steinberg, *Not as a Lamb*, 85–95; Kedward, *Resistance in Vichy France*, 173–174; Ernst Papanek with Edward Linn, *Out of the Fire* (New York: William Morrow, 1975).

107. Yerahmiel Cohen, "French Jewry's Dilemma on the Orientation of Its Leadership (From Polemics to Conciliation: 1942–1944)," *Yad Vashem Studies* 14 (1981): 167–204.

108. Amy Latour, *The Jewish Resistance in France (1940–1944)*, trans. Irene R. Ilton (New York: Holocaust Library, 1981); Steinberg, *Not as a Lamb*, 106–118; Syrkin, *Blessed Is the Match*, 291–306.

109. Marrus and Paxton, *Vichy France*, xi.

110. Susan Zuccotti, *The Italians and the Holocaust: Persecution, Rescue, and Survival* (New York: Basic Books, 1987), xv–xviii. Compare Zuccotti's statistics with Hilberg, *The Destruction*, vol. 2, 665–679.

111. Alan Cassels, *Fascist Italy* (New York: Thomas Y. Crowell, 1968); Ivone Kirkpatrick, *Mussolini: A Study in Power* (New York: Hawthorne, 1964); MacGregor Knox, *Mussolini Unleashed: Politics and Strategy in Fascist Italy's Late War 1939–1941* (New York: Cambridge University Press, 1982); Denis Mack Smith, *Mussolini's Roman Empire* (New York: Viking Press, 1976); Denis Mack Smith, *Mussolini* (New York: Knopf, 1982); Edward R. Tannenbaum, *The Fascist Experience: Italian Society and Culture, 1922–1945* (New York: Basic Books, 1972).

112. Cecil Roth, *The History of the Jews of Italy* (Philadelphia: Jewish Publication Society, 1946), 474; Zoccotti, *The Italians and the Holocaust*, 12–27. A recent article argues that it was the high level of Jewish participation in the unification and emancipation movement that guaranteed Jewish acceptance. See Andrew M. Canepa, "Emancipation and Jewish Response in Mid-19th Century Italy," *European History Quarterly* 16, no. 4 (October 1986): 403–439.

113. Meir Michaelis, *Mussolini and the Jews: German-Italian Relations and the Jewish Question in Italy, 1922–1945* (Oxford, England: Oxford University Press, 1978), 3–103; Michael A. Ledeen, "The Evolution of Italian Fascist Anti-Semitism," *Jewish Social Studies* 37, no. 1 (January 1975): 3–17.

114. Michaelis, *Mussolini and the Jews*, 107–170; Zuccotti, *The Italians and the Holocaust*, 26–38.

115. Michaelis, *Mussolini and the Jews*, 171–275; Zuccotti, *The Italians and the Holocaust*, 36–64.

116. Hilberg, *The Destruction*, vol. 2, 666–668.

117. Laqueur, *The Terrible Secret*, 34–35; according to Laqueur, Mussolini knew what the Germans were doing to the Jews in early 1942.

118. R. Anthony Pedatella, "Italian Attitudes Toward Jewry in the Twentieth

Century," *Jewish Social Studies* 47, no. 1 (Winter 1985): 59; Michaelis, *Mussolini and the Jews,* 295–303.

119. Poliakov and Sabille, *Jews Under the Italian Occupation;* Daniel Carpi, "The Rescue of Jews in the Italian Zone of Occupied Croatia," in *Rescue Attempts During the Holocaust,* Proceedings of the Second Yad Vashem International Historical Conference, Jerusalem, 8–11 April 1974 (New York: Ktav Publishing House, 1978) 465–507; Michael Marrus, *The Unwanted: European Refugees in the Twentieth Century* (New York: Oxford University Press, 1985), 278–281; Zuccotti, *The Italians and the Holocaust,* 74–100.

120. Robert Katz, *Black Sabbath* (New York: Macmillan, 1969); Michaelis, *Mussolini and the Jews,* 337–370; Zuccotti, *The Italians and the Holocaust,* 101–138.

121. Michaelis, *Mussolini and the Jews,* 377–406; Zuccotti, *The Italians and the Holocaust,* 139–200.

122. Zuccotti, *The Italians and the Holocaust,* 229–240, 272–276.

123. Ibid., 201–228; Sam Waagenar, *The Pope's Jews* (LaSalle, Ill.: Alcove, 1974), 377–406.

124. Alexander Ramati, *The Assisi Underground: The Priests Who Rescued Jews* (New York: Stein & Day, 1978).

125. Steinberg, *Not as a Lamb,* 69–78; Masimo Adolfo Vitale, "The Destruction and Resistance of the Jews in Italy," in *They Fought Back: The Story of the Jewish Resistance in Nazi Europe,* ed. Y. Suhl (New York: Schocken Books, 1975) 298–303. For an overview of the Italian resistance, see Charles F. Delzell, *Mussolini's Enemies: The Italian Anti-Fascist Resistance* (Princeton, N.J.: Princeton University Press, 1961). For an account of Jewish participation in the anti-Fascist resistance, see Zuccotti, *The Italians and the Holocaust,* 241–271.

CHAPTER 3   The Acts of Heroism

1. Our quotations from respondents are given with primary consideration to faithfulness to their own words and their recollections of dates and events.

2. J. Presser (*The Destruction of the Dutch Jews* [New York: E. P. Dutton, 1969]) estimates that finding hiding places for Jews was five and a half times more difficult than finding them for non-Jews.

CHAPTER 5   Saving Others: Was It Opportunity or Character?

1. Philip Paul Hallie, *Lest Innocent Blood Be Shed: The Story of Le Chambon and How Goodness Happened There* (New York: Harper & Row, 1979).

CHAPTER 6   The Key to Altruism: Values of Caring

1. The influence of values on human behavior is a matter of some dispute. The eminent sociologist, Talcott Parsons (*The Structure of Social Action* [New York: Free Press, 1939]) perceived them as the heart of social life, but his was a philosophical argument. Although not yet conclusive, more recent empirical findings tend to support Parsons's assertion (Milton Rokeach, *The Nature of Human Values* [New York: Free Press, 1973]).

2. J. P. Meyer and A. Mulherin, "From Attribution to Helping: An Analysis of the Mediating Effects of Affect and Expectancy," *Journal of Personality and Social Psychology* 39 (1980): 201–210.

3. B. Weiner, "A Cognitive (Attribution)-Emotion-Action Model of Motivated Behavior: An Analysis of Judgments of Help Giving," *Journal of Personality and Social Psychology* 39 (1980): 186–200.

4. The association of adult "babylike" features with kindness and lovability were demonstrated in studies done by Ullrich (*Zoopsychologia* [Warsaw: PWN, 1976], cited in J. Reykowski, "Dimensions of Development in Moral Values: Two Approaches to the Development of Morality," in *Social and Moral Values: Individual and Societal Perspectives,* ed. N. Eisenberg, J. Reykowski, and E. Staub [Hillsdale, N.J.: Lawrence Erlbaum, 1987]), and L. Z. MacArthur and K. Apatow ("Impressions of Baby-Faced Adults," *Social Cognition* 2, no. 4 [1983–84]: 315–342).

5. Daniel Levinson, "The Study of Ethnocentric Ideology," in *The Authoritarian Personality,* ed. T. W. Adorno et al. (New York: W. W. Norton, 1950).

6. Viola W. Bernard, Perry Ottenberg, and Fritz Redl, "Dehumanization," in *Sanctions for Evil,* ed. R. Nevitt Sanford and Craig Comstock (San Francisco: Jossey-Bass, 1971), 102–135. Bernard, Ottenberg and Redl further note that the tendency toward dehumanization of others increases in periods of uncertainty because it provides a sense that one has coped with the situation without really confronting it.

7. T. W. Adorno (*The Authoritarian Personality,* ed. T. W. Adorno et al. [New York: W. W. Norton, 1950]).

8. C. Glock and R. Stark, *Christian Beliefs and Anti-Semitism* (New York: Harper & Row, 1966); M. Rokeach, "A Mighty Fortress: Faith, Hope and Bigotry," *Psychology Today* (April 1970): 33–58; J. E. Dittes, *Bias and the Pious* (Minneapolis, Minn.: Augsburg Publishing, 1973). Glock explains this as a result of Christian particularism, "a disposition to see Christian truth as the *only* religious truth," 208. Particularism results in two responses—missionary zealousness in converting others, which, if not successful, results in an expression of the latent hostility implied in particularism. Rokeach explains it as a self-centered preoccupation with personal salvation that results in an otherworldly orientation coupled with indifference toward social inequality and injustice.

9. Jan Tomasz Gross, *Polish Society under German Occupation: The Generalgouvernement, 1939–1944* (Princeton, N.J.: Princeton University Press, 1979).

10. Lucien Steinberg, *Not as a Lamb: The Jews Against Hitler,* trans. M. Hunter (Farnborough, England: Saxon House, 1974).

11. More than sixty political parties were named by our respondents. The following are representative examples of identified parties and their categorization:

Economic Left

France   Section Française de l'Internationale Ouvrière (SFIO)
            Parti Communiste Français (PCF)

Germany Sozialdemokratische Partei Deutschlands (SPD)

Holland   Nieuwenhuis, Domela (1846–1919)
            Sociaal–Democratische Arbeiders Partij (SDAP)
            Onafhankelijke Socialistsche Partij (OSP)

Poland   Polska Partia Socjalistyczna (PPS)
            Polska Partia Robotnicza

Democratic

France	Section Française de l'Internationale Ouvrière (SFIO)
	Action Catholique
Germany	Sozialdemokratische Partei Deutschlands (SPD)
	Deutsche Demokratische Partei (DDP)
	Deutsche Volkspartei (DVP)
Holland	Nieuwenhuis, Domela (1846–1919)
	Anti-Revolutionaire Partij (ARP)
	Vrijzinnig-Democratische Bond (VDB)
	Christelijk Historische Unie (CHU)
	Sociaal-Democratische Arbeiders Partij (SDAP)
Poland	Polska Partia Socjalistyzna (PPS)
	OMTUR
	Stronnictwo Ludowe

All the above parties, with the exception of Stronnictwo Ludowe, were at least tolerant toward minorities and Jews. Stronnictwo Ludowe abstained from opposing anti-Semitism and saw voluntary immigration as a solution to the Jewish problem—they did, however, support Zegota. Economically leftist groups noted above did more than tolerate Jews—they were advocates of Jewish rights. Most affiliated Polish rescuers in our sample were members of PPS. A small percentage of rescuers say that they or their parents (sometimes both) belonged to Nazi parties in Germany, the Fascist party in Italy, and assorted right-wing groups in France (for example, Croix de Feu, Action Française) and Poland (for example, Stronnictwo Narodowe/ Endecja).

12. Bruno Bettelheim, *The Informed Heart: Autonomy in a Mass Age* (New York: Avon, 1971), 69.

13. Else Frenkel-Brunswik, "Parents and Childhood," in *The Authoritarian Personality,* ed. T. W. Adorno et al. (New York: W. W. Norton, 1950), 337–389.

14. Nechama Tec (*Dry Tears: The Story of a Lost Childhood* [New York: Oxford University Press, 1984]) reports that financial gain was the critical factor for some of her helpers. Survivor accounts in the files of the Altruistic Personality Project also refer to those who exploited the victims. For further discussion of those who helped for money in Poland, see Tec, *When Light Pierced the Darkness: Christian Rescue of Jews in Nazi-Occupied Poland* (New York: Oxford University Press, 1986).

15. Frances G. Grossman ("A Psychological Study of Gentiles Who Saved the Lives of Jews During the Holocaust," in *Toward the Understanding and Prevention of Genocide,* ed. Israel W. Charny [Boulder, Colo.: Westview Press, 1984], 202–216), who had the opportunity to study nine rescuers in depth during the course of therapeutic sessions, also agreed that they were essentially conventional people.

16. Alice Miller, *For Your Own Good: Hidden Cruelty in Child-Rearing and the Roots of Violence* (New York: Farrar, Straus & Giroux, 1984).

17. B. R. Schlenker, J. R. Hallam, and N. E. McCown, "Motives and Social Evaluation: Actor–Observer Differences in the Delineation of Motives for a Beneficial Act," *Journal of Experimental Social Psychology* 19 (1983): 254–273.

18. Immanuel Kant, *Observations on the Feeling of the Beautiful and the Sublime,* trans. J. T. Goldwait (Berkeley: University of California Press, 1965); Kant, *The Doctrine of Virtue,* trans. Mary Gregor (New York: Harper & Row, 1964);

Kant, *Foundations of the Metaphysics of Morals,* trans. L. W. Beck (New York: Bobbs-Merrill, 1959); John A. Rawls, *A Theory of Justice* (Cambridge, Mass.: Harvard University Press, 1971); C. Fried, An *Anatomy of Values: Problems of Personal and Social Choice* (Cambridge, Mass.: Harvard University Press, 1970); David A. J. Richards, *A Theory of Reasons for Action* (New York: Oxford University Press, 1971); L. Kohlberg, "Stage and Sequence: The Cognitive-Developmental Approach to Socialization," in *Handbook of Socialization Theory and Research,* ed. D. A. Goslin (New York: Rand McNally, 1969); Kohlberg, "From Is to Ought; How to Commit the Naturalistic Fallacy and Get Away With It in the Study of Moral Development," in *Cognitive Development and Epistemology,* ed. T. Mischel (New York: Academic Press, 1971); Kohlberg, "Moral Stages and Moralization: The Cognitive-Developmental Approach," in *Moral Development and Behavior,* ed. T. Lickona (New York: Holt, Rinehart & Winston, 1976).

19. *Justice* is the preferred term among several social scientists. As generally used, it includes many of the same components. K. S. Cook and K. A. Hegtvedt (in "Distributive Justice, Equity, and Equality," *Annual Review of Sociology* 9 [1983]: 217–241) identified five different uses of the concept of justice in social science literature: (1) as equity or fair exchange, (2) as distributive justice or fair allocation, (3) as fair procedures, (4) as retributive or just compensation, and (5) as principles of equality. We prefer the term *equity,* because the term *justice* has frequently been associated with the philosophical or psychological viewpoint of a particular author—*equity* is less subject to such particularistic interpretation.

20. Iris Murdoch, *The Sovereignty of Good* (London: Routledge & Kegan Paul, 1970); Lawrence A. Blum, *Friendship, Altruism and Morality* (London: Routledge & Kegan Paul, 1980); Nel Noddings, *Caring: A Feminine Approach to Ethics and Moral Education* (Berkeley: University of California Press, 1984); Carol Gilligan, *In a Different Voice: Psychological Theory and Women's Development* (Cambridge, Mass.: Harvard University Press, 1982); Jean Baker Miller, *Toward a New Psychology of Women* (Boston: Beacon Press, 1976); Nancy Chodorow, "Family Structure and Feminine Personality," in *Women, Culture and Society,* ed. M. Z. Rosaldo and L. Lamphere (Stanford, Calif.: Stanford University Press, 1974).

CHAPTER 7   The Roots of Human Attachments

1. Definitions of personality vary, depending largely on theoretical orientations. Most commonly, *personality* refers to relatively enduring internally determined predispositions underlying behavior rather than behavior itself (Irvin L. Child, "Personality in Culture," in *Handbook of Personality Theory and Research,* ed. E. F. Borgatta and W. W. Lambert [New York: Rand McNally, 1968]; Robert LeVine, *Culture, Behavior, and Personality* [New York: Aldine Publishing, 1982]). This would include diverse internal psychological processes, including perception, cognition, emotional reactions as well as attitudes and values. Our use of the word *personality* as distinct from *attitudes* and *values* is somewhat arbitrary. In making this distinction, we do not mean to imply that the latter are not part of personality, but rather that they represent cognitive representations of appropriate behavior—standards regarding what one *should* do. Our emphasis here is on the affective components of personality a manifested in emotional drives and demonstrated in behavior itself.

2. J. Bowlby, *Attachment* (New York: Basic Books, 1969); *Separation* (New York: Basic Books, 1973).

3. M. D. S. Ainsworth (*Infancy in Uganda: Infant Care and the Growth of Attachment* [Baltimore, Md.: Johns Hopkins University Press, 1967]) distinguishes between securely attached and nonsecurely attached children. Securely attached children do not experience the same anxiety when their mothers leave. This may be due to differing needs of individual children as well as the varied responses of their mothers.

4. S. Freud, *An Autobiographical Study*, trans. J. Strachey (London: Hogarth Press, 1935).

5. E. H. Erikson, *Childhood and Society* (New York: W. W. Norton, 1950).

6. H. R. Schaffer and P. E. Emerson, "The Development of Social Attachments in Infancy," *Monographs of the Society for Research in Child Development* 29, no. 3 (1964); Arlene S. Skolnick, *The Psychology of Human Development* (New York: Harcourt Brace Jovanovich, 1986).

7. A. Freud and S. Dann, "An Experiment in Group Upbringing," in *Psychoanalytic Study on the Child*, ed. R. S. Eissler et al. (New York: International Universities Press, 1951), 127–168.

8. Cited in W. W. Hartup, "Peer Relations," in *Handbook of Child Psychology: Socialization, Personality and Social Development*, vol. 4, ed. P. H. Mussen (New York: John Wiley & Sons, 1983), 103–196.

9. A family closeness factor was derived from four questions. (See Table 7.16.) The mean score of rescuers on this factor was significantly higher than that of bystanders as well as all nonrescuers.

10. The Social Responsibility Scale was developed by L. Berkowitz and K. Lutterman; see "The Traditionally Socially Responsible Personality," *Public Opinion Quarterly* 32 (1968): 169–185.

11. The term empathy has been used to mean a cognitive response, an affective response, and sometimes both. As a cognitive process, it is the ability to understand what others are feeling, discriminating among cues to assess others' emotional states and, at a more advanced level, assuming the perspective of the other so as to understand his or her very thoughts and intentions. As an affective reaction, empathy means being emotionally aroused by the feelings of others. The Empathy Scale we used measures emotional empathy only.

12. See Nancy Eisenberg, *Altruistic Emotion, Cognition, and Behavior* (Hillsdale, N.J.: Erlbaum, 1986), chap. 3, for a good summary of empathy research. Empathy has been identified by several investigators as contributing to rescue behavior specifically (S. P. Oliner, "The Unsung Heroes in Nazi-Occupied Europe: The Antidote for Evil," *Nationalities Papers* 12 [Spring 1984]: 129–136; F. G. Grossman, "A Psychological Study of Gentiles Who Saved the Lives of Jews During the Holocaust," in *Toward the Understanding and Prevention of Genocide*, ed. I. Charny [Boulder, Colo.: Westview Press, 1984]).

13. The abbreviated scale we used was adapted by E. Midlarsky from the Empathy Scale developed by A. Mehrabian and N. A. Epstein ("A Measure of Emotional Empathy," *Journal of Personality* 40 [1972]: 525–543); it includes nineteen items.

14. This difference emerged when we did a factor analysis using all forty-two items in all personality scales. This analysis produced three highly intercor-

related factors. One, which we labeled a "prosocial action orientation," distinguished rescuers significantly from all other groups (Table 7.3). The prosocial action factor consisted of twelve intercorrelated variables of which eight were empathy items. (See Table 7.16, Prosocial Action Orientation, for factor loadings.) Of these, five items related to the pain or helplessness of others. Four items related to feelings of social responsibility.

15. The "detachment" factor consisted of seven intercorrelated items. (See Table 7.16, Detachment, for factor loadings.)

16. In general, the more like oneself others are perceived to be, the greater one's inclination to think well of them and help them. Events that endanger people perceived as similar are more likely to be perceived as threats to the self. A number of studies demonstrate the cogency of this hypothesis, showing, for example, that people are more likely to help those who share similar interests, belong to similar social groups, or even come from the same town. See J. Karylowski, *Z Badan Nad Mechanizmani Pozytywnych Ustosunkowan Interpersonalnych* (Wroclaw, Poland: Ossolineaum, 1975), cited in Reykowski, "Spatial Organization"; M. A. Smoleńska, "Dystans Psychologiczny Partnera A Dzialanie Na Jego Rzecz," Ph.D. diss. (University of Warsaw, 1979), cited in Reykowski, "Spatial Organization"; J. A. Piliavin and J. M. Piliavin, *The Good Samaritan: Why Does He Help?* (unpublished manuscript, n. d.).; for a summary of studies showing the tendency to help those perceived as similar, see E. Staub, *Positive Social Behavior and Morality* (New York: Academic Press, 1979).

Stated another way, one might say that those perceived as close to the self are humanized; conversely, those perceived as remote from the self are susceptible to dehumanization. Dehumanization facilitates the perpetration of atrocities on remote others; but, of course, it need not be manifested in such extreme behavior. Dehumanization also allows remote others to be "written off," with or without malicious intent. As Bernard, Ottenberg, and Redl point out:

> Under the impact of ... dehumanization, one stops identifying with others by seeing them as essentially non-similar to oneself in basic human qualities. Relationships to others become stereotyped, rigid, and above all, unexpressive of mutuality. People in "out groups" are apt to be reacted to en bloc; feelings of concern for them have become anesthetized. ... The indifference resulting from that form of dehumanization which causes one to view others as inanimate objects enables one, without conscious malice or selfishness, to write off their misery, injustices, and death as something that "just couldn't be helped."

See Viola W. Bernard, Perry Ottenberg, and Fritz Redl, "Dehumanization," in *Sanctions for Evil*, ed. R. N. Sanford, C. Comstock, and associates (San Francisco: Jossey-Bass Publishers, 1971), 102–135, 112, 116.

17. P. London ("The Rescuers: Motivational Hypotheses About Christians Who Saved Jews from the Nazis," in *Altruism and Helping Behavior*, ed. J. Macaulay and L. Berkowitz [New York: Academic Press, 1970], 241–250) emphasized marginality as a particular characteristic of one type of rescuer, among whom it was induced by virtue of some disability or by having parents differing from others in religion, politics, life style or birthplace. Tec (*When Light Pierced the Darkness*) also maintained that "separateness" distinguished the Polish rescuers she interviewed. They did not fit into their milieus, even

if they were not consciously aware that they did not. Marginality has also been linked with aggressive behavior. J. M. Steiner (*Power Politics and Social Change in National Socialist Germany: A Process of Escalation into Mass Destruction* [The Hague: Mouton; Atlantic Highlands, N.J.: Humanities Press, 1976]), for example, found that marginality was characteristic of many who joined the SS.

18. The Internal/External Locus of Control Scale was developed by J. B. Rotter ("Generalized Expectancies for Internal Versus External Control of Reinforcement," *Psychological Monographs* 80, no. 1, [1966]). We used an adaptation developed by G. Gurin, P. Gurin, and B. M. Morrison ("Personal and Ideological Aspects of Internal and External Control," *Social Psychology* 41, no. 4 [1978]: 275–296) derived from a factor analysis of Rotter's scale on a national probability sample.

19. The Self-Esteem Scale we used was developed by M. Rosenberg (*Society and the Adolescent Self-Image* [Princeton, N.J.: Princeton University Press, 1965]). It includes ten items measuring the self-acceptance aspect of self-esteem. Strong agreement with statements such as, "I feel that I have a number of good qualities," "I take a positive attitude toward myself," and strong disagreement with "I feel I do not have much to be proud of," and "I certainly feel useless at times" are scored as high self-esteem responses.

20. W. James, *The Principles of Psychology*, vol. 1 (New York: Henry Holt & Co., 1896), 310.

21. C. Minton, J. Kagan, and J. Levine, "Maternal Control and Obedience in the Two-year-old," *Child Development* 62 (1971), 1873–1894; H. Lytton, "Disciplinary Encounters Between Young Boys and Their Mothers and Fathers: Is There a Contingency System?," *Developmental Psychology* 15 (1979), 256–268; P. Schoggen, "Environmental Forces in the Everyday Lives of Children," in *The Stream of Behavior: Explorations of Its Structure and Content*, ed. R. G. Barker (New York: Appleton-Century-Crofts, 1963).

22. M. L. Hoffman, "Conscience, Personality and Socialization Techniques," *Human Development* 13 (1970): 90–126; "Moral Internalization: Current Theory and Research" in *Advances in Experimental Social Psychology*, ed. L. Berkowitz (New York: Academic Press, 1977).

23. Each type was derived from a summary factor analysis of synthesized variables which included a field matrix of 27 variables. These synthesized variables, reflecting more than 100 single variables, were derived in one of two ways: simple linear summation (adding scores) of responses to combined variables or through a factor analysis of a set of variables and the creation of factor scores for each set. (For a description of the field matrix, see Table 7.16. For factor loadings relevant to each type, see Table 7.15.)

24. An ANOVA analysis showed rescuers to be significantly different from nonrescuers and bystanders with respect to all four factors.

25. A notable exception with respect to this factor were active nonrescuers. Their score on this measure was higher than that of rescuers. We interpret this to mean that active nonrescuers valued social involvement highly and accepted broad social responsibilities but that their failure to act on behalf of Jews in a more consistent fashion largely stemmed from the nature of their formal resistance networks, whose objectives did not include or accommodate this task.

CHAPTER 8   Concern into Action

1. With the exception of the term "normocentric," Reykowski ("Dimensions of Development in Moral Values: Two Approaches to the Development of Morality," in *Social and Moral Values: Individual and Societal Perspectives,* ed. N. Eisenberg, J. Reykowski, E. Staub [Hillsdale, N.J.: Lawrence Erlbaum, 1987]) uses other labels to describe these motivational mechanisms: *allocentric* for empathy, *axiological* for principled, and *ipsocentric* for self-enhancement. He prefers *allocentric* because an empathic reaction is most commonly interpreted to mean that the individual recognizes the feelings and thoughts of another. He argues, however, that people can be motivated to care for others despite the fact that they do not take their perspectives or even in ignorance of others' feelings. The term *allocentric* simply means having one's attention centered on other persons without reference to the psychological mechanisms that may explain it. Whereas *principles* refer to fundamental and guiding doctrines or truths in varied forms of discourse, including science and ethics, *axiological* generally refers to values and ethics only. Although we prefer Reykowski's terms because of their conceptual clarity, we have used more familiar words to facilitate communication.

   While Reykowski's motivational categories have their roots in the work of others who have studied prosocial behavior (see for example, N. Eisenberg, "The Development of Reasoning Regarding Prosocial Behavior," in *Development of Prosocial Behavior,* ed. N. Eisenberg [New York: Academic Press, 1982], 219–251), not all authors acknowledge a difference between allocentric, normocentric, and axiological motives. S. H. Schwartz and J. A. Howard ("Internalized Values as Motivators of Altruism," in *Development and Maintenance of Prosocial Behavior: International Perspectives on Positive Morality,* ed. Ervin Staub et al. [New York: Plenum Press, 1984], 229–253), for example, contend that personal norms—immediate rules for action in specific situations—derive from values. Reykowski agrees with Schwartz that rules for behavior in specific situations derive from more general abstractions but claims that they can derive from allocentric concern with another person's welfare, from general norms, or from moral principles.

2. Reykowski distinguishes between two types of empathic reactions, primary and secondary. Primary and secondary empathic reactions are due to different types of sensitivity to cues about others' distress. M. L. Hoffman ("Empathy and Prosocial Activism," in *Social and Moral Values: Individual and Societal Perspectives,* ed. N. Eisenberg, J. Reykowski, and E. Staub [Hillsdale, N.J.: Lawrence Erlbaum, 1987]) also distinguishes between two kinds of empathy: "empathy for another's feelings" and "empathy for another's life conditions." The former appears as the result of direct exposure to expressive or verbal cues; the latter depends on information about the distressing situation of another person.

3. The explanation of prosocial and altruistic behavior in terms of conformity to social norms is popular among social psychologists. See L. Berkowitz, "Social Norms, Feelings, and Other Factors Affecting Helping and Altruism," *Advances in Experimental Social Psychology,* vol. 6 (New York: Academic Press, 1972); Daniel Bar Tal, *Prosocial Behavior: Theory and Research* (New York: John Wiley & Sons, 1976); D. L. Krebs and D. T. Miller, "Altruism and Aggression," *Handbook of Social Psychology,* vol. 2 (New York: Random House, 1985).

4. Carol Gilligan, *In a Different Voice: Psychological Theory and Women's Development* (Cambridge, Mass.: Harvard University Press, 1982).

5. Categorizing motives was a lengthy and complicated procedure. Five coders (psychology and sociology students) met jointly with P. Oliner for a period of twelve weeks. The first few weeks were used as training sessions and for conceptual refinements. Coders were instructed to focus on the motivation orientation that appeared to characterize the first helping act only. Coders then began to do independent ratings, reserving group meeting for highly problematic cases. Interrater reliability (.75) was calculated for 110 cases not discussed by the group.

In making their determination, coders relied on several sources: the rescue story itself, specific questions relating to the conditions under which the first helping act occurred (for example, where the person was living; others living in the household, position in the household; if they were asked to help or initiated it; if asked, who asked them; the relationship of the asker to the rescuer; whether they were members of resistance groups) as well as the reasons rescuers gave for helping. Hence, it was not a single item or phrase that determined the categorization of motivation but rather several interrelated items.

Nonetheless, these procedures were accompanied by many problems, not all of which were resolved conclusively. Sufficient details were not always provided, and translations themselves were not of uniform quality. Knowledge of the particular culture and national conditions was sometimes needed to make sense of given phrases. Many of the latter problems were overcome by virtue of becoming accustomed to a particular national style; the first set of French, Poles, and so on was usually more difficult to deal with than subsequent ones.

Most troublesome were uncertainties regarding distinctions between given categories as they applied to concrete cases. Discriminating between a generalized empathic response and a principled motivation of caring was sometimes quite difficult—in several cases, discrepancies regarding such distinctions were not resolved. Where consensus did not emerge after considerable discussion, we simply alternated assignment to these respective categories, calling one empathic and the other principled.

It was equally difficult at times to discriminate between an internalized normocentric orientation and a principled one. Both orientations can generate highly independent actions—behaviors undertaken without any apparent social support. Moreover, principled-like statements would sometimes appear conjointly with references to authoritative social groups—for example, "Christians must help all persons in need." We concluded that if the authoritative social source could be identified and, moreover, was mentioned throughout the rescue story, it represented an internalized normocentric response. If, however, the social authoritative source was omitted from the narrative or reasons or mentioned in a cursory fashion only (a passing reference such as, "I felt God would approve") and a principled statement involving justice or care was given either in the narrative or reasons, it represented a principled motivation.

The coders, too, had to overcome some psychological biases. Group members developed strong feelings of admiration—sometimes intense affection—for particular individuals. It was tempting to place such people in those categories sometimes presumed to be of "higher" moral virtue. Coders needed to be reminded repeatedly that people in a variety of categories were capable of great self-sacrifice and noble character.

6. I. Murdoch, *The Sovereignty of Good* (London: Routledge & Kegan Paul, 1970).

CHAPTER 10   Moral Heroism and Extensivity

1. Scholars from assorted disciplines have supported this tradition, including L. Kohlberg ("Moral Stages and Moralization: The Cognitive-Developmental Approach," in *Moral Development and Behavior,* ed. T. Lickona [New York: Holt, Rinehart & Winston, 1976]); J. Piaget (*The Moral Judgment of the Child* [New York: Free Press, 1948]); David Riesman, Reuel Denney, and Nathan Glazer (*The Lonely Crowd: A Study of The Changing American Character* [New Haven: Yale University Press, 1950]); and D. A. J. Richards (*A Theory of Reasons for Action* [New York: Oxford University Press, 1971]). It has penetrated much of popular culture, so that desired behaviors are routinely advocated as forms of autonomy.

2. N. Tec, *When Light Pierced the Darkness: Christian Rescue of Jews in Nazi-Occupied Poland* (New York: Oxford University Press, 1986); P. London, "The Rescuers: Motivational Hypotheses about Christians who Saved Jews from the Nazis," in *Altruism and Helping Behavior,* ed. J. Macaulay and L. Berkowitz (New York: Academic Press, 1970).

3. T. W. Adorno et al. *The Authoritarian Personality* (New York: W. W. Norton, 1950).

4. Vassily Grossman, *Life and Fate* (New York: Harper & Row, 1985).

5. H. D. Forbes, *Nationalism, Ethnocentrism and Personality: Social Science and Critical Theory* (Chicago: University of Chicago Press, 1985), 181.

6. Lawrence Blum, *Friendship, Altruism and Morality* (London: Routledge & Kegan Paul, 1980).

7. Carol Gilligan, *In a Different Voice: Psychological Theory and Women's Development* (Cambridge, Mass.: Harvard University Press, 1982).

8. Nel Noddings, *Caring: A Feminine Approach to Ethics and Moral Education* (Berkeley: University of California Press, 1984).

9. For a discussion of how caring schools promote citizenship education, see Pearl Oliner, "Putting 'Community' Into Citizenship Education: The Need for Prosociality," *Theory and Research in Social Education* 11, no. 2 (Summer 1983): 65–84. For a discussion of how education for caring is different from values education and education for moral development, see Pearl Oliner, "Implementing and Legitimating Prosocial Education," *Humboldt Journal of Social Relations* 13 (1985/86): 389–408. Practical suggestions for incorporating caring content into the social studies curriculum can be found in Pearl Oliner, "Compassion and Caring: Missing Concepts in Social Studies Programs," *Journal of Education* 161, no. 4 (Fall 1979): 36–60; and "Putting Compassion and Caring into Social Studies Classrooms," *Social Education* 47, no. 4 (April 1983): 273–277.

10. W. I. Thomas and D. S. Thomas, *The Child in America* (New York: Knopf, 1928), 572.

APPENDIX A   Methodology

1. Jack Botwinick, *Aging and Behavior: A Comprehensive Integration of Research Findings* (New York: Springer, 1984).

Selected Bibliography

Abramsky, C., Jachimczyk, M., and Polonsky, A., eds. *The Jews in Poland.* New York: Basil Blackwell Ltd., 1986.

Abramson, L. Y, Seligman, M. E. P.; and Teasdale, J. D. "Learned Helplessness in Humans: a Critique and Reformulation." *Journal of Abnormal Psychology* 87, no. 1 (1978): 49–74.

Adam, U. D. *Judenpolitik im Dritten Reich.* Düsseldorf: Droste Verlag, 1972.

Adorno, T. W.; Frenkel-Brunswik, E.; Levinson, D. J.; and Sanford, R. N. *The Authoritarian Personality.* New York: W. W. Norton, 1950.

Agar, H. *The Saving Remnant: An Account of Jewish Survival.* New York: Viking, 1960.

Ainsworth, M. D. S. *Infancy in Uganda: Infant Care and the Growth of Attachment.* Baltimore, Md.: Johns Hopkins University Press, 1967.

Ainsztein, R. "Jewish Tragedy and Heroism in Soviet War Literature." *Jewish Social Studies* 23, no. 2, (April 1961): 67–84.

Ainsztein, R. *Jewish Resistance in Nazi-Occupied Eastern Europe.* New York: Barnes & Noble, 1975.

Allen, L. "Jews and Catholics." In *Vichy France and the Resistance: Culture and Ideology.* Ed. H. R. Kedward and R. Austin. New York: Barnes & Noble, 1985.

Allen, W. S. "Objective and Subjective Inhibitants in the German Resistance." In *The German Church Struggle and the Holocaust.* Ed. F. H. Littell and H. G. Locke. Detroit, Mich.: Wayne State University Press, 1974.

Anger, P. *With Raoul Wallenberg in Budapest: Memories of the War Years in Hungary.* Trans. D. M. Paul and M. Paul. New York: Holocaust Library, 1981.

Angress, W. T. "The German Jews, 1933–1939." In *The Holocaust: Ideology, Bureaucracy and Genocide.* Ed. H. Friedlander and S. Milton. Millwood, N.Y.: Kraus International Publications, 1980.

Arad, Y. *Belzec, Sobibor, Treblinka.* Bloomington: Indiana University Press, 1987.

Arad, Y. "The 'Final Solution' in Lithuania in the Light of German Documentation." *Yad Vashem Studies* 11 (1976): 234–272.

Arad, Y., Gutman, Y., and Margaliot, A., eds. *Documents on the Holocaust.* Jerusalem: Yad Vashem, 1981.

Arczyński, M. "Rada Pomocy Żydom W Polsce" (Council for aid to Jews). *Biuletyn Żydowskiego Instytutu Historycznego* 65–66 (1968): 173–185.

Arendt, H. "From the Dreyfus Affair to France Today." *Jewish Social Studies* 4, no. 3 (July 1942): 195–240.

Arendt, H. *Eichmann in Jerusalem.* New York: Viking Compass, 1965.

Arendt, H. *The Origins of Totalitarianism.* New York: Harcourt Brace Jovanovich, 1973.

Arkin, R. M.; Gleason, J. M.; and Johnsten, S. "Effects of Perceived Choice, Expected Outcome, and Observed Outcome of an Actor on the Causal Attributions of Actors." *Journal of Experimental Social Psychology* 12 (1976) : 151–158.

Aronsfeld, C. C. *The Text of the Holocaust: A Study of the Nazis' Extermination Propaganda:* 1919–1945. Marblehead, Mass.: Micah Publications, 1985.

Atkinson, J. W., and Birch, D. *Introduction to Motivation.* 2d ed. New York: D. Van Nostrand Co., 1978.

Avni, H. "The Zionist Underground in Holland and France and the Escape to Spain." In *Rescue Attempts During the Holocaust,* Proceedings of the Second Yad Vashem International Historical Conference, Jerusalem, 8–11 April 1974. New York: Ktav Publishing House, 1978.

Baltes, P. B., and Reese, H. W. "The Life-Span Perspective in Developmental Psychology." In *Developmental Psychology: An Advanced Textbook.* Ed. M. H. Bornstein and M. E. Lamb. Hillsdale, N.J.: Lawrence Erlbaum, 1984.

Bandura, A. *Social Learning Theory.* Englewood Cliffs, N.J.: Prentice-Hall, 1977.

Bar-Tal, D. *Prosocial Behavior: Theory and Research.* New York: John Wiley & Sons, 1976.

Bar-Tal, D., and Raviv, A. "A Cognitive-Learning Model of Helping Behavior Development: Possible Implications and Applications." In *The Development of Prosocial Behavior.* Ed. N. Eisenberg. New York: Academic Press, 1982.

Bar-Tal, D.; Raviv, A.; and Leiser, T. "The Development of Altruistic Behavior: Empirical Evidence." *Developmental Psychology* 16 (1980): 516–524.

Bar-Tal, D.; Sharabany, R.; and Raviv, A. "Cognitive Basis of the Development of Altruistic Behavior." In *Cooperation and Helping Behavior: Theories and Research.* Eds. V. J. Derlega and J. Grzelak. New York: Academic Press, 1982.

Barkai, M., ed. *The Fighting Ghettos.* Philadelphia: Lippincott, 1962.

Barnett, K.; Darcie, G.; Holland, C. J.; and Kobasigawa, A. "Children's Cognitions About Effective Helping." *Developmental Psychology* 18 (1982): 267–277.

Baron, L. "Interview with Marion P. Pritchard." *Sh'ma* 14 (April 27, 1984): 97.

Baron, L. "Post-Holocaust Resistance to Righteousness." Unpublished manuscript, 1984.

Baron, L. "Restoring Faith in Humankind." *Sh'ma* 14 (Sept. 7, 1984): 124–128.

Baron, L. "Teaching the Holocaust to Non-Jews." *Shoah* 2, no. 2 (Sping 1981): 14–15.

Baron, L. "The Holocaust and Human Decency: A Review of Research on the Rescue of Jews in Nazi Occupied Europe." *Humboldt Journal of Social Relations* 13, no. 1–2 (1985/86): 237–251.

Baron, S. W. "Changing Patterns in Anti-Semitism." *Jewish Social Studies* 38, no. 1 (Winter 1976) : 5–38.

Barrett, D. E., and Yarrow, M. R. "Prosocial Behavior, Social Inferential Ability, and Assertiveness in Young Children." *Child Development* 48 (1977) : 475–481.

Bartoszewski, W., and Lewin, Z. *The Righteous Among the Nations.* London: Earls Court, 1969.

Bartoszewski, W., and Lewin, Z., eds. *The Samaritans: Heroes of the Holocaust.* New York: Twayne Publishers, 1970.

Batson, C. D., and Coke, J. S. "Empathy: A Source of Altruistic Motivation for Helping?" In *Altruism and Helping Behavior: Social, Personality, and Developmental Perspectives.* Ed. J. P. Rushton and R. M. Sorrentino. Hillsdale, N.J.: Lawrence Erlbaum, 1981.

Bauer, Y. "Genocide: Was It The Nazis' Original Plan?" *Annals of the American Academy of Political and Social Science* 450 (July 1980): 35–45.

Bauer, Y. *A History of the Holocaust.* New York: Franklin Watts, 1982.

Bauer, Y. *American Jewry and the Holocaust: The American Joint Distribution Committee, 1939–1945.* Detroit, Mich.: Wayne State University Press, 1981.

Bauer, Y. *Flight and Rescue: Brichah—The Organized Escape of the Jewish Survivors of Eastern Europe, 1944–1948.* New York: Random House, 1970.

Bauer, Y. *The Holocaust in Historical Perspective.* Seattle: University of Washington Press, 1978.

Bauer, Y. *They Chose Life.* New York: American Jewish Committee, 1973.

Baum, R. *Holocaust and the German Elite: Genocide and National Suicide in Germany.* New York: Rowman & Littlefield, 1981.

Bauminger, A. "Righteous Gentiles." *Jewish Spectator* 27–31 (September 1964) : 9–10.

Bauminger, A. *The Righteous.* Jerusalem: Yad Vashem, 1983.

Bejski, M. "The 'Righteous Among the Nations' and Their Part in the Rescue of Jews." In *Rescue Attempts During the Holocaust,* Proceedings of the Second Yad Vashem International Historical Conference, Jerusalem, 8–11 April 1974. New York: Ktav Publishing House, 1978.

Belinfante, J. C. E. *Joods Historisch Museum.* Haarlem: Joh. Enschede en Zonen Grafische Inrichting, 1978.

Bellah, R. N. "Organic Solidarity and Contractual Solidarity." In *Emile Durkheim: On Morality and Society.* Ed. R. N. Bellah. Chicago: University of Chicago Press, 1973.

Bellah, R. N. *Tokugawa Religion.* Glencoe, Ill.: Free Press, 1957.

Bellah, R. N., ed. *Emile Durkheim: On Morality and Society.* Chicago: University of Chicago Press, 1973.

Belshaw, C. S. "The Identification of Values in Anthropology." *American Journal of Sociology* 64 (1959): 555–562.

Berenstein, T., and Rutkowski, A. "O Ratowaniu Żydów Przez Polaków W Okresie Okupacji Hitlerowskiej" (Polish rescue of Jews during the occupation). *Biuletyn Żydowskiego Instytutu Historycznego.* 35 (1960): 3–46.

Berenstein, T., and Rutkowski, A. *Assistance to the Jews in Poland (1939–1945).* Warsaw: Polonia Foreign Languages Publishing House, 1963.

Berkowitz, L. "Social Norms, Feelings, and Other Factors Affecting Helping and Altruism." In *Advances in Experimental Social Psychology,* vol. 6. Ed. L. Berkowitz. New York: Academic Press, 1972.

Berkowitz, L. "The Self, Selfishness, and Altruism." In *Altruism and Helping Behavior.* Ed. J. Macaulay and L. Berkowitz. New York: Academic Press, 1970.

Berkowitz, L. and Lutterman, K. "The Traditionally Socially Responsible Personality." *Public Opinion Quarterly* 32 (1968): 169–185.

Bernard, R., Sanford, R. N., Comstock, C., and associates. "The Problems of Information Accuracy: Validity of Retrospective Data." *Annual Review of Anthropology* 13 (1984): 495–517.

Bernard, V. W.; Ottenberg, P.; and Redl, F. "Dehumanization." In *Sanctions for Evil.* Ed. R. N. Sanford, C. Comstock, and associates. San Francisco: Jossey-Bass Publishers, 1971.

Bertelsen, A. *October '43.* New York: Putnam, 1954.

Bethell, N. *The War Hitler Won: The Fall of Poland, September 1939.* New York: Holt, Rinehart & Winston, 1972.

Bettelheim, B. *Surviving and Other Essays.* New York: Knopf, 1979.

Bettelheim, B. *The Informed Heart: Autonomy in a Mass Age.* New York: Avon, 1971.

Bierman, J. *Righteous Gentile: The Story of Raoul Wallenberg.* New York: Viking, 1981.

"Big Kids Teach Little Kids: What We Know About Cross-Age Tutoring." *Harvard Education Letter* 3, no. 3 (1987).

Birnbaum, H. *Hope is the Last to Die.* New York: Twayne Publishers, 1971.

Biss, A. *A Million Jews to Save.* New York: Barnes & Noble, 1975.

Blackburn, G. W. *Education in the Third Reich: Race and History in Nazi Textbooks.* Albany: State University of New York Press, 1984.

Blasi, A. "Bridging Moral Cognition and Moral Action: A Critical Review of the Literature." *Psychological Bulletin* 88, (1980): 1–45.

Blau, P. M. "Social Exchange." In *International Encyclopedia of the Social Sciences.* Ed. D. L. Sills. New York: Macmillan, 1968.

Blond, S. *The Righteous Gentiles.* Tel Aviv: S. Blond, 1983.

Blum, L. A. *Friendship, Altruism and Morality.* London: Routledge & Kegan Paul, 1980.

Blumenthal, D. "Religious Jews and Christians in the Holocaust: A Review Essay: 'The Holocaust and Halakha' and 'The Hiding Place.'" In *Emory Studies on the Holocaust: An Interfaith Inquiry.* Atlanta, Ga.: Emory University, 1985.

Blumenthal, N. *Materiały Z Czasów Okupcjit Niemieckiej W Polsce.* Centralna Żdowska Komisja Historyczna W Polsce, 1946.

Boas, J. *Boulevard des Misères: The Story of Transit Camp Westerbork.* Hamden, Conn.: Archon Books, 1985.

Boehm, E. H. *We Survived: The Stories of Fourteen of the Hidden and the Hunted of Nazi Germany.* New Haven, Conn.: Yale University Press, 1949.

Borkin, J. *The Crime and Punishment of I. G. Farben.* New York: Free Press, 1978.

Borwicz, M. *Les vies interdites* (Forbidden lives). Paris: Casterman, 1969.

Borzykowski, T. *Between Tumbling Walls.* Israel: Kibbutz Lohamei Haghettaot (Ghetto fighter's house), 1972.

Botwinick, J. *Aging and Behavior: A Comprehensive Integration of Research Findings.* 3d ed. New York: Springer-Verlag, 1984.

Bowlby, J. *Attachment.* New York: Basic Books, 1969.

Bowlby, J. *Separation.* New York: Basic Books, 1973.

Boyens, A. F. C. "The Ecumenical Community and the Holocaust." *Annals of the American Academy of Political and Social Science* 450 (July 1980): 143–147.

Braham, R. L. *The Destruction of Hungarian Jewry.* 2 vols. New York: World Federation of Hungarian Jews, 1963.

Braham, R. L., ed. *Contemporary Views on the Holocaust.* Boston: Kluwer-Nijhoff, 1984.

Braham, R. L., ed. *Genocide and Retribution.* Boston: Kluwer-Nijhoff, 1983.

Braham, R. L., ed. *Perspectives on the Holocaust.* Boston: Kluwer-Nijhoff, 1983.

Brand, J. *Desperate Mission.* New York: Criterion Books, 1958.

Brand, S. *I Dared to Live.* New York: Shengold, 1978.

Bredin, J. D. *The Affair: The Case of Alfred Dreyfus.* Trans. J. Mehlman. New York: Braziller, 1986.

Brenner, R. R. *The Faith and Doubt of Holocaust Survivors.* New York: Free Press, 1980.

Briskin, M. "Rescue Italian Style." *Jewish Monthly,* May 1986, 20–25.

Browning, C. R. "A Reply to Martin Broszat Regarding the Origins of the Final Solution." *Simon Wiesenthal Center Annual* 1 (1984): 113–132.

Browning, C. R. "Nazi Resettlement Policy and the Search for a Solution to the Jewish Question, 1939–1941." *German Studies Review* 9, no. 3 (October 1986): 497–519.

Bryan, J. H. "Model Affect and Children's Imitative Altruism." *Child Development* 42 (1971): 2061–2065.

Budd, L. J. "Altruism Arrives in America." *American Quarterly* 8 (1956): 40–52.

Buthman, W. *The Rise of Integral Nationalism in France.* New York: Columbia University Press, 1939.

Butler, R. N. "The Life Review: An Interpretation of Reminiscence in the Aged." In *Middle Age and Aging: A Reader in Social Psychology.* Ed. B. L. Neugarten. Chicago: University of Chicago Press, 1968.

Byrnes, R. F. *Anti-Semitism in Modern France: The Prologue to the Dreyfus Affair.* New York: Howard Fertig, 1969.

Canepa, A. M. "Emancipation and Jewish Response in Mid-19th Century Italy." *European History Quarterly* 16, no. 4 (October 1986): 403–439.

Caracciolo, N. *Gli Ebrei e l'Italia durante la guerra 1940–45.* Rome: Bonacci Editore, 1986.

Cargas, H. J. *A Christian Response to the Holocaust.* New York: Stonehenge Books, 1982.

Carpi, D. "The Catholic Church and Italian Jewry under the Fascists (to the Death of Pius XI)." *Yad Vashem Studies* 4 (1960): 43–56.

Carpi, D. "The Diplomatic Negotiations over the Transfer of Jewish Children from Croatia to Turkey and Palestine in 1943." *Yad Vashem Studies* 12 (1977): 109–124.

Carpi, D. "The Resuce of Jews in the Italian Zone of Occupied Croatia." In *Rescue Attempts During the Holocaust,* Proceedings of the Second Yad Vashem International Historical Conference, Jerusalem, 8–11 April 1974. New York: Ktav Publishing House, 1978.

Cassels, A. *Fascist Italy.* New York: Thomas Y. Crowell, 1968.

Cavaglion, A. *Nella notte straniera.* Centro di documentazione ebraica contemporanea; Instituto storico della resistenza in Cuneo. Provincia Cuneo: L'arciere, 1981.

Charny, I. W. *How Can We Commit the Unthinkable? Genocide, the Human Cancer.* Boulder, Colo: Westview Press, 1982.

Chartock, R., and Spencer, J., eds. *The Holocaust Years: Society on Trial.* New York: Bantam Books, 1978.

Chary, F. B. *The Bulgarian Jews and the Final Solution, 1940–1944.* Pittsburgh: University of Pittsburgh Press, 1972.

Child, I. L. "Personality in Culture." *Handbook of Personality Theory and Research.* Ed. E. F. Borgatta and W. W. Lambert. New York: Rand McNally, 1968.

Chodorow, N. "Family Structure and Feminine Personality." In *Women, Culture and Society.* Ed. M. Z. Rosaldo and L. Lamphere. Stanford, Calif.: Stanford University Press, 1974.

Chodziński, E. "Pomoc Żydom Udzielana Przez Konspiracyjne Biuro Fałszywych Dokumentów W Okresie Okupacji Hitlerowskiej" (Help offered to Jews during the occupation by the underground office of illegal documents). *Biuletyn Żydowskiego Instytutu Historycznego* 75 (1970): 129–132.

Chorover, S. L. *From Genesis to Genocide.* Cambridge, Mass.: MIT Press, 1979.

Christie, R., and Geis, F., eds. *Studies in Machiavellianism.* New York: Academic Press, 1970.

Chrześcijańskie Stowarzyszenie Społeczne (Christian charity). Warszawa: Dzieło Miłosierdzia Chrześcijańskiego, 1961.

Cialdini, R. B.; Kenrick, D. T.; and Baumann, D. J. "Effects of Mood on Prosocial Behavior in Children and Adults." In *The Development of Prosocial Behavior.* Ed. N. Eisenberg. New York: Academic Press, 1982.

Cohen, E. A. *Human Behavior in the Concentration Camp.* New York: W. W. Norton, 1953.

Cohen, E. A. *The Abyss.* New York: W. W. Norton, 1973.

Cohen, E. A., and Assa, A. *Saving of the Jews in Bulgaria 1941–1944.* Sofia: State Printing House "Georgy Dimitrov," 1977.

Cohen, N. "The Myth of the Jewish World Conspiracy; A Case Study in Collective Psychopathology. *Commentary Reprint,* 1966.

Cohen, Y. "French Jewry's Dilemma on the Orientation of Its Leadership (From Polemics to Conciliation: 1942–1944)." *Yad Vashem Studies* 14 (1981): 167–204.

Cohn, N. *Warrant for Genocide: The Myth of the Jewish World Conspiracy and the Protocols of the Elders of Zion.* New York: Harper & Row, 1967.

Coles, R. "How Do You Measure a Child's Level of Morality?" *Learning,* July/August, 1981, 70–72.

Comte, A. *System of Positive Polity.* New York: Ben Franklin, 1973.

Conway, J. S. *The Nazi Persecution of the Churches.* London: Weidenfeld and Nicolson, 1968.

Cook, K. S., and Hegtvedt, K. A. "Distributive Justice, Equity, and Equality." *Annual Review of Sociology* 9 (1983): 217–241.

Coopersmith, S. "Some Philosophical and Theoretical Interpretations of Altruism." Unpublished manuscript, 1977.

Coopersmith, S. *The Antecedents of Self-Esteem.* San Francisco: W. H. Freeman & Co., 1967.

Crankshaw, E. *Gestapo: Instrument of Tyranny.* New York: Viking, 1956.

Cunningham, J. D.; Starr, P. A.; and Kanouse, D. E. "Self as Actor, Active Observer and Passive Observer: Implications for Causal Attribution." *Journal of Personality and Social Psychology* 37 (1979): 1146–1152.

Czajka, I. S. *Ocalił Mnie Kowal* (I was saved by a blacksmith). Warszawa: Czytelnik, 1956.

Czapska, M. *Gwiazda Dawida Dzieje Jednej Rodziny (The Star of David,* the story of one family). Londyn: Oficyna Poetów I Malarzy, 1975.

Czarnowski, T. "Pomoc Ludnosci Zysowskiej Przez Pracownikow Wydzialu Ludnosci Zarzadu M. St. Warszawy W Okresie Okupacji, 1939–1945" (Help offered to Jews by employees of the Warsaw population department during the occupation). *Biuletyn Zydowskiego Instytutu Historycznego* 75 (1970): 119–128.

Datner, S. *Las Sprawiedliwych* (The forest of the righteous). Warszawa: Ksiażka I Wiedza, 1968.

Davies, A. "Racism and German Protestant Theology: A Prelude to the Holocaust." *The Annals—Reflections on the Holocaust: Historical, Philosophical and Educational Dimensions.* Ed. I. G. Shur, F. H. Littel, and M. E. Wolfgang. 1980, 20–34.

Dawidowicz, L. S. "Lies About the Holocaust." *Commentary* 70, no. 6 (December 1980): 31–37.

Dawidowicz, L. S. *The Golden Tradition: Jewish Life and Thought in Eastern Europe.* Boston: Beacon Press, 1972.

Dawidowicz, L. S. *The Holocaust and the Historians.* Cambridge, Mass.: Harvard University Press, 1981.

Dawidowicz, L. S. *The Jewish Presence: Essays on Identity and History.* New York: Holt, Rinehart & Winston, 1977.

Dawidowicz, L. S. *The War Against the Jews 1933–1945.* New York: Holt, Rinehart & Winston, 1975.

Dawidowicz, L. S., ed. *A Holocaust Reader.* New York: Behrman House, 1976.

De Jong, L. "Help to People in Hiding." *Delta: A Review of Arts, Life, and Thought in the Netherlands* 8, no. 19 (Spring 1965): 37–79.

De Jong, L. *Het Koninkrijk der Nederlanden in de Tweede Wereldoorlog.* 10 vols. The Hague: Staatsuitgeverij, 1969–1982.

De Jong, P. "Responses of the Churches in the Netherlands to the Nazi Occupation." In *Human Responses to the Holocaust: Perpetrators and Victims—Bystanders and Resisters.* Ed. M. D. Ryan. New York and Toronto: Edwin Mellen Press, 1981.

Delzell, C. F. *Mussolini's Enemies: The Italian Anti-Fascist Resistance.* Princeton, N.J.: Princeton University Press, 1961.

Des Pres, T. *The Survivor.* New York: Oxford University Press, 1976.

Deutsch, H. C. *The Conspiracy Against Hitler in the Twilight War.* Minneapolis: University of Minnesota Press, 1968.

Diamant, D. *Les Juifs dans la Résistance française 1940–1944.* Paris: Roger Maria, 1971.

Dimsdale, J. *Survivors, Victims and Perpetrators: Essays on the Nazi Holocaust.* Washington, D.C.: Hemisphere, 1981.

Dinnerstein, L. *America and the Survivors of the Holocaust.* New York: Columbia University Press, 1982.

Dipper, C. "Der Deutsche Widerstand und das Judentum." *Geschichte und Gesellschaft* 9, no. 3 (1983): 349–380.

Dittes, J. E. *Bias and the Pious.* Minneapolis, Minn. Augsburg Publishing, 1973.

Dobroszycki, L. "Jewish Elites Under German Rule." In *The Holocaust: Ideology, Bureaucracy, and Genocide.* Ed. H. Friedlander and S. Milton. Millwood, N.Y.: Kraus International Publications, 1980.

Dobroszycki, L., ed. *The Chronicle of the Lodz Ghetto, 1941–1944.* New Haven, Conn.: Yale University Press, 1984.

Documents of the Persecution of the Dutch Jewry 1940–1945. Ed. Joods Historisch Museum. Amsterdam: Athenaeum—Polak and Van Gennep, 1979.

Donat, A. *The Holocaust Kingdom: A Memoir.* New York: Holt, Rinehart & Winston, 1965.

Du Bois, C. "The Dominant Value Profile of American Culture." *American Anthropologist* 57 (1955): 1232–1239.

Durkheim, É. *Suicide: A Study in Sociology.* Trans. J. A. Spaulding and G. Simpson. Glencoe, Ill.: Free Press, 1951.

Dweck, C. S. "The Role of Expectations and Attributions in the Alleviation of Learned Helplessness." *Journal of Personality and Social Psychology* 31, no. 4 (1975); 674–685.

Edelheit, A. J. *Bibliography on Holocaust Literature.* Boulder, Colo.: Westview Press, 1986.

Eisenbach, A. "Operation Reinhard-Mass Extermination of the Jewish Population in Poland." *Polish Western Affairs* 3, no. 1 (1962): 80–124.

Eisenberg, A. *Witness to the Holocaust.* New York: The Pilgrim Press, 1981.

Eisenberg, N. "The Development of Reasoning Regarding Prosocial Behavior." In *The Development of Prosocial Behavior.* Ed. N. Eisenberg. New York: Academic Press, 1982.

Eisenberg, N. "The Development of Prosocial Values." In *Social and Moral Values: Individual and Societal Perspectives.* Ed. N. Eisenberg, J. Reykowski, and E. Staub. Hillsdale, N.J.: Lawrence Erlbaum, 1987.

Eisenberg, N. *Altruistic Emotion, Cognition, and Behavior.* Hillsdale, N.J.: Lawrence Erlbaum, 1986.

Eisenberg, N.; Cameron, E.; and Tryon, K. "Prosocial Behavior in the Preschool Years: Methodological and Conceptual Issues." In *The Development and Maintenance of Prosocial Behavior: International Perspectives on Positive Morality.* Ed. E. Staub, S. Bar-Tal, J. Karylowski, and J. Reykowski. New York: Plenum Press, 1984.

Eisenberg, N.; Cameron, E.; Tryon, K.; and Dodez, R. "Socialization of Prosocial Behavior in the Preschool Classroom." *Developmental Psychology* 17 (1981): 773–782.

Eisenberg-Berg, N., and Hand. M. "The Relationship of Preschoolers' Reasoning About Prosocial Moral Conflicts to Prosocial Behavior." *Child Development* 50 (1979): 356–363.

Eitinger, L. *Concentration Camp Survivors in Norway and Israel.* London: George Allen & Unwin, 1964.

Eliach, Y. *Hasidic Tales of the Holocaust.* New York: Oxford University Press, 1982.

Epstein, S. "The Self-Concept: A Review and the Proposal of an Integrated Theory of Personality." In *Personality: Basic Aspects and Current Research.* Ed. E. Staub. Englewood Cliffs, N.J.: Prentice-Hall, 1980.

Erikson, E. H. *Childhood and Society.* New York: W. W. Norton, 1950.

Erikson, E. H. *Identity and the Life Cycle.* New York: W. W. Norton, 1980.

Ettinger, S. "Jews and Non-Jews in Eastern and Central Europe Between the Wars: An Outline." In *Jews and Non-Jews in Eastern Europe 1918–1945.* Ed. B. Vago and G. L. Mosse. New York: Halsted Press, 1974.

Extermination of Polish Jews: Album of Pictures. Lodz: Wydawnictwa Centralnej Zydowskiej Komisji Historycznej Przy C.K., 1945.

Fabre, E. C., ed. *God's Underground.* St. Louis, Mo.: Bethany, 1970.

Fackenheim, E. L. *The Jewish Return into History: Reflections in the Age of Auschwitz.* New York: Schocken Books, 1978.

Feig, K. G. *Hitler's Death Camps: The Sanity of Madness.* New York: Holmes and Meier, 1981.

Fein, H. "A Formula for Genocide: Comparison of Turkish Genocide (1915) and German Holocaust (1939–1945)." *Comparative Studies in Sociology* 1 (1978): 271–293.

Fein, H. "Reviewing the Toll: Jewish Dead, Losses and Victims of the Holocaust." *Shoah* 2, no. 2 (Spring 1981): 20–27.

Fein, H. "The Treatment of Genocide in U.S. Sociology Textbooks." *Patterns of Prejudice* 13, no. 2–3 (March–June 1979): 31–36.

Fein, H. *Accounting for Genocide: National Responses and Jewish Victimization During the Holocaust.* New York: Free Press, 1979.

Feingold, H. *The Politics of Rescue: The Roosevelt Administration and the Holocaust, 1938–1945.* New York: Holocaust Library, 1981.

Ferencz, B. *Less than Slaves.* Cambridge, Mass.: Harvard University Press, 1979.

Feschbach, N. D. "Studies of Empathic Behavior in Children." In *Progress in Experimental Personality Research,* vol. 8. Ed. B. A. Maher. New York: Academic Press, 1978.

Fiske, D. W. *Strategies for Personality Research.* San Francisco: Jossey-Bass Publishers, 1978.

Fitch, G. "Effects of Self-Esteem, Perceived Performance and Choice on Causal Attributions." *Journal of Personality and Social Psychology* 16, no. 2 (1970): 311–315.

Flannery, E. H. *The Anguish of the Jews.* New York: Macmillan, 1965.

Fleischner, E. *Judaism in German Christian Theology since 1945.* Metuchen, N.J.: Scarecrow Press, 1975.

Fleischner, E., ed. *Auschwitz: Beginning of a New Era?* New York: Ktav Publishing House, 1977.

Fleming, Gerald. *Hitler and the Final Solution.* Berkeley and Los Angeles: University of California Press, 1984.

Flender, H. *Rescue in Denmark.* New York: Manor Books, 1964.

Fogelman, E., and Wiener, V. L. "The Few, the Brave, the Noble." *Psychology Today* 19, no. 8 (August 1985): 60–65.

Forbes, H. D. *Nationalism, Ethnocentrism and Personality: Social Science and Critical Theory.* Chicago: University of Chicago Press, 1985.

Ford, H. *Flee the Captor.* Nashville, Tenn.: Southern Publishing Assoc., 1966.

Frank, A. *The Diary of a Young Girl.* Garden City, N.Y.: Doubleday, 1967.

Frankl, V. *Man's Search for Meaning.* Boston: Beacon Press, 1963.

Frenkel-Brunswik, E. "Parents and Childhood." In *The Authoritarian Personality.* Ed. T. W. Adorno, E. Frenkel-Brunswik, D. J. Levinson, and R. N. Sanford. New York: W. W. Norton, 1950.

Freud, A., and Dann, S. "An Experiment in Group Upbringing." In *Psychoanalytic Study of the Child.* Ed. R. S. Eissler. New York: International Universities Press, 1951, 127–168.

Freud, S. "The Ego and the Id." In *The Standard Edition of the Complete Psychological Works of Sigmund Freud,* vol. 19 Ed. J. Strachey. London: Hogarth Press, 1961 (originally published in 1923).

Freud, S. "The Psychopathology of Everyday Life." In *The Standard Edition of the Complete Psychological Works of Sigmund Freud,* vol. 6 Ed. J. Strachey. London: Hogarth Press, 1960 (originally published in 1901).

Freud, S. *An Autobiographical Study.* Trans. J. Strachey. London: Hogarth Press, 1935.

Fried, C. *An Anatomy of Values: Problems of Personal and Social Choice.* Cambridge, Mass.: Harvard University Press, 1970.

Friedlaender, S. *Kurt Gerstein: The Ambiguity of Good.* New York: Knopf, 1969.

Friedlaender, S. *Pius XII and the Third Reich.* New York: Knopf, 1966.

Friedlaender, S. *Reflections of Nazism: An Essay on Kitsch and Death.* New York: Harper & Row, 1984.

Friedlaender, S. *When Memory Comes.* New York: Farrar, Straus & Giroux, 1978.

Friedlander, A. H. *Out of the Whirlwind: A Reader of Holocaust Literature.* Garden City, N.Y.: Doubleday, 1968.

Friedlander, A. H., and Milton, S., eds. *The Holocaust: Ideology, Bureaucracy and Genocide—The San Jose Papers.* Millwood, N.Y.: Kraus International Publications, 1980.

Friedman, F. "Zagłada Żydow Polskich W Latach 1939–1945" (Destruction of Polish Jewry, 1939–1945). *Biuletyn Głownej Komisji Badania Zbrodni Niemieckiej W Polsce* 6 (1946): 165–208.

Friedman, P. "How the Gypsies Were Persecuted." *Wiener Library Bulletin* 3–4 (1950).

Friedman, P. "The Lublin Reservation and the Madagascar Plan." *YIVO Annual of Jewish Social Science* 8 (1953): 151–177.

Friedman, P. "Ukrainian-Jewish Relations During the Nazi Occupation." *YIVO Annual of Jewish Social Science* 7 (1958–1959): 259–296.

Friedman, P. "Was There an 'Other Germany' During the Nazi Period?" *YIVO Annual of Jewish Social Science* 10 (1955): 82–127.

Friedman, P. *Roads to Extinction.* Ed. A. J. Friedman. Philadelphia: Jewish Publication Society, 1980.

Friedman, P. *Their Brothers' Keepers.* New York: Holocaust Library, 1978.

Friedman, S. S. *No Haven for the Oppressed.* Detroit, Mich.: Wayne State University Press, 1973.

Fromm, E. "The Psychology of Nazism." In *Escape from Freedom.* New York: Holt, Rinehart & Winston, 1961.

Fromm, E. *The Art of Loving.* New York: Bantam Books, 1967.

Gabor, G. M. *My Destiny.* California: Borden Publishing Co., 1982.

Gaertner, S. L., and Dovidio, J. F. "The Subtlety of White Racism, Arousal, and Helping Behavior." *Journal of Personality and Social Psychology* 35, no. 10 (1977): 691–707.

Gerth, H. H., and Mills, C. W., eds. and trans. *From Max Weber: Essays in Sociology.* New York: Oxford University Press, 1946.

Gilbert, M. *Auschwitz and Allies.* New York: Holt, Rinehart & Winston, 1982.

Gilbert, M. *The Holocaust: A History of the Jews of Europe During the Second World War.* New York: Holt, Rinehart & Winston, 1985.

Gilbert, M. *The Macmillan Atlas of the Holocaust.* New York: Macmillan, 1982.

Gilligan, C. *In a Different Voice: Psychological Theory and Women's Development.* Cambridge, Mass.: Harvard University Press, 1982.

Glock, C. Y., and Stark, R. *Christian Beliefs and Anti-Semitism.* New York: Harper & Row, 1966.

Golczewski, F. *Polnisch-Jüdische Beziehungen, 1881–1922.* Wiesbaden: Franz Steiner Verlag, 1981.

Goldstein, B. *Five Years in the Warsaw Ghetto.* Garden City, N.Y.: Doubleday, 1961.

Goodall, J. *In the Shadow of Man.* Boston: Houghton Mifflin, 1983.

Gordon, B. M. *Collaborationism in France During the Second World War.* Ithaca, N.Y.: Cornell University Press, 1980.

Gordon, J. *Hitler and the Beer Hall Putsch.* Princeton, N.J.: Princeton University Press, 1972.

Gordon, S. *Hitler, Germans and the "Jewish Question."* Princeton, N.J.: Princeton University Press, 1984.

Green, G. *The Artists of Terezin.* New York: Schocken Books, 1978.

Green, G. *The Legion of Noble Christians: Or the Sweeney Survey.* New York: Trident Press, 1965.

Grim, P.; Kohlberg, L.; and White, S. "Some Relationships Between Conscience and Attentional Processes." *Journal of Personality and Social Psychology* 8 (1968): 239–253.

Grobman, A., and Landes, D., eds. *Genocide: Critical Issues of the Holocaust.* Los Angeles: Simon Wiesenthal Center, 1983.

Gross, J. T. *Polish Society Under German Occupation: The Generalgouvernement 1939–1944.* Princeton, N.J.: Princeton University Press, 1979.

Gross, L. *The Last Jews in Berlin.* New York: Simon & Schuster, 1982.

Grossman, F. G. "A Psychological Study of Gentiles Who Saved the Lives of Jews During the Holocaust." In *Toward the Understanding and Prevention of Genocide.* Ed. I. W. Charny. Boulder, Colo.: Westview Press, 1984.

Grossman, K. *Die Unbesungenen Helden* (The unsung heroes). Berlin-Grunewald: Arani Verlag, 1961.

Grossman, K. R. "The Humanitarian Who Cheated Hitler." *Coronet* (September 1959): 66–71.

Grossman, K. R. "What Were the Jewish Losses?" *Congress Weekly,* 12 October 1953, 9–11.

Grossman, Vassily. *Life and Fate.* New York: Harper & Row, 1985.

Gruber, R. "The Heroism of Staszek Jackowski." *Saturday Review* 50, no. 50 (15 April 1967): 19–21.

Grusec, J. E., and Dix, T. "The Socialization of Prosocial Behavior: Theory and Reality." In *Altruism and Aggression: Biological and Social Origins.* Ed. C. Zahn-Waxler, E. M. Cummings, and R. Iannotti. New York: Cambridge University Press, 1986.

Gurdus-Krugman, L. K. *The Death Train: A Personal Account of a Holocaust Survivor.* New York: Holocaust Library, 1978.

Gurin, P.; Gurin, G.; and Morrison, B. M. "Personal and Ideological Aspects of Internal and External Control." *Social Psychology* 41, no. 4 (1978): 275–296.

Gutman, Y. "Jews in General Anders' Army in the Soviet Union." *Yad Vashem Studies* 12 (1977): 231–296.

Gutman, Y. "The Genesis of the Resistance in the Warsaw Ghetto." *Yad Vashem Studies* 9 (1973): 29–70.

Gutman, Y. *The Jews of Warsaw 1939–1943: Ghetto, Underground, Revolt.* Trans. I. Friedman. Bloomington: Indiana University Press, 1982.

Gutman, Y., and Rothkirchen, L., eds. *The Catastrophe of European Jewry.* Jerusalem: Yad Vashem, 1976.

Gutman, Y., and Zuroff, E., eds. *Rescue Attempts During the Holocaust.* Proceedings of the Second Yad Vashem International Historical Conference, Jerusalem, 8–11 April 1974. New York: Ktav Publishing House, 1978.

Gutteridge, R. *The German Evangelical Church and the Jews, 1879–1950.* Oxford, England: Blackwell, 1976.

Haas, G. *These Do I Remember: Fragments from the Holocaust.* Freeport, Me.: Cumberland Press, 1983.

Haesler, A. *The Lifeboat Is Full: Switzerland and the Refugees, 1933–1945.* New York: Funk & Wagnalls, 1969.

Halasz, N. *Captain Dreyfus: The Story of a Mass Hysteria.* New York: Simon & Schuster, 1955.

Halivni, T. H. "The Birkenau Revolt: The Poles Prevent a Timely Insurrection." *Jewish Social Studies* 41, no. 2 (Spring 1979): 123–154.

Hallie, P. *Lest Innocent Blood Be Shed: The Story of Le Chambon and How Goodness Happened There.* New York: Harper & Row, 1979.

Halls, B. "Catholicism Under Vichy: A Study in Diversity and Ambiguity." In *Vichy France and the Resistance.* Ed. H. R. Kedward and R. Austin. New York: Barnes & Noble, 1985.

Hamerow, T. S. "The Hidden Holocaust." *Commentary* 79 (March 1985): 32–42.

Handler, A., ed. *The Holocaust in Hungary: An Anthology of Jewish Response.* University, Ala.: University of Alabama Press, 1982.

Hardin, G. *The Limits of Altruism: An Ecologist's View of Survival.* Bloomington: Indiana University Press, 1977.

Harris, M. B. "The Effects of Performing One Altruistic Act on the Likelihood of Performing Another." *Journal of Social Psychology* 88 (1972): 65–73.

Harris, M. B., and Huang, L. C. "Competence and Helping." *Journal of Social Psychology* 89 (1973): 203–210.

Hartman, E. *War Without Friends.* Trans. P. Crampton. New York: Crown, 1982.

Hartup, W. W. "Peer Relations." In *Handbook of Child Psychology: Socialization, Personality and Social Development,* vol. 4. Ed. P. H. Mussen. New York: John Wiley & Sons, 1983.

Hausner, G. *Justice in Jerusalem.* New York: Holocaust Library, 1977.

Hay, M. *The Foot of Pride: The Pressure of Christendom on the People of Israel for 1900 Years.* Boston: Beacon Press, 1951.

Heider, F. *The Psychology of Interpersonal Relations.* New York: John Wiley & Sons, 1958.

Heine, P. J. *Personality in Social Theory.* New York: Aldine Publishing Company, 1971.

Heller, C. S. *On the Edge of Destruction: Jews of Poland Between the Two World Wars.* New York: Schocken Books, 1980.

Hellman, P. *Avenue of the Righteous.* New York: Bantam Books, 1981.

Hellman, P. *The Auschwitz Album.* New York: Random House, 1981.

Helmreich, E. C. *The German Churches Under Hitler: Background to Struggle.* Detroit, Mich.: Wayne State University Press, 1978.

Henry, F. *Victims and Neighbors: A Small Town in Germany Remembered.* South Hadley, Mass.: Bergin and Garvey, 1984.

Herzer, I. "How Italians Rescued Jews." *Midstream* (June/July 1983): 35–38.

Hilberg, R. "The Ghetto as a Form of Government." *Annals of the American Academy of Political and Social Science* 450 (July 1980): 98–112.

Hilberg, R. *The Destruction of the European Jews,* vols. 1–3. New York: Holmes and Meier, 1985.

Hilberg, R., ed. *Documents of Destruction, 1933–1945.* New York: Quadrangle, 1971.

Hilberg, R.; Staron, S.; and Kermisz, J. *The Warsaw Diary of Adam Czerniakow: Prelude to Doom.* New York: Stein & Day, 1979.

Hirschfeld, G. *Fremdherrschaft und Kollaboration: Die Niederlande unter Deutscher Besatzung, 1940–1945.* Stuttgart: Deutsche Verlagsanstalt, 1984.

Hirschfeld, G. *The Policies of Genocide: Jews and Soviet Prisoners of War in Nazi Germany.* London: George Allen & Unwin, 1986.

Hochhuth, R. *The Deputy.* New York: Grove Press, 1964.

Hoehne, H. *The Order of the Death's Head.* New York: Coward, McCann & Geoghegan, 1970.

Hoffman, M. L. "Conscience, Personality and Socialization Techniques." *Human Development* 13 (1970): 90–126.

Hoffman, M. L. "Empathy and Prosocial Activism." In *Social and Moral Values: Individual and Societal Perspectives.* Ed. N. Eisenberg, J. Reykowski, and E. Staub. Hillsdale, N.J.: Lawrence Erlbaum, 1987.

Hoffman, M. L. "Empathy, Its Development and Prosocial Implications." In *Nebraska Symposium on Motivation,* vol. 25. Lincoln: University of Nebraska Press, 1977.

Hoffman, M. L. "Empathy, Role Taking, Guilt, and Development of Altruistic Motives." In *Moral Development and Behavior: Theory, Research and Social Issues.* Ed. T. Lickona. New York: Holt, Rinehart & Winston, 1976.

Hoffman, M. L. "Is Altruism Part of Human Nature?" *Journal of Personality and Social Psychology* 40, no. 5 (1981): 121–137.

Hoffman, M. L. "Moral Internalization: Current Theory and Research." In *Advances in Experimental Psychology.* vol. 10. Ed. L. Berkowitz. New York: Academic Press, 1977.

Hoffman, M. L. "Parent Discipline, Moral Internalization, and Development of Prosocial Motivation." In *Development and Maintenance of Prosocial Behavior: International Perspectives on Positive Morality.* Ed. E Staub, D. Bar-Tal, J. Karylowski, and J. Reykowski. New York: Plenum Press, 1984.

Hoffman, P. "Problems of Resistance in National Socialist Germany." In *The German Church Struggle and The Holocaust.* Ed. F. H. Littell and H. G. Locke. Detroit, Mich.: Wayne State University Press, 1974.

Hoffmann, P. *The History of the German Resistance, 1933–1945.* Cambridge, Mass.: MIT Press, 1978.

Hoffman, R. L. *More Than a Trial: The Struggle Over Captain Dreyfus.* New York: Free Press, 1980.

Hoffmann, S. *Decline or Renewal? France since the 1930's.* New York: Viking, 1974.

Holt, H. R. R. "A Review of Some of Freud's Biological Assumptions and their Influence on his Theories." In *Psychoanalysis and Current Biological Thought.* Ed. N. S. Greenfield and W. C. Lewis. Madison: University of Wisconsin Press, 1965.

Holt, H. R. R. "Drive or Wish? A Reconsideration of the Psychoanalytic Theory of Motivation." In *Psychology versus Metapsychology: Psychoanalytic Essays in Memory of George S. Klein—Psychological Issues,* no. 36. Ed. M. M. Gill and P. S. Holzman. New York: International Universities Press, 1976.

Hook, S. *The Hero in History.* Boston: Beacon Press, 1943.

Horbach, M. *Out of the Night.* New York: Frederick Fell, 1967.

Hornstein, H. A. *Cruelty and Kindness: A New Look at Aggression and Altruism.* Englewood Cliffs, N.J.: Prentice-Hall, 1976.

Huneke, D. "A Study of Christians Who Rescued Jews During the Nazi Era." *Humboldt Journal of Social Relations* 9, no. 1 (Fall/Winter 1981–82): 144–149.

Huneke, D. "In the Darkness ... Glimpses of Light: A Study of Nazi Era Rescuers." A Report to the Oregon Committee for the Humanities, privately printed, 1980.

Huneke, D. *The Moses of Rovno.* New York: Dodd, Mead & Co., 1985.

Hyman, P. *From Dreyfus to Vichy: The Remaking of French Jewry, 1906–1939.* New York: Columbia University Press, 1979.

Ickes, W., and Knowles, E. S., eds. *Personality, Roles, and Social Behavior.* New York: Springer-Verlag, 1982.

Ickes, W., and Layden, M. A. "Atttibutional Styles." In *New Directions in Attribution*

Research. vol. 2. Ed. J. H. Harvey, W. Ickes, and R. F. Kidd. Hillsdale, N.J.: Lawrence Erlbaum, 1978.

Iranek-Osmecki, K. *He Who Saves One Life: A Documented Story of the Poles Who Struggled to Save the Jews During World War II.* New York: Crown, 1971.

Jaffe, R. "The Sense of Guilt Within Holocaust Survivors." *Jewish Social Studies* 32, no. 4 (October 1970): 307–314.

James, W. *The Principles of Psychology,* vol. 1. New York: Henry Holt & Co., 1896.

Jaranyi, E. *The Flowers from my Mother's Garden.* Berkeley, Calif.: Judah L. Magnes Memorial Museum, 1985.

Jarymowicz, M. *Modification of 'Self' Cognitions for the Increase of the Readiness for Prosocial Behavior.* Wroclaw, Poland: Ossolineum, 1979.

Jarymowicz, M. "Modification of Self-Worth and Increment of Prosocial Sensitivity." *Polish Psychological Bulletin* 8 (1977): 45–53.

Jaspers, K. *Reason and Anti-Reason in Our Time.* Trans. S. Godman. Hamden, Conn.: Archon Books, 1971.

Jaspers, K. The Question of German Guilt. Trans. E. B. Ashton. Westport, Conn.: Greenwood Press, 1978.

Joffroy, P. *A Spy for God—The Ordeal of Kurt Gerstein.* Trans. N. Denny. New York: Grosset & Dunlap, 1970.

Johnpoll, B. K. *The Politics of Futility: The General Jewish Workers Bund of Poland, 1917–1943.* Ithaca, N.Y.: Cornell University Press, 1967.

Jones, E. E. and Nisbett, R. E. *The Actor and the Observer: Divergent Perceptions of the Causes of Behaviors.* Morristown, N.J.: General Learning Press, 1971.

Ka-Tzetnik 135638. *Sunrise over Hell.* London: A. Howard & Wyndman, 1977.

Kahle, L. R., ed. *Social Values and Social Change: Adaptation to Life in America.* New York: Praeger Publishers, 1983.

Kamenetsky, I. *Secret Nazi Plans for Eastern Europe: A Study of Lebensraum Policies.* New Haven, Conn.: College and University Press, 1961.

Kant, I. *Foundations of the Metaphysics of Morals.* Trans. L. W. Beck. New York: Bobbs-Merrill, 1959.

Kant, I. *Lectures on Ethics.* Trans. L. Infield. New York: Harper & Row, 1963.

Kant, I. *Observations on the Feeling of Beautiful and Sublime.* Trans. J. T. Goldwait. Berkeley: University of California Press, 1965.

Kant, I. *The Doctrine of Virtue.* Trans. M. Gregor. New York: Harper & Row, 1964.

Kaplan, C. A. *The Scroll of Agony.* New York: Macmillan, 1965.

Karski, J. *Story of a Secret State.* Boston: Houghton Mifflin, 1944.

Karylowski, J. "Focus of Attention and Altruism: Endocentric and Exocentric Sources of Altruistic Behavior." In *Development and Maintenance of Prosocial Behavior: International Perspectives on Positive Morality.* Ed. E. Staub, D. Bar-Tal, J. Karylowski, and J. Reykowski. New York: Plenum Press, 1984.

Karylowski, J. "Prosocial Norms, Self-Focused Attention and Prosocial Behavior. *Polish Psychological Bulletin* 8 (1979): 27–34

Karylowski, J. "Two Types of Altruistic Behavior: Doing Good or to Make the Other Feel Good." In *Cooperation and Helping Behavior: Theories and Research.* Ed. V. J. Derlega and J. Grzelak. New York: Academic Press, 1982.

Karylowski, J. *Z Badan Nad Mechanizmani Pozytywnych Ustosunkowan Interpersonal-nych*. Wroclaw, Poland: Ossolineaum, 1975.

Katz, J. "Altruism and Sympathy: Their History in Philosophy and Some Implications for Psychology." *The Journal of Social Issues* 28, no. 3 (1972): 59–70.

Katz, J. "Was the Holocaust Predictable?" *Commentary* 59 (May 1975): 41–48.

Katz, J. *From Prejudice to Destruction: Anti-Semitism, 1900–1933*. Cambridge, Mass.: Harvard University Press, 1980.

Katz, J. *Out of the Ghetto: The Social Background of Jewish Emancipation*. Cambridge, Mass.: Harvard University Press, 1973.

Katz, R. *Black Sabbath*. New York: Macmillan, 1969.

Kedward, H. R. *Resistance in Vichy France: A Study of Ideas and Motivation in the Southern Zone 1940–1942*. New York: Oxford University Press, 1978.

Kelly, E. L. "Consistency of the Adult Personality." *American Psychologist* 10 (1955): 659–681.

Keneally, T. *Schindler's List*. New York: Simon & Schuster, 1982.

Kenrich, D., and Puxon, G. *The Destiny of Europe's Gypsies*. New York: Basic Books, 1972.

Kermish, J. "The Activities of the Council of Aid to Jews ("Zegota") in Occupied Poland." In *Rescue Attempts During the Holocaust*. Proceedings of the Second Yad Vashem International Historical Conference, Jerusalem, 8–11 April 1974. New York: Ktav Publishing House, 1978.

Kershaw, I. *Popular Opinion and Political Dissent in the Third Reich: Bavaria 1933–1945*. New York: Oxford University Press, 1983.

Kershaw, I. *The Nazi Dictatorship: Problems and Perspectives of Interpretation*. Baltimore, Md.: E. Arnold, 1985.

Kielar, W. *Anus Mundi: 1500 Days in Auschwitz/Birkenau*. New York: Times Books, 1980.

Kirkpatrick, I. *Mussolini: A Study in Power*. New York: Hawthorn, 1964.

Klarsfeld, B. *Wherever They May Be!* New York: Vanguard Press, 1975.

Klarsfeld, S. *Memorial to the Jews Deported From France, 1942–1944*. New York: Beate Klarsfeld Foundation, 1983.

Klein, G. *All But My Life*. New York: Hill & Wang, 1957.

Kluckhohn, C. "The Study of Values." In *Values in America*. Ed. D. N. Barrett. South Bend, Ind.: University of Notre Dame Press, 1961.

Kluckhohn, F. "Dominant and Substitute Profiles of Cultural Orientations." *Social Forces* 28 (1950): 376–393.

Knout, D. *Contribution à l'histoire de la Résistance juive en France 1940–1944*. Paris: Éditions du Centre, 1947.

Knox, M. G. *Mussolini Unleashed: Politics and Strategy in Fascist Italy's Late War 1939–1941*. New York: Cambridge University Press, 1982.

Koehl, R. L. *The Black Corps: The Structure and Power Struggles of the Nazi SS*. Madison: University of Wisconsin Press, 1983.

Kogan, E. *The Theory and Practice of Hell*. New York: Octagon, 1972.

Kohlberg, L. "From Is to Ought; How to Commit the Naturalistic Fallacy and Get Away With It in the Study of Moral Development." In *Cognitive Development and Epistemology*. Ed. T. Mischel. New York: Academic Press, 1971.

Kohlberg, L. "Moral Stages and Moralization: The Cognitive-Developmental Approach." In *Moral Development and Behavior.* Ed. T. Lickona. New York: Holt, Rinehart & Winston, 1976.

Kolhberg, L. "Stage and Sequence: The Cognitive-Developmental Approach to Socialization." In *Handbook of Socialization Theory and Research.* Ed. D. A. Goslin. New York: Rand McNally, 1969.

Kohn, M. L. *Class and Conformity: A Study in Values.* Chicago: University of Chicago Press, 1977.

Korbonski, S. *The Polish Underground State: A Guide to the Underground, 1939–1945.* Boulder, Colo.: East European Quarterly, 1978.

Korczak, J. *Ghetto Diary.* New York: Holocaust Library, 1978.

Korczak, J. *The Ghetto Years.* Israel: Kibbutz Lohamei Haghettaot (Ghetto fighter's house), 1972.

Kosinski, J. *The Painted Bird.* Boston: Houghton Mifflin, 1965.

Krakowski, S. *War of the Doomed: Jewish Armed Resistance in Poland 1942–1944.* New York: Holmes and Meier, 1983.

Kranzler, D. *Japanese, Nazis and the Jews: The Jewish Refugee Community of Shanghai, 1938–1945.* New York: Yeshiva University Press, 1979.

Krausnick H., and Broszat, M. *Anatomy of the SS-State.* New York: Walter and Co., 1968.

Krebs, D. "Empathy and Altruism". *Journal of Personality and Social Psychology* 32, no. 6 (1975): 1134–1146.

Krebs, D. L., and Miller, D. T. "Altruism and Aggression." In *Handbook of Social Psychology,* vol. 2. Ed. G. L. Lindzey and E. Aronson. New York: Random House, 1985.

Kren, G. M., and Rappoport, L. *The Holocaust and the Crisis of Human Behavior.* New York: Holmes and Meier, 1980.

Kruk, H. *Diary of the Vilna Ghetto.* New York: YIVO Institute for Jewish Research, 1961.

Kulka, E. "Attempts by Jewish Escapees to Stop Mass Extermination." *Jewish Social Studies* 47, no. 3–4 (Summer/Fall 1985): 295–306.

Kulka, E., ed. *Collection of Testimonies and Documents on the Participation of Czechoslovak Jews in the Second World War.* Jerusalem: Yad Vashem, 1976.

Kuper, J. *Child of the Holocaust.* Garden City, N.Y.: Doubleday, 1968.

Kuper, L. *Genocide: Its Political Use in the Twentieth Century.* New Haven, Conn.: Yale University Press, 1982.

Kuper, L. *The Prevention of Genocide.* New Haven, Conn.: Yale University Press, 1985.

Kurbacz, J. *List Do Wojtka* (A letter to Wojtek). Warszawa: Ludowa Spółdzielnia Wydawnicza, 1963.

Kurtines, W. M., and Gewirtz, J. L. *Morality, Moral Behavior, and Moral Development.* New York: John Wiley & Sons, 1984.

Kurzman, D. *The Bravest Battle.* New York: Putnam, 1976.

Kuznetsov, A. *Babi Yar.* Trans. G. Guralsky. New York: Dell, 1966.

Kwiet, K. *Reichskommissariat Niederlande.* Stuttgart: Deutsche Verlags Anstalt, 1968.

Langer, L. *Versions of Survival: The Holocaust and the Human Spirit.* Albany: State University of New York Press, 1982.

Langmuir, G. I. "Tradition, History and Prejudice." *Jewish Social Studies* 30, no. 3 (July 1968): 157–168.

Laqueur, W. *The Terrible Secret: Suppression of the Truth about Hitler's "Final Solution."* New York: Penguin, 1982.

Larrieu, J. A. "Prosocial Values, Assertiveness, and Sex: Predictors of Children's Naturalistic Helping." Paper presented at the biennial meeting of the Southwestern Society for the Research in Human Development, Denver, March 1984.

Latane, B., and Darley, J. M. "Social Determinants of Bystander Intervention in Emergencies." In *Altruism and Helping Behavior.* Ed. J. Macaulay and L. Berkowitz. New York: Acadmic Press, 1970.

Latour, A. *The Jewish Resistance in France 1940–1944.* Trans. I. R. Ilton. New York: Holocaust Library, 1981.

Lavi. T. "Documents on the Struggle of Rumanian Jewry for Its Rights During the Second World War, Part One." *Yad Vashem Studies* 4 (1960): 261–316.

Le Boucher, F. *The Incredible Mission of Father Bénoit.* Trans. J. F. Bernard. Garden City, N.Y.: Doubleday, 1969.

Ledeen, M. A. "The Evolution of Italian Fascist Anti-Semitism." *Jewish Social Studies* 37, no. 1 (January 1975): 3–17.

Leeds, R. "Altruism and the Norm of Giving." *Merrill-Palmer Quarterly* 9 (1963): 229–240.

Lengyel, O. *Five Chimneys.* New York: Ziff-Davis, 1947.

Lepley, R., ed. *The Language of Value.* New York: Columbia University Press, 1957.

Lerner, M. J., and Simmons, C. H. "Observer's Reaction to the 'Innocent Victim': Compassion or Rejection." *Journal of Personality and Social Psychology* 4, no. 2 (1966): 203–210.

Lerski, G. J., and Lerski, H. T. *Jewish-Polish Coexistence, 1772–1939.* Westport, Conn.: Greenwood Press, 1986.

Lester, E. *Wallenberg: The Man in the Iron Web.* Englewood Cliffs, N.J.: Prentice-Hall, 1982.

Leuner, H. D. *Gerettet vor dem Holocaust: Menschen, die halfen.* Munich: Herbig, 1979.

Leuner, H. D. *When Compassion Was a Crime: Germany's Silent Heroes 1933–1945.* London: Oswald Wolf, 1966.

Levin, D. *Lithuanian Jewry's Armed Resistance to the Nazis.* New York: Holmes and Meier, 1983.

Levin, M. "They Saved the Children; French Keep 8000 Jewish Children Out of Gestapo's Murderous Hands." *Saturday Evening Post* 217, no. 34 (20 January 1945): 34ff.

Levin, N. *The Holocaust: The Destruction of European Jewry, 1933–1945,* New York: Schocken Books, 1973.

LeVine, R. *Culture, Behavior, and Personality.* New York: Aldine Publishing, 1982.

Levinson, D. "The Study of Ethnocentric Ideology." In *The Authoritarian Personality.* Ed. T. W. Adorno, Else Frenkel-Brunswik, Daniel J. Levinson, and R. Nevitt Sanford. New York: W. W. Norton, 1950.

Levy, C., and Tillard, P. Betrayal at the Vel d'Hiv. New York: Hill and Wang, 1969.

Levy, R. S. *The Downfall of the Anti-Semitic Political Parties in Imperial Germany.* New Haven, Conn.: Yale University Press, 1975.

Lewin, K. "Self-Hatred Among Jews." *Contemporary Jewish Record* 4 (June 1941): 219–232.

Lewy, G. *The Catholic Church and Nazi Germany.* New York: Holt, Rinehart & Winston, 1964.

Lichten, J. L. "Did Polish Jews Die Forsaken?" *The Polish Review* 4, no. 1–2 (1959): 119–126.

Lipset, S. M., and Lowenthal, L., eds. *Culture and Social Character.* New York: Free Press, 1961.

Littell, F. H. "Christian Anti-Semitism and the Holocaust." In *Perspectives on the Holocaust.* Ed. Randolph L. Braham. Boston: Kluwer-Nijhoff, 1983.

Littell, F. H. *The Crucifixion of the Jews.* New York: Harper & Row, 1974.

Littell, F. H. *The German Phoenix.* Garden City, N.Y.: Doubleday, 1960.

Littell, F. H., and Locke, H. G., eds. *The German Church Struggle and the Holocaust.* Detroit, Mich.: Wayne State University Press, 1974.

London, P. "The Rescuers: Motivational Hypotheses about Christians who Saved Jews from the Nazis." In *Altruism and Helping Behavior.* Ed. J. Macaulay and L. Berkowitz. New York: Academic Press, 1970.

Love, S. *Jewish Holocaust Survivors' Attitudes Toward Contemporary Beliefs about Themselves.* Ann Arbor: University of Michigan Publications, 1984.

Lowrie, D. A. *The Hunted Children: The Dramatic Story of the Heroic Men and Women Who Outwitted the Nazis to Save Thousands of Helpless Refugees in Southern France During World War II.* New York: W. W. Norton, 1963.

Lukas, R. *The Forgotten Holocaust: The Poles Under German Occupation 1939–1944.* Lexington: University Press of Kentucky, 1986.

Luther, M. "The Jews and Their Lies." In *The Christian Society.* Vol. 4, of *Luther's Works.* Ed. F. Sherman. Philadelphia: Fortress Press, 1971.

Lytton, H. "Disciplinary Encounters Between Young Boys and Their Mothers and Fathers: Is There a Contingency System?" *Developmental Psychology* 15 (1979): 256–268.

Maas, W. B. *Austria Under Nazi Rule, 1938–1945.* New York: Frederick Ungar, 1978.

MacArthur, L. Z., and Apatow, K. "Impressions of Baby-Faced Adults." *Social Cognition* 2, no. 4 (1983–84): 315–342.

Macaulay, J. R., and Berkowitz, L. "Overview." In *Altruism and Helping Behavior.* Ed. J. Macaulay and L. Berkowitz. New York: Academic Press, 1970.

Maccoby, E. E. *Social Development: Psychological Growth and the Parent-Child Relationship.* New York: Harcourt Brace Jovanovich, 1980.

MacIntyre, A. *After Virtue: A Study in Moral Theory.* South Bend, Ind.: University of Notre Dame Press, 1984.

Malcolm, H. *Thy Brother's Blood* New York: Hart, 1975 (originally published as *Europe and the Jews.* Boston: Beacon Press, 1962).

Marcus J. *Social and Political History of the Jews in Poland 1919–1939.* New York: Mouton Publishers, 1983.

Mark, B. *Ruch Oporu W Getcie Białostockim.* Warszawa, 1952.

Mark, B. *Uprising in the Warsaw Ghetto.* New York: Schocken Books, 1975.

Marrus, M. *The Politics of Assimilation.* New York: Oxford University Press, 1971.

Marrus, M. *The Unwanted: European Refugees in the Twentieth Century.* New York: Oxford University Press, 1985.

Marrus, M. R. "The History of the Holocaust: A Survey of Recent Literature." *The Journal of Modern History* 59 (March 1987): 114–159.

Marrus, M. R., and Paxton, R. O. *Vichy France and the Jews.* New York: Schocken Books, 1983.

Marton, K. *Wallenberg.* New York: Random House, 1982.

Mason, H. "Testing Human Bonds Within Nations: Jews in the Occupied Netherlands." *Political Science Quarterly* 99, no. 2 (Summer 1984): 315–343.

Mason, H. L. *Mass Demonstrations Against Foreign Regimes.* New Orleans: Tulane Studies in Political Science, 1966.

Massing, P. *Rehearsal for Destruction: A Study of the Political Anti-Semitism in Imperial Germany.* New York: Harper & Row, 1949.

Matter, J. A. *Love, Altruism, and World Crisis: The Challenge of Pitirim Sorokin.* Chicago: Nelson-Hall Company, 1974.

Mayer, M., ed. *They Thought They Were Free: The Germans, 1933–1945.* Chicago: University of Chicago Press, 1966.

McClelland, D. C. *Human Motivation.* Glenview, Ill: Scott, Foresman and Company, 1985.

McCrae, R. R., and Costa, P. T., Jr. *Emerging Lives, Enduring Dispositions.* Boston: Little, Brown & Co., 1984.

McKeon, R., ed. *The Basic Works of Aristotle.* New York: Random House, 1941.

Mehrabian, A., and Epstein, N. "A Measure of Emotional Empathy". *Journal of Personality* 40 (1972): 525–543.

Meltzer, M. *Never to Forget.* New York: Dell, 1976.

Mendelsohn, E. "The Dilemma of Jewish Politics in Poland: Four Responses." In *Jews and Non-Jews in Eastern Europe 1918–1945.* Ed. B. Vago and G. L. Mosse. New York: Halsted Press, 1974.

Mendelsohn, E. *The Jews of East Central Europe Between the World Wars.* Bloomington: Indiana University Press, 1983.

Mermelstein, M. *By Bread Alone—The Story of A-4685.* Los Angeles: Crescent Publications, 1979.

Meyer, J. P., and Mulherin, A. "From Attribution to Helping: An Analysis of the Mediating Effects of Affect and Expectancy." *Journal of Personality and Social Psychology* 39 (1980): 201–210.

Michaelis, M. *Mussolini and the Jews: German-Italian Relations and the Jewish Question in Italy, 1922–1945.* New York: Oxford University Press, 1978.

Michman, D. "The Committee for Jewish Refugees in Holland, 1933–1940." *Yad Vashem Studies* 14 (1981): 205–232.

Michman, J. "The Controversial Stand of the Joodse Raad in the Netherlands: Lodewijk Visser's Struggle." *Yad Vashem Studies* 10 (1974): 9–68.

Midlarsky, E. "Aiding Under Stress: The Effects of Competence, Dependency, Visibility, and Fatalism." *Journal of Personality* 39 (1971): 132–149.

Midlarsky, E. "Competence and Helping: Notes Toward a Model." In *Development and Maintenance of Prosocial Behavior: International Perspectives on Positive Moral-ity.* Ed. E. Staub, D. Bar-Tal, J. Karylowski and J. Reykowski. New York: Ple-num Press, 1984.

Midlarsky, E., and Bryan, J. H. "Affect Expressions and Children's Imitative Altru-ism." *Journal of Experimental Research in Personality* 6 (1972): 195–203.

Midlarsky, E., and Kahana, E. *Altruism and Helping among the Elderly.* Paper pre-sented at the American Psychological Association, Los Angeles, May 1981.

Midlarsky, E.; Kahana, E.; and Corley, R. "Personal and Situational Influences on Late Life Helping." *Humboldt Journal of Social Relations* 13, no. 1–2 (1985/86): 217–233.

Midlarsky, E., and Midlarsky, M. I. "Some Determinants of Aiding Under Exper-imentally-Induced Stress." *Journal of Personality* 41 (1973): 305–327.

Midlarsky, M. I. "Helping during the Holocaust: The Role of Political, Theologi-cal and Socioeconomic Identifications." *Humboldt Journal of Social Relations* 13, no. 1–2 (1985/86): 285–305.

Milgram, S. *Obedience to Authority.* New York: Harper & Row, 1973.

Miller, A. *For Your Own Good: Hidden Cruelty in Child-Rearing and the Roots of Violence.* New York: Farrar, Straus & Giroux, 1984.

Miller, D. T., and Ross, M. "Self-Serving Biases in the Attribution of Causality: Fact or Fiction?" *Psychological Bulletin* 2 (1975): 213–225.

Miller, J. B. *Toward a New Psychology of Women.* Boston: Beacon Press, 1976.

Milton, S. "The Righteous Who Helped Jews." In *Genocide: Critical Issues of the Holocaust.* Ed. A. Grobman and D. Landes. Los Angeles: Simon Wiesenthal Center, 1983.

Minton, C., Kagan, J., and Levine, J. "Maternal Control and Obedience in the Two-Year-Old," *Child Development* 62 (1971): 1873–1894.

Mischel, W. *Personality and Assessment.* New York: John Wiley & Sons, 1968.

Monte, C. *Beneath the Mask: An Introduction to Theories of Personality.* New York: Holt, Rinehart & Winston, 1980.

Moore, B. "Jewish Refugees in the Netherlands 1933–1940: The Structure and Pattern of Immigration from Nazi Germany." *Leo Baeck Institute Year Book* 29 (1984): 73–101.

Morgan, D. N. *Love: Plato, the Bible and Freud.* Englewood Cliffs, N.J.: Prentice-Hall, 1964.

Morse, A. D. *Die Wasser teilten sich nicht.* Berne, Munich, Vienna: Ruetten und Loening Verlag, 1968.

Morse, A. D. *While Six Million Died: A Chronicle of American Apathy.* New York: Ran-dom House, 1967.

Moser, J. "Nisko: The First Experiment in Deportation." *Simon Wiesenthal Center Annual* 2 (1985): 1–30.

Moskowitz, S. *Love Despite Hate: Child Survivors of the Holocaust and Their Adult Lives.* New York: Schocken Books, 1982.

Mosse, G. L. *The Crisis of German Ideology.* New York: Grosset & Dunlap, 1964.

Mosse, G. L. *Toward the Final Solution: A History of European Racism.* New York: Howard Fertig, 1978.

Mowrer, O. H. *Learning Theory and the Symbolic Processes.* New York: John Wiley & Sons, 1960.

Murdoch, I. *The Sovereignty of Good.* London: Routledge & Kegan Paul, 1970.

Mussen, P. and Eisenberg-Berg, N. *Roots of Caring, Sharing, and Helping: The Development of Prosocial Behavior in Children.* San Francisco: W. H. Freeman and Co., 1977.

Nedoncelle, M. *Love and the Person.* Trans. Sr. R. Adelaide, S.C. New York: Sheed & Ward, 1966.

Neugarten, B. L. "Adult Personality: Toward a Psychology of the Life Cycle." In *Middle Age and Aging: A Reader in Social Psychology.* Ed. B. L. Neugarten. Chicago: University of Chicago Press, 1968.

Niebuhr, R. *Moral Man and Immoral Society: A Study in Ethics and Politics.* New York: Charles Scribner's Sons, 1952.

Noddings, N. *Caring: A Feminine Approach to Ethics and Moral Education.* Berkeley: University of California Press, 1984.

Norton, D. L., and Kille, M. F. *Philosophies of Love.* New York: Rowman & Allanheld Publishers, 1983.

Nowak, J. *Courier from Warsaw.* Foreword by Z. Brzezinski. Detroit, Mich.: Wayne State Unversity Press, 1982.

Nyiszli, M. *Auschwitz: An Eyewitness Account.* New York: Frederick Fell, 1960.

Oliner, P. "Compassion and Caring: Missing Concepts in Social Studies Programs." *Journal of Education* 161, no.4 (1979): 36–60.

Oliner, P. "Implementing and Legitimating Prosocial Education." *Humboldt Journal of Social Relations* 13, no. 1-2 (1985/86): 389–408.

Oliner, P. "Putting 'Community' Into Citizenship Education: The Need for Prosociality." *Theory and Research in Social Education* 11, no. 2 (1983): 65–84.

Oliner, P. "Putting Compassion and Caring into Social Studies Classrooms." *Social Education* 47, no. 4 (1983): 273–277.

Oliner, S. P. "The Heroes of the Nazi-Era: A Plea for Recognition." *Reconstructionist* 48 (June 1982): 7–14.

Oliner, S. P. "The Unsung Heroes in Nazi-Occupied Europe: The Antidote for Evil." *Nationalities Papers* 12, no. 1 (Spring 1984): 129–136.

Oliner, S. P. *Restless Memories: Recollections of the Holocaust Years.* Berkeley, Calif.: Judah L. Magnes Memorial Museum, 1986.

Oliner, S. P., and Hallum, K. "Minority Contempt for Oppressors: A Comparative Analysis of Jews and Gypsies." *California Sociologist* 1, no. 1 (Winter 1978): 41–57.

Oliver, H. D. *Wir, die Geretteten.* Sofia, Bulgaria: Fremdsprachen Verlag, 1967.

Paldiel, M. "Hesed and the Holocaust." *Journal of Ecumenical Studies* 23, no. 1 (Winter 1986): 90–106.

Paldiel, M. "Radical Altruism: Three Case Studies." *Midstream* 33 (April 1987): 35–39.

Panksepp, J. "The Psychobiology of Prosocial Behaviors: Separation Distress, Play, and Altruism." In *Altruism and Aggression: Biological and Social Origins.* Ed. C. Zahn-Waxler, E. M. Cummings, and R. Iannotti. New York: Cambridge University Press, 1986.

Papanek, E., and Linn, E. *Out of the Fire.* New York: William Morrow, 1975.

Paris, E. *Genocide in Satellite Croatia, 1941–1945.* Chicago: American Institute for Baltic Affairs, n.d.

Paris, E. *Unhealed Wounds: France and The Klaus Barbie Affair.* New York: Grove Press, 1985.

Park, R. E. *Race and Culture.* Glencoe, Ill.: Free Press, 1950.

Parkes, J. *The Conflict of the Church and the Synagogue.* New York: Atheneum, 1974.

Parkes, J. W. *An Enemy of the People: Anti-Semitism.* New York: Quadrangle, 1964.

Parsons, T. *The Structure of Social Action.* New York: Free Press, 1939.

Parsons, T., and Shils, E. A., eds. *Toward a General Theory of Action.* New York: Harper and Row, 1951.

Pat, J. *Ashes and Fire.* New York: International Universities Press, 1947.

Patterson, C. "Yad Vashem Conference: 35 Educators Learn How to Teach the Holocaust." *Jewish World* (14–20 October 1983): 8+.

Pawlikowski, J. T. "The Holocaust and Catholic Theology: Some Reflections." *Shoah* 2, no. 1 (Spring/Summer 1980): 6–9.

Pawlowicz, S., and Klose, K. *I Will Survive.* New York: W. W. Norton, 1962.

Paxton, R. O. *Vicy France: Old Guard and New Order, 1940–1944.* New York: Knopf, 1972.

Pedatella, R. A. "Italian Attitudes Toward Jewry in the Twentieth Century." *Jewish Social Studies* 47, no. 1 (Winter 1985): 51–62.

Penkower, M. N. *The Jews Were Expendable: Free World Diplomacy and the Holocaust.* Chicago: University of Illinois Press, 1983.

Percival, J. *For Valour.* London: Thames Methuen, 1985.

Perl, G. *I Was a Doctor at Auschwitz.* New York: International Universities Press, 1948.

Pervin, L. A. *Current Controversies and Issues in Personality.* New York: John Wiley & Sons, 1978.

Peters, R. S. *Reason and Compassion.* London: Routledge & Kegan Paul, 1973.

Peterson, L. "Influence of Age, Task Competence, and Responsibility Focus on Children's Altruism." *Developmental Psychology* 19 (1983): 141–148.

Peterson, L. "Role of Donor Competence, Donor Age, and Peer Presence on Helping in an Emergency." *Developmental Psychology* 19 (1983): 873–880.

Phares, E. J. *Locus of Control in Personality.* Morristown, N.J.: General Learning Press, 1976.

Piaget, J. *The Moral Judgment of the Child.* Glencoe, Ill.: Free Press, 1948.

Piliavin, I. M.; Rodin, J.; and Piliavin, J. A. "Good Samaritanism: An Underground Phenomenon? *Journal of Personality and Social Psychology* 13 (1969): 289–299.

Piliavin, J.; Dovidio, J. F.; Gaertner, S. L.; and Clark, R. D. III. *Emergency Intervention.* New York: Academic Press, 1981.

Piliavin, J. A., and Piliavin, I. M. "The Effects of Blood on Reactions to a Victim". *Journal of Personality and Social Psychology* 23 (1972): 253–261.

Piliavin, J. A., and Piliavin, I. M. "The Good Samaritan: Why Does He Help?" Unpublished manuscript, n. d.

Pinkus, O. *The House of Ashes.* New York: World Publishing House, 1964.

Pisar, S. *Of Blood and Hope.* Boston: Little, Brown & Co., 1980.

Poliakov, L. "Human Morality and the Nazi Terror." *Commentary* (August 1950): 111–116.

Poliakov, L. "The Vatican and the Jewish Question." *Commentary* (November 1950): 439–449.

Poliakov, L. *Harvest of Hate.* New York: Holocaust Library, 1979.

Poliakov, L. *L'Auberge des musiciens.* Paris: Mazarine, 1981.

Poliakov, L. *The Aryan Myth: A History of Racist and Nationalist Ideas in Europe.* New York: Basic Books, 1971.

Poliakov, L. *The History of Anti-Semitism.* New York: Schocken Books, 1965.

Poliakov, L., and Sabille, J. *Jews Under the Italian Occupation.* New York: Howard Fertig, 1983.

Porter, J. N. *Genocide and Human Rights: A Global Anthology.* Lanham, Md.: University Press of America, 1982.

Prekerowa, T. *Konspiracyjna Rada Pomocy, Żydom W Warszawie 1942–1945* (Illegal help to Jews in Warsaw). Warszawa: Państwowy Instytut Wydawniczy, 1982.

Presser, J. *The Destruction of the Dutch Jews.* New York: E. P. Dutton, 1969.

Prus, R. C. "Resisting Designations: An Extension of Attribution Theory into a Negotiated Context." *Sociological Inquiry* 45, no. 1 (1975): 3–14.

Pulzer, P. *The Rise of Political Anti-Semitism in Germany and Austria.* New York: John Wiley & Sons, 1964.

Puxon, G. *Rom: Europe's Gypsies* (report no. 14) London: Minority Rights Group, March 1973.

Raab, E. *The Anatomy of Nazism.* New York: ADL, 1961.

Rabinowitz, D. *About the Holocaust: What We Know and How We Know It.* New York: American Jewish Committee, 1979.

Ramati, A. *The Assisi Underground: The Priests Who Rescued Jews.* New York: Stein & Day, 1978.

Ratcliffe, J. M. *The Good Samaritan and the Law.* New York: Anchor Books, 1966.

Rawls, J. *A Theory of Justice.* Cambridge, Mass.: Harvard University Press, 1971.

Rector, F. *The Nazi Extermination of Homosexuals.* New York: Stein & Day, 1981.

Reichmann, E. *Hostages of Civilization: The Sources of National Socialist Anti-Semitism.* Westport, Conn.: Greenwood Press, 1970.

Reid, J. B. "Social-Interactional Patterns in Families of Abused and Nonabused Children." In *Altruism and Aggression: Biological and Social Origins.* Ed. C. Zahn-Waxler, E. M. Cummings, and R. Iannotti. New York: Cambridge University Press, 1986.

Reiss, J. *The Upstairs Room.* New York: Thomas Y. Crowell, 1972;

Reitlinger, G. *The Final Solution: The Attempt to Exterminate the Jews of Europe, 1939–1945.* New York: Beechhurst Press, 1953.

Reitlinger, G. *The SS: Alibi of a Nation: 1922–1945.* New York: Viking, 1957.

Rescue Attempts During the Holocaust. Proceedings of the Second Yad Vashem International Historical Conference, Jerusalem, 8–11 April 1974. New York: Ktav Publishing House, 1978.

Reykowski, J. "Activation of Helping Motivation: The Role of Extensivity." Unpublished paper, 1987.

Reykowski, J. "Dimensions of Development in Moral Values: Two Approaches to the Development of Morality." In *Social and Moral Values: Individual and Societal Perspectives*. Ed. N. Eisenberg, J. Reykowski, and E. Staub. Hillsdale, N.J.: Lawrence Erlbaum, 1987.

Reykowski, J. "Motivation of Prosocial Behavior." In *Cooperation and Helping Behavior: Theories and Research*. Ed. V. J. Derlaga and J. Grzelak. New York: Academic Press, 1982.

Reykowski, J. "Spatial Organization of a Cognitive System and Intrinsic Prosocial Motivation." In *Development and Maintenance of Prosocial Behavior: International Perspectives on Positive Morality*. Ed. E. Staub, D. Bar-Tal, J. Karylowski, and J. Reykowski. New York: Plenum Press, 1984.

Reykowski, J. "Who is my Neighbor?: The Case of Descriptive and Affective Judgment." Paper delivered at the Conférence de la Psychologie Social et les Émotions, Paris, Fall 1987.

Reykowski, J. *Motywacja, Postawy Prospoleczne A Osobowość (Prosocial motivation, prosocial attitudes and personality)* Warszawa: PWN, 1979.

Richards, D. A. J. *A Theory of Reasons for Action*. New York: Oxford University Press, 1971.

Riesman, D. *The Lonely Crowd*. New Haven, Conn.: Yale University Press, 1950.

Riesman, David; Denney, Reuel; and Glazer, Nathan. *The Lonely Crowd: A Study of the Changing American Character*. New Haven, Conn.: Yale University Press, 1950.

Ringelblum, E. *Notes from the Warsaw Ghetto: The Journal of Emmanuel Ringelblum*. New York: McGraw-Hill, 1958.

Ringelblum, E. *Polish-Jewish Relations During the Second World War*. Ed. J. Kermish and S. Krakowski. New York: Howard Fertig, 1976.

Rings, W. *Life with the Enemy: Collaboration and Resistance in Hitler's Europe 1939–1945*. Garden City, N.Y.: Doubleday, 1982.

Rittner, C., and Myers, S., eds. *The Courage to Care*. New York: New York University Press, 1986.

Robinson, J. *And the Crooked Shall Be Straight*. New York: Macmillan, 1965.

Rok, A. "Jedno Ludzkie Zycie." *Folks Sztyme*, Warszawa (September 1978): 11–12.

Rokeach, M. "A Mighty Fortress: Faith, Hope and Bigotry." *Psychology Today* (April 1970): 33–58.

Rokeach, M. *The Nature of Human Values*. New York: Free Press, 1973.

Rokeach, M. *The Open and Closed Mind*. New York: Basic Books, 1960.

Rokeach, M., ed. *Understanding Human Values: Individual and Societal*. New York: Free Press, 1979.

Rose, L. *The Tulips Are Red*. New York: A. S. Barnes & Co., 1978.

Rosen, D. *The Forest My Friend*. Trans. M. S. Chertoff. New York: World Federation of Bergen-Belsen Association, 1971.

Rosenberg, M. *Society and the Adolescent Self-Image*. Princeton, N.J.: Princeton University Press, 1965.

Rosenberg, M., and Kaplan, H. B. *Social Psychology of the Self-Concept.* Arlington Heights, Ill.: H. Davidson, 1982.

Rosenfeld, H. *Raoul Wallenberg: Angel of Rescue—Heroism and Torment in the Gulag.* Buffalo, N.Y.: Prometheus Books, 1982.

Rosenhan, D. "Learning Theory and Prosocial Behavior." *Journal of Social Issues* 28 (1972): 151–164.

Rosenhan, D. L. "Some Origins of Concern for Others." In *Trends and Issues in Developmental Psychology.* Ed. P. Mussen, J. Langer, and M. Covington. New York: Academic Press, 1969.

Rosenhan, D. L. "The Natural Socialization of Altruistic Autonomy." In *Altruism and Helping Behavior.* Ed. J. Macaulay and L. Berkowitz. New York: Academic Press, 1970.

Rosenhan, D. L. "Toward Resolving the Altruistic Paradox: Affect, Self-Reinforcement and Cognition." In *Altruism, Sympathy and Helping: Psychological and Sociological Principles.* Ed. L. Wispe. New York: Academic Press, 1978.

Rosenthal, L. *How Was It Possible?* Berkeley, Calif.: Judah L. Magnes Memorial Museum, 1971.

Rosenthal, L. *The Final Solution to the Jewish Question: Mass-Murder or Hoax?* Berkeley, Calif.: Judah L. Magnes Memorial Museum, 1979.

Rossel, S. *The Holocaust.* New York: Franklin Watts, 1981.

Roth, C. "The Last Days of Jewish Salonica." *Commentary* 10 (July 1950): 49–55.

Roth, C. *The History of the Jews of Italy.* Philadelphia: Jewish Publication Society, 1946.

Roth, J. K. "The Holocaust and Freedom to Choose." *Shoah* 2, no. 1 (Spring/Summer 1980): 19–22.

Rothchild, S., ed. *Voices from the Holocaust.* New York: New American Library, 1981.

Rothkirchen, L. "Czech Attitudes Towards the Jews During the Nazi Regime." *Yad Vashem Studies* 13 (1979): 287–320.

Rotter, J. B. "Generalized Expectancies for Internal Versus External Control of Reinforcement." *Psychological Monographs* 80, no. 1 (1966).

Rubenstein, R. L. *The Age of Triage: Fear and Hope in an Overcrowded World.* New York: Harper & Row, 1982.

Rubenstein, R. L. *The Cunning of History: The Holocaust and the American Future.* New York: Harper & Row, 1975.

Rubinowicz, D. *The Diary of Dawid Rubinowicz.* Trans. D. Bowman. Edmonds, Wash.: Creative Options, 1982.

Rudashevski, Y. *The Diary of the Vilna Ghetto: June 1941–April 1943.* Trans. P. Matenko. Israel: Kibbutz Lohamei Haghettaot (Ghetto fighter's house), 1972.

Ruether, R. R. "Anti-Semitism and Christian Theology." In *Auschwitz: Beginning of a New Era? Reflections on the Holocaust.* Ed. Eva Fleischner. New York: Ktav Publishing House, 1977.

Rushton, J. P. "The Altruistic Personality: Evidence from Laboratory, Naturalistic, and Self-Report Perspectives." In *Development and Maintenance of Prosocial Behavior: International Perspectives on Positive Morality.* Ed. E. Staub, D. Bar-Tal, J. Karylowski, and J. Reykowski. New York: Plenum Press, 1984.

Rushton, J. P. *Altruism, Socialization and Society.* Englewood Cliffs, N.J.: Prentice-Hall, 1980.

Rushton, J. P., and Wiener, J. "Altruism and Cognitive Development in Children". *British Journal of Social and Clinical Psychology* 14 (1975): 341–349.

Sanford, R. N., Comstock, C., and associates. *Sanctions for Evil: The Sources of Social Destructiveness.* San Francisco: Jossey-Bass Publishers, 1971.

Sartre, J. *Anti-Semite and Jew.* New York: Schocken Books, 1965, 1976.

Sauvage, P. "A Most Persistent Haven: Le Chambon-Sur-Lignon." *Moment* (October 1983): 30–35.

Sauvage, P. "Ten Things I would Like to Know About Righteous Conduct in Le Chambon and Elsewhere During the Holocaust." *Humboldt Journal of Social Relations* 13 no. 1–2 (1985/86): 252–259.

Schaffer, H. R., and Emerson, P. E. "The Development of Social Attachments in Infancy." *Monographs of the Society for Research in Child Development* 29, no. 3 (1964): 1–77.

Scheffler, W. "The Forgotten Part of the 'Final Solution': The Liquidation of the Ghettos." *Simon Wiesenthal Center Annual* 2 (1985): 31–47.

Schlenker, B. R.; Hallam, J. R.; and McCown, N. E. "Motives and Social Evaluation: Actor Observer Differences in the Delineation of Motives for a Beneficial Act." *Journal of Experimental Social Psychology* 19 (1983): 254–273.

Schlesinger, W. "On a Reappraisal of the *Shtadlan* During the Holocaust: The Activity and Correspondence of Dr. Wilhelm Filderman on Behalf of Roumania's Jews." *Centerpoint: A Journal of Interdisciplinary Studies* 4, no. 1 (Fall 1980): 113–121.

Schleunes, K. A. *The Twisted Road to Auschwitz: Nazi Policy Toward German Jews.* Chicago: University of Illinois Press, 1970.

Schneider, G. *Journey into Terror: Story of the Riga Ghetto.* New York: Ark House, 1980.

Schoggen, P. "Environmental Forces in the Everyday Lives of Children." In *The Stream of Behavior.* Ed. R. G. Barker. New York: Appelton-Century-Crofts, 1963.

Schulweis, H. "The Holocaust Dybbuk." *Moment* 1 (Feb. 1976): 4.

Schwartz, S. H. "Normative Influences on Altruism." In *Advances in Experimental Social Psychology,* Vol. 10. Ed. L. Berkowitz. New York: Academic Press, 1977.

Schwartz, S. H., and Howard, J. A. "Helping and Cooperation: A Self-Based Motivational Model." In *Cooperation and Helping Behavior: Theories and Research.* Ed. V. J. Derlega and J. Grzelak. New York: Academic Press, 1982.

Schwartz, S. H., and Howard, J. A. "Internalized Values as Motivators of Altruism." In *Development and Maintenance of Prosocial Behavior: International Perspectives on Positive Morality.* Ed. E. Staub, D. Bar-Tal, J. Karylowski, and J. Reykowski. New York: Plenum Press, 1984.

Schwarz, S. *The Jews in the Soviet Union.* New York: Arno Press, 1951, 1972.

Seeman, M. "Intellectual Perspective and Adjustment to Minority Status." *Social Problems* 3 (1956): 142–153.

Seeman, M. "On the Meaning of Alienation." *American Sociological Review* 24 (1959): 783–791.

Sereny, G. *Into That Darkness.* New York: McGraw-Hill, 1974.

Shaver, P., ed. *Self, Situations, and Social Behavior.* Beverly Hills, Calif.: Sage Publications, 1985.

Shibutani, T. *Society and Personality: An Interactionist Approach to Social Psychology.* Englewood Cliffs, N.J.: Prentice-Hall, 1961.

Shirer, W. L. *The Rise and Fall of the Third Reich.* New York: Simon & Schuster, 1960.

Siegler, I. C. "Psychological Aspects of the Duke Longitudinal Studies." In *Longitudinal Studies of Adult Psychological Development.* Ed. K. W. Schaie. New York: Guilford Press, 1983.

Sierakowski, D. "Pamietnik Z Ghetta Łódzkiego" (Diary from Lodz Ghetto). *ZIH* 28 (1958): 79–110.

Sijes, B. A. *De Februari-Staking.* The Hague: Martinus Nijhoff, 1954.

Silberschein, A. (L. R.) "Rescue Efforts with the Assistance of International Organizations-Documents from the Archives of Dr. A. Silberschein." *Yad Vashem Studies* 8 (1970): 69–80.

Sim, K. *Women at War: Five Heroines Who Defied the Nazis and Survived.* New York: William Morrow, 1982.

Simmel, G. *Conflict.* Trans. K. H. Wolff, *The Web of Group Affiliations.* Trans. R. Bendix. Glencoe, Ill.: Free Press, 1955.

Simpson, E. L. "Moral Development Research: A Case of Scientific Cultural Bias." *Human Development* 17 (1974): 81–106.

Skinner, B. F. *Science and Human Behavior.* New York: Macmillan, 1974.

Skolnick, A. S. *The Psychology of Human Development.* New York: Harcourt Brace Jovanovich, 1986.

Smith, D. M. *Mussolini's Roman Empire.* New York: Viking, 1976.

Smith, D. M. *Mussolini.* New York: Knopf, 1982.

Smith, M. B. *Social Psychology and Human Values.* New York: Aldine Publishing, 1969.

Smoleńska, M. A. "Dystans Psychologiczny Partnera a Dzialanie Na Jego Rzecz." Ph.D. dissertation, University of Warsaw, 1979.

Smolski, W. *Za To Grazita Śmierć* (Death threatened for this). Warszawa: Pax, 1981.

Sobiesiak, J. *Ziemia Płonie* (The soil burns). Lublin, Poland: Wydawnictwo Lubelskie, 1974.

Sorokin, P. "Factors of Altruism and Egoism." *Sociology and Social Research* 32 (1948): 674–678.

Sorokin, P. *Altruistic Love: A Study of American "Good Neighbors" and Christian Saints.* Boston: Beacon Press, 1950.

Sorokin, P. *Explorations in Altruistic Love and Behavior: A Symposium.* Boston: Beacon Press, 1950.

Sorokin, P. *Forms and Techniques of Altruistic and Spiritual Growth.* Boston: Beacon Press, 1954.

Sorokin, P. *The Reconstruction of Humanity.* Boston: Beacon Press, 1948.

Sorokin, P. *The Ways and Powers of Love.* Chicago: H. Regnery, 1967.

Soucy, R. *Fascism in France: The Case of Maurice Barrès.* Berkeley: University of California Press, 1972.

Staub, E. "Social and Prosocial Behavior: Personal and Situational Influences and Their Interactions." In *Personality: Basic Aspects and Current Research.* Ed. E. Staub. Englewood Cliffs, N.J.: Prentice-Hall, 1980.

Staub, E. *Positive Social Behavior and Morality.* New York: Academic Press, 1979.

Staub, E., and Baer, R. S. "Stimulus Characteristics of Sufferer and Difficulty of Escape as Determinants of Helping." *Journal of Personality and Social Psychology* 30, no. 2 (1974): 279–284.

Staub, E.; Bar-Tal, D.; Karylowski, J.; and Reykowski, J., eds. *Development and Maintenance of Prosocial Behavior: International Perspectives on Positive Morality.* New York: Plenum Press, 1984.

Stein, A. *Quiet Heroes: Dutch-Canadian Rescuers of Jews.* In press.

Stein, J. B. "Britain and the Jews of Danzig: 1938–1939." *Wiener Library Bulletin* 32, no. 49–50 (1979): 29–33.

Steinberg, L. *Not as a Lamb: The Jews Against Hitler.* Trans. M. Hunter. Farnborough, England: Saxon House, 1974.

Steiner, G. "Postscript to a Tragedy." *Encounter* 28, no. 2 (February 1967): 33–39.

Steiner, J. F. *Treblinka.* Trans. H. Weaver. New York: Simon & Schuster, 1967.

Steiner, J. M. "The SS Yesterday and Today: A Sociopsychological View." In *Survivors, Victims, and Perpetrators: Essays on the Nazi Holocaust.* Ed. J. E. Dimsdale. Washington, D.C.: Hemisphere, 1980.

Steiner, J. M. *Power Politics and Social Change in National Socialist Germany: A Process of Escalation into Mass Destruction.* The Hague: Mouton; Atlantic Highlands, N.J.: Humanities Press, 1976.

Steinitz, L., and Szonyi, D., eds. *Living After the Holocaust: Reflections of the Post-War Generation in America.* New York: Bloch, 1979.

Stern, F. *The Politics of Cultural Despair.* Berkeley: University of California Press, 1961.

Sternhell, Z. *La droite révolutionnaire, 1885–1914: Les origines françaises du fascisme.* Paris: Éditions du Seuil, 1978.

Stokes, L. D. "The German People and the Destruction of the European Jews." *Central European History* 6, no. 2 (June 1973): 167–192.

Stone, G. P., and Farberman, H. A. *Social Psychology Through Symbolic Interaction.* New York: John Wiley & Sons, 1981.

Stoodley, B. H., ed. *Society and Self.* New York: Free Press, 1962.

Stotland, E. "Exploratory Studies in Empathy." In *Advances in Experimental Social Psychology,* vol. 4. Ed. L. Berkowitz. New York: Academic Press, 1969.

Strauss, H. A. "Jewish Emigration from Germany-Nazi Policies and Jewish Responses." *Leo Baeck Institute Year Book* 25–26 (1980/81): 313–361, 343–409.

Strom, M. S., and Parsons, W. S. *Facing History and Ourselves: Holocaust and Human Behavior.* Brookline, Mass.: Intentional Educations, Inc., 1982.

Suhl, Y., ed. *They Fought Back: The Story of the Jewish Resistance in Nazi Europe.* New York: Schocken Books, 1975.

Syrkin, M. *Blessed Is the Match: The Story of Jewish Resistance.* Philadelphia: Jewish Publication Society, 1976.

Szajkowski, Z. *An Illustrated Sourcebook of Russian Anti-Semitism, 1881–1978,* 2 vols. New York: Ktav Publishing House, 1980.

Szonyi, D. M. *The Holocaust: An Annotated Bibliography and Resource Guide.* New York: The National Jewish Resource Center, 1985.

Szymańska, Z. "Ratunek W Klasztorze" (Rescue in the Convent). *ZIH* 4, no. 88 (1973): 33–44.

Szymańska, Z. *Bylam Tylko Lekarzen* (I was only a physician). Warszawa: Pax, 1979.

Tal, U. *Christians and Jews in Germany: Religion, Politics and Ideology in the Second Reich, 1870–1914.* Ithaca, N.Y.: Cornell University Press, 1975.

Tannenbaum, E. R. *The Fascist Experience: Italian Society and Culture, 1922–1945.* New York: Basic Books, 1972.

Tec, N. "Polish Anti-Semitism and the Rescuing of Jews." *East European Quarterly* 20, no. 3 (1986): 299–315.

Tec, N. "Righteous Christians in Poland." *International Social Science Review* (Winter 1983): 12–19.

Tec, N. "Righteous Christians—Who Are They?" In *Book of Proceedings, Eighth World Congress of Jewish Studies.* Jerusalem: 1982, 167–172.

Tec, N. "Sex Distinctions and Passing as Christians During the Holocaust." *East European Quarterly* 18, no. 1 (March 1984): 113–123.

Tec, N. *Dry Tears: The Story of a Lost Childhood.* New York: Oxford University Press, 1984.

Tec, N. *When Light Pierced the Darkness: Christian Rescue of Jews in Nazi-Occupied Poland.* New York: Oxford University Press, 1986.

Ten Boom, C. *The Hiding Place.* London: Hodder & Stoughton, 1971.

Tenenbaum, J. *Underground.* New York: Philosophical Library, 1952.

Thalmann, R., and Feinermann, E. *Crystal Night: 9–10 November 1938.* Trans. G. Cremonesi. New York: Coward, McCann & Geoghegan, 1974.

The Path to Dictatorship 1918–1933: Ten Essays. Trans. J. Conway. New York: Anchor Books, 1966.

Thomas, G., and Witts, M. *Voyage of the Damned.* New York: Stein & Day, 1974.

Thomas, W. I., and Thomas, D. S. *The Child in America.* New York: Knopf, 1928.

Tikayer, M., and Swartz, M. *The Fugu Plan: Japanese and Jews During WWII.* New York: Paddington, 1979.

Tillich, P. *Morality and Beyond.* New York: Harper & Row, 1963.

Toi, M., and Batson, D. C. "More Evidence That Empathy is a Source of Altruistic Motivation." *Journal of Personality and Social Psychology* 43, no. 2 (1982): 281–292.

Toland, J. *Adolf Hitler.* Garden City, N.Y.: Doubleday, 1976.

Trimakas, K. A., and Nicolay, R. C. "Self-Concept and Altruism in Old Age." *Journal of Gerontology* 29 no. 4 (1974): 434–439.

Trunk, I. *Jewish Responses to Nazi Persecution.* New York: Stein & Day, 1980.

Trunk, I. *Judenrat: The Jewish Councils in Eastern Europe Under Nazi Occupation.* Trans. J. Robinson, New York: Stein & Day, 1977.

Tushnet, L. *The Pavements of Hell.* New York: St. Martin's Press, 1972.

Tusk-Schweinwechslerowa, F. "Cena Jednego Życia, Wspomienia Z Czasów Okupacji." *Biuletyn Żydowskiego Instytutu Historycznego* 33 (1960): 88–104.

Valentin, H. "Rescue and Relief Acting in Behalf of Jewish Victims of Nazism in Scandinavia." *YIVO Annual* 8 (1953): 224–251.

Vitale, M. A. "The Destruction and Resistance of the Jews in Italy." In *They Fought*

Back: The Story of the Jewish Resistance in Nazi Europe. Ed. Y. Suhl. New York: Schocken Books, 1975.

Vrba, R., and Bestie, A. *I Cannot Forgive.* New York: Grove Press, 1964.

Waagenar, S. "Unknown War Hero: Rescue of the Jews by a Capuchin Priest." *America* 131, no. 11 (19 October 1974): 210–212.

Waagenar, S. *The Pope's Jews.* La Salle, Ill.: Alcove, 1974.

Waite, R. G. *The Psychopathic God Adolf Hitler.* New York: Basic Books, 1977.

Wallach, M. A., and Wallach, L. *Psychology's Sanction for Selfishness: The Error of Egoism in Theory and Therapy.* San Francisco: W. H. Freeman & Co., 1983.

Walton, D. N. *Courage.* Berkeley: University of California Press, 1986.

Warmbrunn, W. *The Dutch Under German Occupation 1940–1945.* Stanford, Calif.: Stanford University Press, 1963.

Wasserstein, B. *Great Britain and the Jews of Europe, 1939–1945.* New York: Oxford University Press, 1979.

Weber, E. "France." In *The European Right: A Historical Profile.* Ed. H. Rogger and E. Weber. Berkeley: University of California Press, 1965.

Weber, E. *Action Française.* Stanford, Calif.: Stanford University Press, 1962.

Weber, E. *The Nationalist Revival in France.* Berkeley: University of California Press, 1959.

Wegner, D. M. "The Self in Prosocial Action". In *The Self in Social Psychology.* Ed. D. M. Wegner and R. R. Vallacher. New York: Oxford University Press, 1980.

Weinberg, D. H. *A Community on Trial: The Jews of Paris in the 1930's.* Chicago: University of Chicago Press, 1977.

Weiner, B. "A Cognitive (Attribution)—Emotion—Action Model of Motivated Behavior: An Analysis of Judgments of Help Giving." *Journal of Personality and Social Psychology* 39 (1980): 186–200.

Weiner, B. *Human Motivation.* New York: Holt, Rinehart & Winston, 1980.

Weinreich, M. *Hitler's Professors.* New York: YIVO Institute for Jewish Research, 1946.

Weinstock, E., and Wilner, H. *The Seven Years.* New York: E. P. Dutton, 1959.

Weiss, A. "Jewish Leadership in Occupied Poland." *Yad Vashem Studies* 12 (1977): 335–366.

Wells, L. *The Janowska Road.* New York: Macmillan, 1963.

Werbell, F., and Clarke, T. *Lost Hero: The Mystery of Raoul Wallenberg.* New York: McGraw-Hill, 1982.

Wiener, V. L.; Fogelman. E.; and Cohen, S. P. "Rescuers: Why Righteous Gentiles Risked Their Lives to Save Jews." *The Jewish Monthly* (January 1985): 16–19.

Wiesel, E. *Night.* New York: Hill and Wang, 1960.

Williams, B. A. O. *Moral Luck: Philosophical Papers 1973–1980.* New York: Cambridge University Press, 1981.

Williams, J. P. "Netherlands' Foreign Policy as a Reflection of Its Political System." In *Papers from the First Interdisciplinary Conference on Netherlandic Studies.* Ed. W. H. Fletcher. Lanham, Md.: University Press of America, 1985.

Williams, R. M. *American Society.* New York: Knopf, 1960.

Wilson, E. O. *Sociobiology: The New Synthesis.* Cambridge, Mass.: Harvard University Press, 1975.

Wispé, L. G., ed. *Altruism, Sympathy and Helping: Psychological and Sociological Principles.* New York: Academic Press, 1978.

Wispé, L. G. "Positive Forms of Social Behavior: An Overview." *The Journal of Social Issues* 28, no. 3 (1972): 1–20.

Wolff, P. H. "The Biology of Morals from a Psychological Perspective." In *Morality as a Biological Phenomenon.* Ed. G. S. Stent. Berlin: Dahlem Konferenzen, 1978.

Wolfson, M. "Zum Widerstand gegen Hitler: Umriss eines Gruppenporträts deutscher Retter von Juden" (Opposition to Hitler: Profile of the German rescuers of Jews). *Tradition und Neubeginn: Internationale Forschungen Deutscher Geschichte im 20. Jahrhundert* 26. (1975): 391–407.

Worchel, S. "The Darker Side of Helping: The Social Dynamics of Helping and Cooperation." In *Development and Maintenance of Prosocial Behavior.* Ed. E. Staub, New York: Plenum Press, 1984.

Wright, G. *The Ordeal of Total War 1939–1945.* New York: Harper & Row, 1968.

Wylie, R. C. *The Self-Concept.* Lincoln: University of Nebraska Press, 1974.

Wyman, D. *Paper Walls: America and the Refugee Crisis, 1938–1941.* Amherst: University of Massachusetts Press, 1969.

Wyman, D. S. *The Abandonment of the Jews: America and the Holocaust, 1941–1945.* New York: Pantheon Books, 1984.

Wynot, E. D., Jr. "A 'Necessary Cruelty': The Emergence of Official Anti-Semitism in Poland, 1936–1939." *American Historical Review* 76, no. 4 (October 1971): 1035–1058.

Wynot, E. D., Jr. *Polish Politics in Transition.* Athens: University of Georgia Press, 1974.

Wytwycky, B. *The Other Holocaust: Many Circles of Hell.* Washington, D.C.: Novak Report, 1981.

Yad Vashem. *Black Book of Localities Whose Jewish Population was Exterminated by the Nazis.* Jerusalem: Yad Vashem, 1965.

Yad Vashem. *Jewish Resistance During the Holocaust.* Jerusalem: Yad Vashem, 1971.

Yahil, L. "Madagascar—Phantom of a Solution for the Jewish Question." In *Jews and Non-Jews in Eastern Europe 1918–1945.* Eds. B. Vago and G. L. Mosse. New York: Halsted Press, 1974.

Yahil, L. "Methods of Persecution: A Comparison of the 'Final Solution' in Holland and Denmark." *Scripta Hierosolymitana* 23 (1972): 283+.

Yahil, L. "Scandinavian Rescue of Prisoners." *Yad Vashem Studies* 6 (1967): 181–220.

Yahil, L. *The Rescue of Danish Jewry: Test of a Democracy.* Trans. M. Gradel. Philadelphia: Jewish Publication Society, 1969.

Yoors, J. *Crossing.* New York: Simon & Schuster, 1971.

Zahn, G. C. *German Catholics and Hitler's Wars.* New York: Sheed & Ward, 1962.

Zahn-Waxler, C., and Radke-Yarrow, M. "The Development of Prosocial Behavior: Alternative Research Strategies." In *The Development of Prosocial Behavior.* Ed. N. Eisenberg-Berg. New York: Academic Press, 1981.

Zahn-Waxler, C. Z., Cummings, E. M., and Iannotti, R., eds. *Altruism and Aggression.* New York: Cambridge University Press, 1986.

Zawodny, J. Z. *Nothing but Honor: The Story of the Warsaw Uprising, 1944.* Stanford, Calif.: Hoover Institution Press, 1979.

Zeller, E. *The Flame of Freedom: The German Struggle Against Hitler.* Trans. R. P. Heller and D. Masters. Coral Gables, Fla.: University of Miami Press 1969.

Ziemian, J. *The Cigarette Sellers of Three Crosses Square.* London: Vallentine & Mitchell, 1970.

Zuccotti, S. *The Italians and the Holocaust: Persecution, Rescue, and Survival.* New York: Basic Books, 1987.

Zuckerman, Y. "From the Warsaw Ghetto." *Commentary* 60. (December 1975): 62–69.

Zuker-Bujanowska, L. *Liliana's Journal: Warsaw 1939–1945.* London: J. Piatkus, 1981.

Zuroff, E. "Rescue Priority and Fund Raising as Issues during the Holocaust: A Case Study of the Relations Between the Vaad Hatzala and the Joint, 1939–1941." *American Jewish Historical Quarterly* 68, no. 3 (March 1979): 305–326.

Index